Simply Scheme

Brian Harvey
Matthew Wright

Foreword by Harold Abelson

Simply Scheme:
Introducing Computer Science

SECOND EDITION

The MIT Press
Cambridge, Massachusetts
London, England

Second printing, 2001
© 1999 by the Massachusetts Institute of Technology

This book was typeset in the Baskerville typeface, using the JOVE text editor and the TEX document formatting system, for which we thank John Baskerville (1706–75), Jonathan Payne (1964–), and Donald Knuth (1938–), respectively.

Library of Congress Cataloging-in-Publication Data

Harvey, Brian, 1949–
   Simply scheme : introducing computer science / Brian Harvey, Matthew Wright ; foreword by Harold Abelson. — 2nd ed.
     p.   cm.
   Includes bibliographic references and index.
   ISBN 0–262–08281–0 (hc : alk. paper)
   1. Scheme (Computer programming language) 2. Computer science.
   I. Wright, Matthew. II. Title.
QA76.H3475 1999
005.13'3–dc21   99-10037
                                           CIP

10 9 8 7 6 5 4 3

Contents

Appendices

Foreword

One of the best ways to stifle the growth of an idea is to enshrine it in an educational curriculum. The textbook publishers, certification panels, professional organizations, the folks who write the college entrance exams—once they've settled on an approach, they become frozen in a straitjacket of interlocking constraints that thwarts the ability to evolve. So it is common that students learn the "modern" geography of countries that no longer exist and practice using logarithm tables when calculators have made tables obsolete. And in computer science, beginning courses are trapped in an approach that was already ten years out of date by the time it was canonized in the mid-1980s, when the College Entrance Examination Board adopted an advanced placement exam based on Pascal.*

This book points the way out of the trap. It emphasizes programming as a way to express ideas, rather than just a way to get computers to perform tasks.

Julie and Gerry Sussman and I are flattered that Harvey and Wright characterize their revolutionary introduction to computer science as a "prequel" to our text *Structure and Interpretation of Computer Programs*. When we were writing *SICP*, we often drew upon the words of the great American computer scientist Alan Perlis (1922–1990). Perlis was one of the designers of the Algol programming language, which, beginning in 1958, established the tradition of formalism and precision that Pascal embodies. Here's what Perlis had to say about this tradition in 1975, nine years *before* the start of the AP exam:

> Algol is a blight. You can't have fun with Algol. Algol is a code that now
> belongs in a plumber's union. It helps you design correct structures that

---

* Since Hal wrote this Foreword, they've switched the AP exam to use C++, but the principle is the same.

don't collapse, but it doesn't have any fun in it. There are no pleasures in writing Algol programs. It's a labor of necessity, a preoccupation with the details of tedium.

Harvey and Wright's introduction to computing emerges from a different intellectual heritage, one rooted in research in artificial intelligence and the programming language Lisp. In approaching computing through this book, you'll focus on two essential techniques.

First is the notion of *symbolic programming*. This means that you deal not only with numbers and letters, but with structured collections of data—a word is a list of characters, a sentence is a list of words, a paragraph is a list of sentences, a story is a list of paragraphs, and so on. You assemble things in terms of natural parts, rather than always viewing data in terms of its tiniest pieces. It's the difference between saying "find the fifth character of the third word in the sentence" and "scan the sentence until you pass two spaces, then scan past four more characters, and return the next character."

The second technique is to work with *higher-order functions*. That means that you don't only write programs, but rather you *write programs that write programs*, so you can bootstrap your methods into more powerful methods.

These two techniques belong at center stage in any beginning programming course, which is exactly where Harvey and Wright put them. The underlying principle in both cases is that you work with general parts that you extend and combine in flexible ways, rather than tiny fragments that you fit together into rigid structures.

You should come to this introduction to computing ready to think about ideas rather than details of syntax, ready to design your own languages rather than to memorize the rules of languages other people have designed. This kind of activity changes your outlook not only on programming, but on any area where design plays an important role, because you learn to appreciate the relations among parts rather than always fixating on the individual pieces. To quote Alan Perlis again,

> You begin to think in terms of patterns and idioms and phrases, and no longer pick up a trowel and some cement and lay things down brick by brick. The Great Wall, standing for centuries, is a monument. But building it must have been a bore.

Hal Abelson
Cambridge, MA

Preface

There are two schools of thought about teaching computer science. We might caricature the two views this way:

- **The conservative view:** Computer programs have become too large and complex to encompass in a human mind. Therefore, the job of computer science education is to teach people how to discipline their work in such a way that 500 mediocre programmers can join together and produce a program that correctly meets its specification.

- **The radical view:** Computer programs have become too large and complex to encompass in a human mind. Therefore, the job of computer science education is to teach people how to expand their minds so that the programs *can* fit, by learning to think in a vocabulary of larger, more powerful, more flexible ideas than the obvious ones. Each unit of programming thought must have a big payoff in the capabilities of the program.

Of course nobody would admit to endorsing the first approach as we've described it. Yet many introductory programming courses seem to spend half their time on obscure rules of the programming language (semicolons go *between* the instructions in Pascal, but *after* each instruction in C) and the other half on stylistic commandments (thou shalt comment each procedure with its preconditions and postconditions; thou shalt not use `goto`). In an article that was *not* intended as a caricature, the noted computer scientist Edsger Dijkstra argues that beginning computer science students *should not be allowed to use computers,* lest they learn to debug their programs interactively instead of writing programs that can be proven correct by formal methods before testing.*

If you are about to be a student in an introductory computer science course, you may already be an experienced programmer of your home computer, or instead you may have only a vague idea of what you're getting into. Perhaps you suspect that programming a computer is like programming a VCR: entering endless obscure numeric codes. Even if you're already a computer programmer, you may not yet have a clear idea of what computer *science* means. In either case, what we want to do in this book is put our best foot forward—introduce you to some new ideas, get you excited, rather than mold you into a disciplined soldier of the programming army.

In order to understand the big ideas, though, we'll also have to expend some effort on technical details; studying computer science without writing computer programs is like trying to study German grammar without learning any of the words in the language. But we'll try to keep the ideas in view while struggling with the details, and we hope you'll remember them too.

One Big Idea: Symbolic Programming

We said that our approach to teaching computer science emphasizes big ideas. Our explanation of symbolic programming in the following paragraphs is in part just an illustration of that approach. But we chose this particular example for another reason also. Scheme, the programming language used in this book, is an unusual choice for an introductory computer science course. You may wonder why we didn't use a more traditional language, such as Pascal, Modula-2, or C. Our discussion of symbolic programming is the beginning of an answer to that question.

Originally computers were about numbers. Scientists used them to solve equations; businesses used them to compute the payroll and the inventory. We were rescued from this boring state of affairs mainly by researchers in *artificial intelligence*—people who wanted to get computers to think more nearly the way people do, about ideas in general rather than just numbers.

What does it mean to represent *ideas* in a computer? Here's a simple example: We want to teach the computer to answer the question, "Was so-and-so a Beatle?" We can't quite ask the question in English; in this book we interact with the computer using Scheme. Our interactions will look like this:

---

* "On the Cruelty of Really Teaching Computer Science," *Communications of the ACM,* vol. 32, no. 12, December, 1989.

You type: `(beatle? 'paul)`
Computer replies: `#t` (computerese for "true")

You type: `(beatle? 'elvis)`
Computer replies: `#f` ("false")

Here's the program that does the job:

```
(define (beatle? person)
  (member? person '(john paul george ringo)))
```

If you examine this program with a (metaphoric) magnifying glass, you'll find that it's really still full of numbers. In fact, each letter or punctuation character is represented in the computer by its own unique number.* But the point of the example is that you don't have to know that! When you see

```
(john paul george ringo)
```

you don't have to worry about the numbers that represent the letters inside the computer; all you have to know is that you're seeing a *sentence* made up of four *words*. Our programming language hides the underlying mechanism and lets us think in terms more appropriate to the problem we're trying to solve. That hiding of details is called *abstraction,* one of the big ideas in this book.

Programming with words and sentences is an example of symbolic programming. In 1960 John McCarthy invented the Lisp programming language to handle symbolic computations like this one. Our programming language, Scheme, is a modern dialect of Lisp.

Lisp and Radical Computer Science

Symbolic programming is one aspect of the reason why we like to teach computer science using Scheme instead of a more traditional language. More generally, Lisp (and therefore Scheme) was designed to support what we've called the radical view of computer science. In this view, computer science is about tools for expressing ideas. Symbolic programming allows *the computer* to express ideas; other aspects of Lisp's design help *the programmer*

---

* The left parenthesis is 40, for example, and the letter d is 100. If it were a capital D it would be 68.

express ideas conveniently. Sometimes that goal comes in conflict with the conservative computer scientist's goal of protection against errors.

Here's an example. We want to tell our computer, "To square a number, multiply it by itself." In Scheme we can say

```
(define (square num)
  (* num num))
```

The asterisk represents multiplication, and is followed by the two operands—in this case, both the same number. This short program works for any number, of course, as we can see in the following dialogue. (The lines with > in front are the ones you type.)

```
> (square 4)
16
> (square 3.14)
9.8596
> (square -0.3)
0.09
```

But the proponents of the 500-mediocre-programmer school* think this straightforward approach is sinful. "What!" they cry. "You haven't said whether num is a whole number or a number with a decimal fraction!" They're afraid that you might write the square program with whole numbers in mind, and then apply it to a decimal fraction *by mistake.* If you're on a team with 499 other programmers, it's easy to have failures of communication so that one programmer uses another's program in unintended ways.

To avoid that danger, they want you to write these two separate programs:

```
function SquareOfWholeNumber(num: integer): integer;
  begin
    SquareOfWholeNumber := num * num
  end;

function SquareOfDecimalNumber(num: real): real;
  begin
    SquareOfDecimalNumber := num * num
  end;
```

---

* Their own names for their approach are *structured programming* and *software engineering.*

Isn't this silly? Why do they pick this particular distinction (whole numbers and decimals) to worry about? Why not positive and negative numbers, for example? Why not odd and even numbers?

That two-separate-program example is written in the Pascal language. Pascal was designed by Niklaus Wirth, one of the leaders of the structured programming school, specifically to *force* programming students to write programs that fit conservative ideas about programming style and technique; you can't write a program in Pascal at all unless you write it in the approved style. Naturally, this language has been very popular with school teachers.* That's why, as we write this in 1993, the overwhelming majority of introductory computer science classes are taught using Pascal, even though no professional programmer would be caught dead using it.**

For fourteen years after the introduction of Pascal in 1970, its hegemony in computer science education was essentially unchallenged. But in 1984, two professors at the Massachusetts Institute of Technology and a programmer at Bolt, Beranek and Newman (a commercial research lab) published the Scheme-based *Structure and Interpretation of Computer Programs* (Harold Abelson and Gerald Jay Sussman with Julie Sussman, MIT Press/McGraw-Hill). That ground-breaking text brought the artificial intelligence approach to a wide audience for the first time. We (Brian and Matt) have been teaching their course together for several years. Each time, we learn something new.

The only trouble with *SICP* is that it was written for MIT students, all of whom love science and are quite comfortable with formal mathematics. Also, most of the students who use *SICP* at MIT have already learned to program computers before they begin. As a result, many other schools have found the book too challenging for a beginning course. We believe that everyone who is seriously interested in computer science must read *SICP* eventually. Our book is a *prequel;* it's meant to teach you what you need to know in order to read that book successfully.*** Generally speaking, our primary goal in Parts I–V has been preparation for *SICP,* while the focus of Part VI is to connect the course with the

---

* Of course, *your* teacher isn't an uptight authoritarian, or you wouldn't be using our book!

** Okay, we're exaggerating. But even Professor Wirth himself has found Pascal so restrictive that he had to design more flexible languages—although not flexible enough—called Modula and Oberon.

*** As the ideas pioneered by *SICP* have spread, we are starting to see other intellectually respectable introductions to computer science that are meant as alternatives to *SICP.* In particular, we should acknowledge *Scheme and the Art of Programming* (George Springer and Daniel P. Friedman, MIT Press/McGraw-Hill, 1989) as a recognized classic. We believe our book will serve as preparation for theirs, too.

kinds of programming used in "real world" application programs like spreadsheets and databases. (These are the last example and the last project in the book.)

Who Should Read This Book

This book is intended as an introduction to computer programming and to computer science for two kinds of students.

For those whose main interest is in some other field, we provide a self-contained, one-semester experience with computer programming in a language with a minimum of complicated notation, so that students can quickly come in contact with high-level ideas about algorithms, functions, and recursion. The book ends with the implementation of a spreadsheet program and a database program, so it complements a computer application course in which the commercial versions of such programs are used.

For those who intend to continue the study of computer science but who have no prior programming experience, we offer a preparatory course, less intense than a traditional CS 1 but not limited to programming technique; we give the flavor of computer science ideas that will be studied in more depth later in the curriculum. We also include an extensive discussion of recursion, which is a stumbling block for many beginning students.

The course at Berkeley for which we wrote this book includes both categories of students. About 90% of the first-year students who intend to major in computer science have already had a programming course in high school, and most of them begin with *SICP.* The other 10% are advised to take this course first. But many of the students in this course aren't computer science majors. A few other departments (business administration and architecture are the main ones) have a specific computer course requirement, and all students must meet a broader "quantitative reasoning" requirement; our course satisfies these requirements. Finally, some students come just out of curiosity about computers.

We assume that you have never programmed a computer. On the other hand, we do assume that you can *use* a computer; we don't talk about how to turn it on, how to edit text, and so on, because those details are too different from one computer model to another. If you've never used a computer before, you may wish to spend a few days with a book written specifically for your machine that will introduce you to its operation. It won't take more than a few days, because you don't have to be an expert before you read our book. As long as you can start up the Scheme interpreter and correct your typing mistakes, you're ready.

We assume that you're not a mathematics lover. (If you are, you might be ready to read *SICP* right away.) The earlier example about squaring a number is about as advanced as we get. And of course you don't have to do any arithmetic at all; computers are good at that. You'll learn how to *tell* the computer to do arithmetic, but that's no harder than using a pocket calculator. Most of our programming examples are concerned with words and sentences rather than with numbers. A typical example is to get Scheme to figure out the plural form of a noun. Usually that means putting an "s" on the end, but not quite always. (What's the plural of "French fry"?)

How to Read This Book

Do the exercises! Whenever we teach programming, we always get students who say, "When I read the book it all makes sense, but on the exams, when you ask me to write a program, I never know where to start." Computer science is two things: a bunch of big ideas, as we've been saying, and also a skill. You can't learn the skill by watching.

Do the exercises on a computer! It's not good enough to solve the exercises on paper, even if you feel sure your solution is correct. Maybe it's 99% correct but there's some little detail you've overlooked. When you run such a program, you won't get 99% of the answer you wanted. By trying the exercise on the computer, you get unambiguous feedback. If your program is correct, you get the response you expected. If not, not.

Don't feel bad if you don't get things right the first time. Even the most experienced programmers have to *debug* their programs—that is, fix the parts that don't work. In fact, an important part of what you'll learn from the exercises is the *process* of debugging your solutions. It would be too bad if all of your programs in this course worked the first time, because that would let you avoid the practice in debugging that you'll certainly need when you write more complicated programs later. Also, don't be afraid or ashamed to ask for help if you get stuck. That, too, is part of the working style of professional programmers.

In some of the chapters, we've divided the exercises into two categories, "boring" and "real." The boring exercises ask you to work through examples mechanically, to make sure you understand the rules. The real exercises ask you to *invent* something, usually a small computer program, but sometimes an explanation of some situation that we present. (In some chapters, the exercises are just labeled "exercises," which means that they're all considered "real.") We don't intend that the boring exercises be handed in; the idea is for you to do as many of them as you need to make sure you understand the mechanics of whatever topic you're learning.

Occasionally we introduce some idea with a simplified explanation, saving the whole truth for later. We warn you when we do this. Also, we sometimes write preliminary, partial, or incorrect example programs, and we always flag these with a comment like

```
(define (something foo baz)                ;; first version
  ...)
```

When we introduce technical terms, we sometimes mention the origin of the word, if it's not obvious, to help prevent the terminology from seeming arbitrary.

This book starts easy but gets harder, in two different ways. One is that we spend some time teaching you the basics of Scheme before we get to two hard big ideas, namely, function as object and recursion. The earlier chapters are short and simple. You may get the idea that the whole book will be trivial. You'll change your mind in Parts III and IV.

The other kind of difficulty in the book is that it includes long programming examples and projects. ("Examples" are programs we write and describe; "projects" are programs we ask you to write.) Writing a long program is quite different from writing a short one. Each small piece may be easy, but fitting them together and remembering all of them at once is a challenge. The examples and projects get longer as the book progresses, but even the first example, tic-tac-toe, is much longer and more complex than anything that comes before it.

As the text explains more fully later, in this book we use some extensions to the standard Scheme language—features that we implemented ourselves, as Scheme programs. If you are using this book in a course, your instructor will provide our programs for you, and you don't have to worry about it. But if you're reading the book on your own, you'll need to follow the instructions in Appendix A.

There are several reference documents at the end of the book. If you don't understand a technical term in the text, try the Glossary for a short definition, or the General Index to find the more complete explanation in the text. If you've forgotten how to use a particular Scheme primitive procedure, look in the Alphabetical Table of Scheme Primitives, or in the General Index. If you've forgotten the name of the relevant primitive, refer to the inside back cover, where all the primitive procedures are listed by category. Some of our example programs make reference to procedures that were defined earlier, either in another example or in an exercise. If you're reading an example program and it refers to some procedure that's defined elsewhere, you can find that other procedure in the Index of Defined Procedures.

To the Instructor

The language that we use in this book isn't exactly standard Scheme. We've provided several extensions that may seem unusual to an experienced Scheme programmer. This may make the book feel weird at first, but there's a pedagogic reason for each extension.

Along with our slightly strange version of Scheme, our book has a slightly unusual order of topics. Several ideas that are introduced very early in the typical Scheme-based text are delayed in ours, most notably recursion. Quite a few people have looked at our table of contents, noted some particular big idea of computer science, and remarked, "I can't believe you wait so long before getting to *such and such!*"

In this preface for instructors, we describe and explain the unusual elements of our approach. Other teaching issues, including the timing and ordering of topics, are discussed in the Instructor's Manual.

Lists and Sentences

The chapter named "Lists" in this book is Chapter 17, about halfway through the book. But really we use lists much earlier than that, almost from the beginning.

Teachers of Lisp have always had trouble deciding when and how to introduce lists. The advantage of an early introduction is that students can then write interesting symbolic programs instead of boring numeric ones. The disadvantage is that students must struggle with the complexity of the implementation, such as the asymmetry between the two ends of a list, while still also struggling with the idea of composition of functions and Lisp's prefix notation.

We prefer to have it both ways. We want to spare beginning students the risk of accidentally constructing ill-formed lists such as

```
((((() . D) . C) . B) . A)
```

but we also want to write natural-language programs from the beginning of the book. Our solution is to borrow from Logo the idea of a *sentence* abstract data type.* Sentences are guaranteed to be flat, proper lists, and they appear to be symmetrical to the user of the abstraction. (That is, it's as easy to ask for the last word of a sentence as to ask for the first word.) The `sentence` constructor accepts either a word or a sentence in any argument position.

We defer *structured* lists until we have higher-order functions and recursion, the tools we need to be able to use the structure effectively.** A structured list can be understood as a tree, and Lisp programmers generally use that understanding implicitly. After introducing `car-cdr` recursion, we present an explicit abstract data type for trees, without reference to its implementation. Then we make the connection between these formal trees and the name "tree recursion" used for structured lists generally. But Chapter 18 can be omitted, if the instructor finds the tree ADT unnecessary, and the reader of Chapter 17 will still be able to use structured lists.

Sentences and Words

We haven't said what a *word* is. Scheme includes separate data types for characters, symbols, strings, and numbers. We want to be able to dissect words into letters, just as we can dissect sentences into words, so that we can write programs like `plural` and `pig-latin`. Orthodox Scheme style would use strings for such purposes, but we want a sentence to look (`like this`) and not (`"like" "this"`). We've arranged that in most contexts symbols, strings, and numbers can be used interchangeably; our readers never see Scheme characters at all.*** Although a word made of letters is represented internally as a symbol, while a word made of digits is represented as a number, above the abstraction line they're both words. (A word that standard Scheme won't accept as a symbol nor as a number is represented as a string.)

---

* Speaking of abstraction, even though that's the name of Part V, we do make an occasion in each of the earlier parts to talk about abstraction as examples come up.

** Even then, we take lists as a primitive data type. We don't teach about pairs or improper lists, except as a potential pitfall.

*** Scheme's primitive I/O facility gives you the choice of expressions or characters. Instead of using `read-char`, we invent `read-line`, which reads a line as a sentence, and `read-string`, which returns the line as one long word.

There is an efficiency cost to treating both words and sentences as abstract aggregates, since it's slow to disassemble a sentence from right to left and slow to disassemble a word in either direction. Many simple procedures that seem linear actually behave quadratically. Luckily, words aren't usually very long, and the applications we undertake in the early chapters don't use large amounts of data in any form. We write our large projects as efficiently as we can without making the programs unreadable, but we generally don't make a fuss about it. Near the end of the book we discuss explicitly the efficient use of data structures.

Overloading in the Text Abstraction

Even though computers represent numbers internally in many different ways (fixed point, bignum, floating point, exact rational, complex), when people visit mathland, they expect to meet numbers there, and they expect that all the numbers will understand how to add, subtract, multiply, and divide with each other. (The exception is dividing by zero, but that's because of the inherent rules of mathematics, not because of the separation of numbers into categories by representation format.)

We feel the same way about visiting textland. We expect to meet English text there. It takes the form of words and sentences. The operations that text understands include `first`, `last`, `butfirst`, and `butlast` to divide the text into its component parts. You can't divide an empty word or sentence into parts, but it's just as natural to divide a word into letters as to divide a sentence into words. (The ideas of mathland and textland, as well as the details of the word and sentence procedures, come from Logo.)

Some people who are accustomed to Scheme's view of data types consider `first` to be badly "overloaded"; they feel that a procedure that selects an element from a list shouldn't also extract a letter from a symbol. Some of them would prefer that we use `car` for lists, use `substring` for strings, and not disassemble symbols at all. Others want us to define `word-first` and `sentence-first`.

To us, `word-first` and `sentence-first` sound no less awkward than `fixnum-+` and `bignum-+`. Everyone agrees that it's reasonable to overload the name `+` because the purposes are so similar. Our students find it just as reasonable that `first` works for words as well as for sentences; they don't get confused by this.

As for the inviolability of symbols—the wall between names and data—we are following an older Lisp tradition, in which it was commonplace to `explode` symbols and to construct new names within a program. Practically speaking, all that prevents us from representing words as strings is that Scheme requires quotation marks around them. But in any case, the abstraction we're presenting is that the data we're dissecting are neither strings nor symbols, but words.

Higher-Order Procedures, Lambda, and Recursion

Scheme relies on procedure invocation as virtually its only control mechanism. In order to write interesting programs, a Scheme user must understand at least one of two hard ideas: recursion or procedure as object (in order to use higher-order procedures). We believe that higher-order procedures are easier to learn, especially because we begin in Chapter 8 by applying them only to named procedures. Using a named procedure as an argument to another procedure is the way to use procedures as objects that's least upsetting to a beginner. After the reader is comfortable with higher-order procedures, we introduce `lambda`; after that we introduce recursion. We do the tic-tac-toe example with higher-order procedures and `lambda`, but not recursion.

In this edition, however, we have made the necessary minor revisions so that an instructor who prefers to begin with recursion can assign Part IV before Part III.

When we get to recursion, we begin with an example of embedded recursion. Many books begin with the simplest possible recursive procedure, which turns out to be a simple sequential recursion, or even a tail recursion. We feel that starting with such examples allows students to invent the "go back" model of recursion as looping.

Mutators and Environments

One of the most unusual characteristics of this book is that there is no assignment to variables in it. The reason we avoid `set!` is that the environment model of evaluation is very hard for most students. We use a pure substitution model throughout most of the book. (With the background they get from this book, students should be ready for the environment model when they see a rigorous presentation, as they will, for example, in Chapter 3 of *SICP*.)

As the last topic in the book, we do introduce a form of mutation, namely `vector-set!`. Mutation of vectors is less problematic than mutation of lists, because lists naturally share storage. You really have to go out of your way to get two pointers to the same vector.* Mutation of data structures is less problematic than assignment to variables because it separates the issue of mutation from the issues of binding and scope. Using vectors raises no new questions about the evaluation process, so we present mutation without reference to any formal model of evaluation. We acknowledge that we're on thin ice here, but it seems to work for our students.

In effect, our model of mutation is the "shoebox" model that you'd find in a mainstream programming language text. Before we get to mutation, we use input/output programming to introduce the ideas of effect and sequence; assigning a value to a vector element introduces the important idea of state. We use the sequential model to write two more or less practical programs, a spreadsheet and a database system. A more traditional approach to assignment in Scheme would be to build an object-oriented language extension, but the use of local state variables would definitely force us to pay attention to environments.

---

* We don't talk about eq? at all. We're careful to write our programs in such a way that the issue of identity doesn't arise for the reader.

Acknowledgments

Obviously our greatest debt is to Harold Abelson, Gerald Jay Sussman, and Julie Sussman. They have inspired us and taught us, and gave birth to the movement to which we are minor contributors. Julie carefully read what we thought was the final draft, made thousands of suggestions, both small and large, improved the book enormously, and set us back two months. Hal encouraged us, read early drafts, and also made this a better book than we could have created on our own.

Mike Clancy, Ed Dubinsky, Dan Friedman, Tessa Harvey, and Yehuda Katz also read drafts and made detailed and very helpful suggestions for improvement. Mike contributed many exercises. (We didn't take their advice about everything, though, so they get none of the blame for anything you don't like here.)

Terry Ehling, Bob Prior, and everyone at the MIT Press have given this project the benefit of their enthusiasm and their technical support. We're happy to be working with them.

The Computer Science Division at the University of California, Berkeley, allowed us to teach a special section of the CS 3 course using the first draft of this book. The book now in your hands is much better because of that experience. We thank Annika Rogers, our teaching assistant in the course, and also the thirty students who served not merely as guinea pigs but as collaborators in pinning down the weak points in our explanations.

Some of the ideas in this book, especially the different approaches to recursion, are taken from Brian's earlier Logo-based textbook.* Many of our explanatory metaphors, especially the "little people" model, were invented by members of the Logo community.

---

* *Computer Science Logo Style, volume 1: Intermediate Programming,* MIT Press, 1985.

We also took the word and sentence data types from Logo. Although this book doesn't use Logo itself, we tried to write it in the Logo spirit.

We wrote much of this book during the summer of 1992, while we were on the faculty of the Institute for Secondary Mathematics and Computer Science Education, an inservice teacher training program at Kent State University. Several of our IFSMACSE colleagues contributed to our ideas both about computer science and about teaching; we are especially indebted to Ed Dubinsky and Uri Leron.

We stole the idea of a "pitfalls" section at the end of each chapter from Dave Patterson and John Hennessy.

We stole some of the ideas for illustrations from Douglas Hofstadter's wonderful *Gödel, Escher, Bach.*

David Zabel helped us get software ready for students, especially with compiling SCM for the PC.

We conclude this list with an acknowledgment of each other. Because of the difference in our ages, it may occur to some readers to suspect that we contributed unequally to this book—either that Matt did all the work and Brian just lent his name and status to impress publishers, or that Brian had all the ideas and Matt did the typing. Neither of these is true. Almost everything in the book was written with both of us in front of the computer, arguing out every paragraph. When we did split up to write some sections separately, each of us read and criticized the other's work. (We're a little surprised that we still like each other, after all the arguments!) Luckily we both like the Beatles, Chinese food, and ice cream, so we had a common ground for programming examples. But when you see an example about Bill Frisell, you can be pretty sure it's Matt's writing, and when the example is about Dave Dee, Dozy, Beaky, Mick, and Tich, it's probably Brian's.

Simply Scheme

Part I
Introduction: Functions

The purpose of these introductory pages before each part of the book is to call attention to a big idea that runs through all the work of several chapters. In the chapters themselves, the big idea may sometimes be hidden from view because of the technical details that we need to make the idea work. If you ever feel lost in the forest, you might want to refer back here.

In these first two chapters, our goal is to introduce the Scheme programming language and the idea of using *functions* as the building blocks of a computation.

The first chapter is a collection of short Scheme programs, presented to show off what Scheme can do. We'll try to explain enough of the mechanism so that you don't feel completely mystified, but we'll defer the details until later. Our goal is not for you to feel that you could re-create these programs, but rather that you get a sense of what *kinds* of programs we'll be working with.

The second chapter explores functions in some detail. Traditionally, computer programs are built out of *actions:* First do this, then do that, and finally print the results. Each step in the program *does* something. Functional programming is different, in that we are less concerned with actions and more concerned with values.

For example, if you have a pocket calculator with a square root button, you could enter the number 3, push the button, and you'll see something like 1.732050808 in the display. How does the calculator know? There are several possible processes that the calculator could carry out. One process, for example, is to make a guess, square it, see if the result is too big or too small, and use that information to make a closer guess. That's a sequence of actions. But ordinarily you don't care what actions the calculator takes;

what interests you is that you want to apply the square root *function* to the *argument* 3, and get back a *value*. We're going to focus on this business of functions, arguments, and result values.

Don't think that functions have to involve numbers. We'll be working with functions like "first name," "plural," and "acronym." These functions have words and sentences as their arguments and values.

Scheme-Brained Hare

1   Showing Off Scheme

We are going to use the programming language Scheme to teach you some big ideas in computer science. The ideas are mostly about *control of complexity*—that is, about how to develop a large computer program without being swamped in details.

For example, once you've solved part of the large problem, you can give that partial solution a *name* and then you can use the named subprogram as if it were an indivisible operation, just like the ones that are built into the computer. Thereafter, you can forget about the details of that subprogram. This is the beginning of the idea of *abstraction,* which we'll discuss in more depth throughout the book.

The big ideas are what this book is about, but first we're going to introduce you to Scheme. (Scheme is a dialect of Lisp, a family of computer programming languages invented for computing with words, sentences, and ideas instead of just numbers.)

Talking to Scheme

The incantations to get Scheme running will be different for each model of computer. Appendix A talks about these details; you can look up the particular version of Scheme that you're using. That appendix will also tell you how to load the file `simply.scm`, which you need to make the examples in this book work.

When Scheme has started up and is ready for you to interact with it, you'll see a message on the screen, something like this:

```
Welcome to XYZ Brand Scheme.
>
```

The > is a *prompt,* Scheme's way of telling you that it's ready for you to type something. Scheme is an *interactive* programming language. In other words, you type a request to Scheme, then Scheme prints the answer, and then you get another prompt. Try it out:

```
> 6
6
```

We just asked Scheme, "What is 6?" and Scheme told us that 6 is 6. Most of the time we ask harder questions:

```
> (+ 4 7)
11
> (- 23 5)
18
> (+ 5 6 7 8)
26
```

Whenever something you type to Scheme is enclosed in parentheses, it indicates a request to carry out a *procedure.* (We'll define "procedure" more formally later, but for now it means something that Scheme knows how to do. A procedure tells Scheme how to compute a particular function.) The first thing inside the parentheses indicates what procedure to use; the others are *arguments,* i.e., values that are used as data by the procedure.

Scheme has non-numeric procedures, too:

```
> (word 'comp 'uter)
COMPUTER
```

(If this last example gives an error message saying that Scheme doesn't understand the name word, it means that you didn't load the file `simply.scm`. Consult Appendix A.)

In these first examples, we've shown what you type in **boldface** and what the computer responds in `lightface`. Hereafter, we will rely on the prompt characters to help you figure out who's talking on which line.

For the most part, Scheme doesn't care about whether you type in UPPER CASE or lower case. For the examples in this book, we'll assume that you always type in lower case and that the computer prints in upper case. Your Scheme might print in lower case; it doesn't matter.

Recovering from Typing Errors

Don't worry if you make a mistake typing these examples in; you can just try again. One of the great things about interactive programming languages is that you can experiment in them.

The parentheses and single quote marks are important; don't leave them out. If Scheme seems to be ignoring you, try typing a bunch of right parentheses,)))))) , and hitting the return or enter key. (That's because Scheme doesn't do anything until you've closed all the parentheses you've opened, so if you have an extra left parenthesis, you can keep typing forever with no response.)

Another problem you might encounter is seeing a long message that you don't understand and then finding yourself with something other than a Scheme prompt. This happens when Scheme considers what you typed as an error. Here's an example; for now, never mind exactly why this is an error. We just want to talk about the result:

```
> (+ 2 a)

Unbound variable a
;Package: (user)

2 Error->
```

The exact form of the message you get will depend on the version of Scheme that you're using. For now, the important point is that some versions deal with errors by leaving you talking to a *debugger* instead of to Scheme itself. The debugger may have a completely different language. It's meant to help you figure out what's wrong in a large program you've written. For a beginner, though, it's more likely to get in the way. Read the documentation for your particular Scheme dialect to learn how to escape from the debugger. (In some versions you don't get trapped in a debugger when you make an error, so this problem may not arise.)

Exiting Scheme

Although there's no official standard way to exit Scheme, most versions use the notation

```
> (exit)
```

for this purpose. If you type in some of the examples that follow and then exit from Scheme, what you type won't be remembered the next time you use Scheme. (Appendix A talks about how to use a text editor along with Scheme to make a permanent record of your work.)

More Examples

We're about to show you a few examples of (we hope) interesting programs in Scheme. Play with them! Type them into your computer and try invoking them with different data. Again, don't worry too much if something doesn't work—it probably just means that you left out a parenthesis, or some such thing.

While you're going through these examples, see how much you can figure out for yourself about how they work. In particular, try guessing what the names of procedures, such as first and keep, mean. Some of them will probably be obvious, some of them harder. The point isn't to see how smart you are, but to get you thinking about the *kinds* of things you want to be able to do in a computer program. Later on we'll go through these examples in excruciating detail and tell you the official meanings of all the pieces.

Besides learning the *vocabulary* of Scheme, another point of this activity is to give you a feeling for the ways in which we put these names together in a program. Every programming language has its own flavor. For example, if you've programmed before in other languages, you may be surprised not to find anything that says print in these examples.

On the other hand, some of these examples are programs that we won't expect you to understand fully until most of the way through this book. So don't worry if something doesn't make sense; just try to get some of the flavor of Scheme programming.

Example: Acronyms

Here's our first new program. So far we have just been using procedures built into Scheme: +, -, and word. When you first start up Scheme, it knows 100–200 procedures. These are called *primitive* procedures. Programming in Scheme means defining new procedures, called *compound* procedures. Right now we're going to invent one that finds the acronym for a title:

```
(define (acronym phrase)
  (accumulate word (every first phrase)))
```

```
> (acronym '(american civil liberties union))
ACLU

> (acronym '(reduced instruction set computer))
RISC

> (acronym '(quod erat demonstrandum))
QED
```

Did you have trouble figuring out what all the pieces do in the **acronym** procedure? Try these examples:

```
> (first 'american)
A

> (every first '(american civil liberties union))
(A C L U)

> (accumulate word '(a c l u))
ACLU
```

Notice that this simple **acronym** program doesn't always do exactly what you might expect:

```
> (acronym '(united states of america))
USOA
```

We can rewrite the program to leave out certain words:

```
(define (acronym phrase)
  (accumulate word (every first (keep real-word? phrase))))

(define (real-word? wd)
  (not (member? wd '(a the an in of and for to with))))

> (acronym '(united states of america))
USA

> (acronym '(structure and interpretation of computer programs))
SICP

> (acronym '(association for computing machinery))
ACM

> (real-word? 'structure)
#T
```

```
> (real-word? 'of)
#F*

> (keep real-word? '(united network command for law and enforcement))
(UNITED NETWORK COMMAND LAW ENFORCEMENT)
```

Example: Pig Latin

Our next example translates a word into Pig Latin.**

```
(define (pigl wd)
  (if (member? (first wd) 'aeiou)
      (word wd 'ay)
      (pigl (word (butfirst wd) (first wd)))))

> (pigl 'spaghetti)
AGHETTISPAY

> (pigl 'ok)
OKAY
```

(By the way, if you've used other programming languages before, don't fall into the trap of thinking that each line of the `pigl` definition is a "statement" and that the

---

* In some versions of Scheme you might see ( ) instead of #F.

** Pig Latin is a not-very-secret secret language that many little kids learn. Each word is translated by moving all the initial consonants to the end of the word, and adding "ay" at the end. It's usually spoken rather than written, but that's a little harder to do on a computer.

statements are executed one after the other. That's not how it works in Scheme. The entire thing is a single expression, and what counts is the grouping with parentheses. Starting a new line is no different from a space between words as far as Scheme is concerned. We could have defined `pigl` on one humongous line and it would mean the same thing. Also, Scheme doesn't care about how we've indented the lines so that subexpressions line up under each other. We do that only to make the program more readable for human beings.)

The procedure follows one of two possible paths, depending on whether the first letter of the given word is a vowel. If so, `pigl` just adds the letters `ay` at the end:

```
> (pigl 'elephant)
ELEPHANTAY
```

The following examples might make it a little more clear how the starting-consonant case works:

```
> (first 'spaghetti)
S

> (butfirst 'spaghetti)
PAGHETTI

> (word 'paghetti 's)
PAGHETTIS

> (define (rotate wd)
    (word (butfirst wd) (first wd)))

> (rotate 'spaghetti)
PAGHETTIS

> (rotate 'paghettis)
AGHETTISP

> (pigl 'aghettisp)
AGHETTISPAY
```

You've seen **every** before, in the **acronym** example, but we haven't told you what it does. Try to guess what Scheme will respond when you type this:

```
(every pigl '(the ballad of john and yoko))
```

Example: Ice Cream Choices

Here's a somewhat more complicated program, but still pretty short considering what it accomplishes:

```
(define (choices menu)
  (if (null? menu)
      '(())
      (let ((smaller (choices (cdr menu))))
        (reduce append
                (map (lambda (item) (prepend-every item smaller))
                     (car menu))))))

(define (prepend-every item lst)
  (map (lambda (choice) (se item choice)) lst))

> (choices '((small medium large)
             (vanilla (ultra chocolate) (rum raisin) ginger)
             (cone cup)))
((SMALL VANILLA CONE)
 (SMALL VANILLA CUP)
 (SMALL ULTRA CHOCOLATE CONE)
 (SMALL ULTRA CHOCOLATE CUP)
 (SMALL RUM RAISIN CONE)
 (SMALL RUM RAISIN CUP)
 (SMALL GINGER CONE)
 (SMALL GINGER CUP)
 (MEDIUM VANILLA CONE)
 (MEDIUM VANILLA CUP)
 (MEDIUM ULTRA CHOCOLATE CONE)
 (MEDIUM ULTRA CHOCOLATE CUP)
 (MEDIUM RUM RAISIN CONE)
 (MEDIUM RUM RAISIN CUP)
 (MEDIUM GINGER CONE)
 (MEDIUM GINGER CUP)
 (LARGE VANILLA CONE)
 (LARGE VANILLA CUP)
 (LARGE ULTRA CHOCOLATE CONE)
 (LARGE ULTRA CHOCOLATE CUP)
 (LARGE RUM RAISIN CONE)
 (LARGE RUM RAISIN CUP)
 (LARGE GINGER CONE)
 (LARGE GINGER CUP))
```

Notice that in writing the program we didn't have to say how many menu categories there are, or how many choices in each category. This one program will work with any menu—try it out yourself.

Example: Combinations from a Set

Here's a more mathematical example. We want to know all the possible combinations of, let's say, three things from a list of five possibilities. For example, we want to know all the teams of three people that can be chosen from a group of five people. "Dozy, Beaky, and Tich" counts as the same team as "Beaky, Tich, and Dozy"; the order within a team doesn't matter.

Although this will be a pretty short program, it's more complicated than it looks. We don't expect you to be able to figure out the algorithm yet.* Instead, we just want you to marvel at Scheme's ability to express difficult techniques succinctly.

```
(define (combinations size set)
  (cond ((= size 0) '(()))
        ((empty? set) '())
        (else (append (prepend-every (first set)
                                     (combinations (- size 1)
                                                   (butfirst set)))
                      (combinations size (butfirst set))))))

> (combinations 3 '(a b c d e))
((A B C) (A B D) (A B E) (A C D) (A C E)
 (A D E) (B C D) (B C E) (B D E) (C D E))

> (combinations 2 '(john paul george ringo))
((JOHN PAUL) (JOHN GEORGE) (JOHN RINGO)
 (PAUL GEORGE) (PAUL RINGO) (GEORGE RINGO))
```

(If you're trying to figure out the algorithm despite our warning, here's a hint: All the combinations of three letters shown above can be divided into two groups. The first group consists of the ones that start with the letter A and contain two more letters; the second group has three letters not including A. The procedure finds these two groups separately and combines them into one. If you want to try to understand all the pieces, try playing with them separately, as we encouraged you to do with the pigl and acronym procedures.)

---

* What's an *algorithm*? It's a method for solving a problem. The usual analogy is to a recipe in cooking, although you'll see throughout this book that we want to get away from the aspect of that analogy that emphasizes the *sequential* nature of a recipe—first do this, then do that, etc. There can be more than one algorithm to solve the same problem.

If you've taken a probability course, you know that there is a formula for the *number* of possible combinations. The most traditional use of computers is to work through such formulas and compute numbers. However, not all problems are numeric. Lisp, the programming language family of which Scheme is a member, is unusual in its emphasis on *symbolic* computing. In this example, listing the actual combinations instead of just counting them is part of the flavor of symbolic computing, along with our earlier examples about manipulating words and phrases. We'll try to avoid numeric problems when possible, because symbolic computing is more fun for most people.

Example: Factorial

Scheme can handle numbers, too. The factorial of n (usually written in mathematical notation as $n!$) is the product of all the numbers from 1 to n:

```
(define (factorial n)
  (if (= n 0)
      1
      (* n (factorial (- n 1))))))
```

```
> (factorial 4)
24
```

```
> (factorial 1000)
402387260077093773543702433923003985719374864210714632543799910429938
512398629020592044208486969404800479988610197196058631666872994808558901
323829669944590997424504087073759918823627271887325197795059509952760
120874975462497043601418278094646496291056393887437886487337119181045820
257836478499770124766328898359557354325131853239584630755574091142624180
747434934753428646576611667797396668820291207379143853719588249808126080
867838375459731746136085379534524221586593201928090878297308431392844400
032812315586110369768013573042161687476096758713483120254785893207671600
913244884262361314125087802080002616831510273418279777047846358681701600
365024153691398281264810213092761244896359928705114964975419909342221500
668325720808213331861168115536158365469840467089756029009505376164758400
772842188967964624494516076535340819890138544248798495995331910172335500
556602139450399736280750137837615307127761926849034352625200015888535100
473316117021039681759215109077880193931781141945452572238655414610628900
218796022383897147608850627686296714667469756291123408243920816015378000
889893964518263243671616762179168909779911903754031274622289988005195400
444142820121873617459926429565817466283029557029902432415318161721046000
583203678690611726015878352075151628422554026517048330422614397428693300
061690897968482590125458327168226458066526769958652682272807075781391800
```

```
58178889652208164348344825993266043367660176999612831860788386150279946
59551311565520360939881806121385586003014356945272242063446317974605 94
68257310379008402443243846565724501440282188525247093519062092902313 64
93273497565513958720559654228749774011413346962715422845862377387538 23
04838656889764619273838149001407673104466402598994902222217659043399 01
88601856652648506179970235619389701786004081188972991831102117122984 59
01641921068884387121855646124960798722908519296819372388642614839657 38
22911231250241866493531439701374285319266498753372189406942814341185 20
15801412334482801505139969429015348307764456909907315243327828826986 46
02789864321139083506217095002597389863554277196742822487575867657523 4
42202075736305694988250879689281627538488633969099598262809561214509 94
87170124451646126037902930912088908694202851064018215439945715680594 18
72748998094254742173582401063677404595741785160829230135358081840096 99
63725242305608559037006242712434169090041536901059339838357779394109 70
02775347200000000000000000000000000000000000000000000000000000000000 00
00000000000000000000000000000000000000000000000000000000000000000000 00
00000000000000000000000000000000000000000000000000000000000000000000 00
00000000000000000000000000000000000000000000000000000000
```

If this doesn't work because your computer is too small, try a more reasonably sized example, such as the factorial of 200.

Play with the Procedures

This chapter has introduced a lot of new ideas at once, leaving out all the details. Our hope has been to convey the *flavor* of Scheme programming, before we get into Chapter 2, which is full of those missing details. But you can't absorb the flavor just by reading; take some time out to play with these examples before you go on.

Exercises

1.1 Do 20 push-ups.

1.2 Calculate 1000 factorial by hand and see if the computer got the right answer.

1.3 Create a file called `acronym.scm` containing our acronym program, using the text editor provided for use with your version of Scheme. Load the file into Scheme and run the program. Produce a transcript file called `acronym.log`, showing your interaction with Scheme as you test the program several times, and print it.

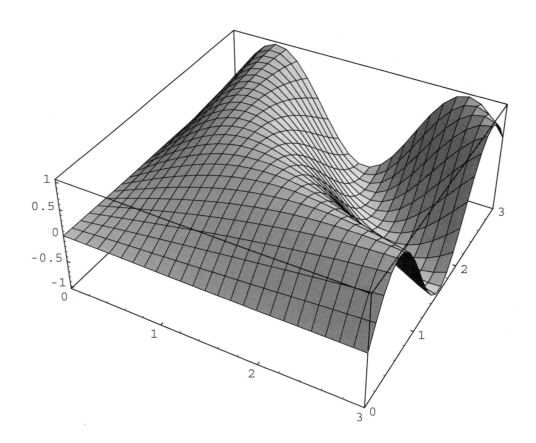

The function $f(x, y) = \sin xy$ plotted by computer

2   Functions

Throughout most of this book we're going to be using a technique called *functional programming*. We can't give a complete definition of this term yet, but in this chapter we introduce the building block of functional programming, the *function*.

Basically we mean by "function" the same thing that your high school algebra teacher meant, except that our functions don't necessarily relate to numbers. But the essential idea is just like the kind of function described by $f(x) = 6x - 2$. In that example, f is the name of a function; that function takes an *argument* called x, which is a number, and *returns* some other number.

In this chapter you are going to use the computer to explore functions, but you are *not* going to use the standard Scheme notation as in the rest of the book. That's because, in this chapter, we want to separate the idea of functions from the complexities of programming language notation. For example, real Scheme notation lets you write expressions that involve more than one function, but in this chapter you can only use one at a time.

To get into this chapter's special computer interface, first start running Scheme as you did in the first chapter, then type

```
(load "functions.scm")
```

to tell Scheme to read the program you'll be using. (If you have trouble loading the program, look in Appendix A for further information about load.) Then, to start the program, type

```
(functions)
```

You'll then be able to carry out interactions like the following.* In the text below we've printed what *you* type in **boldface** and what the *computer* types in `lightface` printing:

```
Function: +
Argument: 3
Argument: 5

The result is: 8

Function: sqrt
Argument: 144

The result is: 12
```

As you can see, different functions can have different numbers of arguments. In these examples we added two numbers, and we took the square root of one number. However, every function gives exactly one result each time we use it.

To leave the `functions` program, type `exit` when it asks for a function.

Arithmetic

Experiment with these arithmetic functions: `+`, `-`, `*`, `/`, `sqrt`, `quotient`, `remainder`, `random`, `round`, `max`, and `expt`. Try different kinds of numbers, including integers and numbers with decimal fractions. What if you try to divide by zero? Throughout this chapter we are going to let you experiment with functions rather than just give you a long, boring list of how each one works. (The boring list is available for reference on page 553.)

Try these:

```
Function: /
Argument: 1
Argument: 987654321987654321

Function: remainder
Argument: 12
Argument: -5
```

---

* If you get no response at all after you type `(functions)`, just press the Return or Enter key again. Tell your instructor to read Appendix A to see how to fix this.

```
Function: round
Argument: 17.5
```

These are just a few suggestions. Be creative; don't just type in our examples.

Words

Not all Scheme functions deal with numbers. A broader category of argument is the *word,* including numbers but also including English words like `spaghetti` or `xylophone`. Even a meaningless sequence of letters and digits such as `glo87rp` is considered a word.* Try these functions that accept words as arguments: `first`, `butfirst`, `last`, `butlast`, `word`, and `count`. What happens if you use a number as the argument to one of these?

```
Function: butfirst
Argument: a

Function: count
Argument: 765432
```

So far most of our functions fall into one of two categories: the arithmetic functions, which require numbers as arguments and return a number as the result; and the word functions, which accept words as arguments and return a word as the result. The one exception we've seen is `count`. What kind of argument does `count` accept? What kind of value does it return? The technical term for "a kind of data" is a *type.*

In principle you could think of almost anything as a type, such as "numbers that contain the digit 7." Such *ad hoc* types are legitimate and sometimes useful, but there are also official types that Scheme knows about. Types can overlap; for example, numbers are also considered words.

```
Function: word
Argument: 3.14
Argument: 1592654

Function: +
Argument: 6
Argument: seven
```

---

* Certain punctuation characters can also be used in words, but let's defer the details until you've gotten to know the word functions with simpler examples.

Domain and Range

The technical term for "the things that a function accepts as an argument" is the *domain* of the function. The name for "the things that a function returns" is its *range*. So the domain of `count` is words, and the range of `count` is numbers (in fact, nonnegative integers). This example shows that the range may not be exactly one of our standard data types; there is no "nonnegative integer" type in Scheme.

How do you talk about the domain and range of a function? You could say, for example, "The `cos` function has numbers as its domain and numbers between −1 and 1 as its range." Or, informally, you may also say "`Cos` takes a number as its argument and returns a number between −1 and 1."*

For functions of two or more arguments, the language is a little less straightforward. The informal version still works: "`Remainder` takes two integers as arguments and returns an integer." But you can't say "The domain of `remainder` is two integers," because the domain of a function is the *set* of all possible arguments, not just a statement about the characteristics of legal arguments.**

(By the way, we're making certain simplifications in this chapter. For example, Scheme's + function can actually accept any number of arguments, not just two. But we don't want to go into all the bells and whistles at once, so we'll start with adding two numbers at a time.)

Here are examples that illustrate the domains of some functions:

```
Function: expt
Argument: -3
Argument: .5

Function: expt
Argument: -3
Argument: -3

Function: remainder
Argument: 5
Argument: 0
```

---

* Unless your version of Scheme has complex numbers.

** Real mathematicians say, "The domain of `remainder` is the Cartesian cross product of the integers and the integers." In order to avoid that mouthful, we'll just use the informal wording.

More Types: Sentences and Booleans

We're going to introduce more data types, and more functions that include those types in their domain or range. The next type is the *sentence:* a bunch of words enclosed in parentheses, such as

```
(all you need is love)
```

(Don't include any punctuation characters within the sentence.) Many of the functions that accept words in their domain will also accept sentences. There is also a function `sentence` that accepts words and sentences. Try examples like `butfirst` of a sentence.

```
Function: sentence
Argument: (when i get)
Argument: home

Function: butfirst
Argument: (yer blues)

Function: butlast
Argument: ()
```

Other important functions are used to ask yes-or-no questions. That is, the range of these functions contains only two values, one meaning "true" and the other meaning "false." Try the numeric comparisons =, <, >, <=, and >=, and the functions `equal?` and `member?` that work on words and sentences. (The question mark is part of the name of the function.) There are also functions `and`, `or`, and `not` whose domain and range are both true-false values. The two values "true" and "false" are called *Booleans,* named after George Boole (1815–1864), who developed the formal tools used for true-false values in mathematics.

What good are these true-false values? Often a program must choose between two options: If the number is positive, do this; if negative, do that. Scheme has functions to make such choices based on true-false values. For now, you can experiment with the `if` function. Its first argument must be true or false; the others can be anything.

Our Favorite Type: Functions

So far our data types include numbers, words, sentences, and Booleans. Scheme has several more data types, but for now we'll just consider one more. A *function* can be used as data. Here's an example:

```
Function: number-of-arguments
Argument: equal?

The result is: 2
```

The range of `number-of-arguments` is nonnegative integers. But its domain is *functions*. For example, try using it as an argument to itself!

If you've used other computer programming languages, it may seem strange to use a function—that is, a part of a computer program—as data. Most languages make a sharp distinction between program and data. We'll soon see that the ability to treat functions as data helps make Scheme programming very powerful and convenient.

Try these examples:

```
Function: every
Argument: first
Argument: (the long and winding road)

Function: keep
Argument: vowel?
Argument: constantinople
```

Think carefully about these. You aren't applying the function `first` to the sentence (`the long and winding road`); you're applying the function `every` to a function and a sentence.

Other functions that can be used with `keep` include `even?` and `odd?`, whose domains are the integers, and `number?`, whose domain is everything.

Play with It

If you've been reading the book but not trying things out on the computer as you go along, get to work! Spend some time getting used to these ideas and thinking about them. When you're done, read ahead.

Thinking about What You've Done

The idea of *function* is at the heart of both mathematics and computer science. For example, when mathematicians want to think very formally about the system of numbers, they use functions to create the integers. They say, let's suppose we have one number, called zero; then let's suppose we have the *function* given by $f(x) = x + 1$. By applying that function repeatedly, we can create $1 = f(0)$, then $2 = f(1)$, and so on.

Functions are important in computer science because they give us a way to think about *process*—in simple English, a way to think about something happening, something changing. A function embodies a *transformation* of information, taking in something we know and returning something we didn't know. That's what computers do: They transform information to produce new results.

A lot of the mathematics taught in school is about numbers, but we've seen that functions don't have to be about numbers. We've used functions of words and sentences, such as `first`, and even functions of functions, such as `keep`. You can imagine functions that transform information of any kind at all, such as the function French(window)=fenêtre or the function capital(California)=Sacramento.

You've done a lot of thinking about the *domain* and *range* of functions. You can add two numbers, but it doesn't make sense to add two words that aren't numbers. Some two-argument functions have complicated domains because the acceptable values for one argument depend on the specific value used for the other one. (The function `expt` is an example; make sure you've tried both positive and negative numbers, and fractional as well as whole-number powers.)

Part of the definition of a function is that you always get the same answer whenever you call a function with the same argument(s). The value returned by the function, in other words, shouldn't change regardless of anything else you may have computed meanwhile. One of the "functions" you've explored in this chapter isn't a real function according to this rule; which one? The rule may seem too restrictive, and indeed it's often convenient to use the name "function" loosely for processes that can give different results in different circumstances. But we'll see that sometimes it's important to stick with the strict definition and refrain from using processes that aren't truly functions.

We've hinted at two different ways of thinking about functions. The first is called *function as process*. Here, a function is a rule that tells us how to transform some information into some other information. The function is just a rule, not a thing in its own right. The actual "things" are the words or numbers or whatever the function manipulates. The second way of thinking is called *function as object*. In this view, a function is a perfectly good "thing" in itself. We can use a function as an argument to another function, for example. Research with college math students shows that this second idea is hard for most people, but it's worth the effort because you'll see that *higher-order functions* (functions of functions) like `keep` and `every` can make programs much easier to write.

As a homey analogy, think about a carrot peeler. If we focus our attention on the carrots—which are, after all, what we want to eat—then the peeler just represents a process. We are peeling carrots. We are applying the function peel to carrots. It's the carrot that counts. But we can also think about the peeler as a thing in its own right, when we clean it, or worry about whether its blade is sharp enough.

The big idea that we *haven't* explored in this chapter (although we used it a lot in Chapter 1) is the *composition* of functions: using the result from one function as an argument to another function. It's a crucial idea; we write large programs by defining a bunch of small functions and then composing them with each other to produce the desired result. We'll start doing that in the next chapter, where we return to real Scheme notation.

Exercises

Use the functions *program for all these exercises.*

2.1 In each line of the following table we've left out one piece of information. Fill in the missing details.

function	arg 1	arg 2	result
word	now	here	
sentence	now	here	
first	blackbird	none	
first	(blackbird)	none	
	3	4	7
every		(thank you girl)	(hank ou irl)
member?	e	aardvark	
member?	the		#t
keep	vowel?	(i will)	
keep	vowel?		eieio*
last	( )	none	
	last	(honey pie)	(y e)
		taxman	aa

2.2 What is the domain of the vowel? function?

---

* Yes, there is an English word. It has to do with astronomy.

2.3 One of the functions you can use is called `appearances`. Experiment with it, and then describe fully its domain and range, and what it does. (Make sure to try lots of cases. Hint: Think about its name.)

2.4 One of the functions you can use is called `item`. Experiment with it, and then describe fully its domain and range, and what it does.

The following exercises ask for functions that meet certain criteria. For your convenience, here are the functions in this chapter: `+`, `-`, `/`, `<=`, `<`, `=`, `>=`, `>`, `and`, `appearances`, `butfirst`, `butlast`, `cos`, `count`, `equal?`, `every`, `even?`, `expt`, `first`, `if`, `item`, `keep`, `last`, `max`, `member?`, `not`, `number?`, `number-of-arguments`, `odd?`, `or`, `quotient`, `random`, `remainder`, `round`, `sentence`, `sqrt`, `vowel?`, and `word`.

2.5 List the one-argument functions in this chapter for which the type of the return value is always different from the type of the argument.

2.6 List the one-argument functions in this chapter for which the type of the return value is sometimes different from the type of the argument.

2.7 Mathematicians sometimes use the term "operator" to mean a function of two arguments, both of the same type, that returns a result of the same type. Which of the functions you've seen in this chapter satisfy that definition?

2.8 An operator f is *commutative* if $f(a, b) = f(b, a)$ for all possible arguments a and b. For example, `+` is commutative, but `word` isn't. Which of the operators from Exercise 2.7 are commutative?

2.9 An operator f is *associative* if $f(f(a, b), c) = f(a, f(b, c))$ for all possible arguments a, b, and c. For example, `*` is associative, but not `/`. Which of the operators from Exercise 2.7 are associative?

Part II
Composition of Functions

The big idea in this part of the book is deceptively simple. It's that we can take the value returned by one function and use it as an argument to another function. By "hooking up" two functions in this way, we invent a new, third function. For example, let's say we have a function that adds the letter **s** to the end of a word:

$$add\text{-}s(\text{``run''}) = \text{``runs''}$$

and another function that puts two words together into a sentence:

$$sentence(\text{``day''}, \text{``tripper''}) = \text{``day tripper''}$$

We can combine these to create a new function that represents the third person singular form of a verb:

$$third\text{-}person(\text{verb}) = sentence(\text{``she''}, add\text{-}s(\text{verb}))$$

That general formula looks like this when applied to a particular verb:

$$third\text{-}person(\text{``sing''}) = \text{``she sings''}$$

The way we say it in Scheme is

```
(define (third-person verb)
  (sentence 'she (add-s verb)))
```

(When we give an example like this at the beginning of a part, don't worry about the fact that you don't recognize the notation. The example is meant as a preview of what you'll learn in the coming chapters.)

We know that this idea probably doesn't look like much of a big deal to you. It seems obvious. Nevertheless, it will turn out that we can express a wide variety of computational algorithms by linking functions together in this way. This linking is what we mean by "functional programming."

In a bucket brigade, each person hands a result to the next.

3   Expressions

The interaction between you and Scheme is called the "read-eval-print loop." Scheme reads what you type, *evaluates* it, and prints the answer, and then does the same thing over again. We're emphasizing the word "evaluates" because the essence of understanding Scheme is knowing what it means to evaluate something.

Each question you type is called an *expression*.* The expression can be a single value, such as 26, or something more complicated in parentheses, such as (+ 14 7). The first kind of expression is called an *atom* (or *atomic expression*), while the second kind of expression is called a *compound expression,* because it's made out of the smaller expressions +, 14, and 7. The metaphor is from chemistry, where atoms of single elements are combined to form chemical compounds. We sometimes call the expressions within a compound expression its *subexpressions.*

Compound expressions tell Scheme to "do" a procedure. This idea is so important that it has a lot of names. You can *call* a procedure; you can *invoke* a procedure; or you can *apply* a procedure to some numbers or other values. All of these mean the same thing.

If you've programmed before in some other language, you're probably accustomed to the idea of several different types of statements for different purposes. For example, a "print statement" may look very different from an "assignment statement." In Scheme,

---

* In other programming languages, the name for what you type might be a "command" or an "instruction." The name "expression" is meant to emphasize that we are talking about the notation in which you ask the question, as distinct from the idea in your head, just as in English you express an idea in words. Also, in Scheme we are more often asking questions rather than telling the computer to take some action.

everything is done by calling procedures, just as we've been doing here. Whatever you want to do, there's only one notation: the compound expression.

Notice that we said a compound expression contains expressions. This means that you can't understand what an expression is until you already understand what an expression is. This sort of circularity comes up again and again and again and again* in Scheme programming. How do you ever get a handle on this self-referential idea? The secret is that there has to be some simple kind of expression that *doesn't* have smaller expressions inside it—the atomic expressions.

It's easy to understand an expression that just contains one number. Numbers are *self-evaluating;* that is, when you evaluate a number, you just get the same number back.

Once you understand *numbers,* you can understand *expressions that add up* numbers. And once you understand *those* expressions, you can use that knowledge to figure out *expressions that add up* expressions-that-add-up-numbers. Then ... and so on. In practice, you don't usually think about all these levels of complexity separately. You just think, "I know what a number is, and I know what it means to add up *any* expressions."

So, for example, to understand the expression

```
(+ (+ 2 3) (+ 4 5))
```

you must first understand 2 and 3 as self-evaluating numbers, then understand (+ 2 3) as an expression that adds those numbers, then understand how the sum, 5, contributes to the overall expression.

By the way, in ordinary arithmetic you've gotten used to the idea that parentheses can be optional; $3 + 4 \times 5$ means the same as $3 + (4 \times 5)$. But in Scheme, parentheses are *never* optional. Every procedure call must be enclosed in parentheses.

Little People

You may not have realized it, but inside your computer there are thousands of little people. Each of them is a specialist in one particular Scheme procedure. The head little person, Alonzo, is in charge of the read-eval-print loop.

When you enter an expression, such as

```
(- (+ 5 8) (+ 2 4))
```

---

* and again

Alonzo reads it, hires other little people to help him evaluate it, and finally prints 7, its value. We're going to focus on the evaluation step.

Three little people work together to evaluate the expression: a minus person and two plus people. (To make this account easier to read, we're using the ordinary English words "minus" and "plus" to refer to the procedures whose Scheme names are - and +. Don't be confused by this and try to type `minus` to Scheme.)

Since the overall expression is a subtraction, Alonzo hires Alice, the first available minus specialist. Here's how the little people evaluate the expression:

- Alice wants to be given some numbers, so before she can do any work, she complains to Alonzo that she wants to know which numbers to subtract.

- Alonzo looks at the subexpressions that should provide Alice's arguments, namely, (+ 5 8) and (+ 2 4). Since both of these are addition problems, Alonzo hires two plus specialists, Bernie and Cordelia, and tells them to report their results to Alice.

- The first plus person, Bernie, also wants some numbers, so he asks Alonzo for them.

- Alonzo looks at the subexpressions of (+ 5 8) that should provide Bernie's arguments, namely, 5 and 8. Since these are both atomic, Alonzo can give them directly to Bernie.

- Bernie adds his arguments, 5 and 8, to get 13. He does this in his head—we don't have to worry about how he knows how to add; that's his job.

- The second plus person, Cordelia, wants some arguments; Alonzo looks at the subexpressions of (+ 2 4) and gives the 2 and 4 to Cordelia. She adds them, getting 6.

- Bernie and Cordelia hand their results to the waiting Alice, who can now subtract them to get 7. She hands that result to Alonzo, who prints it.

How does Alonzo know what's the argument to what? That's what the grouping of subexpressions with parentheses is about. Since the plus expressions are inside the minus expression, the plus people have to give their results to the minus person.

We've made it seem as if Bernie does his work before Cordelia does hers. In fact, the *order of evaluation* of the argument subexpressions is not specified in Scheme; different implementations may do it in different orders. In particular, Cordelia might do her work before Bernie, or they might even do their work at the same time, if we're using a *parallel processing* computer. However, it *is* important that both Bernie and Cordelia finish their work before Alice can do hers.

The entire call to – is itself a single expression; it could be a part of an even larger expression:

```
> (* (- (+ 5 8) (+ 2 4))
     (/ 10 2))
35
```

This says to multiply the numbers 7 and 5, except that instead of saying 7 and 5 explicitly, we wrote expressions whose values are 7 and 5. (By the way, we would say that the above expression has three subexpressions, the * and the two arguments. The argument subexpressions, in turn, have their own subexpressions. However, these sub-subexpressions, such as (+ 5 8), don't count as subexpressions of the whole thing.)

We can express this organization of little people more formally. If an expression is atomic, Scheme just knows the value.* Otherwise, it is a compound expression, so Scheme first evaluates all the subexpressions (in some unspecified order) and then applies the value of the first one, which had better be a procedure, to the values of the rest of them. Those other subexpressions are the arguments.

We can use this rule to evaluate arbitrarily complex expressions, and Scheme won't get confused. No matter how long the expression is, it's made up of smaller subexpressions to which the same rule applies. Look at this long, messy example:

```
> (+ (* 2 (/ 14 7) 3)
     (/ (* (- (* 3 5) 3) (+ 1 1))
        (- (* 4 3) (* 3 2)))
     (- 15 18))
13
```

Scheme understands this by looking for the subexpressions of the overall expression, like this:

```
(+ (...)
   (...        ; One of them takes two lines but you can tell by
      ...)     ; matching parentheses that they're one expression.
   (...))
```

(Scheme ignores everything to the right of a semicolon, so semicolons can be used to indicate comments, as above.)

---

* We'll explain this part in more detail later.

Notice that in the example above we asked + to add *three* numbers. In the `functions` program of Chapter 2 we pretended that every Scheme function accepts a fixed number of arguments, but actually, some functions can accept any number. These include +, *, `word`, and `sentence`.

Result Replacement

Since a little person can't do his or her job until all of the necessary subexpressions have been evaluated by other little people, we can "fast forward" this process by skipping the parts about "Alice waits for Bernie and Cordelia" and starting with the completion of the smaller tasks by the lesser little people.

To keep track of which result goes into which larger computation, you can write down a complicated expression and then *rewrite* it repeatedly, each time replacing some small expression with a simpler expression that has the same value.

```
(+ (* [(- 10 7)] (+ 4 1)) (- 15 (/ 12 3)) 17)
(+ (* 3        [(+ 4 1)]) (- 15 (/ 12 3)) 17)
(+ [(* 3       5        )] (- 15 (/ 12 3)) 17)
(+ 15                     (- 15 [(/ 12 3)]) 17)
(+ 15                     [(- 15 4        )] 17)
[(+ 15                    11              17)]
43
```

In each line of the diagram, the boxed expression is the one that will be replaced with its value on the following line.

If you like, you can save some steps by evaluating *several* small expressions from one line to the next:

```
(+ (* [(- 10 7)] [(+ 4 1)]) (- 15 [(/ 12 3)]) 17)
(+ [(* 3        5         )] [(- 15 4        )] 17)
[(+ 15                      11               17)]
43
```

Plumbing Diagrams

Some people find it helpful to look at a pictorial form of the connections among subexpressions. You can think of each procedure as a machine, like the ones they drew on the chalkboard in junior high school.

Each machine has some number of input hoppers on the top and one chute at the bottom. You put something in each hopper, turn the crank, and something else comes out the bottom. For a complicated expression, you hook up the output chute of one machine to the input hopper of another. These combinations are called "plumbing diagrams." Let's look at the plumbing diagram for (- (+ 5 8) (+ 2 4)):

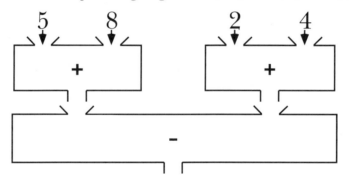

You can annotate the diagram by indicating the actual information that flows through each pipe. Here's how that would look for this expression:

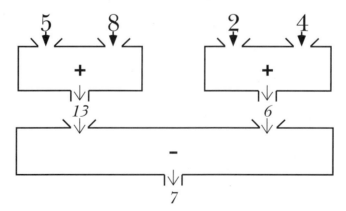

Pitfalls

⇒ One of the biggest problems that beginning Lisp programmers have comes from trying to read a program from left to right, rather than thinking about it in terms of expressions and subexpressions. For example,

```
(square (cos 3))
```

doesn't mean "square three, then take the cosine of the answer you get." Instead, as you know, it means that the argument to `square` is the return value from `(cos 3)`.

⇒ Another big problem that people have is thinking that Scheme cares about the spaces, tabs, line breaks, and other "white space" in their Scheme programs. We've been indenting our expressions to illustrate the way that subexpressions line up underneath each other. But to Scheme,

```
(+ (* 2 (/ 14 7) 3) (/ (* (- (* 3 5) 3) (+ 1
1)) (- (* 4 3) (* 3 2))) (- 15 18))
```

means the same thing as

```
(+ (* 2 (/ 14 7) 3)
   (/ (* (- (* 3 5) 3) (+ 1 1))
      (- (* 4 3) (* 3 2)))
   (- 15 18))
```

So in this expression:

```
(+ (* 3 (sqrt 49)                       ;; weirdly formatted
      (/ 12 4)))
```

there aren't two arguments to +, even though it looks that way if you think about the indenting. What Scheme does is look at the parentheses, and if you examine these carefully, you'll see that there are three arguments to *: the atom 3, the compound expression `(sqrt 49)`, and the compound expression `(/ 12 4)`. (And there's only one argument to +.)

⇒ A consequence of Scheme's not caring about white space is that when you hit the return key, Scheme might not do anything. If you're in the middle of an expression, Scheme waits until you're done typing the entire thing before it evaluates what you've typed. This is fine if your program is correct, but if you type this in:

```
(+ (* 3 4)
   (/ 8 2)                                    ; note missing right paren
```

then *nothing* will happen. Even if you type forever, until you close the open parenthesis next to the + sign, Scheme will still be reading an expression. So if Scheme seems to be ignoring you, try typing a zillion close parentheses. (You'll probably get an error message about too many parentheses, but after that, Scheme should start paying attention again.)

⇒ You might get into the same sort of trouble if you have a double-quote mark (") in your program. Everything inside a pair of quotation marks is treated as one single *string*. We'll explain more about strings later. For now, if your program has a stray quotation mark, like this:

```
(+ (* 3 " 4)                                  ; note extra quote mark
   (/ 8 2))
```

then you can get into the same predicament of typing and having Scheme ignore you. (Once you type the second quotation mark, you may still need some close parentheses, since the ones you type inside a string don't count.)

⇒ One other way that Scheme might seem to be ignoring you comes from the fact that you don't get a new Scheme prompt until you type in an expression and it's evaluated. So if you just hit the **return** or **enter** key without typing anything, most versions of Scheme won't print a new prompt.

Boring Exercises

3.1 Translate the arithmetic expressions $(3+4)\times5$ and $3+(4\times5)$ into Scheme expressions, and into plumbing diagrams.

3.2 How many little people does Alonzo hire in evaluating each of the following expressions:

```
(+ 3 (* 4 5) (- 10 4))
```

```
(+ (* (- (/ 8 2) 1) 5) 2)
```

```
(* (+ (- 3 (/ 4 2))
      (sin (* 3 2))
      (- 8 (sqrt 5)))
   (- (/ 2 3)
      4))
```

3.3 Each of the expressions in the previous exercise is compound. How many subexpressions (not including subexpressions of subexpressions) does each one have?

For example,

```
(* (- 1 (+ 3 4)) 8)
```

has three subexpressions; you wouldn't count `(+ 3 4)`.

3.4 Five little people are hired in evaluating the following expression:

```
(+ (* 3 (- 4 7))
   (- 8 (- 3 5)))
```

Give each little person a name and list her specialty, the argument values she receives, her return value, and the name of the little person to whom she tells her result.

3.5 Evaluate each of the following expressions using the result replacement technique:

```
(sqrt (+ 6 (* 5 2)))
```

```
(+ (+ (+ 1 2) 3) 4)
```

3.6 Draw a plumbing diagram for each of the following expressions:

```
(+ 3 4 5 6 7)
```

```
(+ (+ 3 4) (+ 5 6 7))
```

```
(+ (+ 3 (+ 4 5) 6) 7)
```

3.7 What value is returned by `(/ 1 3)` in your version of Scheme? (Some Schemes return a decimal fraction like `0.33333`, while others have exact fractional values like `1/3` built in.)

3.8   Which of the functions that you explored in Chapter 2 will accept variable numbers of arguments?

Real Exercises

3.9   The expression (+ 8 2) has the value 10. It is a compound expression made up of three atoms. For this problem, write five other Scheme expressions whose values are also the number ten:

- An atom

- Another compound expression made up of three atoms

- A compound expression made up of four atoms

- A compound expression made up of an atom and two compound subexpressions

- Any other kind of expression

In the old days, they "defined procedures" like this.

4 Defining Your Own Procedures

Until now we've been using procedures that Scheme already knows when you begin working with it. In this chapter you'll find out how to create new procedures.

How to Define a Procedure

A Scheme program consists of one or more *procedures*. A procedure is a description of the process by which a computer can work out some result that we want. Here's how to define a procedure that returns the square of its argument:

```
(define (square x)
  (* x x))
```

(The value returned by define may differ depending on the version of Scheme you're using. Many versions return the name of the procedure you're defining, but others return something else. It doesn't matter, because when you use define you aren't interested in the returned value, but rather in the fact that Scheme remembers the new definition for later use.)

This is the definition of a procedure called square. Square takes one argument, a number, and it returns the square of that number. Once you have defined square, you can use it just the same way as you use primitive procedures:

```
> (square 7)
49

> (+ 10 (square 2))
14
```

```
> (square (square 3))
81
```

This procedure definition has four parts. The first is the word **define**, which indicates that you are defining something. The second and third come together inside parentheses: the name that you want to give the procedure and the name(s) you want to use for its argument(s). This arrangement was chosen by the designers of Scheme because it looks like the form in which the procedure will be invoked. That is, (**square x**) looks like (**square 7**). The fourth part of the definition is the *body:* an expression whose value provides the function's return value.

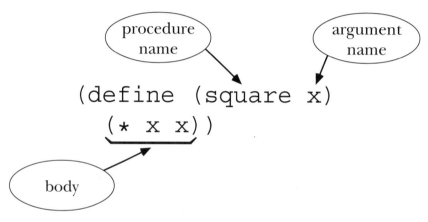

Special Forms

Define is a *special form,* an exception to the evaluation rule we've been going on about.* Usually, an expression represents a procedure invocation, so the general rule is that Scheme first evaluates all the subexpressions, and then applies the resulting procedure to the resulting argument values. The specialness of special forms is that Scheme *doesn't* evaluate all the subexpressions. Instead, each special form has its own particular evaluation rule. For example, when we defined **square**, no part of the definition was evaluated: not **square**, not **x**, and not (*** x x**). It wouldn't make sense to evaluate (**square x**) because you can't invoke the **square** procedure before you define it!

---

* Technically, the entire expression (**define (square x) ...**) is the special form; the word **define** itself is called a *keyword.* But in fact Lispians are almost always loose about this distinction and say "**define** is a special form," just as we've done here. The word "form" is an archaic synonym for "expression," so "special form" just means "special expression."

It would be possible to describe special forms using the following model: "Certain procedures want their arguments unevaluated, and Scheme recognizes them. After refraining from evaluating define's arguments, for example, Scheme invokes the define procedure with those unevaluated arguments." But in fact the designers of Scheme chose to think about it differently. The entire special form that starts with define is just a completely different kind of thing from a procedure call. In Scheme there is no procedure named define. In fact, define is not the name of anything at all:

```
> +
#<PRIMITIVE PROCEDURE +>

> define
ERROR -- INVALID CONTEXT FOR KEYWORD DEFINE
```

Nevertheless, in this book, unless it's really important to make the distinction, we'll talk as if there were a procedure called define. For example, we'll talk about "define's arguments" and "the value returned by define" and "invoking define."

Functions and Procedures

Throughout most of this book, our procedures will describe processes that compute *functions*. A function is a connection between some values you already know and a new value you want to find out. For example, the *square* function takes a number, such as 8, as its input value and returns another number, 64 in this case, as its output value. The *plural* function takes a noun, such as "computer," and returns another word, "computers" in this example. The technical term for the function's input value is its *argument*. A function may take more than one argument; for example, the remainder function takes two arguments, such as 12 and 5. It returns one value, the remainder on dividing the first argument by the second (in this case, 2).

We said earlier that a procedure is "a description of the process by which a computer can work out some result that we want." What do we mean by *process?* Consider these two definitions:

$$f(x) = 3x + 12$$
$$g(x) = 3(x + 4)$$

The two definitions call for different arithmetic operations. For example, to compute $f(8)$ we'd multiply 8 by 3, then add 12 to the result. To compute $g(8)$, we'd add 4 to

8, then multiply the result by 3. But we get the same answer, 36, either way. These two equations describe different *processes,* but they compute the same *function.* The function is just the association between the starting value(s) and the resulting value, no matter how that result is computed. In Scheme we could say

```
(define (f x)
  (+ (* 3 x) 12))

(define (g x)
  (* 3 (+ x 4)))
```

and we'd say that f and g are two procedures that represent the same function.

In real life, functions are not always represented by procedures. We could represent a function by a *table* showing all its possible values, like this:

Alabama	Montgomery
Alaska	Juneau
Arizona	Phoenix
Arkansas	Little Rock
California	Sacramento
...	...

This table represents the State Capital function; we haven't shown all the lines of the complete table, but we could. There are only a finite number of U.S. states. Numeric functions can also be represented by *graphs,* as you probably learned in high school algebra. In this book our focus is on the representation of functions by procedures. The only reason for showing you this table example is to clarify what we mean when we say that a function *is represented by* a procedure, rather than that a function *is* the procedure.

We'll say "the procedure f" when we want to discuss the operations we're telling Scheme to carry out. We'll say "the function represented by f" when our attention is focused on the value returned, rather than on the mechanism. (But we'll often abbreviate that lengthy second phrase with "the function f" unless the context is especially confusing.)*

---

* Also, we'll sometimes use the terms "domain" and "range" when we're talking about procedures, although technically, only functions have domains and ranges.

Argument Names versus Argument Values

> "It's long," said the Knight, "but it's very, *very* beautiful. Everybody that hears me sing it—either it brings the *tears* into their eyes, or else—"
>
> "Or else what?" said Alice, for the Knight had made a sudden pause.
>
> "Or else it doesn't, you know. The name of the song is called '*Haddock's Eyes.*'"
>
> "Oh, that's the name of the song, is it?" Alice said, trying to feel interested.
>
> "No, you don't understand," the Knight said, looking a little vexed. "That's what the name is *called*. The name really is '*The Aged Aged Man.*'"
>
> "Then I ought to have said 'That's what the *song* is called'?" Alice corrected herself.
>
> "No, you oughtn't; that's quite another thing! The *song* is called '*Ways And Means*': but that's only what it's *called,* you know!"
>
> "Well, what *is* the song, then?" said Alice, who was by this time completely bewildered.
>
> "I was coming to that," the Knight said. "The song really is '*A-sitting On A Gate*': and the tune's my own invention."
>
> —Lewis Carroll, *Through the Looking-Glass, and What Alice Found There*

Notice that when we *defined* the `square` procedure we gave a *name*, `x`, for its argument. By contrast, when we *invoked* `square` we provided a *value* for the argument (e.g., 7). The word `x` is a "place holder" in the definition that stands for whatever value you use when you call the procedure. So you can read the definition of `square` as saying, "In order to `square` a number, multiply *that number* by *that number.*" The name `x` holds the place of the particular number that you mean.

Be sure you understand this distinction between defining a procedure and calling it. A procedure represents a general technique that can be applied to many specific cases. We don't want to build any particular case into the procedure definition; we want the definition to express the general nature of the technique. You wouldn't want a procedure that only knew how to take the square of 7. But when you actually get around to using `square`, you have to be specific about which number you're squaring.

The name for the name of an argument (whew!) is *formal parameter*. In our `square` example, `x` is the formal parameter. (You may hear people say either "formal" alone or "parameter" alone when they're feeling lazy.) The technical term for the actual value of the argument is the *actual argument*. In a case like

```
(square (+ 5 9))
```

you may want to distinguish the *actual argument expression* `(+ 5 9)` from the *actual argument value* 14. Most of the time it's perfectly clear what you mean, and you just say "argument" for all of these things, but right now when you're learning these ideas it's important to be able to talk more precisely.

The `square` procedure takes one argument. If a procedure requires more than one argument, then the question arises, which actual argument goes with which formal parameter? The answer is that they go in the order in which you write them, like this:

```
(define (f a b)
  (+ (* 3 a) b))

> (f 5 8)
23

> (f 8 5)
29
```

Procedure as Generalization

What's the average of 17 and 25? To answer this question you could add the two numbers, getting 42, and divide that by two, getting 21. You could ask Scheme to do this for you:

```
> (/ (+ 17 25) 2)
21
```

What's the average of 14 and 68?

```
> (/ (+ 14 68) 2)
41
```

Once you understand the technique, you could answer any such question by typing an expression of the form

```
(/ (+ _____ _____) 2)
```

to Scheme.

But if you're going to be faced with more such problems, an obvious next step is to *generalize* the technique by defining a procedure:

```
(define (average a b)
  (/ (+ a b) 2))
```

With this definition, you can think about the next problem that comes along in terms of the problem itself, rather than in terms of the steps required for its solution:

```
> (average 27 4)
15.5
```

This is an example of what we meant when we defined "abstraction" as noticing a pattern and giving it a name. It's not so different from the naming of such patterns in English; when someone invented the name "average" it was, probably, after noticing that it was often useful to find the value halfway between two other values.

This naming process is more important than it sounds, because once we have a name for some idea, we can use that idea without thinking about its pieces. For example, suppose that you want to know not only the average of some numbers but also a measure of whether the numbers are clumped together close to the average, or widely spread out. Statisticians have developed the "standard deviation" as a measure of this second property. You'd rather not have to think about this mysterious formula:

$$\sigma_x = \sqrt{\frac{\sum_{i=1}^{n} x_i^2 - \left(\sum_{i=1}^{n} x_i\right)^2}{n}}$$

but you'd be happy to use a procedure `standard-deviation` that you found in a collection of statistical programs.

After all, there's no law of nature that says computers automatically know how to add or subtract. You could imagine having to instruct Scheme to compute the sum of two large numbers digit by digit, the way you did in elementary school. But instead someone has "taught" your computer how to add before you get to it, giving this technique the name `+` so that you can ask for the sum of two numbers without thinking about the steps required. By inventing `average` or `standard-deviation` we are extending the repertoire of computations that you can ask for without concerning yourself with the details.

Composability

We've suggested that a procedure you define, such as `average`, is essentially similar to one that's built into Scheme, such as `+`. In particular, the rules for building expressions are the same whether the building blocks are primitive procedures or defined procedures.

```
> (average (+ 10 8) (* 3 5))
16.5

> (average (average 2 3) (average 4 5))
3.5

> (sqrt (average 143 145))
12
```

Any return value can be used as an end in itself, as the return value from `sqrt` was used in the last of these examples, or it can provide an argument to another procedure, as the return value from `*` was used in the first of these examples.

These small examples may seem arbitrary, but the same idea, composition of functions, is the basis for all Scheme programming. For example, the complicated formula we gave for standard deviation requires computing the squares of several numbers. So if we were to write a `standard-deviation` procedure, it would invoke `square`.

The Substitution Model

We've paid a lot of attention to the details of formal parameters and actual arguments, but we've been a little handwavy* about how a procedure actually computes a value when you invoke it.

We're going to explain what happens when you invoke a user-defined procedure. Every explanation is a story. No story tells the entire truth, because there are always some details left out. A *model* is a story that has just enough detail to help you understand whatever it's trying to explain but not so much detail that you can't see the forest for the trees.

Today's story is about the *substitution* model. When a procedure is invoked, the goal is to carry out the computation described in its body. The problem is that the body is written in terms of the formal parameters, while the computation has to use the actual argument values. So what Scheme needs is a way to associate actual argument values with formal parameters. It does this by making a new copy of the body of the procedure, in

---

* You know, that's when you wave your hands around in the air instead of explaining what you mean.

which it substitutes the argument values for every appearance of the formal parameters, and then evaluating the resulting expression. So, if you've defined `square` with

```
(define (square x)
  (* x x))
```

then the body of `square` is `(* x x)`. When you want to know the square of a particular number, as in `(square 5)`, Scheme substitutes the 5 for `x` everywhere in the body of square and evaluates the expression. In other words, Scheme takes

```
(* x x)
```

then does the substitution, getting

```
(* 5 5)
```

and then evaluates that expression, getting 25.

If you just type `(* x x)` into Scheme, you will get an error message complaining that `x` doesn't mean anything. Only after the substitution does this become a meaningful expression.

By the way, when we talk about "substituting into the body," we don't mean that the procedure's definition is changed in any permanent way. The body of the procedure doesn't change; what happens, as we said before, is that Scheme constructs a new expression that looks like the body, except for the substitutions.*

There are little people who specialize in `square`, just as there are little people who specialize in `+` and `*`. The difference is that the little people who do primitive procedures can do the work "in their head," all at once. The little people who carry out user-defined procedures have to go through this substitution business we're talking about here. Then they hire other little people to help evaluate the resulting expression, just as Alonzo hires people to help him evaluate the expressions you type directly to Scheme.

Let's say Sam, a little person who specializes in `square`, has been asked to compute `(square 6)`. Sam carries out the substitution, and is left with the expression `(* 6 6)` to

---

* You may be thinking that this is rather an inefficient way to do things—all this copying and replacement before you can actually compute anything. Perhaps you're afraid that your Scheme programs will run very slowly as a result. Don't worry. It really happens in a different way, but the effect is the same except for the speed.

evaluate. Sam then hires Tessa, a multiplication specialist, to evaluate this new expression. Tessa tells Sam that her answer is 36, and, because the multiplication is the entire problem to be solved, this is Sam's answer also.

Here's another example:

```
(define (hypotenuse a b)
  (sqrt (+ (square a) (square b))))

> (hypotenuse 5 12)
```

Suppose Alonzo hires Harry to compute this expression. Harry must first substitute the actual argument values (5 and 12) into the body of hypotenuse:

```
(sqrt (+ (square 5) (square 12)))
```

Now he evaluates that expression, just as Alonzo would evaluate it if you typed it at a Scheme prompt. That is, Harry hires four little people: one sqrt expert, one + expert, and two square experts.* In particular, some little person has to evaluate (square 5), by substituting 5 for x in the body of square, as in the earlier example. Similarly, we substitute 12 for x in order to evaluate (square 12):

```
(hypotenuse 5 12)                      ; substitute into HYPOTENUSE body
(sqrt (+ (square 5) (square 12)))      ; substitute for (SQUARE 5)
         (* 5 5)
          25
(sqrt (+ 25           (square 12)))    ; substitute for (SQUARE 12)
                      (* 12 12)
                       144
(sqrt (+ 25           144))
      (+ 25           144)             ; combine the results as before
      169
(sqrt 169)
13
```

---

* Until we started defining our own procedures in this chapter, all of the little people were hired by Alonzo, because all expressions were typed directly to a Scheme prompt. Now expressions can come from the bodies of procedures, and so the little people needed to compute those expressions are hired by the little person who's computing that procedure. Notice also that each little person *reports to* another little person, not necessarily the one who *hired* her. In this case, if Harry hires Shari for sqrt, Paul for +, and Slim and Sydney for the two squares, then Slim reports to Paul, not to Harry. Only Shari reports directly to Harry.

Don't forget, in the heady rush of learning about the substitution model, what you already knew from before: Each piece of this computation is done by a little person, and some other little person is waiting for the result. In other words, the substitution model tells us how *each compound procedure* is carried out, but doesn't change our picture of the way in which procedure invocations are *composed* into larger expressions.

Pitfalls

⇒ Don't forget that a function can have only *one* return value. For example, here's a program that's supposed to return the sum of the squares of its two arguments:

```
(define (sum-of-squares x y)                    ;; wrong!
  (square x)
  (square y))
```

The problem is that the body of this procedure has two expressions, instead of just one. As it turns out, Scheme just ignores the value of the first expression in cases like this, and returns the value of the last one. What the programmer wants is the *sum* of these two values, so the procedure should say

```
(define (sum-of-squares x y)
  (+ (square x)
     (square y)))
```

⇒ Another pitfall comes from thinking that a procedure call changes the value of a parameter. Here's a faulty program that's supposed to compute the function described by $f(x) = 3x + 10$:

```
(define (f x)                                   ;; wrong!
  (* x 3)
  (+ x 10))
```

Again, the first expression has no effect and Scheme will just return the value $x + 10$.*

⇒ A very common pitfall in Scheme comes from choosing the name of a procedure as a parameter. It doesn't come up very often with procedures like the ones in this chapter

---

* This is especially problematic for people who used to program in a language like Pascal or BASIC, where you say things like "X = X * 3" all the time.

whose domains and ranges are both numbers, but it will be more likely later. If you have a program like this:

```
(define (square x)
  (* x x))

(define (area square)                      ;; wrong!
  (square square))
```

then you'll get in trouble when you invoke the procedure, for example, by saying `(area 8)`. The `area` little person will substitute 8 for `square` everywhere in the procedure definition, leaving you with the expression `(8 8)` to evaluate. That expression would mean to apply the procedure 8 to the argument 8, but 8 isn't a procedure, so an error message results.

It isn't a problem if the formal parameter is the name of a procedure that you don't use inside the body. The problem arises when you try to use the same name, e.g., `square`, with two meanings within a single procedure. But special forms are an exception; you can never use the name of a special form as a parameter.

⇒ A similar problem about name conflicts comes up if you try to use a keyword (the name of a special form, such as `define`) as some other kind of name—either a formal parameter or the name of a procedure you're defining. We're listing this separately because the result is likely to be different. Instead of getting the wrong value substituted, as above, you'll probably see a special error message along the lines of "improper use of keyword."

⇒ Formal parameters *must* be words. Some people try to write procedures that have compound expressions as the formal parameters, like this:

```
(define (f (+ 3 x) y)                      ;; wrong!
  (* x y))
```

Remember that the job of the procedure definition is only to provide a *name* for the argument. The *actual* argument isn't pinned down until you invoke the procedure. People who write programs like the one above are trying to make the procedure definition do some of the job of the procedure invocation.

Boring Exercises

4.1 Consider this procedure:

```
(define (ho-hum x y)
  (+ x (* 2 y)))
```

Show the substitution that occurs when you evaluate

```
(ho-hum 8 12)
```

4.2 Given the following procedure:

```
(define (yawn x)
  (+ 3 (* x 2)))
```

list all the little people that are involved in evaluating

```
(yawn (/ 8 2))
```

(Give their names, their specialties, their arguments, who hires them, and what they do with their answers.)

4.3 Here are some procedure definitions. For each one, describe the function in English, show a sample invocation, and show the result of that invocation.

```
(define (f x y) (- y x))

(define (identity x) x)

(define (three x) 3)

(define (seven) 7)

(define (magic n)
  (- (/ (+ (+ (* 3 n)
             13)
          (- n 1))
       4)
    3))
```

Real Exercises

4.4   Each of the following procedure definitions has an error of some kind. Say what's wrong and why, and fix it:

```
(define (sphere-volume r)
  (* (/ 4 3) 3.141592654)
  (* r r r))

(define (next x)
  (x + 1))

(define (square)
  (* x x))

(define (triangle-area triangle)
  (* 0.5 base height))

(define (sum-of-squares (square x) (square y))
  (+ (square x) (square y)))
```

4.5   Write a procedure to convert a temperature from Fahrenheit to Celsius, and another to convert in the other direction. The two formulas are $F = \frac{9}{5}C + 32$ and $C = \frac{5}{9}(F - 32)$.

4.6   Define a procedure `fourth` that computes the fourth power of its argument. Do this two ways, first using the multiplication function, and then using `square` and not (directly) using multiplication.

4.7   Write a procedure that computes the absolute value of its argument by finding the square root of the square of the argument.

4.8   "Scientific notation" is a way to represent very small or very large numbers by combining a medium-sized number with a power of 10. For example, 5×10^7 represents the number 50000000, while 3.26×10^{-9} represents 0.00000000326 in scientific notation. Write a procedure `scientific` that takes two arguments, a number and an exponent of 10, and returns the corresponding value:

```
> (scientific 7 3)
7000
```

```
> (scientific 42 -5)
0.00042
```

Some versions of Scheme represent fractions in a/b form, and some use scientific notation, so you might see 21/50000 or 4.2E-4 as the result of the last example instead of 0.00042, but these are the same value.

(A harder problem for hotshots: Can you write procedures that go in the other direction? So you'd have

```
> (sci-coefficient 7000)
7

> (sci-exponent 7000)
3
```

You might find the primitive procedures log and floor helpful.)

4.9 Define a procedure discount that takes two arguments: an item's initial price and a percentage discount. It should return the new price:

```
> (discount 10 5)
9.50

> (discount 29.90 50)
14.95
```

4.10 Write a procedure to compute the tip you should leave at a restaurant. It should take the total bill as its argument and return the amount of the tip. It should tip by 15%, but it should know to round up so that the total amount of money you leave (tip plus original bill) is a whole number of dollars. (Use the ceiling procedure to round up.)

```
> (tip 19.98)
3.02

> (tip 29.23)
4.77

> (tip 7.54)
1.46
```

5   Words and Sentences

We started out, in Part I, with examples about acronyms and so on, but since then we've been working with numbery old numbers. That's because the discussions about evaluation and procedure definition were complicated enough without introducing extra ideas at the same time. But now we're ready to get back to symbolic programming.

As we mentioned in Chapter 3, everything that you type into Scheme is evaluated and the resulting value is printed out. Let's say you want to use "square" as a word in your program. For example, you want your program to solve the problem, "Give me an adjective that describes Barry Manilow." If you just type `square` into Scheme, you will find out that `square` is a procedure:

```
> square
#<PROCEDURE>
```

(Different versions of Scheme will have different ways of printing out procedures.)

What you need is a way to say that you want to use the word "*square*" *itself*, rather than the *value* of that word, as an expression. The way to do this is to use `quote`:

```
> (quote square)
SQUARE

> (quote (tomorrow never knows))
(TOMORROW NEVER KNOWS)

> (quote (things we said today))
(THINGS WE SAID TODAY)
```

`Quote` is a special form, since its argument isn't evaluated. Instead, it just returns the argument as is.

Scheme programmers use `quote` a lot, so there is an abbreviation for it:

```
> 'square
SQUARE

> '(old brown shoe)
(old brown shoe)
```

(Since Scheme uses the apostrophe as an abbreviation for `quote`, you can't use one as an ordinary punctuation mark in a sentence. That's why we've been avoiding titles like `(can't buy me love)`. To Scheme this would mean `(can (quote t) buy me love)`!)*

This idea of quoting, although it may seem arbitrary in the context of computer programming, is actually quite familiar from ordinary English. What is a book? It's a bunch of pieces of paper, with printing on them, bound together. What is "a book"? It's a noun phrase, made up of an article and a noun. See? Similarly, what's 2 + 3? It's five. What's "2 + 3"? It's an arithmetic formula. When you see words inside quotation marks, you understand that you're supposed to think about the words themselves; you don't evaluate what they mean. Scheme is the same way.

(It's no accident that kids who make jokes like

> Matt: "Say your name."

> Brian: "Your name."

grow up to be computer programmers. The difference between a thing and its name is one of the important ideas that programmers need to understand.)

---

* Actually, it *is* possible to put punctuation inside words as long as the entire word is enclosed in double-quote marks, like this:

```
> '("can't" buy me love)
("can't" BUY ME LOVE)
```

Words like that are called *strings*. We're not going to use them in any examples until almost the end of the book. Stay away from punctuation and you won't get in trouble. However, question marks and exclamation points are okay. (Ordinary words, the ones that are neither strings nor numbers, are officially called *symbols*.)

Selectors

So far all we've done with words and sentences is quote them. To do more interesting work, we need tools for two kinds of operations: We have to be able to take them apart, and we have to be able to put them together.* We'll start with the take-apart tools; the technical term for them is *selectors*.

```
> (first 'something)
S

> (first '(eight days a week))
EIGHT

> (first 910)
9

> (last 'something)
G

> (last '(eight days a week))
WEEK

> (last 910)
0

> (butfirst 'something)
OMETHING

> (butfirst '(eight days a week))
(DAYS A WEEK)

> (butfirst 910)
10

> (butlast 'something)
SOMETHIN
```

---

* The procedures we're about to show you are not part of standard, official Scheme. Scheme does provide ways to do these things, but the regular ways are somewhat more complicated and error-prone for beginners. We've provided a simpler way to do symbolic computing, using ideas developed as part of the Logo programming language.

```
> (butlast '(eight days a week))
(EIGHT DAYS A)

> (butlast 910)
91
```

Notice that the `first` of a sentence is a word, while the `first` of a word is a letter. (But there's no separate data type called "letter"; a letter is the same as a one-letter word.) The `butfirst` of a sentence is a sentence, and the `butfirst` of a word is a word. The corresponding rules hold for `last` and `butlast`.

The names `butfirst` and `butlast` aren't meant to describe ways to sled; they abbreviate "all but the `first`" and "all but the `last`."

You may be wondering why we're given ways to find the first and last elements but not the 42nd element. It turns out that the ones we have are enough, since we can use these primitive selectors to define others:

```
(define (second thing)
  (first (butfirst thing)))

> (second '(like dreamers do))
DREAMERS

> (second 'michelle)
I
```

There is, however, a primitive selector `item` that takes two arguments, a number n and a word or sentence, and returns the nth element of the second argument.

```
> (item 4 '(being for the benefit of mister kite!))
BENEFIT

> (item 4 'benefit)
E
```

Don't forget that a sentence containing exactly one word is different from the word itself, and selectors operate on the two differently:

```
> (first 'because)
B

> (first '(because))
BECAUSE
```

```
> (butfirst 'because)
ECAUSE

> (butfirst '(because))
()
```

The value of that last expression is the *empty sentence*. You can tell it's a sentence because of the parentheses, and you can tell it's empty because there's nothing between them.

```
> (butfirst 'a)
""

> (butfirst 1024)
"024"
```

As these examples show, sometimes `butfirst` returns a word that has to have double-quote marks around it. The first example shows the *empty word*, while the second shows a number that's not in its ordinary form. (Its numeric value is 24, but you don't usually see a zero in front.)

```
> 024
24

> "024"
"024"
```

We're going to try to avoid printing these funny words. But don't be surprised if you see one as the return value from one of the selectors for words. (Notice that you don't have to put a single quote in front of the double quotes. Strings are self-evaluating, just as numbers are.)

Since `butfirst` and `butlast` are so hard to type, there are abbreviations `bf` and `bl`. You can figure out which is which.

Constructors

Functions for putting things together are called *constructors*. For now, we just have two of them: `word` and `sentence`. `Word` takes any number of words as arguments and joins them all together into one humongous word:

```
> (word 'ses 'qui 'pe 'da 'lian 'ism)
SESQUIPEDALIANISM
```

```
> (word 'now 'here)
NOWHERE

> (word 35 893)
35893
```

Sentence is similar, but slightly different, since it can take both words and sentences as arguments:

```
>  (sentence 'carry 'that 'weight)
(CARRY THAT WEIGHT)

> (sentence '(john paul) '(george ringo))
(JOHN PAUL GEORGE RINGO)
```

Sentence is also too hard to type, so there's the abbreviation se.

```
> (se '(one plus one) 'makes 2)
(ONE PLUS ONE MAKES 2)
```

By the way, why did we have to quote makes in the last example, but not 2? It's because numbers are self-evaluating, as we said in Chapter 3. We have to quote makes because otherwise Scheme would look for something named makes instead of using the word itself. But numbers can't be the names of things; they represent themselves. (In fact, you could quote the 2 and it wouldn't make any difference—do you see why?)

First-Class Words and Sentences

If Scheme isn't your first programming language, you're probably accustomed to dealing with English text on a computer quite differently. Many other languages treat a sentence, for example, as simply a collection (a "string") of *characters* such as letters, spaces, and punctuation. Those languages don't help you maintain the two-level nature of English text, in which a sentence is composed of words, and a word is composed of letters.

Historically, computers just dealt with numbers. You could add two numbers, move a number from one place in the computer's memory to another place, and so on. Since each instruction in the computer's native *machine language* couldn't process anything larger than a number, programmers developed the attitude that a single number is a "real thing" while anything more complicated has to be considered as a collection of things, rather than as a single thing in itself.

The computer represents a text character as a single number. In many programming languages, therefore, a character is a "real thing," but a word or sentence is understood only as a collection of these character-code numbers.

But this isn't the way in which human beings normally think about their own language. To you, a word isn't primarily a string of characters (although it may temporarily seem like one if you're competing in a spelling bee). It's more like a single unit of meaning. Similarly, a sentence is a linguistic structure whose parts are words, not letters and spaces.

A programming language should let you express your ideas in terms that match *your* way of thinking, not the computer's way. Technically, we say that words and sentences should be *first-class data* in our language. This means that a sentence, for example, can be an argument to a procedure; it can be the value returned by a procedure; we can give it a name; and we can build aggregates whose elements are sentences. So far we've seen how to do the first two of these. We'll finish the job in Chapter 7 (on *variables*) and Chapter 17 (on *lists*).

Pitfalls

⇒ We've been avoiding apostrophes in our words and sentences because they're abbreviations for the quote special form. You must also avoid periods, commas, semicolons, quotation marks, vertical bars, and, of course, parentheses, since all of these have special meanings in Scheme. You may, however, use question marks and exclamation points.

⇒ Although we've already mentioned the need to avoid names of primitives when choosing formal parameters, we want to remind you specifically about the names word and sentence. These are often very tempting formal parameters, because many procedures have words or sentences as their domains. Unfortunately, if you choose these names for parameters, you won't be able to use the corresponding procedures within your definition.

```
(define (plural word)                          ;; wrong!
  (word word 's))

> (plural 'george)
ERROR: GEORGE isn't a procedure
```

The result of substitution was not, as you might think,

```
(word 'george 's)
```

but rather

```
('george 'george 's)
```

We've been using `wd` and `sent` as formal parameters instead of `word` and `sentence`, and we recommend that practice.

⇒ There's a difference between a word and a single-word sentence. For example, people often fall into the trap of thinking that the `butfirst` of a two-word sentence such as (`sexy sadie`) is the second word, but it's not. It's a one-word-long sentence. For example, its `count` is one, not five.*

```
> (bf '(sexy sadie))
(SADIE)

> (first (bf '(sexy sadie)))
SADIE
```

⇒ We mentioned earlier that sometimes Scheme has to put double-quote marks around words. Just ignore them; don't get upset if your procedure returns `"6-of-hearts"` instead of just `6-of-hearts`.

⇒ Quote doesn't mean "print." Some people look at interactions like this:

```
> '(good night)
(GOOD NIGHT)
```

and think that the quotation mark was an instruction telling Scheme to print what comes after it. Actually, Scheme *always* prints the value of each expression you type, as part of the read-eval-print loop. In this case, the value of the entire expression is the subexpression that's being quoted, namely, the sentence (`good night`). That value wouldn't be printed if the quotation were part of some larger expression:

```
> (bf '(good night))
(NIGHT)
```

---

* You met `count` in Chapter 2. It takes a word or sentence as its argument, returning either the number of letters in the word or the number of words in the sentence.

⇒ If you see an error message like

```
> (+ 3 (bf 1075))
ERROR: INVALID ARGUMENT TO +: "075"
```

try entering the expression

```
> (strings-are-numbers #t)
OKAY
```

and try again. (The extension to Scheme that allows arithmetic operations to work on nonstandard numbers like `"075"` makes ordinary arithmetic slower than usual. So we've provided a way to turn the extension on and off. Invoking `strings-are-numbers` with the argument `#f` turns off the extension.)*

Boring Exercises

5.1 What values are printed when you type these expressions to Scheme? (Figure it out in your head before you try it on the computer.)

```
(sentence 'I '(me mine))

(sentence '() '(is empty))

(word '23 '45)

(se '23 '45)

(bf 'a)

(bf '(aye))

(count (first '(maggie mae)))

(se "" '() "" '())

(count (se "" '() "" '()))
```

---

* See Appendix A for a fuller explanation.

5.2 For each of the following examples, write a procedure of two arguments that, when applied to the sample arguments, returns the sample result. Your procedures may not include any quoted data.

```
> (f1 '(a b c) '(d e f))
(B C D E)

> (f2 '(a b c) '(d e f))
(B C D E AF)

> (f3 '(a b c) '(d e f))
(A B C A B C)

> (f4 '(a b c) '(d e f))
BE
```

5.3 Explain the difference in meaning between (first 'mezzanine) and (first '(mezzanine)).

5.4 Explain the difference between the two expressions (first (square 7)) and (first '(square 7)).

5.5 Explain the difference between (word 'a 'b 'c) and (se 'a 'b 'c).

5.6 Explain the difference between (bf 'zabadak) and (butfirst 'zabadak).

5.7 Explain the difference between (bf 'x) and (butfirst '(x)).

5.8 Which of the following are legal Scheme sentences?

```
(here, there and everywhere)
(help!)
(all i've got to do)
(you know my name (look up the number))
```

5.9 Figure out what values each of the following will return *before* you try them on the computer:

```
(se (word (bl (bl (first '(make a))))
          (bf (bf (last '(baseball mitt)))))
    (word (first 'with) (bl (bl (bl (bl 'rigidly))))
          (first 'held) (first (bf 'stitches)))))

(se (word (bl (bl 'bring)) 'a (last 'clean))
    (word (bl (last '(baseball hat))) (last 'for) (bl (bl 'very))
          (last (first '(sunny days)))))
```

5.10 What kinds of argument can you give `butfirst` so that it returns a word? A sentence?

5.11 What kinds of argument can you give `last` so that it returns a word? A sentence?

5.12 Which of the functions `first`, `last`, `butfirst`, and `butlast` can return an empty word? For what arguments? What about returning an empty sentence?

Real Exercises

5.13 What does ' 'banana stand for?

What is (`first` ' 'banana) and why?

5.14 Write a procedure `third` that selects the third letter of a word (or the third word of a sentence).

5.15 Write a procedure `first-two` that takes a word as its argument, returning a two-letter word containing the first two letters of the argument.

```
> (first-two 'ambulatory)
AM
```

5.16 Write a procedure `two-first` that takes two words as arguments, returning a two-letter word containing the first letters of the two arguments.

```
> (two-first 'brian 'epstein)
BE
```

Now write a procedure `two-first-sent` that takes a two-word sentence as argument, returning a two-letter word containing the first letters of the two words.

```
> (two-first-sent '(brian epstein))
BE
```

5.17 Write a procedure `knight` that takes a person's name as its argument and returns the name with "Sir" in front of it.

```
> (knight '(david wessel))
(SIR DAVID WESSEL)
```

5.18 Try the following and explain the result:

```
(define (ends word)
  (word (first word) (last word)))

> (ends 'john)
```

5.19 Write a procedure `insert-and` that takes a sentence of items and returns a new sentence with an "and" in the right place:

```
> (insert-and '(john bill wayne fred joey))
(JOHN BILL WAYNE FRED AND JOEY)
```

5.20   Define a procedure to find somebody's middle names:

```
> (middle-names '(james paul mccartney))
(PAUL)

> (middle-names '(john ronald raoul tolkien))
(RONALD RAOUL)

> (middle-names '(bugs bunny))
()

> (middle-names '(peter blair denis bernard noone))
(BLAIR DENIS BERNARD)
```

5.21   Write a procedure `query` that turns a statement into a question by swapping the first two words and adding a question mark to the last word:

```
> (query '(you are experienced))
(ARE YOU EXPERIENCED?)

> (query '(i should have known better))
(SHOULD I HAVE KNOWN BETTER?)
```

"Contrariwise," continued Tweedledee, "if it was so, it might be; and if it were so, it would be; but as it isn't, it ain't. That's logic."

6 True and False

We still need one more thing before we can write more interesting programs: the ability to make decisions. Scheme has a way to say "if this is true, then do this thing, otherwise do something else."

Here's a procedure that greets a person:

```
(define (greet name)
  (if (equal? (first name) 'professor)
      (se '(i hope i am not bothering you) 'professor (last name))
      (se '(good to see you) (first name))))

> (greet '(matt wright))
(GOOD TO SEE YOU MATT)

> (greet '(professor harold abelson))
(I HOPE I AM NOT BOTHERING YOU PROFESSOR ABELSON)
```

The program greets a person by checking to see if that person is a professor. If so, it says, "I hope I am not bothering you" and then the professor's name. But if it's a regular person, the program just says, "Good to see you," and then the person's first name.

If takes three arguments. The first has to be either true or false. (We'll talk in a moment about exactly what true and false look like to Scheme.) In the above example, the first word of the person's name might or might not be equal to the word "Professor." The second and third arguments are expressions; one or the other of them is evaluated depending on the first argument. The value of the entire if expression is the value of either the second or the third argument.

You learned in Chapter 2 that Scheme includes a special data type called *Booleans* to represent true or false values. There are just two of them: #t for "true" and #f for "false."*

We said that the first argument to `if` has to be true or false. Of course, it would be silly to say

```
> (if #t (+ 4 5) (* 2 7))
9
```

because what's the point of using `if` if we already know which branch will be followed? Instead, as in the `greet` example, we call some procedure whose return value will be either true or false, depending on the particular arguments we give it.

Predicates

A function that returns either `#t` or `#f` is called a *predicate*.** You've already seen the `equal?` predicate. It takes two arguments, which can be of any type, and returns `#t` if the two arguments are the same value, or `#f` if they're different. It's a convention in Scheme that the names of predicates end with a question mark, but that's just a convention. Here are some other useful predicates:

```
> (member? 'mick '(dave dee dozy beaky mick and tich))
#T
> (member? 'mick '(john paul george ringo))
#F
> (member? 'e 'truly)
#F
```

---

* In *some* versions of Scheme, the empty sentence is considered false. That is, ( ) and #f may be the same thing. The reason that we can't be definite about this point is that older versions of Scheme follow the traditional Lisp usage, in which the empty sentence is false, but since then a standardization committee has come along and insisted that the two values should be different. In this book we'll consider them as different, but we'll try to avoid examples in which it matters. The main point is that you shouldn't be surprised if you see something like this:

```
> (= 3 4)
()
```

in the particular implementation of Scheme that you're using.

** Why is it called that? Think about an English sentence, such as "Ringo is a drummer." As you may remember from elementary school, "Ringo" is the *subject* of that sentence, and "is a drummer" is the *predicate*. That predicate could be truthfully attached to some subjects but not others. For example, it's true of "Neil Peart" but not of "George Harrison." So the predicate "is a drummer" can be thought of as a function whose value is true or false.

```
> (member? 'y 'truly)
#T
> (= 3 4)
#F
> (= 67 67)
#T
> (> 98 97)
#T
> (before? 'zorn 'coleman)
#F
> (before? 'pete 'ringo)
#T
> (empty? '(abbey road))
#F
> (empty? '())
#T
> (empty? 'hi)
#F
> (empty? (bf (bf 'hi)))
#T
> (empty? "")
#T
```

Member? takes two arguments; it checks to see if the first one is a member of the second. The =, >, <, >=, and <= functions take two numbers as arguments and do the obvious comparisons. (By the way, these are exceptions to the convention about question marks.) Before? is like <, but it compares two words alphabetically. Empty? checks to see if its argument is either the empty word or the empty sentence.

Why do we have both equal? and = in Scheme? The first of these works on any kind of Scheme data, while the second is defined only for numbers. You could get away with always using equal?, but the more specific form makes your program more self-explanatory; people reading the program know right away that you're comparing numbers.

There are also several predicates that can be used to test the type of their argument:

```
> (number? 'three)
#F
> (number? 74)
#T
> (boolean? #f)
#T
> (boolean? '(the beatles))
#F
```

```
> (boolean? 234)
#F
> (boolean? #t)
#T
> (word? 'flying)
#T
> (word? '(dig it))
#F
> (word? 87)
#T
> (sentence? 'wait)
#F
> (sentence? '(what goes on))
#T
```

Of course, we can also define new predicates:

```
(define (vowel? letter)
  (member? letter 'aeiou))

(define (positive? number)
  (> number 0))
```

Using Predicates

Here's a procedure that returns the absolute value of a number:

```
(define (abs num)
  (if (< num 0)
      (- num)
      num))
```

(If you call – with just one argument, it returns the negative of that argument.) Scheme actually provides abs as a primitive procedure, but we can redefine it.

Do you remember how to play buzz? You're all sitting around the campfire and you go around the circle counting up from one. Each person says a number. If your number is divisible by seven or if one of its digits is a seven, then instead of calling out your number, you say "buzz."

```
(define (buzz num)
  (if (or (divisible? num 7) (member? 7 num))
      'buzz
      num))
```

```
(define (divisible? big little)
  (= (remainder big little) 0))
```

Or can take any number of arguments, each of which must be true or false. It returns true if any of its arguments are true, that is, if the first argument is true *or* the second argument is true *or...* (Remainder, as you know, takes two integers and tells you what the remainder is when you divide the first by the second. If the remainder is zero, the first number is divisible by the second.)

Or is one of three functions in Scheme that combine true or false values to produce another true or false value. And returns true if all of its arguments are true, that is, the first *and* second *and...* Finally, there's a function not that takes exactly one argument, returning true if that argument is false and vice versa.

In the last example, the procedure we really wanted to write was buzz, but we found it useful to define divisible? also. It's quite common that the easiest way to solve some problem is to write a *helper procedure* to do part of the work. In this case the helper procedure computes a function that's meaningful in itself, but sometimes you'll want to write procedures with names like buzz-helper that are useful only in the context of one particular problem.

Let's write a program that takes a word as its argument and returns the plural of that word. Our first version will just put an "s" on the end:

```
(define (plural wd)
  (word wd 's))

> (plural 'beatle)
BEATLES

> (plural 'computer)
COMPUTERS

> (plural 'fly)
FLYS
```

This works for most words, but not those that end in "y." Here's version two:

```
(define (plural wd)
  (if (equal? (last wd) 'y)
      (word (bl wd) 'ies)
      (word wd 's)))
```

This isn't exactly right either; it thinks that the plural of "boy" is "boies." We'll ask you to add some more rules in Exercise 6.12.

If Is a Special Form

There are a few subtleties that we haven't told you about yet. First of all, if is a special form. Remember that we're going to need the value of only one of its last two arguments. It would be wasteful for Scheme to evaluate the other one. So if you say

```
(if (= 3 3)
    'sure
    (factorial 1000))
```

if won't compute the factorial of 1000 before returning sure.

The rule is that if always evaluates its first argument. If the value of that argument is true, then if evaluates its second argument and returns its value. If the value of the first argument is false, then if evaluates its third argument and returns that value.

So Are And and Or

And and or are also special forms. They evaluate their arguments in order from left to right* and stop as soon as they can. For or, this means returning true as soon as any of the arguments is true. And returns false as soon as any argument is false. This turns out to be useful in cases like the following:

```
(define (divisible? big small)
  (= (remainder big small) 0))

(define (num-divisible-by-4? x)
  (and (number? x) (divisible? x 4)))

> (num-divisible-by-4? 16)
#T
```

---

* Since you can start a new line in the middle of an expression, in some cases the arguments will be "top to bottom" rather than "left to right," but don't forget that Scheme doesn't care about line breaks. That's why Lisp programmers always talk as if their programs were written on one enormously long line.

```
> (num-divisible-by-4? 6)
#F

> (num-divisible-by-4? 'aardvark)
#F

> (divisible? 'aardvark 4)
ERROR: AARDVARK IS NOT A NUMBER
```

We want to see if x is a number, and, if so, if it's divisible by 4. It would be an error to apply `divisible?` to a nonnumber. If `and` were an ordinary procedure, the two tests (`number?` and `divisible?`) would both be evaluated before we would have a chance to pay attention to the result of the first one. Instead, if x turns out not to be a number, our procedure will return #f without trying to divide it by 4.

Everything That Isn't False Is True

#T isn't the only true value. In fact, *every* value is considered true except for #f.

```
> (if (+ 3 4) 'yes 'no)
YES
```

This allows us to have *semipredicates* that give slightly more information than just true or false. For example, we can write an integer quotient procedure. That is to say, our procedure will divide its first argument by the second, but only if the first is evenly divisible by the second. If not, our procedure will return #f.

```
(define (integer-quotient big little)
  (if (divisible? big little)
      (/ big little)
      #f))

> (integer-quotient 27 3)
9

> (integer-quotient 12 5)
#F
```

And and or are also semipredicates. We've already explained that or returns a true result as soon as it evaluates a true argument. The particular true value that or returns is the value of that first true argument:

```
> (or #f 3 #f 4)
3
```

And returns a true value only if all of its arguments are true. In that case, it returns the value of the last argument:

```
> (and 1 2 3 4 5)
5
```

As an example in which this behavior is useful, we can rewrite `integer-quotient` more tersely:

```
(define (integer-quotient big little)          ;; alternate version
  (and (divisible? big little)
       (/ big little)))
```

Decisions, Decisions, Decisions

If is great for an either-or choice. But sometimes there are several possibilities to consider:

```
(define (roman-value letter)
  (if (equal? letter 'i)
      1
      (if (equal? letter 'v)
          5
          (if (equal? letter 'x)
              10
              (if (equal? letter 'l)
                  50
                  (if (equal? letter 'c)
                      100
                      (if (equal? letter 'd)
                          500
                          (if (equal? letter 'm)
                              1000
                              'huh?)))))))))
```

That's pretty hideous. Scheme provides a shorthand notation for situations like this in which you have to choose from among several possibilities: the special form cond.

```
(define (roman-value letter)
  (cond ((equal? letter 'i) 1)
        ((equal? letter 'v) 5)
        ((equal? letter 'x) 10)
        ((equal? letter 'l) 50)
        ((equal? letter 'c) 100)
        ((equal? letter 'd) 500)
        ((equal? letter 'm) 1000)
        (else 'huh?)))
```

The tricky thing about cond is that it doesn't use parentheses in quite the same way as the rest of Scheme. Ordinarily, parentheses mean procedure invocation. In cond, *most* of the parentheses still mean that, but *some* of them are used to group pairs of tests and results. We've reproduced the same cond expression below, indicating the funny ones in boldface.

```
(define (roman-value letter)
  (cond ((equal? letter 'i) 1)
        ((equal? letter 'v) 5)
        ((equal? letter 'x) 10)
        ((equal? letter 'l) 50)
        ((equal? letter 'c) 100)
        ((equal? letter 'd) 500)
        ((equal? letter 'm) 1000)
        (else 'huh?) ))
```

Cond takes any number of arguments, each of which is *two expressions* inside a pair of parentheses. Each argument is called a *cond clause*. In the example above, one typical clause is

```
((equal? letter 'l) 50)
```

The outermost parentheses on that line enclose two expressions. The first of the two expressions (the *condition*) is taken as true or false, just like the first argument to if. The second expression of each pair (the *consequent*) is a candidate for the return value of the entire cond invocation.

Cond examines its arguments from left to right. Remember that since cond is a special form, its arguments are not evaluated ahead of time. For each argument, cond evaluates the first of the two expressions within the argument. If that value turns out to be true, then cond evaluates the second expression in the same argument, and returns

```
```

that value without examining any further arguments. But if the value is false, then `cond` does *not* evaluate the second expression; instead, it goes on to the next argument.

By convention, the last argument always starts with the word `else` instead of an expression. You can think of this as representing a true value, but `else` doesn't mean true in any other context; you're only allowed to use it as the condition of the last clause of a `cond`.*

Don't get into bad habits of thinking about the appearance of `cond` clauses in terms of "two parentheses in a row." That's often the case, but not always. For example, here is a procedure that translates Scheme true or false values (`#t` and `#f`) into more human-readable words `true` and `false`.

```
(define (truefalse value)
  (cond (value 'true)
        (else 'false)))

> (truefalse (= 2 (+ 1 1)))
TRUE

> (truefalse (= 5 (+ 2 2)))
FALSE
```

When a `cond` tests several possible conditions, they might not be mutually exclusive.** This can be either a source of error or an advantage in writing efficient programs. The trick is to make the *most restrictive* test first. For example, it would be an error to say

```
(cond ((number? (first sent)) ...)           ;; wrong
      ((empty? sent) ...)
      ...)
```

because the first test only makes sense once you've already established that there *is* a first word of the sentence. On the other hand, you don't have to say

```
(cond ((empty? sent) ...)
      ((and (not (empty? sent)) (number? (first sent))) ...)
      ...)
```

---

* What if you don't use an `else` clause at all? If none of the clauses has a true condition, then the return value is unspecified. In other words, always use `else`.

** Conditions are mutually exclusive if only one of them can be true at a time.

because you've already established that the sentence is nonempty if you get as far as the second clause.

If Is Composable

Suppose we want to write a `greet` procedure that works like this:

```
> (greet '(brian epstein))
(PLEASED TO MEET YOU BRIAN -- HOW ARE YOU?)

> (greet '(professor donald knuth))
(PLEASED TO MEET YOU PROFESSOR KNUTH -- HOW ARE YOU?)
```

The response of the program in these two cases is almost the same; the only difference is in the form of the person's name.

This procedure could be written in two ways:

```
(define (greet name)
  (if (equal? (first name) 'professor)
      (se '(pleased to meet you)
          'professor
          (last name)
          '(-- how are you?))
      (se '(pleased to meet you)
          (first name)
          '(-- how are you?))))

(define (greet name)
  (se '(pleased to meet you)
      (if (equal? (first name) 'professor)
          (se 'professor (last name))
          (first name))
      '(-- how are you?)))
```

The second version avoids repeating the common parts of the response by using `if` within a larger expression.

Some people find it counterintuitive to use `if` as we did in the second version. Perhaps the reason is that in some other programming languages, `if` is a "command" instead of a function like any other. A mechanism that selects one part of a program to run, and leaves out another part, may seem too important to be a mere argument subexpression. But in Scheme, the value returned by *every* function can be used as part of a larger expression.*

We aren't saying anything new here. We've already explained the idea of composition of functions, and we're just making the same point again about `if`. But we've learned that many students expect `if` to be an exception, so we're taking the opportunity to emphasize the point: There are no exceptions to this rule.

Pitfalls

⇒   The biggest pitfall in this chapter is the unusual notation of `cond`. Keeping track of the parentheses that mean function invocation, as usual, and the parentheses that just group the parts of a `cond` clause is tricky until you get accustomed to it.

⇒   Many people also have trouble with the asymmetry of the `member?` predicate. The first argument is something small; the second is something big. (The order of arguments is the same as the order of a typical English sentence about membership: "Is Mick a member of the Beatles?") It seems pretty obvious when you look at an example in which both arguments are quoted constant values, but you can get in trouble when you define a procedure and use its parameters as the arguments to `member?`. Compare writing a procedure that says, "does the letter E appear in this word?" with one that says, "is this letter a vowel?"

⇒   Many people try to use `and` and `or` with the full flexibility of the corresponding English words. Alas, Scheme is not English. For example, suppose you want to know whether the argument to a procedure is either the word `yes` or the word `no`. You can't say

```
(equal? argument (or 'yes 'no))                ; wrong!
```

This sounds promising: "Is the `argument` `equal` to the word `yes` or the word `no`?" But the arguments to `or` must be true-or-false values, not things you want to check for

---

* Strictly speaking, since the argument expressions to a special form aren't evaluated, `if` is a function whose domain is expressions, not their values. But many special forms, including `if`, `and`, and `or`, are designed to act as if they were ordinary functions, the kind whose arguments Scheme evaluates in advance. The only difference is that it is sometimes possible for Scheme to figure out the correct return value after evaluating only some of the arguments. Most of the time we'll just talk about the domains and ranges of these special forms as if they were ordinary functions.

equality with something else. You have to make two separate equality tests:

```
(or (equal? argument 'yes) (equal? argument 'no))
```

In this particular case, you could also solve the problem by saying

```
(member? argument '(yes no))
```

but the question of trying to use or as if it were English comes up in other cases for which member? won't help.

⇒ This isn't exactly a pitfall, because it won't stop your program from working, but programs like

```
(define (odd? n)
  (if (not (even? n)) #t #f))
```

are redundant. Instead, you could just say

```
(define (odd? n)
  (not (even? n)))
```

since the value of (not (even? n)) is already #t or #f.

Boring Exercises

6.1 What values are printed when you type these expressions to Scheme? (Figure it out in your head before you try it on the computer.)

```
(cond ((= 3 4) '(this boy))
      ((< 2 5) '(nowhere man))
      (else '(two of us)))

(cond (empty? 3)
      (square 7)
      (else 9))

(define (third-person-singular verb)
  (cond ((equal? verb 'be) 'is)
        ((equal? (last verb) 'o) (word verb 'es))
        (else (word verb 's))))

(third-person-singular 'go)
```

6.2 What values are printed when you type these expressions to Scheme? (Figure it out in your head before you try it on the computer.)

```
(or #f #f #f #t)

(and #f #f #f #t)

(or (= 2 3) (= 4 3))

(not #f)

(or (not (= 2 3)) (= 4 3))

(or (and (= 2 3) (= 3 3)) (and (< 2 3) (< 3 4)))
```

6.3 Rewrite the following procedure using a cond instead of the ifs:

```
(define (sign number)
  (if (< number 0)
      'negative
      (if (= number 0)
          'zero
          'positive)))
```

6.4 Rewrite the following procedure using an if instead of the cond:

```
(define (utensil meal)
  (cond ((equal? meal 'chinese) 'chopsticks)
        (else 'fork)))
```

Real Exercises

Note: Writing helper procedures may be useful in solving some of these problems.

6.5 Write a procedure european-time to convert a time from American AM/PM notation into European 24-hour notation. Also write american-time, which does the opposite:

```
> (european-time '(8 am))
8
```

```
> (european-time '(4 pm))
16

> (american-time 21)
(9 PM)

> (american-time 12)
(12 PM)

> (european-time '(12 am))
24
```

Getting noon and midnight right is tricky.

6.6 Write a predicate `teen?` that returns true if its argument is between 13 and 19.

6.7 Write a procedure `type-of` that takes anything as its argument and returns one of the words `word`, `sentence`, `number`, or `boolean`:

```
> (type-of '(getting better))
SENTENCE

> (type-of 'revolution)
WORD

> (type-of (= 3 3))
BOOLEAN
```

(Even though numbers are words, your procedure should return `number` if its argument is a number.)

Feel free to check for more specific types, such as "positive integer," if you are so inclined.

6.8 Write a procedure `indef-article` that works like this:

```
> (indef-article 'beatle)
(A BEATLE)

> (indef-article 'album)
(AN ALBUM)
```

Don't worry about silent initial consonants like the h in `hour`.

6.9 Sometimes you must choose the singular or the plural of a word: `1 book` but `2 books`. Write a procedure `thismany` that takes two arguments, a number and a singular noun, and combines them appropriately:

```
> (thismany 1 'partridge)
(1 PARTRIDGE)

> (thismany 3 'french-hen)
(3 FRENCH-HENS)
```

6.10 Write a procedure `sort2` that takes as its argument a sentence containing two numbers. It should return a sentence containing the same two numbers, but in ascending order:

```
> (sort2 '(5 7))
(5 7)

> (sort2 '(7 5))
(5 7)
```

6.11 Write a predicate `valid-date?` that takes three numbers as arguments, representing a month, a day of the month, and a year. Your procedure should return `#t` if the numbers represent a valid date (e.g., it isn't the 31st of September). February has 29 days if the year is divisible by 4, except that if the year is divisible by 100 it must also be divisible by 400.

```
> (valid-date? 10 4 1949)
#T

> (valid-date? 20 4 1776)
#F

> (valid-date? 5 0 1992)
#F

> (valid-date? 2 29 1900)
#F

> (valid-date? 2 29 2000)
#T
```

6.12 Make `plural` handle correctly words that end in **y** but have a vowel before the **y**, such as **boy**. Then teach it about words that end in **x** (box). What other special cases can you find?

6.13 Write a better `greet` procedure that understands as many different kinds of names as you can think of:

```
> (greet '(john lennon))
(HELLO JOHN)

> (greet '(dr marie curie))
(HELLO DR CURIE)

> (greet '(dr martin luther king jr))
(HELLO DR KING)

> (greet '(queen elizabeth))
(HELLO YOUR MAJESTY)

> (greet '(david livingstone))
(DR LIVINGSTONE I PRESUME?)
```

6.14 Write a procedure `describe-time` that takes a number of seconds as its argument and returns a more useful description of that amount of time:

```
> (describe-time 45)
(45 SECONDS)

> (describe-time 930)
(15.5 MINUTES)

> (describe-time 30000000000)
(9.506426344208686 CENTURIES)
```

Trombone players produce different pitches partly by varying the length of a tube.

7   Variables

A *variable* is a connection between a name and a value.* That sounds simple enough, but some complexities arise in practice. To avoid confusion later, we'll spend some time now looking at the idea of "variable" in more detail.

The name *variable* comes from algebra. Many people are introduced to variables in high school algebra classes, where the emphasis is on solving equations. "If $x^3 - 8 = 0$, what is the value of x?" In problems like these, although we call x a variable, it's really a *named constant!* In this particular problem, x has the value 2. In any such problem, at first we don't know the value of x, but we understand that it does have some particular value, and that value isn't going to change in the middle of the problem.

In functional programming, what we mean by "variable" is like a named constant in mathematics. Since a variable is the connection between a name and a value, a formal parameter in a procedure definition isn't a variable; it's just a name. But when we invoke the procedure with a particular argument, that name is associated with a value, and a variable is created. If we invoke the procedure again, a *new* variable is created, perhaps with a different value.

There are two possible sources of confusion about this. One is that you may have programmed before in a programming language like BASIC or Pascal, in which a variable often *does* get a new value, even after it's already had a previous value assigned to it. Programs in those languages tend to be full of things like "X = X + 1." Back in Chapter 2 we told you that this book is about something called "functional programming," but we haven't yet explained exactly what that means. (Of course we *have* introduced a lot

---

* The term "variable" is used by computer scientists to mean several subtly different things. For example, some people use "variable" to mean just a holder for a value, without a name. But what we said is what *we* mean by "variable."

of functions, and that is an important part of it.) Part of what we mean by functional programming is that once a variable exists, we aren't going to *change* the value of that variable.

The other possible source of confusion is that in Scheme, unlike the situation in algebra, we may have more than one variable with the same name at the same time. That's because we may invoke one procedure, and the body of that procedure may invoke another procedure, and each of them might use the same formal parameter name. There might be one variable named **x** with the value 7, and another variable named **x** with the value 51, at the same time. The pitfall to avoid is thinking "**x** has changed its value from 7 to 51."

As an analogy, imagine that you are at a party along with Mick Jagger, Mick Wilson, Mick Avory, and Mick Dolenz. If you're having a conversation with one of them, the name "Mick" means a particular person to you. If you notice someone else talking with a different Mick, you wouldn't think "Mick has become a different person." Instead, you'd think "there are several people here all with the name Mick."

How Little People Do Variables

You can understand variables in terms of the little-people model. A variable, in this model, is the association in the little person's mind between a formal parameter (name) and the actual argument (value) she was given. When we want to know (square 5), we hire Srini and tell him his argument is 5. Srini therefore substitutes 5 for **x** in the body of **square**. Later, when we want to know the square of 6, we hire Samantha and tell her that her argument is 6. Srini and Samantha have two different variables, both named **x**.

Part II   Composition of Functions

Srini and Samantha do their work separately, one after the other. But in a more complicated example, there could even be more than one value called x at the same time:

```
(define (square x) (* x x))

(define (hypotenuse x y)
  (sqrt (+ (square x) (square y))))

> (hypotenuse 3 4)
5
```

Consider the situation when we've hired Hortense to evaluate that expression. Hortense associates the name x with the value 3 (and also the name y with the value 4, but we're going to pay attention to x). She has to compute two squares. She hires Solomon to compute (square 3). Solomon associates the name x with the value 3. This happens to be the same as Hortense's value, but it's still a separate variable that could have had a different value—as we see when Hortense hires Sheba to compute (square 4). Now, simultaneously, Hortense thinks x is 3 and Sheba thinks x is 4.

(Remember that we said a variable is a connection between a name and a value. So x isn't a variable! The association of the name x with the value 5 is a variable. The reason we're being so fussy about this terminology is that it helps clarify the case in which several variables have the same name. But in practice people are generally sloppy about this fine point; we can usually get away with saying "x is a variable" when we mean "there is some variable whose name is x.")

Another important point about the way little people do variables is that they can't read each others' minds. In particular, they don't know about the values of the local variables that belong to the little people who hired them. For example, the following attempt to compute the value 10 won't work:

```
(define (f x)
  (g 6))

(define (g y)
  (+ x y))

> (f 4)
ERROR -- VARIABLE X IS UNBOUND.
```

We hire Franz to compute (f 4). He associates x with 4 and evaluates (g 6) by hiring Gloria. Gloria associates y with 6, but she doesn't have any value for x, so she's in trouble. The solution is for Franz to tell Gloria that x is 4:

```
(define (f x)
  (g x 6))

(define (g x y)
  (+ x y))

> (f 4)
10
```

Global and Local Variables

Until now, we've been using two very different kinds of naming. We have names for procedures, which are created permanently by `define` and are usable throughout our programs; and we have names for procedure arguments, which are associated with values temporarily when we call a procedure and are usable only inside that procedure.

These two kinds of naming seem to be different in every way. One is for procedures, one for data; the one for procedures makes a permanent, global name, while the one for data makes a temporary, local name. That picture does reflect the way that procedures and other data are *usually* used, but we'll see that really there is only one kind of naming. The boundaries can be crossed: Procedures can be arguments to other procedures, and any kind of data can have a permanent, global name. Right now we'll look at that last point, about global variables.

Just as we've been using `define` to associate names with procedures globally, we can also use it for other kinds of data:

```
> (define pi 3.141592654)

> (+ pi 5)
8.141592654

> (define song '(I am the walrus))

> (last song)
WALRUS
```

Once defined, a global variable can be used anywhere, just as a defined procedure can be used anywhere. (In fact, defining a procedure creates a variable whose value is the procedure. Just as `pi` is the name of a variable whose value is 3.141592654, `last` is the name of a variable whose value is a primitive procedure. We'll come back to this point in Chapter 9.) When the name of a global variable appears in an expression, the corresponding value must be substituted, just as actual argument values are substituted for formal parameters.

When a little person is hired to carry out a compound procedure, his or her first step is to substitute actual argument values for formal parameters in the body. The same little person substitutes values for global variable names also. (What if there is a global variable whose name happens to be used as a formal parameter in this procedure? Scheme's rule is that the formal parameter takes precedence, but even though Scheme knows what to do, conflicts like this make your program harder to read.)

How does this little person know what values to substitute for global variable names? What makes a variable "global" in the little-people model is that *every* little person knows its value. You can imagine that there's a big chalkboard, with all the global definitions written on it, that all the little people can see. If you prefer, you could imagine that whenever a global variable is defined, the `define` specialist climbs up a huge ladder, picks up a megaphone, and yells something like "Now hear this! `Pi` is 3.141592654!"

The association of a formal parameter (a name) with an actual argument (a value) is called a *local variable*.

It's awkward to have to say "Harry associates the value 7 with the name `foo`" all the time. Most of the time we just say "`foo` has the value 7," paying no attention to whether this association is in some particular little person's head or if everybody knows it.

The Truth about Substitution

We said earlier in a footnote that Scheme doesn't actually do all the copying and substituting we've been talking about. What actually happens is more like our model of global variables, in which there is a chalkboard somewhere that associates names with values—except that instead of making a new copy of every expression with values substituted for names, Scheme works with the original expression and looks up the value for each name at the moment when that value is needed. To make local variables work, there are several chalkboards: a global one and one for each little person.

The fully detailed model of variables using several chalkboards is what many people find hardest about learning Scheme. That's why we've chosen to use the simpler substitution model.*

Let

We're going to write a procedure that solves quadratic equations. (We know this is the prototypical boring programming problem, but it illustrates clearly the point we're about to make.)

We'll use the quadratic formula that you learned in high school algebra class:

$$ax^2 + bx + c = 0 \quad \text{when} \quad x = \frac{-b \pm \sqrt{b^2 - 4ac}}{2a}$$

```
(define (roots a b c)
  (se (/ (+ (- b) (sqrt (- (* b b) (* 4 a c))))
         (* 2 a))
      (/ (- (- b) (sqrt (- (* b b) (* 4 a c))))
         (* 2 a))))
```

Since there are two possible solutions, we return a sentence containing two numbers. This procedure works fine,** but it does have the disadvantage of repeating a lot of the

---

* The reason that all of our examples work with the substitution model is that this book uses only functional programming, in the sense that we never change the value of a variable. If we started doing the X = X + 1 style of programming, we would need the more complicated chalkboard model.

** That is, it works if the equation has real roots, or if your version of Scheme has complex

work. It computes the square root part of the formula twice. We'd like to avoid that inefficiency.

One thing we can do is to compute the square root and use that as the actual argument to a helper procedure that does the rest of the job:

```
(define (roots a b c)
  (roots1 a b c (sqrt (- (* b b) (* 4 a c)))))

(define (roots1 a b c discriminant)
  (se (/ (+ (- b) discriminant) (* 2 a))
      (/ (- (- b) discriminant) (* 2 a))))
```

This version evaluates the square root only once. The resulting value is used as the argument named `discriminant` in `roots1`.

We've solved the problem we posed for ourselves initially: avoiding the redundant computation of the discriminant (the square-root part of the formula). The cost, though, is that we had to define an auxiliary procedure `roots1` that doesn't make much sense on its own. (That is, you'd never invoke `roots1` for its own sake; only `roots` uses it.)

Scheme provides a notation to express a computation of this kind more conveniently. It's called `let`:

```
(define (roots a b c)
  (let ((discriminant (sqrt (- (* b b) (* 4 a c)))))
    (se (/ (+ (- b) discriminant) (* 2 a))
        (/ (- (- b) discriminant) (* 2 a)))))
```

Our new program is just an abbreviation for the previous version: In effect, it creates a temporary procedure just like `roots1`, but without a name, and invokes it with the specified argument value. But the `let` notation rearranges things so that we can say, in the right order, "let the variable `discriminant` have the value (`sqrt`...) and, using that variable, compute the body."

`Let` is a special form that takes two arguments. The first is a sequence of name-value pairs enclosed in parentheses. (In this example, there is only one name-value pair.) The second argument, the *body* of the `let`, is the expression to evaluate.

---

numbers. Also, the limited precision with which computers can represent irrational numbers can make this particular algorithm give wrong answers in practice even though it's correct in theory.

Now that we have this notation, we can use it with more than one name-value connection to eliminate even more redundant computation:

```
(define (roots a b c)
  (let ((discriminant (sqrt (- (* b b) (* 4 a c))))
        (minus-b (- b))
        (two-a (* 2 a)))
    (se (/ (+ minus-b discriminant) two-a)
        (/ (- minus-b discriminant) two-a))))
```

In this example, the first argument to let includes three name-value pairs. It's as if we'd defined and invoked a procedure like the following:

```
(define (roots1 discriminant minus-b two-a) ...)
```

Like cond, let uses parentheses both with the usual meaning (invoking a procedure) and to group sub-arguments that belong together. This grouping happens in two ways. Parentheses are used to group a name and the expression that provides its value. Also, an additional pair of parentheses surrounds the entire collection of name-value pairs.

Pitfalls

⇒ If you've programmed before in other languages, you may be accustomed to a style of programming in which you *change* the value of a variable by assigning it a new value. You may be tempted to write

```
> (define x (+ x 3))                           ;; no-no
```

Although some versions of Scheme do allow such redefinitions, so that you can correct errors in your procedures, they're not strictly legal. A definition is meant to be *permanent* in functional programming. (Scheme does include other mechanisms for non-functional programming, but we're not studying them in this book because once you allow reassignment you need a more complex model of the evaluation process.)

⇒ When you create more than one temporary variable at once using let, all of the expressions that provide the values are computed before any of the variables are created. Therefore, you can't have one expression depend on another:

```
> (let ((a (+ 4 7))                            ;; wrong!
        (b (* a 5)))
    (+ a b))
```

Don't think that a gets the value 11 and therefore b gets the value 55. That let expression is equivalent to defining a helper procedure

```
(define (helper a b)
  (+ a b))
```

and then invoking it:

```
(helper (+ 4 7) (* a 5))
```

The argument expressions, as always, are evaluated *before* the function is invoked. The expression (* a 5) will be evaluated using the *global* value of a, if there is one. If not, an error will result. If you want to use a in computing b, you must say

```
> (let ((a (+ 4 7)))
    (let ((b (* a 5)))
      (+ a b)))
66
```

⇒ Let's notation is tricky because, like cond, it uses parentheses that don't mean procedure invocation. Don't teach yourself magic formulas like "two open parentheses before the let variable and three close parentheses at the end of its value." Instead, think about the overall structure:

```
(let variables body)
```

Let takes exactly two arguments. The first argument to let is one or more name-value groupings, all in parentheses:

```
((name1 value1) (name2 value2) (name3 value3) ...)
```

Each name is a single word; each value can be any expression, usually a procedure invocation. If it's a procedure invocation, then parentheses are used with their usual meaning.

The second argument to let is the expression to be evaluated using those variables.

Now put all the pieces together:

```
(let ((name1 (fn1 arg1))
      (name2 (fn2 arg2))
      (name3 (fn3 arg3)))
  body)
```

Boring Exercises

7.1 The following procedure does some redundant computation.

```
(define (gertrude wd)
  (se (if (vowel? (first wd)) 'an 'a)
      wd
      'is
      (if (vowel? (first wd)) 'an 'a)
      wd
      'is
      (if (vowel? (first wd)) 'an 'a)
      wd))

> (gertrude 'rose)
(A ROSE IS A ROSE IS A ROSE)

> (gertrude 'iguana)
(AN IGUANA IS AN IGUANA IS AN IGUANA)
```

Use `let` to avoid the redundant work.

7.2 Put in the missing parentheses:

```
> (let pi 3.14159
       pie 'lemon meringue
    se 'pi is pi 'but pie is pie)
(PI IS 3.14159 BUT PIE IS LEMON MERINGUE)
```

Real Exercises

7.3 The following program doesn't work. Why not? Fix it.

```
(define (superlative adjective word)
  (se (word adjective 'est) word))
```

It's supposed to work like this:

```
> (superlative 'dumb 'exercise)
(DUMBEST EXERCISE)
```

7.4 What does this procedure do? Explain how it manages to work.

```
(define (sum-square a b)
  (let ((+ *)
        (* +))
    (* (+ a a) (+ b b))))
```

Part III
Functions as Data

By now you're accustomed to the idea of expressing a computational process in terms of the function whose value you want to compute, rather than in terms of a sequence of actions. But you probably think of a function (or the procedure that embodies it) as something very different from the words, sentences, numbers, or other data that serve as arguments to the functions. It's like the distinction between verbs and nouns in English: A verb represents something *to do,* while a noun represents something *that is.*

In this part of the book our goal is to overturn that distinction.

Like many big ideas, this one seems simple at first. All we're saying is that a function can have *functions* as its domain or range. One artificially simple example that you've seen earlier was the `number-of-arguments` function in Chapter 2. That function takes a function as argument and returns a number. It's not so different from `count`, which takes a word or sentence as argument and returns a number.

But you'll see that this idea leads to an enormous rise in the length and complexity of the processes you can express in a short procedure, because now a process can give rise to several other processes. A typical example is the `acronym` procedure that we introduced in Chapter 1 and will examine now in more detail. Instead of applying the `first` procedure to a single word, we use `first` as an argument to a procedure, `every`, that automatically applies it to every word of a sentence. A single `every` process gives rise to several `first` processes.

The same idea of function as data allows us to write procedures that create and return new procedures. At the beginning of Part II we showed a Scheme representation of a function that computes the third person singular of a verb. Now, to illustrate the idea of function as data, we'll show how to represent in Scheme a function `make-conjugator` whose range is *the whole family* of verb-conjugation functions:

```
(define (make-conjugator prefix ending)
  (lambda (verb) (sentence prefix (word verb ending))))
```

Never mind the notation for now; the idea to think about is that we can use
`make-conjugator` to create many functions similar to the `third-person` example of
the Part II introduction:

```
> (define third-person (make-conjugator 'she 's))

> (third-person 'program)
(SHE PROGRAMS)

> (define third-person-plural-past (make-conjugator 'they 'ed))

> (third-person-plural-past 'play)
(THEY PLAYED)

> (define second-person-future-perfect
    (make-conjugator '(you will have) 'ed))

> (second-person-future-perfect 'laugh)
(YOU WILL HAVE LAUGHED)
```

We'll explore only a tiny fraction of the area opened up by the idea of allowing a
program as data. Further down the same road is the study of *compilers* and *interpreters,* the
programs that translate your programs into instructions that computers can carry out. A
Scheme compiler is essentially a function whose domain is Scheme programs.

Turning function machines into plowshares

8 Higher-Order Functions

Note: If you read Part IV before this one, pretend you didn't; we are going to develop a different technique for solving similar problems.

You can use the function `first` to find the first letter of a word. What if you want to find the first letters of several words? You did this in the first chapter, as part of the process of finding acronyms.

To start with a simple case, suppose you have two words (that is, a sentence of length two). You could apply the `first` procedure to each of them and combine the results:

```
(define (two-firsts sent)
  (se (first (first sent))
      (first (last sent))))

> (two-firsts '(john lennon))
(J L)

> (two-firsts '(george harrison))
(G H)
```

Similarly, here's the version for three words:

```
(define (three-firsts sent)
  (se (first (first sent))
      (first (first (bf sent)))
      (first (last sent))))

> (three-firsts '(james paul mccartney))
(J P M)
```

But this approach would get tiresome if you had a sentence of five words—you'd have to write a procedure specifically for the case of exactly five words, and that procedure would have five separate subexpressions to extract the first word, the second word, and so on. Also, you don't want a separate procedure for every sentence length; you want one function that works no matter how long the sentence is. Using the tools you've already learned about, the only possible way to do that would be pretty hideous:

```
(define (first-letters sent)
  (cond ((= (count sent) 1) (one-first sent))
        ((= (count sent) 2) (two-firsts sent))
        ((= (count sent) 3) (three-firsts sent))
        ... and so on ...)))
```

But even this won't work because there's no way to say "and so on" in Scheme. You could write a version that works for all sentences up to, let's say, length 23, but you'd be in trouble if someone tried to use your procedure on a 24-word sentence.

Every

To write a better any-length first-letter procedure, you need to be able to say "apply the function `first` to *every* word in the sentence, no matter how long the sentence is." Scheme provides a way to do this:*

```
(define (first-letters sent)
  (every first sent))

> (first-letters '(here comes the sun))
(H C T S)

> (first-letters '(lucy in the sky with diamonds))
(L I T S W D)
```

Every takes two arguments. The second argument is a sentence, but the first is something new: a *procedure* used as an argument to another procedure.** Notice that

---

* Like all the procedures in this book that deal with words and sentences, **every** and the other procedures in this chapter are part of our extensions to Scheme. Later, in Chapter 17, we'll introduce the standard Scheme equivalents.

** Talking about **every** strains our resolve to distinguish functions from the procedures that implement them. Is the argument to **every** a function or a procedure? If we think of **every** itself

there are no parentheses around the word `first` in the body of `first-letters`! By now you've gotten accustomed to seeing parentheses whenever you see the name of a function. But parentheses indicate an *invocation* of a function, and we aren't invoking `first` here. We're using `first`, the procedure itself, as an argument to `every`.

```
> (every last '(while my guitar gently weeps))
(E Y R Y S)

> (every - '(4 5 7 8 9))
(-4 -5 -7 -8 -9)
```

These examples use `every` with primitive procedures, but of course you can also define procedures of your own and apply them to `every` word of a sentence:

```
(define (plural noun)
  (if (equal? (last noun) 'y)
      (word (bl noun) 'ies)
      (word noun 's)))

> (every plural '(beatle turtle holly kink zombie))
(BEATLES TURTLES HOLLIES KINKS ZOMBIES)
```

You can also use a word as the second argument to `every`. In this case, the first-argument procedure is applied to every letter of the word. The results are collected in a sentence.

```
(define (double letter) (word letter letter))

> (every double 'girl)
(GG II RR LL)

> (every square 547)
(25 16 49)
```

In all these examples so far, the first argument to `every` was a function that returned a *word,* and the value returned by `every` was a sentence containing all the returned

---

as a procedure—that is, if we're focusing on how it does its job—then of course we must say that it does its job by repeatedly invoking the *procedure* that we supply as an argument. But it's equally valid for us to focus attention on the function that the `every` procedure implements, and that function takes *functions* as arguments.

words. The first argument to every can also be a function that returns a *sentence*. In this case, every returns one long sentence:

```
(define (sent-of-first-two wd)
  (se (first wd) (first (bf wd))))

> (every sent-of-first-two '(the inner light))
(T H IN L I)

> (every sent-of-first-two '(tell me what you see))
(T E ME WH YOU SE)

> (define (g wd)
    (se (word 'with wd) 'you))

> (every g '(in out))
(WITHIN YOU WITHOUT YOU)
```

A function that takes another function as one of its arguments, as every does, is called a *higher-order function*. If we focus our attention on procedures, the mechanism through which Scheme computes functions, we think of every as a procedure that takes another procedure as an argument—a *higher-order procedure*.

A Pause for Reflection

Earlier we used the metaphor of the "function machine," with a hopper at the top into which we throw data, and a chute at the bottom from which the result falls, like a meat grinder. Well, every is a function machine into whose hopper we throw *another function machine!* Instead of a meat grinder, we have a metal grinder.*

Do you see what an exciting idea this is? We are accustomed to thinking of numbers and sentences as "real things," while functions are less like things and more like activities. As an analogy, think about cooking. The real foods are the meats, vegetables, ice cream, and so on. You can't eat a recipe, which is analogous to a function. A recipe has to be applied to ingredients, and the result of carrying out the recipe is an edible meal. It

---

* You can get in trouble mathematically by trying to define a function whose domain includes *all* functions, because applying such a function to itself can lead to a paradox. In programming, the corresponding danger is that applying a higher-order procedure to *itself* might result in a program that runs forever.

would seem weird if a recipe used other recipes as ingredients: "Preheat the oven to 350 and insert your *Joy of Cooking*." But in Scheme we can do just that.*

Cooking your cookbook is unusual, but the general principle isn't. In some contexts we do treat recipes as things rather than as algorithms. For example, people write recipes on cards and put them into a recipe file box. Then they perform operations such as searching for a particular recipe, sorting the recipes by category (main dish, dessert, etc.), copying a recipe for a friend, and so on. The same recipe is both a process (when we're cooking with it) and the object of a process (when we're filing it).

Keep

Once we have this idea, we can use functions of functions to provide many different capabilities.

For instance, the `keep` function takes a predicate and a sentence as arguments. It returns a sentence containing only the words of the argument sentence for which the predicate is true.

```
> (keep even? '(1 2 3 4 5))
(2 4)

> (define (ends-e? word) (equal? (last word) 'e))

> (keep ends-e? '(please put the salami above the blue elephant))
(PLEASE THE ABOVE THE BLUE)

> (keep number? '(1 after 909))
(1 909)
```

Keep will also accept a word as its second argument. In this case, it applies the predicate to every letter of the word and returns another word:

```
> (keep number? 'zonk23hey9)
239

> (define (vowel? letter) (member? letter '(a e i o u)))

> (keep vowel? 'piggies)
IIE
```

---

* Some recipes may seem to include other recipes, because they say things like "add pesto (recipe on p. 12)." But this is just composition of functions; the *result* of the pesto procedure is used as an argument to this recipe. The pesto recipe itself is not an ingredient.

When we used **every** to select the first letters of words earlier, we found the first letters even of uninteresting words such as "the." We're working toward an acronym procedure, and for that purpose we'd like to be able to discard the boring words.

```
(define (real-word? wd)
  (not (member? wd '(a the an in of and for to with))))

> (keep real-word? '(lucy in the sky with diamonds))
(LUCY SKY DIAMONDS)

> (every first (keep real-word? '(lucy in the sky with diamonds)))
(L S D)
```

Accumulate

In **every** and **keep**, each element of the second argument contributes *independently* to the overall result. That is, **every** and **keep** apply a procedure to a single element at a time. The overall result is a collection of individual results, with no interaction between elements of the argument. This doesn't let us say things like "Add up all the numbers in a sentence," where the desired output is a function of the entire argument sentence taken as a whole. We can do this with a procedure named **accumulate**. Accumulate takes a procedure and a sentence as its arguments. It applies that procedure to two of the words of the sentence. Then it applies the procedure to the result we got back and another element of the sentence, and so on. It ends when it's combined all the words of the sentence into a single result.

```
> (accumulate + '(6 3 4 -5 7 8 9))
32

> (accumulate word '(a c l u))
ACLU

> (accumulate max '(128 32 134 136))
136

> (define (hyphenate word1 word2)
    (word word1 '- word2))

> (accumulate hyphenate '(ob la di ob la da))
OB-LA-DI-OB-LA-DA
```

(In all of our examples in this section, the second argument contains at least two elements. In the "pitfalls" section at the end of the chapter, we'll discuss what happens with smaller arguments.)

Accumulate can also take a word as its second argument, using the letters as elements:

```
> (accumulate + 781)
16

> (accumulate sentence 'colin)
(C O L I N)
```

Combining Higher-Order Functions

What if we want to add up all the numbers in a sentence but ignore the words that aren't numbers? First we keep the numbers in the sentence, then we accumulate the result with +. It's easier to say in Scheme:

```
(define (add-numbers sent)
  (accumulate + (keep number? sent)))

> (add-numbers '(4 calling birds 3 french hens 2 turtle doves))
9

> (add-numbers '(1 for the money 2 for the show 3 to get ready
                 and 4 to go))
10
```

We also have enough tools to write a version of the count procedure, which finds the number of words in a sentence or the number of letters in a word. First, we'll define a procedure always-one that returns 1 no matter what its argument is. We'll every always-one over our argument sentence,* which will result in a sentence of as many ones as there were words in the original sentence. Then we can use accumulate with + to add up the ones. This is a slightly roundabout approach; later we'll see a more natural way to find the count of a sentence.

```
(define (always-one arg)
  1)
```

---

* We mean, of course, "We'll invoke every with the procedure always-one and our argument sentence as its two arguments." After you've been programming computers for a while, this sort of abuse of English will come naturally to you.

```
(define (count sent)
  (accumulate + (every always-one sent)))

> (count '(the continuing story of bungalow bill))
6
```

You can now understand the `acronym` procedure from Chapter 1:

```
(define (acronym phrase)
  (accumulate word (every first (keep real-word? phrase))))

> (acronym '(reduced instruction set computer))
RISC

> (acronym '(structure and interpretation of computer programs))
SICP
```

Choosing the Right Tool

So far you've seen three higher-order functions: `every`, `keep`, and `accumulate`. How do you decide which one to use for a particular problem?

`Every` transforms each element of a word or sentence individually. The result sentence usually contains as many elements as the argument.*

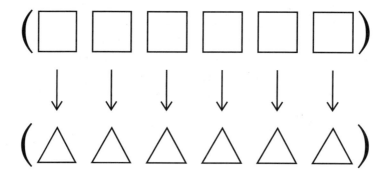

---

* What we mean by "usually" is that `every` is most often used with an argument function that returns a single word. If the function returns a sentence whose length might not be one, then the number of words in the overall result could be anything!

`Keep` selects certain elements of a word or sentence and discards the others. The elements of the result are elements of the argument, without transformation, but the result may be smaller than the original.

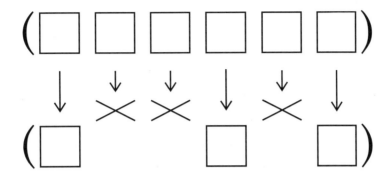

`Accumulate` transforms the entire word or sentence into a single result by combining all of the elements in some way.

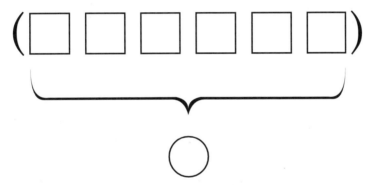

These three pictures represent graphically the differences in the meanings of `every`, `keep`, and `accumulate`. In the pictures, we're applying these higher-order procedures to sentences, but don't forget that we could have drawn similar pictures in which the higher-order procedures process the letters of a word.

Here's another way to compare these three higher-order functions:

function	purpose	first argument is a ...
`every`	transform	one-argument *transforming* function
`keep`	select	one-argument *predicate* function
`accumulate`	combine	two-argument *combining* function

To help you understand these differences, we'll look at specific examples using each of them, with each example followed by an equivalent computation done without the higher-order procedure. Here is an example for **every**:

```
> (every double 'girl)
(GG II RR LL)

> (se (double 'g)
      (double 'i)
      (double 'r)
      (double 'l))
(GG II RR LL)
```

You can, if you like, think of the first of these expressions as abbreviating the second.

An expression using **keep** can also be replaced with an expression that performs the same computation without using **keep**. This time it's a little messier:

```
> (keep even? '(1 2 3 4 5))
(2 4)

> (se (if (even? 1) 1 '())
      (if (even? 2) 2 '())
      (if (even? 3) 3 '())
      (if (even? 4) 4 '())
      (if (even? 5) 5 '()))
(2 4)
```

Here's how an **accumulate** can be expressed the long way:

```
> (accumulate word '(a c l u))
ACLU

> (word 'a (word 'c (word 'l 'u)))
ACLU
```

(Of course **word** will accept any number of arguments, so we could have computed the same result with all four letters as arguments to the same invocation. But the version we've shown here indicates how **accumulate** actually works; it combines the elements one by one.)

First-Class Functions and First-Class Sentences

If Scheme (or any dialect of Lisp) is your first programming language, having procedures that operate on entire sentences at once may not seem like a big deal. But if you used to program in some lesser language, you're probably accustomed to writing something like `first-letters` as a *loop* in which you have some variable named I and you carry out some sequence of steps for I=1, I=2, and so on, until you get to N, the number of elements. The use of higher-order functions allows us to express this problem all at once, rather than as a sequence of events. Once you're accustomed to the Lisp way of thinking, you can tell yourself "just take `every first` of the sentence," and that feels like a single step, not a complicated task.

Two aspects of Scheme combine to permit this mode of expression. One, which we've mentioned earlier, is that sentences are first-class data. You can use an entire sentence as an argument to a procedure. You can type a quoted sentence in, or you can compute a sentence by putting words together.

The second point is that functions are also first-class. This lets us write a procedure like `pigl` that applies to a single word, and then combine that with `every` to translate an entire sentence to Pig Latin. If Scheme didn't have first-class functions, we couldn't have general-purpose tools like `keep` and `every`, because we couldn't say which function to extend to all of a sentence. You'll see later that without `every` it would still be possible to write a specific `pigl-sent` procedure and separately write a `first-letters` procedure. But the ability to use a procedure as argument to another procedure lets us *generalize* the idea of "apply this function to every word of the sentence."

Repeated

All the higher-order functions you've seen so far take functions as arguments, but none of them have functions as return values. That is, we have machines that can take machines in their input hoppers, but now we'd like to think about machines that drop *other machines* out of their output chutes—machine factories, so to speak.

In the following example, the procedure `repeated` returns a procedure:

```
> ((repeated bf 3) '(she came in through the bathroom window))
(THROUGH THE BATHROOM WINDOW)

> ((repeated plural 4) 'computer)
COMPUTERSSSS
```

```
> ((repeated square 2) 3)
81

> (define (double sent)
    (se sent sent))

> ((repeated double 3) '(banana))
(BANANA BANANA BANANA BANANA BANANA BANANA BANANA BANANA)
```

The procedure `repeated` takes two arguments, a procedure and a number, and returns a new procedure. The returned procedure is one that invokes the original procedure repeatedly. For example, (`repeated bf 3`) returns a function that takes the butfirst of the butfirst of the butfirst of its argument.

Notice that all our examples start with two open parentheses. If we just invoked `repeated` at the Scheme prompt, we would get back a procedure, like this:

```
> (repeated square 4)
#<PROCEDURE>
```

The procedure that we get back isn't very interesting by itself, so we invoke it, like this:

```
> ((repeated square 4) 2)
65536
```

To understand this expression, you must think carefully about its two subexpressions. Two subexpressions? Because there are two open parentheses next to each other, it would be easy to ignore one of them and therefore think of the expression as having four atomic subexpressions. But in fact it has only two. The first subexpression, (`repeated square 4`), has a procedure as its value. The second subexpression, 2, has a number as its value. The value of the entire expression comes from applying the procedure to the number.

All along we've been saying that you evaluate a compound expression in two steps: First, you evaluate all the subexpressions. Then you apply the first value, which has to be a procedure, to the rest of the values. But until now the first subexpression has always been just a single word, the name of a procedure. Now we see that the first expression might be an invocation of a higher-order function, just as any of the argument subexpressions might be function invocations.

We can use `repeated` to define `item`, which returns a particular element of a sentence:

```
(define (item n sent)
  (first ((repeated bf (- n 1)) sent)))

> (item 1 '(a day in the life))
A

> (item 4 '(a day in the life))
THE
```

Pitfalls

⇒ Some people seem to fall in love with **every** and try to use it in all problems, even when **keep** or **accumulate** would be more appropriate.

⇒ If you find yourself using a predicate function as the first argument to **every**, you almost certainly mean to use **keep** instead. For example, we want to write a procedure that determines whether any of the words in its argument sentence are numbers:

```
(define (any-numbers? sent)                   ;; wrong!
  (accumulate or (every number? sent)))
```

This is wrong for two reasons. First, since Boolean values aren't words, they can't be members of sentences:

```
> (sentence #T #F)
ERROR: ARGUMENT TO SENTENCE NOT A WORD OR SENTENCE: #F

> (every number? '(a b 2 c 6))
ERROR: ARGUMENT TO SENTENCE NOT A WORD OR SENTENCE: #T
```

Second, even if you could have a sentence of Booleans, Scheme doesn't allow a special form, such as **or**, as the argument to a higher-order function.* Depending on your version of Scheme, the incorrect **any-numbers?** procedure might give an error message about either of these two problems.

Instead of using **every**, select the numbers from the argument and count them:

```
(define (any-numbers? sent)
  (not (empty? (keep number? sent))))
```

---

* As we said in Chapter 4, special forms aren't procedures, and aren't first-class.

⇒ The keep function always returns a result of the same type (i.e., word or sentence) as its second argument. This makes sense because if you're selecting a subset of the words of a sentence, you want to end up with a sentence; but if you're selecting a subset of the letters of a word, you want a word. Every, on the other hand, always returns a sentence. You might think that it would make more sense for every to return a word when its second argument is a word. Sometimes that *is* what you want, but sometimes not. For example:

```
(define (spell-digit digit)
  (item (+ 1 digit)
        '(zero one two three four five six seven eight nine)))

> (every spell-digit 1971)
(ONE NINE SEVEN ONE)
```

In the cases where you do want a word, you can just accumulate word the sentence that every returns.

⇒ Remember that every expects its first argument to be a function of just one argument. If you invoke every with a function such as quotient, which expects two arguments, you will get an error message from quotient, complaining that it only got one argument and wanted to get two.

Some people try to get around this by saying things like

```
(every (quotient 6) '(1 2 3))                    ;; wrong!
```

This is a sort of wishful thinking. The intent is that Scheme should interpret the first argument to every as a fill-in-the-blank template, so that every will compute the values of

```
(quotient 6 1)
(quotient 6 2)
(quotient 6 3)
```

But of course what Scheme really does is the same thing it always does: It evaluates the argument expressions, then invokes every. So Scheme will try to compute (quotient 6) and will give an error message.

We picked quotient for this example because it requires exactly two arguments. Many Scheme primitives that ordinarily take two arguments, however, will accept only one. Attempting the same wishful thinking with one of these procedures is still wrong, but the error message is different. For example, suppose you try to add 3 to each of several numbers this way:

```
(every (+ 3) '(1 2 3))                    ;; wrong!
```

The first argument to **every** in this case isn't "the procedure that adds 3," but the result returned by invoking + with the single argument 3. (+ 3) returns the number 3, which isn't a procedure. So you will get an error message like "Attempt to apply non-procedure 3."

The idea behind this mistake—looking for a way to "specialize" a two-argument procedure by supplying one of the arguments in advance—is actually a good one. In the next chapter we'll introduce a new mechanism that does allow such specialization.

⇒ If the procedure you use as the argument to **every** returns an empty sentence, then you may be surprised by the results:

```
(define (beatle-number n)
  (if (or (< n 1) (> n 4))
      '()
      (item n '(john paul george ringo))))

> (beatle-number 3)
GEORGE

> (beatle-number 5)
()

> (every beatle-number '(2 8 4 0 1))
(PAUL RINGO JOHN)
```

What happened to the 8 and the 0? Pretend that **every** didn't exist, and you had to do it the hard way:

```
(se (beatle-number 2) (beatle-number 8) (beatle-number 4)
    (beatle-number 0) (beatle-number 1))
```

Using result replacement, we would get

```
(se 'paul '() 'ringo '() 'john)
```

which is just (PAUL RINGO JOHN).

On the other hand, if **every**'s argument procedure returns an empty *word,* it will appear in the result.

```
> (every bf '(i need you))
("" EED OU)
```

The sentence returned by **every** has three words in it: the empty word, **eed**, and **ou**.

⇒ Don't confuse

```
(first '(one two three four))
```

with

```
(every first '(one two three four))
```

In the first case, we're applying the procedure **first** to a sentence; in the second, we're applying **first** four separate times, to each of the four words separately.

⇒ What happens if you use a one-word sentence or one-letter word as argument to **accumulate**? It returns that word or that letter, without even invoking the given procedure. This makes sense if you're using something like + or **max** as the accumulator, but it's disconcerting that

```
(accumulate se '(one-word))
```

returns the *word* **one-word**.

⇒ What happens if you give **accumulate** an empty sentence or word? **Accumulate** accepts empty arguments for some combiners, but not for others:

```
> (accumulate + '())
0

> (accumulate max '())
ERROR: CAN'T ACCUMULATE EMPTY INPUT WITH THAT COMBINER
```

The combiners that can be used with an empty sentence or word are +, *, **word**, and **sentence**. **Accumulate** checks specifically for one of these combiners.

Why should these four procedures, and no others, be allowed to **accumulate** an empty sentence or word? The difference between these and other combiners is that you can invoke them with no arguments, whereas `max`, for example, requires at least one number:

```
> (+)
0

> (max)
ERROR: NOT ENOUGH ARGUMENTS TO #<PROCEDURE>.
```

`Accumulate` actually invokes the combiner with no arguments in order to find out what value to return for an empty sentence or word. We would have liked to implement `accumulate` so that *any* procedure that can be invoked with no arguments would be accepted as a combiner to accumulate the empty sentence or word. Unfortunately, Scheme does not provide a way for a program to ask, "How many arguments will this procedure accept?" The best we could do was to build a particular set of zero-argument-okay combiners into the definition of `accumulate`.

Don't think that the returned value for an empty argument is always zero or empty.

```
> (accumulate * '())
1
```

The explanation for this behavior is that any function that works with no arguments returns its *identity element* in that case. What's an identity element? The function `+` has the identity element 0 because (`+` *anything* 0) returns the *anything*. Similarly, the empty word is the identity element for `word`. In general, a function's identity element has the property that when you invoke the function with the identity element and something else as arguments, the return value is the something else. It's a Scheme convention that a procedure with an identity element returns that element when invoked with no arguments.*

⇒ The use of two consecutive open parentheses to invoke the procedure returned by a procedure is a strange-looking notation:

```
((repeated bf 3) 987654)
```

---

* PC Scheme returns zero for an invocation of `max` with no arguments, but that's the wrong answer. If anything, the answer would have to be $-\infty$.

Don't confuse this with the similar-looking `cond` notation, in which the outer parentheses have a special meaning (delimiting a `cond` clause). Here, the parentheses have their usual meaning. The inner parentheses invoke the procedure `repeated` with arguments `bf` and 3. The value of that expression is a procedure. It doesn't have a name, but for the purposes of this paragraph let's pretend it's called `bfthree`. Then the outer parentheses are basically saying (`bfthree` 987654); they apply the unnamed procedure to the argument 987654.

In other words, there are two sets of parentheses because there are two functions being invoked: `repeated` and the function returned by `repeated`. So don't say

```
(repeated bf 3 987654)                          ;; wrong
```

just because it looks more familiar. `Repeated` isn't a function of three arguments.

Boring Exercises

8.1 What does Scheme return as the value of each of the following expressions? Figure it out for yourself before you try it on the computer.

```
> (every last '(algebra purple spaghetti tomato gnu))

> (keep number? '(one two three four))

> (accumulate * '(6 7 13 0 9 42 17))

> (member? 'h (keep vowel? '(t h r o a t)))

> (every square (keep even? '(87 4 7 12 0 5)))

> (accumulate word (keep vowel? (every first '(and i love her))))

> ((repeated square 0) 25)

> (every (repeated bl 2) '(good day sunshine))
```

8.2 Fill in the blanks in the following Scheme interactions:

```
> (_____ vowel? 'birthday)
IA
```

```
> (_____ first '(golden slumbers))
(G S)

> (_____ '(golden slumbers))
GOLDEN

> (_____ _____ '(little child)))
(E D)

> (_____ _____ (_____ _____ '(little child)))
ED

> (_____ + '(2 3 4 5))
(2 3 4 5)

> (_____ + '(2 3 4 5))
14
```

8.3 Describe each of the following functions in English. Make sure to include a description of the domain and range of each function. Be as precise as possible; for example, "the argument must be a function of one numeric argument" is better than "the argument must be a function."

```
(define (f a)
  (keep even? a))

(define (g b)
  (every b '(blue jay way)))


(define (h c d)
  (c (c d)))

(define (i e)
  (/ (accumulate + e) (count e)))

accumulate

sqrt

repeated

(repeated sqrt 3)
```

```
(repeated even? 2)

(repeated first 2)

(repeated (repeated bf 3) 2)
```

Real Exercises

Note: Writing helper procedures may be useful in solving some of these problems. *If you read Part IV before this, do not use recursion in solving these problems; use higher order functions instead.*

8.4   Write a procedure `choose-beatles` that takes a predicate function as its argument and returns a sentence of just those Beatles (John, Paul, George, and Ringo) that satisfy the predicate. For example:

```
(define (ends-vowel? wd) (vowel? (last wd)))

(define (even-count? wd) (even? (count wd)))

> (choose-beatles ends-vowel?)
(GEORGE RINGO)

> (choose-beatles even-count?)
(JOHN PAUL GEORGE)
```

8.5   Write a procedure `transform-beatles` that takes a procedure as an argument, applies it to each of the Beatles, and returns the results in a sentence:

```
(define (amazify name)
  (word 'the-amazing- name))


> (transform-beatles amazify)
(THE-AMAZING-JOHN THE-AMAZING-PAUL THE-AMAZING-GEORGE
 THE-AMAZING-RINGO)

> (transform-beatles butfirst)
(OHN AUL EORGE INGO)
```

8.6 When you're talking to someone over a noisy radio connection, you sometimes have to spell out a word in order to get the other person to understand it. But names of letters aren't that easy to understand either, so there's a standard code in which each letter is represented by a particular word that starts with the letter. For example, instead of "B" you say "bravo."

Write a procedure words that takes a word as its argument and returns a sentence of the names of the letters in the word:

```
> (words 'cab)
(CHARLIE ALPHA BRAVO)
```

(You may make up your own names for the letters or look up the standard ones if you want.)

Hint: Start by writing a helper procedure that figures out the name for a single letter.

8.7 [14.5]* Write a procedure letter-count that takes a sentence as its argument and returns the total number of letters in the sentence:

```
> (letter-count '(fixing a hole))
11
```

8.8 [12.5] Write an exaggerate procedure which exaggerates sentences:

```
> (exaggerate '(i ate 3 potstickers))
(I ATE 6 POTSTICKERS)

> (exaggerate '(the chow fun is good here))
(THE CHOW FUN IS GREAT HERE)
```

It should double all the numbers in the sentence, and it should replace "good" with "great," "bad" with "terrible," and anything else you can think of.

---

* Exercise 14.5 in Part IV asks you to solve this same problem using recursion. Here we are asking you to use higher-order functions. Whenever we pose the same problem in both parts, we'll cross-reference them in brackets as we did here. When you see the problem for the second time, you might want to consult your first solution for ideas.

8.9 What procedure can you use as the first argument to every so that for any sentence used as the second argument, every returns that sentence?

What procedure can you use as the first argument to keep so that for any sentence used as the second argument, keep returns that sentence?

What procedure can you use as the first argument to accumulate so that for any sentence used as the second argument, accumulate returns that sentence?

8.10 Write a predicate true-for-all? that takes two arguments, a predicate procedure and a sentence. It should return #t if the predicate argument returns true for *every* word in the sentence.

```
> (true-for-all? even? '(2 4 6 8))
#T

> (true-for-all? even? '(2 6 3 4))
#F
```

8.11 [12.6] Write a GPA procedure. It should take a sentence of grades as its argument and return the corresponding grade point average:

```
> (gpa '(A A+ B+ B))
3.67
```

Hint: write a helper procedure base-grade that takes a grade as argument and returns 0, 1, 2, 3, or 4, and another helper procedure grade-modifier that returns −.33, 0, or .33, depending on whether the grade has a minus, a plus, or neither.

8.12 [11.2] When you teach a class, people will get distracted if you say "um" too many times. Write a count-ums that counts the number of times "um" appears in a sentence:

```
> (count-ums
    '(today um we are going to um talk about functional um programming))
3
```

8.13 [11.3] Write a procedure phone-unspell that takes a spelled version of a phone number, such as POPCORN, and returns the real phone number, in this case 7672676. You will need to write a helper procedure that uses an 8-way cond expression to translate a single letter into a digit.

8.14 Write the procedure `subword` that takes three arguments: a word, a starting position number, and an ending position number. It should return the subword containing only the letters between the specified positions:

```
> (subword 'polythene 5 8)
THEN
```

Alonzo Church
inventor of lambda calculus

9 Lambda

Let's say we want to add three to each of the numbers in a sentence. Using the tools from Chapter 8, we would do it like this:

```
(define (add-three number)
  (+ number 3))

(define (add-three-to-each sent)
  (every add-three sent))

> (add-three-to-each '(1 9 9 2))
(4 12 12 5)
```

It's slightly annoying to have to define a helper procedure `add-three` just so we can use it as the argument to `every`. We're never going to use that procedure again, but we still have to come up with a name for it. We'd like a general way to say "here's the function I want you to use" without having to give the procedure a name. In other words, we want a general-purpose procedure-generating procedure!

Lambda is the name of a special form that generates procedures. It takes some information about the function you want to create as arguments and it returns the procedure. It'll be easier to explain the details after you see an example.

```
(define (add-three-to-each sent)
  (every (lambda (number) (+ number 3)) sent))

> (add-three-to-each '(1 9 9 2))
(4 12 12 5)
```

The first argument to every is, in effect, the same procedure as the one we called add-three earlier, but now we can use it without giving it a name. (Don't make the mistake of thinking that lambda is the argument to every. The argument is *the procedure returned by* lambda.)

Perhaps you're wondering whether "lambda" spells something backward. Actually, it's the name of the Greek letter L, which looks like this: λ. It would probably be more sensible if lambda were named something like make-procedure, but the name lambda is traditional.*

Creating a procedure by using lambda is very much like creating one with define, as we've done up to this point, except that we don't specify a name. When we create a procedure with define, we have to indicate the procedure's name, the names of its arguments (i.e., the formal parameters), and the expression that it computes (its body). With lambda we still provide the last two of these three components.

As we said, lambda is a special form. This means, as you remember, that its arguments are not evaluated when you invoke it. The first argument is a sentence containing the formal parameters; the second argument is the body. What lambda returns is an unnamed procedure. You can invoke that procedure:

```
> ((lambda (a b) (+ (* 2 a) b)) 5 6)
16

> ((lambda (wd) (word (last wd) (first wd))) 'impish)
HI
```

In real life, though, you're not likely to create a procedure with lambda merely to invoke it once. More often, we use lambda as in the first example in this chapter, to provide a procedure as argument to a higher-order function. Here are some more examples:

```
> (every (lambda (wd) (se (first wd) wd (last wd)))
         '(only a northern song))
(O ONLY Y A A A N NORTHERN N S SONG G)
```

---

* It comes from a branch of mathematical logic called "lambda calculus" that's about the formal properties of functions. The inclusion of first-class functions in Lisp was inspired by this mathematical work, so Lisp borrowed the name lambda.

```
> (keep (lambda (n) (member? 9 n)) '(4 81 909 781 1969 1776))
(909 1969)

> (accumulate (lambda (this that)
                (if (> (count this) (count that)) this that))
              '(wild honey pie))
HONEY

> (keep (lambda (person) (member? person '(john paul george ringo)))
        '(mick smokey paul diana bill geddy john yoko keith reparata))
(PAUL JOHN)

> (keep (lambda (person) (member? 'e person))
        '(mick smokey paul diana bill geddy john yoko keith reparata))
(SMOKEY GEDDY KEITH REPARATA)
```

Procedures That Return Procedures

An even more powerful use of lambda is to provide the value returned by some procedure
that you write. Here's the classic example:

```
(define (make-adder num)
  (lambda (x) (+ x num)))

> ((make-adder 4) 7)
11

> (every (make-adder 6) '(2 4 8))
(8 10 14)
```

The value of the expression (make-adder 4) is a *procedure,* not a number. That
unnamed procedure is the one that adds 4 to its argument. We can understand this by
applying the substitution model to make-adder. We substitute 4 for num in the body of
make-adder; we end up with

```
(lambda (x) (+ x 4))
```

and then we evaluate that expression to get the desired procedure.

Here's a procedure whose argument is a procedure:

```
(define (same-arg-twice fn)
  (lambda (arg) (fn arg arg)))
```

```
> ((same-arg-twice word) 'hello)
HELLOHELLO

> ((same-arg-twice *) 4)
16
```

When we evaluate (same-arg-twice word) we substitute the procedure word for the formal parameter fn, and the result is

```
(lambda (arg) (word arg arg))
```

One more example:

```
(define (flip fn)
  (lambda (a b) (fn b a)))

> ((flip -) 5 8)
3

> ((flip se) 'goodbye 'hello)
(HELLO GOODBYE)
```

The Truth about Define

Remember how we said that creating a procedure with lambda was a lot like creating a procedure with define? That's because the notation we've been using with define is an abbreviation that combines two activities: creating a procedure and giving a name to something.

As you saw in Chapter 7, define's real job is to give a name to some value:

```
> (define pi 3.141592654)

> (* pi 10)
31.41592654

> (define drummer '(ringo starr))

> (first drummer)
RINGO
```

When we say

```
(define (square x) (* x x))
```

it's actually an abbreviation for

```
(define square (lambda (x) (* x x)))
```

In this example, the job of `lambda` is to create a procedure that multiplies its argument by itself; the job of `define` is to name that procedure `square`.

In the past, without quite saying so, we've talked as if the name of a procedure were understood differently from other names in a program. In thinking about an expression such as

```
(* x x)
```

we've talked about substituting some actual value for the `x` but took the `*` for granted as meaning the multiplication function.

The truth is that we have to substitute a value for the `*` just as we do for the `x`. It just happens that `*` has been predefined to have the multiplication procedure as its value. This definition of `*` is *global*, like the definition of `pi` above. "Global" means that it's not a formal parameter of a procedure, like `x` in `square`, but has a permanent value established by `define`.

When an expression is evaluated, every name in the expression must have some value substituted for it. If the name is a formal parameter, then the corresponding actual argument value is substituted. Otherwise, the name had better have a global definition, and *that* value is substituted. It just so happens that Scheme has predefined a zillion names before you start working, and most of those are names of primitive procedures.

(By the way, this explains why when you make a typing mistake in the name of a procedure you might see an error message that refers to variables, such as "variable `frist` not bound." You might expect it to say "`frist` is not a procedure," but the problem is no different from that of any other name that has no associated value.)

Now that we know the whole truth about `define`, we can use it in combination with the function-creating functions in these past two chapters.

```
> (define square (same-arg-twice *))

> (square 7)
49
```

```
> (define fourth-power (repeated square 2))

> (fourth-power 5)
625
```

The Truth about Let

In Chapter 7 we introduced `let` as an abbreviation for the situation in which we would otherwise define a helper procedure in order to give names to commonly-used values in a calculation. We started with

```
(define (roots a b c)
  (roots1 a b c (sqrt (- (* b b) (* 4 a c)))))

(define (roots1 a b c discriminant)
  (se (/ (+ (- b) discriminant) (* 2 a))
      (/ (- (- b) discriminant) (* 2 a))))
```

and introduced the new notation

```
(define (roots a b c)
  (let ((discriminant (sqrt (- (* b b) (* 4 a c)))))
    (se (/ (+ (- b) discriminant) (* 2 a))
        (/ (- (- b) discriminant) (* 2 a)))))
```

to avoid creating an otherwise-useless named procedure. But now that we know about unnamed procedures, we can see that `let` is merely an abbreviation for creating and invoking an anonymous procedure:

```
(define (roots a b c)
  ((lambda (discriminant)
     (se (/ (+ (- b) discriminant) (* 2 a))
         (/ (- (- b) discriminant) (* 2 a))))
   (sqrt (- (* b b) (* 4 a c)))))
```

What's shown in boldface above is the part that invokes the procedure created by the lambda, including the actual argument expression.

Just as the notation to define a procedure with parentheses around its name is an abbreviation for a `define` and a `lambda`, the `let` notation is an abbreviation for a `lambda` and an invocation.

Name Conflicts

When a procedure is created inside another procedure, what happens if you use the same formal parameter name in both?

```
(define (f x)
  (lambda (x) (+ x 3)))
```

Answer: Don't do it.

What actually happens is that the inner **x** wins; that's the one that is substituted into the body. But if you find yourself in this situation, you are almost certainly doing something wrong, such as using nondescriptive names like **x** for your variables.

Named and Unnamed Functions

Although you've been running across the idea of function since high school algebra, you've probably never seen an *unnamed* function until now. The high school function notation, $g(x) = 3x + 8$, requires you to give the function a name (g in this case) when you create it. Most of the functions you know, both in math and in programming, have names, such as logarithm or `first`.*

When do you want to name a function, and when not? It may help to think about an analogy with numbers. Imagine if every Scheme number had to have a name before you could use it. You'd have to say

```
> (define three 3)
> (define four 4)
> (+ three four)
7
```

This is analogous to the way we've dealt with procedures until now, giving each one a name. Sometimes it's much easier to use a number directly, and it's silly to have to give it a name.

But sometimes it isn't silly. A common example that we've seen earlier is

---

* Professional mathematicians do have a notation for unnamed functions, by the way. They write $(x \mapsto 3x + 8)$.

```
(define pi 3.141592654)

(define (circle-area radius)
  (* pi radius radius))

(define (circumference radius)
  (* 2 pi radius))

(define (sphere-surface-area radius)
  (* 4 pi radius radius))

(define (sphere-volume radius)
  (* (/ 4 3) pi radius radius radius))
```

If we couldn't give a name to the number 3.141592654, then we'd have to type it over and over again. Apart from the extra typing, our programs would be harder to read and understand. Giving π a name makes the procedures more self-documenting. (That is, someone else who reads our procedures will have an easier time understanding what we meant.)

It's the same with procedures. If we're going to use a procedure more than once, and if there's a meaningful name for it that will help clarify the program, then we define the procedure with define and give it a name.

```
(define (square x) (* x x))
```

Square deserves a name both because we use it often and because there is a good traditional name for it that everyone understands. More important, by giving square a name, we are shifting attention from the process by which it works (invoking the multiplication procedure) to its *purpose*, computing the square of a number. From now on we can think about squaring as though it were a Scheme primitive. This idea of naming something and forgetting the details of its implementation is what we've been calling "abstraction."

On the other hand, if we have an unimportant procedure that we're using only once, we might as well create it with lambda and without a name.

```
> (every (lambda (x) (last (bl x))) '(all together now))
(L E O)
```

We could have defined this procedure with the name next-to-last, but if we're never going to use it again, why bother?

Here's an example in which we use an obscure unnamed function to help us define one that's worth naming:

```
(define (backwards wd) (accumulate (lambda (a b) (word b a)) wd))

> (backwards 'yesterday)
YADRETSEY

> (every backwards '(i saw her standing there))
(I WAS REH GNIDNATS EREHT)
```

Pitfalls

⇒ It's very convenient that **define** has an abbreviated form to define a procedure using a hidden **lambda**, but because there are two notations that differ only subtly—one has an extra set of parentheses—you could use the wrong one by mistake. If you say

```
(define (pi) 3.141592654)
```

you're not defining a variable whose value is a number. Instead the value of **pi** will be a *procedure*. It would then be an error to say

```
(* 2 pi)
```

⇒ When should the body of your procedure be a **lambda** expression? It's easy to go overboard and say "I'm writing a procedure so I guess I need **lambda**" even when the procedure is supposed to return a word.

The secret is to remember the ideas of *domain* and *range* that we talked about in Chapter 2. What is the range of the function you're writing? Should it return a procedure? If so, its body might be a **lambda** expression. (It might instead be an invocation of a higher-order procedure, such as **repeated**, that returns a procedure.) If your procedure doesn't return a procedure, its body won't be a **lambda** expression. (Of course your procedure might still use a **lambda** expression as an argument to some *other* procedure, such as **every**.)

For example, here is a procedure to keep the words of a sentence that contain the letter h. The domain of the function is sentences, and its range is also sentences. (That is, it takes a sentence as argument and returns a sentence as its value.)

```
(define (keep-h sent)
  (keep (lambda (wd) (member? 'h wd)) sent))
```

By contrast, here is a function of a letter that returns a *procedure* to keep words containing that letter.

```
(define (keeper letter)
  (lambda (sent)
    (keep (lambda (wd) (member? letter wd)) sent)))
```

The procedure keeper has letters as its domain and procedures as its range. The procedure *returned by* keeper has sentences as its domain and as its range, just as keep-h does. In fact, we can use keeper to define keep-h:

```
(define keep-h (keeper 'h))
```

⇒ Don't confuse the *creation* of a procedure with the *invocation* of one. Lambda creates a procedure. The procedure is invoked in response to an expression whose first subexpression represents that procedure. That is, the first subexpression could be the *name* of the procedure, or it could be a lambda expression if you want to create a procedure and invoke it right away:

```
((lambda (x) (+ x 3)) 6)
```

In particular, when you create a procedure, you specify its formal parameters—the *names* for its arguments. When you invoke the procedure, you specify *values* for those arguments. (In this example, the lambda expression includes the formal parameter x, but the invocation provides the actual argument 6.)

Boring Exercises

9.1 What will Scheme print? Figure it out yourself before you try it on the computer.

```
> (lambda (x) (+ (* x 3) 4))

> ((lambda (x) (+ (* x 3) 4)) 10)

> (every (lambda (wd) (word (last wd) (bl wd)))
         '(any time at all))
```

```
> ((lambda (x) (+ x 3)) 10 15)
```

9.2 Rewrite the following definitions so as to make the implicit `lambda` explicit.

```
(define (second stuff)
  (first (bf stuff)))

(define (make-adder num)
  (lambda (x) (+ num x)))
```

9.3 What does this procedure do?

```
(define (let-it-be sent)
  (accumulate (lambda (x y) y) sent))
```

Real Exercises

9.4 The following program doesn't work. Why not? Fix it.

```
(define (who sent)
  (every describe '(pete roger john keith)))

(define (describe person)
  (se person sent))
```

It's supposed to work like this:

```
> (who '(sells out))
(pete sells out roger sells out john sells out keith sells out)
```

In each of the following exercises, write the procedure in terms of `lambda` and higher-order functions. Do not use named helper procedures. If you've read Part IV, don't use recursion, either.

9.5 Write `prepend-every`:

```
> (prepend-every 's '(he aid he aid))
(SHE SAID SHE SAID)

> (prepend-every 'anti '(dote pasto gone body))
(ANTIDOTE ANTIPASTO ANTIGONE ANTIBODY)
```

9.6 Write a procedure `sentence-version` that takes a function F as its argument and returns a function G. F should take a single word as argument. G should take a sentence as argument and return the sentence formed by applying F to each word of that argument.

```
> ((sentence-version first) '(if i fell))
(I I F)

> ((sentence-version square) '(8 2 4 6))
(64 4 16 36)
```

9.7 Write a procedure called `letterwords` that takes as its arguments a letter and a sentence. It returns a sentence containing only those words from the argument sentence that contain the argument letter:

```
> (letterwords 'o '(got to get you into my life))
(GOT TO YOU INTO)
```

9.8 Suppose we're writing a program to play hangman. In this game one player has to guess a secret word chosen by the other player, one letter at a time. You're going to write just one small part of this program: a procedure that takes as arguments the secret word and the letters guessed so far, returning the word in which the guessing progress is displayed by including all the guessed letters along with underscores for the not-yet-guessed ones:

```
> (hang 'potsticker 'etaoi)
_OT_TI__E_
```

Hint: You'll find it helpful to use the following procedure that determines how to display a single letter:

```
(define (hang-letter letter guesses)
  (if (member? letter guesses)
      letter
      '_))
```

9.9 Write a procedure `common-words` that takes two sentences as arguments and returns a sentence containing only those words that appear both in the first sentence and in the second sentence.

9.10 In Chapter 2 we used a function called `appearances` that returns the number of times its first argument appears as a member of its second argument. Implement `appearances`.

9.11 Write a procedure `unabbrev` that takes two sentences as arguments. It should return a sentence that's the same as the first sentence, except that any numbers in the original sentence should be replaced with words from the second sentence. A number 2 in the first sentence should be replaced with the second word of the second sentence, a 6 with the sixth word, and so on.

```
> (unabbrev '(john 1 wayne fred 4) '(bill hank kermit joey))
(JOHN BILL WAYNE FRED JOEY)

> (unabbrev '(i 3 4 tell 2) '(do you want to know a secret?))
(I WANT TO TELL YOU)
```

9.12 Write a procedure `first-last` whose argument will be a sentence. It should return a sentence containing only those words in the argument sentence whose first and last letters are the same:

```
> (first-last '(california ohio nebraska alabama alaska massachusetts))
(OHIO ALABAMA ALASKA)
```

9.13 Write a procedure `compose` that takes two functions *f* and *g* as arguments. It should return a new function, the composition of its input functions, which computes $f(g(x))$ when passed the argument *x*.

```
> ((compose sqrt abs) -25)
5

> (define second (compose first bf))

> (second '(higher order function))
ORDER
```

9.14 Write a procedure `substitute` that takes three arguments, two words and a sentence. It should return a version of the sentence, but with every instance of the second word replaced with the first word:

```
> (substitute 'maybe 'yeah '(she loves you yeah yeah yeah))
(SHE LOVES YOU MAYBE MAYBE MAYBE)
```

9.15 Many functions are applicable only to arguments in a certain domain and result in error messages if given arguments outside that domain. For example, `sqrt` may require a nonnegative argument in a version of Scheme that doesn't include complex numbers. (In *any* version of Scheme, `sqrt` will complain if its argument isn't a number at all!) Once a program gets an error message, it's impossible for that program to continue the computation.

Write a procedure `type-check` that takes as arguments a one-argument procedure `f` and a one-argument predicate procedure `pred`. `Type-check` should return a one-argument procedure that first applies `pred` to its argument; if that result is true, the procedure should return the value computed by applying `f` to the argument; if `pred` returns false, the new procedure should also return `#f`:

```
> (define safe-sqrt (type-check sqrt number?))

> (safe-sqrt 16)
4

> (safe-sqrt 'sarsaparilla)
#F
```

9.16 In the language APL, most arithmetic functions can be applied either to a number, with the usual result, or to a *vector*—the APL name for a sentence of numbers—in which case the result is a new vector in which each element is the result of applying the function to the corresponding element of the argument. For example, the function `sqrt` applied to 16 returns 4 as in Scheme, but `sqrt` can also be applied to a sentence such as (16 49) and it returns (4 7).

Write a procedure `aplize` that takes as its argument a one-argument procedure whose domain is numbers or words. It should return an APLized procedure that also accepts sentences:

```
> (define apl-sqrt (aplize sqrt))

> (apl-sqrt 36)
6

> (apl-sqrt '(1 100 25 16))
(1 10 5 4)
```

9.17 Write `keep` in terms of `every` and `accumulate`.

Project: Scoring Bridge Hands

At the beginning of a game of bridge, each player assigns a value to his or her hand by counting *points*. Bridge players use these points in the first part of the game, the "bidding," to decide how high to bid. (A bid is a promise about how well you'll do in the rest of the game. If you succeed in meeting your bid you win, and if you don't meet the bid, you lose.) For example, if you have fewer than six points, you generally don't bid anything at all.

You're going to write a computer program to look at a bridge hand and decide how many points it's worth. You won't have to know anything about the rest of the game; we'll tell you the rules for counting points.

A bridge hand contains thirteen cards. Each ace in the hand is worth four points, each king is worth three points, each queen two points, and each jack one. The other cards, twos through tens, have no point value. So if your hand has two aces, a king, two jacks, and eight other cards, it's worth thirteen points.

A bridge hand might also have some "distribution" points, which are points having to do with the distribution of the thirteen cards among the four suits. If your hand has only two cards of a particular suit, then it is worth an extra point. If it has a "singleton," only one card of a particular suit, that's worth two extra points. A "void," no cards in a particular suit, is worth three points.

In our program, we'll represent a card by a word like h5 (five of hearts) or dk (king of diamonds).* A hand will be a sentence of cards, like this:

---

* Why not 5h? Scheme words that begin with a digit but aren't numbers have to be surrounded with double-quote marks. Putting the suit first avoids that.

```
(sa s10 s7 s6 s2 hq hj h9 ck c4 dk d9 d3)
```

This hand is worth 14 points: ace of spades (4), plus queen of hearts (2), plus jack of hearts (1), plus king of clubs (3), plus king of diamonds (3), plus one more for having only two clubs.

To find the suit of a card, we take its `first`, and to find the rank, we take the `butfirst`. (Why not the `last`?)

We have a particular program structure in mind. We'll describe all of the procedures you need to write; if you turn each description into a working procedure, then you should have a complete program. In writing each procedure, take advantage of the ones you've already written. Our descriptions are ordered *bottom-up*, which means that for each procedure you will already have written the helper procedures you need. (This ordering will help you write the project, but it means that we're beginning with small details. If we were describing a project to help you understand its structure, we'd do it in *top-down* order, starting with the most general procedures. We'll do that in the next chapter, in which we present a tic-tac-toe program as a larger Scheme programming example.)

Card-val

Write a procedure `card-val` that takes a single card as its argument and returns the value of that card.

```
> (card-val 'cq)
2

> (card-val 's7)
0

> (card-val 'ha)
4
```

High-card-points

Write a procedure `high-card-points` that takes a hand as its argument and returns the total number of points from high cards in the hand. (This procedure does *not* count distribution points.)

```
> (high-card-points '(sa s10 hq ck c4))
9

> (high-card-points '(sa s10 s7 s6 s2 hq hj h9 ck c4 dk d9 d3))
13
```

Count-suit

Write a procedure `count-suit` that takes a suit and a hand as arguments and returns
the number of cards in the hand with the given suit.

```
> (count-suit 's '(sa s10 hq ck c4))
2

> (count-suit 'c '(sa s10 s7 s6 s2 hq hj h9 ck c4 dk d9 d3))
2

> (count-suit 'd '(h3 d7 sk s3 c10 dq d8 s9 s4 d10 c7 d4 s2))
5
```

Suit-counts

Write a procedure `suit-counts` that takes a hand as its argument and returns a
sentence containing the number of spades, the number of hearts, the number of clubs,
and the number of diamonds in the hand.

```
> (suit-counts '(sa s10 hq ck c4))
(2 1 2 0)

> (suit-counts '(sa s10 s7 s6 s2 hq hj h9 ck c4 dk d9 d3))
(5 3 2 3)

> (suit-counts '(h3 d7 sk s3 c10 dq d8 s9 s4 d10 c7 d4 s2))
(5 1 2 5)
```

Suit-dist-points

Write `suit-dist-points` that takes a number as its argument, interpreting it as the number of cards in a suit. The procedure should return the number of distribution points your hand gets for having that number of cards in a particular suit.

```
> (suit-dist-points 2)
1

> (suit-dist-points 7)
0

> (suit-dist-points 0)
3
```

Hand-dist-points

Write `hand-dist-points`, which takes a hand as its argument and returns the number of distribution points the hand is worth.

```
> (hand-dist-points '(sa s10 s7 s6 s2 hq hj h9 ck c4 dk d9 d3))
1

> (hand-dist-points '(h3 d7 sk s3 c10 dq d8 s9 s4 d10 c7 d4 s2))
3
```

Bridge-val

Write a procedure `bridge-val` that takes a hand as its argument and returns the total number of points that the hand is worth.

```
> (bridge-val '(sa s10 s7 s6 s2 hq hj h9 ck c4 dk d9 d3))
14

> (bridge-val '(h3 d7 sk s3 c10 dq d8 s9 s4 d10 c7 d4 s2))
8
```

This computer, built of Tinker-Toy parts, plays tic-tac-toe.

10   Example: Tic-Tac-Toe

Now that you've learned about higher-order functions, we're going to look at a large example that uses them extensively. Using the techniques you've learned so far, we're going to write a program that plays perfect tic-tac-toe.

You can load our program into Scheme by typing

```
(load "ttt.scm")
```

(See Appendix A if this doesn't work for you.)

A Warning

Programs don't always come out right the first time. One of our goals in this chapter is to show you how a program is developed, so we're presenting early versions of procedures. These include some mistakes that we made, and also some after-the-fact simplifications to make our explanations easier. If you type in these early versions, they won't work. We will show you how we corrected these "bugs" and also will present a complete, correct version at the end of the chapter.

To indicate the unfinished versions of procedures, we'll use comments like "first version" or "not really part of game."

Technical Terms in Tic-Tac-Toe

We'll number the squares of the board this way:

```
1 | 2 | 3
4 | 5 | 6
7 | 8 | 9
```

We'll call a partially filled-in board a "position."

```
  |   | o
  | x | o
x |   | x
```

To the computer, the same position will be represented by the word `__o_xox_x`. The nine letters of the word correspond to squares one through nine of the board. (We're thinking ahead to the possibility of using `item` to extract the nth square of a given position.)

Thinking about the Program Structure

Our top-level procedure, `ttt`, will return the computer's next move given the current position. It takes two arguments: the current position and whether the computer is playing X or O. If the computer is O and the board looks like the one above, then we'd invoke `ttt` like this:

```
(ttt '__o_xox_x 'o)
```

Here is a sample game:

```
> (ttt '____x____ 'o)          ; Human goes first in square 5
1                              ; Computer moves in square 1
> (ttt 'o__xx____ 'o)          ; Human moves in square 4
6                              ; Computer blocks in square 6
> (ttt 'o_xxxo___ 'o)         ; Human moves in square 3
7                              ; Computer blocks again
> (ttt 'o_xxxoox_ 'o)
2
```

This is not a complete game program! Later, when we talk about input and output, you'll see how to write an interactive program that displays the board pictorially, asks the player where to move, and so on. For now, we'll just write the *strategy* procedure that chooses the next move. As a paying customer, you wouldn't be satisfied with this partial program, but from the programmer's point of view, this is the more interesting part.

Let's plan the computer's strategy in English before we start writing a computer program. How do *you* play tic-tac-toe? You have several strategy rules in your head, some of which are more urgent than others. For example, if you can win on this move, then you just do it without thinking about anything else. But if there isn't anything that immediate, you consider less urgent questions, such as how this move might affect what happens two moves later.

So we'll represent this set of rules by a giant `cond` expression:

```
(define (ttt position me)                       ;; first version
  (cond ((i-can-win?)
         (choose-winning-move))
        ((opponent-can-win?)
         (block-opponent-win))
        ((i-can-win-next-time?)
         (prepare-win))
        (else (whatever)))))
```

We're imagining many helper procedures. `I-can-win?` will look at the board and tell if the computer has an immediate winning move. If so, `choose-winning-move` will find that particular move. `Opponent-can-win?` returns true if the human player has an immediate winning move. `Block-opponent-win` will return a move that prevents the computer's opponent from winning, and so on.

We didn't actually start by writing this definition of `ttt`. The particular names of helper procedures are just guesses, because we haven't yet planned the tic-tac-toe strategy in detail. But we did know that this would be the overall structure of our program. This big picture doesn't automatically tell us what to do next; different programmers might fill in the details differently. But it's a framework to keep in mind during the rest of the job.

Our first practical step was to think about the *data structures* in our program. A data structure is a way of organizing several pieces of information into a big chunk. For example, a sentence is a data structure that combines several words in a sequence (that is, in left-to-right order).

In the first, handwavy version of `ttt`, the strategy procedures like `i-can-win?` are called with no arguments, but of course we knew they would need some information about the board position. We began by thinking about how to represent that information within the program.

The First Step: Triples

A person looking at a tic-tac-toe board looks at the rows, columns, and diagonals. The question "do I have a winning move?" is equivalent to the question "are there three squares in a line such that two of them are mine and the last one is blank?" In fact, nothing else matters about the game besides these potential winning combinations.

There are eight potential winning combinations: three rows, three columns, and two diagonals. Consider the combination containing the three squares 1, 5, and 9. If it contains both an x and an o then nobody can win with this combination and there's nothing to think about. But if it contains two xs and a free square, we're very interested in the combination. What we want to know in particular is which square is free, since we want to move in that square to win or block.

More generally, the only squares whose *numbers* we care about are the ones we might want to move into, namely, the free ones. So the only interesting information about a square is whether it has an x or an o, and if not, what its number is.

The information that 1, 5, 9 is a potential winning combination and the information that square 1 contains an x, square 5 is empty, and square 9 contains another x can be combined into the single word x5x. Looking at this word we can see immediately that there are two xs in this "triple" and that the free square is square 5. So when we want to know about a three-square combination, we will turn it into a triple of that form.

Here's a sample board position:

```
   | x | o
  -----------
   | x |
  -----------
 o |   |
```

and here is a sentence of all of its triples:

```
(1xo 4x6 o89 14o xx8 o69 1x9 oxo)
```

Take a minute to convince yourself that this sentence really does tell you everything you need to know about the corresponding board position. Once our strategy procedure finds the triples for a board position, it's never going to look at the original position again.

This technique of converting data from one form to another so that it can be manipulated more easily is an important idea in computer science. There are really three representations of the same thing. There's this picture:

as well as the word `_xo_x_o__` and the sentence (`1xo 4x6 o89 14o xx8 o69 1x9 oxo`). All three of these formats have the same information but are convenient in different ways. The pictorial form is convenient because it makes sense to the person who's playing tic-tac-toe. Unfortunately, you can't type that picture into a computer, so we need a different format, the word `_xo_x_o__`, which contains the *contents* of the nine squares in the picture, but without the lines separating the squares and without the two-dimensional shape.

The third format, the sentence, is quite *inconvenient* for human beings. You'd never want to think about a tic-tac-toe board that way yourself, because the sentence doesn't have the visual simplicity that lets you take in a tic-tac-toe position at a glance. But the sentence of triples is the most convenient representation for our program. `Ttt` will have to answer questions like "can `x` win on the next move?" To do that, it will have to consider an equivalent but more detailed question: "For each of the eight possible winning combinations, can `x` complete that combination on the next move?" It doesn't really matter whether a combination is a row or a column; what does matter is that each of the eight combinations be readily available for inspection by the program. The sentence-of-triples representation obscures part of the available information (which combination is where) to emphasize another part (making the eight combinations explicit, instead of implicit in the nine boxes of the diagram).

The representation of fractions as "mixed numerals," such as $2\frac{1}{3}$, and as "improper fractions," such as $\frac{7}{3}$, is a non-programming example of this idea about multiple representations. A mixed numeral makes it easier for a person to tell how big the number is, but an improper fraction makes arithmetic easier.

Finding the Triples

We said that we would combine the current board position with the numbers of the squares in the eight potential winning combinations in order to compute the things we're calling triples. That was our first task in writing the program.

Our program will start with this sentence of all the winning combinations:

```
(123 456 789 147 258 369 159 357)
```

and a position word such as `_xo_x_o__`; it will return a sentence of triples such as

```
(1xo 4x6 o89 14o xx8 o69 1x9 oxo)
```

All that's necessary is to replace some of the numbers with xs and os. This kind of word-by-word translation in a sentence is a good job for **every**.

```
(define (find-triples position)              ;; first version
  (every substitute-triple '(123 456 789 147 258 369 159 357)))
```

We've made up a name `substitute-triple` for a procedure we haven't written yet. This is perfectly OK, as long as we write it before we try to invoke `find-triples`. The `substitute-triple` function will take three digits, such as `258`, and return a triple, such as `2x8`:

```
(define (substitute-triple combination)      ;; first version
  (every substitute-letter combination))
```

This procedure uses **every** to call `substitute-letter` on all three letters.

There's a small problem, though. **Every** always returns a sentence, and we want our triple to be a word. For example, we want to turn the potential winning combination `258` into the word `2x8`, but **every** would return the sentence `(2 x 8)`. So here's our next version of `substitute-triple`:

```
(define (substitute-triple combination)      ;; second version
  (accumulate word (every substitute-letter combination)))
```

Substitute-letter knows that letter number 3 of the word that represents the board corresponds to the contents of square 3 of the board. This means that it can just call `item` with the given square number and the board to find out what's in that square. If it's empty, we return the square number itself; otherwise we return the contents of the square.

```
(define (substitute-letter square)           ;; first version
  (if (equal? '_ (item square position))
      square
      (item square position)))
```

Whoops! Do you see the problem?

```
> (substitute-letter 5)
ERROR: Variable POSITION is unbound.
```

Using **Every** with Two-Argument Procedures

Our procedure only takes one argument, `square`, but it needs to know the position so it can find out what's in the given square. So here's the real `substitute-letter`:

```
(define (substitute-letter square position)
  (if (equal? '_ (item square position))
      square
      (item square position)))

> (substitute-letter 5 '_xo_x_o__)
X

> (substitute-letter 8 '_xo_x_o__)
8
```

Now `substitute-letter` can do its job, since it has access to the position. But we'll have to modify `substitute-triple` to invoke `substitute-letter` with two arguments.

This is a little tricky. Let's look again at the way we're using `substitute-letter` inside `substitute-triple`:

```
(define (substitute-triple combination)        ;; second version again
  (accumulate word (every substitute-letter combination)))
```

By giving `substitute-letter` another argument, we have made this formerly correct procedure incorrect. The first argument to **every** must be a function of one argument, not two. This is exactly the kind of situation in which `lambda` can help us: We have a function of two arguments, and we need a function of one argument that does the same thing, but with one of the arguments fixed.

The procedure returned by

```
(lambda (square) (substitute-letter square position))
```

does exactly the right thing; it takes a square as its argument and returns the contents of the position at that square.

Here's the final version of `substitute-triple`:

```
(define (substitute-triple combination position)
  (accumulate word
              (every (lambda (square)
                        (substitute-letter square position))
                     combination)))
```

```
> (substitute-triple 456 '_xo_x_o__)
"4X6"
```

```
> (substitute-triple 147 '_xo_x_o__)
"140"
```

```
> (substitute-triple 357 '_xo_x_o__)
OXO
```

As you can see, Scheme prints some of these words with double-quote marks. The rule is that a word that isn't a number but begins with a digit must be double-quoted. But in the finished program we're not going to print such words at all; we're just showing you the working of a helper procedure. Similarly, in this chapter we'll show direct invocations of helper procedures in which some of the arguments are strings, but a user of the overall program won't have to use this notation.

We've fixed the `substitute-letter` problem by giving `substitute-triple` an extra argument, so we're going to have to go through the same process with `find-triples`. Here's the right version:

```
(define (find-triples position)
  (every (lambda (comb) (substitute-triple comb position))
         '(123 456 789 147 258 369 159 357)))
```

It's the same trick. `Substitute-triple` is a procedure of two arguments. We use `lambda` to transform it into a procedure of one argument for use with `every`.

We've now finished `find-triples`, one of the most important procedures in the game.

```
> (find-triples '_xo_x_o__)
("1XO" "4X6" O89 "140" XX8 O69 "1X9" OXO)
```

```
> (find-triples 'x_____oxo)
(X23 456 OXO X40 "25X" "360" X50 "350")
```

Here again are the jobs of all three procedures we've written so far:

Substitute-letter finds the letter in a single square.
Substitute-triple finds all three letters corresponding to three squares.
Find-triples   finds all the letters in all eight winning combinations.

We've done all this because we think that the rest of the program can use the triples we've computed as data. So we'll just compute the triples once for all the other procedures to use:

```
(define (ttt position me)
  (ttt-choose (find-triples position) me))

(define (ttt-choose triples me)                 ;; first version
  (cond ((i-can-win? triples me)
         (choose-winning-move triples me))
        ((opponent-can-win? triples me)
         (block-opponent-win triples me))
        ...))
```

Can the Computer Win on This Move?

The obvious next step is to write i-can-win?, a procedure that should return #t if the computer can win on the current move—that is, if the computer already has two squares of a triple whose third square is empty. The triples x6x and oo7 are examples.

So we need a function that takes a word and a letter as arguments and counts how many times that letter appears in the word. The appearances primitive that we used in Chapter 2 (and that you re-implemented in Exercise 9.10) will do the job:

```
> (appearances 'o 'oo7)
2

> (appearances 'x 'oo7)
0
```

The computer "owns" a triple if the computer's letter appears twice and the opponent's letter doesn't appear at all. (The second condition is necessary to exclude cases like xxo.)

```
(define (my-pair? triple me)
  (and (= (appearances me triple) 2)
       (= (appearances (opponent me) triple) 0)))
```

Notice that we need a function opponent that returns the opposite letter from ours.

```
(define (opponent letter)
  (if (equal? letter 'x) 'o 'x))

> (opponent 'x)
O

> (opponent 'o)
X

> (my-pair? 'oo7 'o)
#T

> (my-pair? 'xo7 'o)
#F

> (my-pair? 'oox 'o)
#F
```

Finally, the computer can win if it owns any of the triples:

```
(define (i-can-win? triples me)                ;; first version
  (not (empty?
        (keep (lambda (triple) (my-pair? triple me))
              triples)))) 

> (i-can-win? '("1xo" "4x6" o89 "14o" xx8 o69 "1x9" oxo) 'x)
#T

> (i-can-win? '("1xo" "4x6" o89 "14o" xx8 o69 "1x9" oxo) 'o)
#F
```

By now you're accustomed to this trick with lambda. My-pair? takes a triple and the computer's letter as arguments, but we want a function of one argument for use with keep.

If So, in Which Square?

Suppose `i-can-win?` returns `#t`. We then have to find the particular square that will win the game for us. This will involve a repetition of some of the same work we've already done:

```
(define (choose-winning-move triples me)      ;; not really part of game
  (keep number? (first (keep (lambda (triple) (my-pair? triple me))
                             triples))))
```

We again use `keep` to find the triples with two of the computer's letter, but this time we extract the number from the first such winning triple.

We'd like to avoid this inefficiency. As it turns out, generations of Lisp programmers have been in just this bind in the past, and so they've invented a kludge* to get around it.

Remember we told you that everything other than `#f` counts as true? We'll take advantage of that by having a single procedure that returns the number of a winning square if one is available, or `#f` otherwise. In Chapter 6 we called such a procedure a "semipredicate." The kludgy part is that `cond` accepts a clause containing a single expression instead of the usual two expressions; if the expression has any true value, then `cond` returns that value. So we can say

```
(define (ttt-choose triples me)               ;; second version
  (cond ((i-can-win? triples me))
        ((opponent-can-win? triples me))
        ...))
```

where each `cond` clause invokes a semipredicate. We then modify `i-can-win?` to have the desired behavior:

```
(define (i-can-win? triples me)
  (choose-win
   (keep (lambda (triple) (my-pair? triple me))
         triples)))
```

---

* A kludge is a programming trick that doesn't follow the rules but works anyway somehow. It doesn't rhyme with "sludge"; it's more like "clue" followed by "j" as in "Jim."

```
(define (choose-win winning-triples)
  (if (empty? winning-triples)
      #f
      (keep number? (first winning-triples))))
```

```
> (i-can-win? '("1xo" "4x6" o89 "14o" xx8 o69 "1x9" oxo) 'x)
8
```

```
> (i-can-win? '("1xo" "4x6" o89 "14o" xx8 o69 "1x9" oxo) 'o)
#F
```

By this point, we're starting to see the structure of the overall program. There will be several procedures, similar to i-can-win?, that will try to choose the next move. I-can-win? checks to see if the computer can win on this turn, another procedure will check to see if the computer should block the opponent's win next turn, and other procedures will check for other possibilities. Each of these procedures will be what we've been calling "semipredicates." That is to say, each will return the number of the square where the computer should move next, or #f if it can't decide. All that's left is to figure out the rest of the computer's strategy and write more procedures like i-can-win?.

Second Verse, Same as the First

Now it's time to deal with the second possible strategy case: The computer can't win on this move, but the opponent can win unless we block a triple right now.

(What if the computer and the opponent both have immediate winning triples? In that case, we've already noticed the computer's win, and by winning the game we avoid having to think about blocking the opponent.)

Once again, we have to go through the complicated business of finding triples that have two of the opponent's letter and none of the computer's letter—but it's already done!

```
(define (opponent-can-win? triples me)
  (i-can-win? triples (opponent me)))
```

```
> (opponent-can-win? '("1xo" "4x6" o89 "14o" xx8 o69 "1x9" oxo) 'x)
#F
```

```
> (opponent-can-win? '("1xo" "4x6" o89 "14o" xx8 o69 "1x9" oxo) 'o)
8
```

Is that amazing or what?

Now the Strategy Gets Complicated

Since our goal here is to teach programming, rather than tic-tac-toe strategy, we're just going to explain the strategy we use and not give the history of how we developed it.

The third step, after we check to see if either player can win on the next move, is to look for a situation in which a move that we make now will give rise to *two* winning triples next time. Here's an example:

```
x │ o │
──┼──┼──
  │ x │
──┼──┼──
  │   │ o
```

Neither x nor o can win on this move. But if the computer is playing x, moving in square 4 or square 7 will produce a situation with two winning triples. For example, here's what happens if we move in square 7:

```
x │ o │
──┼──┼──
  │ x │
──┼──┼──
x │   │ o
```

From this position, x can win by moving either in square 3 or in square 4. It's o's turn, but o can block only one of these two possibilities. By contrast, if (in the earlier position) x moves in square 3 or square 6, that would create a single winning triple for next time, but o could block it.

In other words, we want to find *two* triples in which one square is taken by the computer and the other two are free, with one free square shared between the two triples. (In this example, we might find the two triples x47 and 3x7; that would lead us to move in square 7, the one that these triples have in common.) We'll call a situation like this a "fork," and we'll call the common square the "pivot." This isn't standard terminology; we just made up these terms to make it easier to talk about the strategy.

In order to write the strategy procedure `i-can-fork?` we assume that we'll need a procedure `pivots` that returns a sentence of all pivots of forks currently available to the computer. In this board, 4 and 7 are the pivots, so the `pivots` procedure would return the sentence (4 7). If we assume `pivots`, then writing `i-can-fork?` is straightforward:

```
(define (i-can-fork? triples me)
  (first-if-any (pivots triples me)))
```

```
(define (first-if-any sent)
  (if (empty? sent)
      #f
      (first sent)))
```

Finding the Pivots

`Pivots` should return a sentence containing the pivot numbers. Here's the plan. We'll start with the triples:

```
(xo3 4x6 78o x47 ox8 36o xxo 3x7)
```

We `keep` the ones that have an `x` and two numbers:

```
(4x6 x47 3x7)
```

We mash these into one huge word:

```
4x6x473x7
```

We sort the digits from this word into nine "buckets," one for each digit:

```
("" "" 3 44 "" 6 77 "" "")
```

We see that there are no ones or twos, one three, two fours, and so on. Now we can easily see that four and seven are the pivot squares.

Let's write the procedures to carry out that plan. `Pivots` has to find all the triples with one computer-owned square and two free squares, and then it has to extract the square numbers that appear in more than one triple.

```
(define (pivots triples me)
  (repeated-numbers (keep (lambda (triple) (my-single? triple me))
                          triples)))

(define (my-single? triple me)
  (and (= (appearances me triple) 1)
       (= (appearances (opponent me) triple) 0)))

> (my-single? "4x6" 'x)
#T
```

```
> (my-single? 'xo3 'x)
#F

> (keep (lambda (triple) (my-single? triple 'x))
        (find-triples 'xo__x___o))
("4X6" X47 "3X7")
```

My-single? is just like my-pair? except that it looks for one appearance of the letter instead of two.

Repeated-numbers takes a sentence of triples as its argument and has to return a sentence of all the numbers that appear in more than one triple.

```
(define (repeated-numbers sent)
  (every first
         (keep (lambda (wd) (>= (count wd) 2))
               (sort-digits (accumulate word sent))))))
```

We're going to read this procedure inside-out, starting with the accumulate and working outward.

Why is it okay to accumulate word the sentence? Suppose that a number appears in two triples. All we need to know is that number, not the particular triples through which we found it. Therefore, instead of writing a program to look through several triples separately, we can just as well combine the triples into one long word, keep only the digits of that word, and simply look for the ones that appear more than once.

```
> (accumulate word '("4x6" x47 "3x7"))
"4X6X473X7"
```

We now have one long word, and we're looking for repeated digits. Since this is a hard problem, let's start with the subproblem of finding all the copies of a particular digit.

```
(define (extract-digit desired-digit wd)
  (keep (lambda (wd-digit) (equal? wd-digit desired-digit)) wd))

> (extract-digit 7 "4x6x473x7")
77

> (extract-digit 2 "4x6x473x7")
""
```

Now we want a sentence where the first word is all the 1s, the second word is all the 2s, etc. We could do it like this:

```
(se (extract-digit 1 "4x6x473x7")
    (extract-digit 2 "4x6x473x7")
    (extract-digit 3 "4x6x473x7")
    ...)
```

but that wouldn't be taking advantage of the power of computers to do that sort of repetitious work for us. Instead, we'll use **every**:

```
(define (sort-digits number-word)
  (every (lambda (digit) (extract-digit digit number-word))
         '(1 2 3 4 5 6 7 8 9)))
```

Sort-digits takes a word full of numbers and returns a sentence whose first word is all the ones, second word is all the twos, etc.*

```
> (sort-digits 123456789147258369159357)
(111 22 333 44 5555 66 777 88 999)

> (sort-digits "4x6x473x7")
("" "" 3 44 "" 6 77 "" "")
```

Let's look at **repeated-numbers** again:

```
(define (repeated-numbers sent)
  (every first
         (keep (lambda (wd) (>= (count wd) 2))
               (sort-digits (accumulate word sent)))))

> (repeated-numbers '("4x6" x47 "3x7"))
(4 7)

> (keep (lambda (wd) (>= (count wd) 2))
        '("" "" 3 44 "" 6 77 "" ""))
(44 77)

> (every first '(44 77))
(4 7)
```

---

* Brian thinks this is a kludge, but Matt thinks it's brilliant and elegant.

This concludes the explanation of `pivots`. Remember that `i-can-fork?` chooses the first pivot, if any, as the computer's move.

Taking the Offensive

Here's the final version of `ttt-choose` with all the clauses shown:

```
(define (ttt-choose triples me)
  (cond ((i-can-win? triples me))
        ((opponent-can-win? triples me))
        ((i-can-fork? triples me))
        ((i-can-advance? triples me))
        (else (best-free-square triples))))
```

You already know about the first three possibilities.

Just as the second possibility was the "mirror image" of the first (blocking an opponent's move of the same sort the computer just attempted), it would make sense for the fourth possibility to be blocking the creation of a fork by the opponent. That would be easy to do:

```
(define (opponent-can-fork? triples me)       ;; not really part of game
  (i-can-fork? triples (opponent me)))
```

Unfortunately, although the programming works, the strategy doesn't. Maybe the opponent has *two* potential forks; we can block only one of them. (Why isn't that a concern when blocking the opponent's wins? It *is* a concern, but if we've allowed the situation to reach the point where there are two ways the opponent can win on the next move, it's too late to do anything about it.)

Instead, our strategy is to go on the offensive. If we can get two in a row on this move, then our opponent will be forced to block on the next move, instead of making a fork. However, we want to make sure that we don't accidentally force the opponent *into* making a fork.

Let's look at this board position again, but from o's point of view:

```
x | o |
--+---+--
  | x |
--+---+--
  |   | o
```

X's pivots are 4 and 7, as we discussed earlier; o couldn't take both those squares. Instead, look at the triples 369 and 789, both of which are singles that belong to o. So o should move in one of the squares 3, 6, 7, or 8, forcing x to block instead of setting up the fork. But o *shouldn't* move in square 8, like this:

```
x | o |
-----------
  | x |
-----------
  | o | o
```

because that would force x to block in square 7, setting up a fork!

```
x | o |
-----------
  | x |
-----------
x | o | o
```

The structure of the algorithm is much like that of the other strategy possibilities. We use keep to find the appropriate triples, take the first such triple if any, and then decide which of the two empty squares in that triple to move into.

```
(define (i-can-advance? triples me)
  (best-move (keep (lambda (triple) (my-single? triple me)) triples)
             triples
             me))

(define (best-move my-triples all-triples me)
  (if (empty? my-triples)
      #f
      (best-square (first my-triples) all-triples me)))
```

Best-move does the same job as first-if-any, which we saw earlier, except that it also invokes best-square on the first triple if there is one.

Since we've already chosen the relevant triples before we get to best-move, you may be wondering why it needs *all* the triples as an additional argument. The answer is that best-square is going to look at the board position from the opponent's point of view to look for forks.

```
(define (best-square my-triple triples me)
  (best-square-helper (pivots triples (opponent me))
                      (keep number? my-triple)))
```

```
(define (best-square-helper opponent-pivots pair)
  (if (member? (first pair) opponent-pivots)
      (first pair)
      (last pair)))
```

· We **keep** the two numbers of the triple that we've already selected. We also select the opponent's possible pivots from among all the triples. If one of our two possible moves is a potential pivot for the opponent, that's the one we should move into, to block the fork. Otherwise, we arbitrarily pick the second (**last**) free square.

```
> (best-square "78o" (find-triples 'xo__x___o) 'o)
7

> (best-square "36o" (find-triples 'xo__x___o) 'o)
6

> (best-move '("78o" "36o") (find-triples 'xo__x___o) 'o)
7

> (i-can-advance? (find-triples 'xo__x___o) 'o)
7
```

What if *both* of the candidate squares are pivots for the opponent? In that case, we've picked a bad triple; moving in either square will make us lose. As it turns out, this can occur only in a situation like the following:

If we chose the triple 3o7, then either move will force the opponent to set up a fork, so that we lose two moves later. Luckily, though, we can instead choose a triple like 2o8. We can move in either of those squares and the game will end up a tie.

In principle, we should analyze a candidate triple to see if both free squares create forks for the opponent. But since we happen to know that this situation arises only on the diagonals, we can be lazier. We just list the diagonals *last* in the procedure **find-triples**. Since we take the first available triple, this ensures that we won't take a diagonal if there are any other choices.*

---

* Matt thinks this is a kludge, but Brian thinks it's brilliant and elegant.

Leftovers

If all else fails, we just pick a square. However, some squares are better than others. The center square is part of four triples, the corner squares are each part of three, and the edge squares each a mere two.

So we pick the center if it's free, then a corner, then an edge.

```
(define (best-free-square triples)
  (first-choice (accumulate word triples)
                '(5 1 3 7 9 2 4 6 8)))

(define (first-choice possibilities preferences)
  (first (keep (lambda (square) (member? square possibilities))
               preferences)))

> (first-choice 123456789147258369159357 '(5 1 3 7 9 2 4 6 8))
5

> (first-choice "1xo4x6o8914oxx8o691x9oxo" '(5 1 3 7 9 2 4 6 8))
1

> (best-free-square (find-triples '_____))
5

> (best-free-square (find-triples '____x____))
1
```

Complete Program Listing

```
;;; ttt.scm
;;; Tic-Tac-Toe program

(define (ttt position me)
  (ttt-choose (find-triples position) me))

(define (find-triples position)
  (every (lambda (comb) (substitute-triple comb position))
         '(123 456 789 147 258 369 159 357)))

(define (substitute-triple combination position)
  (accumulate word
              (every (lambda (square)
                       (substitute-letter square position))
                     combination) ))
```

```
(define (substitute-letter square position)
  (if (equal? '_ (item square position))
      square
      (item square position) ))

(define (ttt-choose triples me)
  (cond ((i-can-win? triples me))
        ((opponent-can-win? triples me))
        ((i-can-fork? triples me))
        ((i-can-advance? triples me))
        (else (best-free-square triples)) ))

(define (i-can-win? triples me)
  (choose-win
    (keep (lambda (triple) (my-pair? triple me))
        triples)))

(define (my-pair? triple me)
  (and (= (appearances me triple) 2)
       (= (appearances (opponent me) triple) 0)))

(define (opponent letter)
  (if (equal? letter 'x) 'o 'x))

(define (choose-win winning-triples)
  (if (empty? winning-triples)
      #f
      (keep number? (first winning-triples)) ))

(define (opponent-can-win? triples me)
  (i-can-win? triples (opponent me)) )

(define (i-can-fork? triples me)
  (first-if-any (pivots triples me)) )

(define (first-if-any sent)
  (if (empty? sent)
      #f
      (first sent) ))

(define (pivots triples me)
  (repeated-numbers (keep (lambda (triple) (my-single? triple me))
                        triples)))
```

```
(define (my-single? triple me)
  (and (= (appearances me triple) 1)
       (= (appearances (opponent me) triple) 0)))

(define (repeated-numbers sent)
  (every first
         (keep (lambda (wd) (>= (count wd) 2))
               (sort-digits (accumulate word sent)) )))

(define (sort-digits number-word)
  (every (lambda (digit) (extract-digit digit number-word))
         '(1 2 3 4 5 6 7 8 9) ))

(define (extract-digit desired-digit wd)
  (keep (lambda (wd-digit) (equal? wd-digit desired-digit)) wd))

(define (i-can-advance? triples me)
  (best-move (keep (lambda (triple) (my-single? triple me)) triples)
             triples
             me))

(define (best-move my-triples all-triples me)
  (if (empty? my-triples)
      #f
      (best-square (first my-triples) all-triples me) ))

(define (best-square my-triple triples me)
  (best-square-helper (pivots triples (opponent me))
                      (keep number? my-triple)))

(define (best-square-helper opponent-pivots pair)
  (if (member? (first pair) opponent-pivots)
      (first pair)
      (last pair)))

(define (best-free-square triples)
  (first-choice (accumulate word triples)
                '(5 1 3 7 9 2 4 6 8)))

(define (first-choice possibilities preferences)
  (first (keep (lambda (square) (member? square possibilities))
               preferences)))
```

Exercises

10.1 The `ttt` procedure assumes that nobody has won the game yet. What happens if you invoke `ttt` with a board position in which some player has already won? Try to figure it out by looking through the program before you run it.

A complete tic-tac-toe program would need to stop when one of the two players wins. Write a predicate `already-won?` that takes a board position and a letter (`x` or `o`) as its arguments and returns `#t` if that player has already won.

10.2 The program also doesn't notice when the game has ended in a tie, that is, when all nine squares are already filled. What happens now if you ask it to move in this situation?

Write a procedure `tie-game?` that returns `#t` in this case.

10.3 A real human playing tic-tac-toe would look at a board like this:

```
 o | x | o
---+---+---
 o | x | x
---+---+---
 x | o |
```

and notice that it's a tie, rather than moving in square 9. Modify `tie-game?` from Exercise 10.2 to notice this situation and return `#t`.

(Can you improve the program's ability to recognize ties even further? What about boards with two free squares?)

10.4 Here are some possible changes to the rules of tic-tac-toe:

- What if you could win a game by having three squares forming an L shape in a corner, such as squares 1, 2, and 4?

- What if the diagonals didn't win?

- What if you could win by having *four* squares in a corner, such as 1, 2, 4, and 5?

Answer the following questions for each of these modifications separately: What would happen if we tried to implement the change merely by changing the quoted sentence of potential winning combinations in `find-triples`? Would the program successfully follow the rules as modified?

10.5 Modify `ttt` to play chess.

Part IV
Recursion

By now you're very familiar with the idea of implementing a function by composing other functions. In effect we are breaking down a large problem into smaller parts. The idea of recursion—as usual, it sounds simpler than it actually is—is that one of the smaller parts can be the *same* function we are trying to implement.

At clothes stores they have arrangements with three mirrors hinged together. If you keep the side mirrors pointing outward, and you're standing in the right position, what you see is just three separate images of yourself, one face-on and two with profile views. But if you turn the mirrors in toward each other, all of a sudden you see what looks like infinitely many images of yourself. That's because each mirror reflects a scene that includes an image of the mirror itself. This *self-reference* gives rise to the multiple images.

Recursion is the idea of self-reference applied to computer programs. Here's an example:

> "I'm thinking of a number between 1 and 20."
>
> (Her number is between 1 and 20. I'll guess the halfway point.) "10."
>
> "Too low."
>
> (Hmm, her number is between 11 and 20. I'll guess the halfway point.) "15."
>
> "Too high."
>
> (That means her number is between 11 and 14. I'll guess the halfway point.) "12."
>
> "Got it!"

We can write a procedure to do this:

```
(define (game low high)
  (let ((guess (average low high)))
    (cond ((too-low? guess) (game (+ guess 1) high))
          ((too-high? guess) (game low (- guess 1)))
          (else '(I win!)))))
```

This isn't a complete program because we haven't written `too-low?` and `too-high?`. But it illustrates the idea of a problem that contains a version of itself as a subproblem: We're asked to find a secret number within a given range. We make a guess, and if it's not the answer, we use that guess to create another problem in which the same secret number is known to be within a smaller range. The self-reference of the problem description is expressed in Scheme by a procedure that invokes itself as a subprocedure.

Actually, this isn't the first time we've seen self-reference in this book. We defined "expression" in Chapter 3 self-referentially: An expression is either atomic or composed of smaller expressions.

The idea of self-reference also comes up in some paradoxes: Is the sentence "This sentence is false" true or false? (If it's true, then it must also be false, since it says so; if it's false, then it must also be true, since that's the opposite of what it says.) This idea also appears in the self-referential shapes called *fractals* that are used to produce realistic-looking waves, clouds, mountains, and coastlines in computer-generated graphics.

Print Gallery, by M. C. Escher (lithograph, 1956)

11 Introduction to Recursion

I know an old lady who swallowed a fly.
I don't know why she swallowed the fly.
Perhaps she'll die.

I know an old lady who swallowed a spider
that wriggled and jiggled and tickled inside her.
She swallowed the spider to catch the fly.
I don't know why she swallowed the fly.
Perhaps she'll die.

I know an old lady who swallowed a bird.
How absurd, to swallow a bird!
She swallowed the bird to catch the spider
that wriggled and jiggled and tickled inside her.
She swallowed the spider to catch the fly.
I don't know why she swallowed the fly.
Perhaps she'll die.

I know an old lady who swallowed a cat.
Imagine that, to swallow a cat.

She swallowed the cat to catch the bird.
She swallowed the bird to catch the spider
that wriggled and jiggled and tickled inside her.
She swallowed the spider to catch the fly.
I don't know why she swallowed the fly.
Perhaps she'll die.

I know an old lady who swallowed a dog.
What a hog, to swallow a dog!
She swallowed the dog to catch the cat.
She swallowed the cat to catch the bird.
She swallowed the bird to catch the spider
that wriggled and jiggled and tickled inside her.
She swallowed the spider to catch the fly.
I don't know why she swallowed the fly.
Perhaps she'll die.

I know an old lady who swallowed a horse.
She's dead of course!

100 bottles of beer on the wall,
100 bottles of beer.
If one of those bottles should happen to fall,
99 bottles of beer on the wall.

99 bottles of beer on the wall,
99 bottles of beer.
If one of those bottles should happen to fall,
98 bottles of beer on the wall.

98 bottles of beer on the wall,
98 bottles of beer.
If one of those bottles should happen to fall,
97 bottles of beer on the wall.

97 bottles of beer on the wall,
97 bottles of beer.
If one of those bottles should happen to fall,
96 bottles of beer on the wall. . .

In the next few chapters we're going to talk about *recursion:* solving a big problem by reducing it to a similar, smaller subproblem. Actually that's a little backward from the old lady in the song, who turned her little problem into a similar but *bigger* problem! As the song warns us, this can be fatal.

Here's the first problem we'll solve. We want a function that works like this:

```
> (downup 'ringo)
(RINGO RING RIN RI R RI RIN RING RINGO)

> (downup 'marsupial)
(MARSUPIAL
 MARSUPIA
 MARSUPI
 MARSUP
 MARSU
 MARS
 MAR
 MA
 M
 MA
 MAR
 MARS
 MARSU
 MARSUP
 MARSUPI
 MARSUPIA
 MARSUPIAL)
```

None of the tools that we've used so far will handle this problem. It's not a "compute this function for each letter of the word" problem, for which we could use **every.*** Rather, we have to think about the entire word in a rather complicated way.

We're going to solve this problem using recursion. It turns out that the idea of recursion is both very powerful—we can solve a *lot* of problems using it—and rather tricky to understand. That's why we're going to explain recursion several different ways in the coming chapters. Even after you understand one of them, you'll probably find that thinking about recursion from another point of view enriches your ability to use this idea. The explanation in this chapter is based on the *combining method.*

---

* If your instructor has asked you to read Part IV before Part III, ignore that sentence.

A Separate Procedure for Each Length

Since we don't yet know how to solve the `downup` problem in general, let's start with a particular case that we *can* solve. We'll write a version of `downup` that works only for one-letter words:

```
(define (downup1 wd)
  (se wd))

> (downup1 'a)
(A)
```

So far so good! This isn't a very versatile program, but it does have the advantage of being easy to write.

Now let's see if we can do two-letter words:

```
(define (downup2 wd)
  (se wd (first wd) wd))

> (downup2 'be)
(BE B BE)
```

Moving right along...

```
(define (downup3 wd)
  (se wd
      (bl wd)
      (first wd)
      (bl wd)
      wd))

> (downup3 'foo)
(FOO FO F FO FOO)
```

We could continue along these lines, writing procedures `downup4` and so on. If we knew that the longest word in English had 83 letters, we could write all of the single-length `downup`s up to `downup83`, and then write one overall `downup` procedure that would consist of an enormous `cond` with 83 clauses, one for each length.

Use What You Have to Get What You Need

But that's a terrible idea. We'd get really bored, and start making a lot of mistakes, if we tried to work up to `downup83` this way.

The next trick is to notice that the middle part of what (`downup3 'foo`) does is just like (`downup2 'fo`):

```
> (downup3 'foo)
(FOO  FO F FO  FOO)
         ↑
   (downup2 'fo)
```

So we can find the parts of `downup3` that are responsible for those three words:

```
(define (downup3 wd)
  (se wd
      (bl wd)
      (first wd)
      (bl wd)
      wd))
```

```
(FOO  FO F FO  FOO)
```

and replace them with an invocation of `downup2`:

```
(define (downup3 wd)
  (se wd (downup2 (bl wd)) wd))
```

How about `downup4`? Once we've had this great idea about using `downup2` to help with `downup3`, it's not hard to continue the pattern:

```
(define (downup4 wd)
  (se wd (downup3 (bl wd)) wd))
```

```
> (downup4 'paul)
(PAUL PAU PA P PA PAU PAUL)
```

The reason we can fit the body of `downup4` on one line is that most of its work is done for it by `downup3`. If we continued writing each new `downup` procedure independently, as we did in our first attempt at `downup3`, our procedures would be getting longer and longer. But this new way avoids that.

```
(define (downup59 wd)
  (se wd (downup58 (bl wd)) wd))
```

Also, although it may be harder to notice, we can even rewrite downup2 along the same lines:

```
(define (downup2 wd)
  (se wd (downup1 (bl wd)) wd))
```

Notice That They're All the Same

Although downup59 was easy to write, the problem is that it won't work unless we also define downup58, which in turn depends on downup57, and so on. This is a lot of repetitive, duplicated, and redundant typing. Since these procedures are all basically the same, what we'd like to do is combine them into a single procedure:

```
(define (downup wd)                              ;; first version
  (se wd (downup (bl wd)) wd))
```

Isn't this a great idea? We've written one short procedure that serves as a kind of abbreviation for 59 other ones.

Notice That They're Almost All the Same

Unfortunately, it doesn't work.

```
> (downup 'toe)
ERROR: Invalid argument to BUTLAST: ""
```

What's gone wrong here? Not quite every numbered downup looks like

```
(define (downupn wd)
  (se wd (downupn-1 (bl wd)) wd))
```

The only numbered downup that doesn't follow the pattern is downup1:

```
(define (downup1 wd)
  (se wd))
```

So if we collapse all the numbered downups into a single procedure, we have to treat one-letter words as a special case:

```
(define (downup wd)
  (if (= (count wd) 1)
      (se wd)
      (se wd (downup (bl wd)) wd)))

> (downup 'toe)
(TOE TO T TO TOE)

> (downup 'banana)
(BANANA BANAN BANA BAN BA B BA BAN BANA BANAN BANANA)
```

This version of downup will work for any length word, from a to pneumonoultra-microscopicsilicovolcanoconinosis* or beyond.

Base Cases and Recursive Calls

Downup illustrates the structure of every recursive procedure. There is a choice among expressions to evaluate: At least one is a *recursive* case, in which the procedure (e.g., downup) itself is invoked with a smaller argument; at least one is a *base* case, that is, one that can be solved without calling the procedure recursively. For downup, the base case is a single-letter argument.

How can this possibly work? We're defining downup in terms of downup. In English class, if the teacher asks you to define "around," you'd better not say, "You know, *around!*" But we appear to be doing just that. We're telling Scheme: "In order to find downup of a word, find downup of another word."

The secret is that it's not just any old other word. The new word is *smaller* than the word we were originally asked to downup. So we're saying, "In order to find downup of a word, find downup of a shorter word." We are posing a whole slew of *subproblems* asking for the downup of words smaller than the one we started with. So if someone asks us the downup of happy, along the way we have to compute the downups of happ, hap, ha, and h.

---

* It's a disease. Coal miners get it.

A recursive procedure doesn't work unless every possible argument can eventually be reduced to some base case. When we are asked for `downup` of h, the procedure just knows what to do without calling itself recursively.

We've just said that there has to be a base case. It's also important that each recursive call has to get us somehow closer to the base case. For `downup`, "closer" means that in the recursive call we use a shorter word. If we were computing a numeric function, the base case might be an argument of zero, and the recursive calls would use smaller numbers.

Pig Latin

Let's take another example; we'll write the Pig Latin procedure that we showed off in Chapter 1. We're trying to take a word, move all the initial consonants to the end, and add "ay."

The simplest case is that there are no initial consonants to move:

```
(define (pig10 wd)
  (word wd 'ay))

> (pig10 'alabaster)
ALABASTERAY
```

(This will turn out to be the base case of our eventual recursive procedure.)

The next-simplest case is a word that starts with one consonant. The obvious way to write this is

```
(define (pig11 wd)                        ;; obvious version
  (word (bf wd) (first wd) 'ay))

> (pig11 'salami)
ALAMISAY
```

but, as in the `downup` example, we'd like to find a way to use `pig10` in implementing `pig11`. This case isn't exactly like `downup`, because there isn't a piece of the return value that we can draw a box around to indicate that `pig10` returns that piece. Instead, `pig10` puts the letters `ay` at the end of some word, and so does `pig11`. The difference is that `pig11` puts `ay` at the end of a *rearrangement* of its argument word. To make this point clearer, we'll rewrite `pig11` in a way that separates the rearrangement from the `ay` addition:

```
(define (pig11 wd)
  (word (word (bf wd) (first wd))
        'ay))

> (pig11 'pastrami)
ASTRAMIPAY
```

Now we actually replace the pig10-like part with an invocation. We want to replace (word *something* 'ay) with (pig10 *something*). If we use pig10 to attach the ay at the end, our new version of pig11 looks like this:

```
(define (pig11 wd)
  (pig10 (word (bf wd) (first wd))))
```

How about a word starting with two consonants? By now we know that we're going to try to use pig11 as a helper procedure, so let's skip writing pig12 the long way. We can just move the first consonant to the end of the word, and handle the result, a word with only one consonant in front, with pig11:

```
(define (pig12 wd)
  (pig11 (word (bf wd) (first wd))))

> (pig12 'trample)
AMPLETRAY
```

For a three-initial-consonant word we move one letter to the end and call pig12:

```
(define (pig13 wd)
  (pig12 (word (bf wd) (first wd))))

> (pig13 'chrome)
OMECHRAY
```

So how about a version that will work for any word?* The recursive case will involve

---

* As it happens, there are no English words that start with more than four consonants. (There are only a few even with four; "phthalate" is one, and some others are people's names, such as "Schneider.") So we could solve the problem without recursion by writing the specific procedures up to pig14 and then writing a five-way cond to choose the appropriate specific case. But as you will see, it's easier to solve the more general case! A single recursive procedure, which can handle even nonexistent words with hundreds of initial consonants, is less effort than the conceptually simpler four-consonant version.

taking the `pigl` of `(word (bf wd) (first wd))`, to match the pattern we found in `pigl1`, `pigl2`, and `pigl3`. The base case will be a word that begins with a vowel, for which we'll just add `ay` on the end, as `pigl0` does:

```
(define (pigl wd)
  (if (member? (first wd) 'aeiou)
      (word wd 'ay)
      (pigl (word (bf wd) (first wd)))))
```

It's an unusual sense in which `pigl`'s recursive call poses a "smaller" subproblem. If we're asked for the `pigl` of `scheme`, we construct a new word, `chemes`, and ask for `pigl` of that. This doesn't seem like much progress. We were asked to translate `scheme`, a six-letter word, into Pig Latin, and in order to do this we need to translate `chemes`, another six-letter word, into Pig Latin.

But actually this *is* progress, because for Pig Latin the base case isn't a one-letter word, but rather a word that starts with a vowel. `Scheme` has three consonants before the first vowel; `chemes` has only two consonants before the first vowel.

`Chemes` doesn't begin with a vowel either, so we construct the word `hemesc` and try to `pigl` that. In order to find `(pigl 'hemesc)` we need to know `(pigl 'emesch)`. Since `emesch` *does* begin with a vowel, `pigl` returns `emeschay`. Once we know `(pigl 'emesch)`, we've thereby found the answer to our original question.

Problems for You to Try

You've now seen two examples of recursive procedures that we developed using the combining method. We started by writing special-case procedures to handle small problems of a particular size, then simplified the larger versions by using smaller versions as helper procedures. Finally we combined all the nearly identical individual versions into a single recursive procedure, taking care to handle the base case separately.

Here are a couple of problems that can be solved with recursive procedures. Try them yourself before reading further. Then we'll show you our solutions.

```
> (explode 'dynamite)
(D Y N A M I T E)

> (letter-pairs 'george)
(GE EO OR RG GE)
```

Our Solutions

What's the smallest word we can `explode`? There's no reason we can't explode an empty word:

```
(define (explode0 wd)
  '())
```

That wasn't very interesting, though. It doesn't suggest a pattern that will apply to larger words. Let's try a few larger cases:

```
(define (explode1 wd)
  (se wd))

(define (explode2 wd)
  (se (first wd) (last wd)))

(define (explode3 wd)
  (se (first wd) (first (bf wd)) (last wd)))
```

With `explode3` the procedure is starting to get complicated enough that we want to find a way to use `explode2` to help. What `explode3` does is to pull three separate letters out of its argument word, and collect the three letters in a sentence. Here's a sample:

```
> (explode3 'tnt)
(T N T)
```

`Explode2` pulls *two* letters out of a word and collects them in a sentence. So we could let `explode2` deal with two of the letters of our three-letter argument, and handle the remaining letter separately:

```
(define (explode3 wd)
  (se (first wd) (explode2 (bf wd))))
```

We can use similar reasoning to define `explode4` in terms of `explode3`:

```
(define (explode4 wd)
  (se (first wd) (explode3 (bf wd))))
```

Now that we see the pattern, what's the base case? Our first three numbered `explode`s are all different in shape from `explode3`, but now that we know what the pattern should be we'll find that we can write `explode2` in terms of `explode1`, and even `explode1` in terms of `explode0`:

```
(define (explode2 wd)
  (se (first wd) (explode1 (bf wd))))

(define (explode1 wd)
  (se (first wd) (explode0 (bf wd))))
```

We would never have thought to write `explode1` in that roundabout way, especially since `explode0` pays no attention to its argument, so computing the `butfirst` doesn't contribute anything to the result, but by following the pattern we can let the recursive case handle one-letter and two-letter words, so that only zero-letter words have to be special:

```
(define (explode wd)
  (if (empty? wd)
      '()
      (se (first wd) (explode (bf wd)))))
```

Now for `letter-pairs`. What's the smallest word we can use as its argument? Empty and one-letter words have no letter pairs in them:

```
(define (letter-pairs0 wd)
  '())

(define (letter-pairs1 wd)
  '())
```

This pattern is not very helpful.

```
(define (letter-pairs2 wd)
  (se wd))

(define (letter-pairs3 wd)
  (se (bl wd) (bf wd)))

(define (letter-pairs4 wd)
  (se (bl (bl wd))
      (bl (bf wd))
      (bf (bf wd))))
```

Again, we want to simplify `letter-pairs4` by using `letter-pairs3` to help. The problem is similar to `explode`: The value returned by `letter-pairs4` is a three-word sentence, and we can use `letter-pairs3` to generate two of those words.

```
> (letter-pairs4 'nems)
(NE  EM MS )
```

This gives rise to the following procedure:

```
(define (letter-pairs4 wd)
  (se (bl (bl wd))
      (letter-pairs3 (bf wd))))
```

Does this pattern work for defining `letter-pairs5` in terms of `letter-pairs4`?

```
(define (letter-pairs5 wd)                    ;; wrong
  (se (bl (bl wd))
      (letter-pairs4 (bf wd))))

> (letter-pairs5 'bagel)
(BAG AG GE EL)
```

The problem is that `(bl (bl wd))` means "the first two letters of `wd`" only when `wd` has four letters. In order to be able to generalize the pattern, we need a way to ask for the first two letters of a word that works no matter how long the word is. You wrote a procedure to solve this problem in Exercise 5.15:

```
(define (first-two wd)
  (word (first wd) (first (bf wd))))
```

Now we can use this for `letter-pairs4` and `letter-pairs5`:

```
(define (letter-pairs4 wd)
  (se (first-two wd) (letter-pairs3 (bf wd))))

(define (letter-pairs5 wd)
  (se (first-two wd) (letter-pairs4 (bf wd))))
```

This pattern *does* generalize.

```
(define (letter-pairs wd)
  (if (<= (count wd) 1)
      '()
      (se (first-two wd)
          (letter-pairs (bf wd))))))
```

Note that we treat two-letter and three-letter words as recursive cases and not as base cases. Just as in the example of `explode`, we noticed that we could rewrite `letter-pairs2` and `letter-pairs3` to follow the same pattern as the larger cases:

```
(define (letter-pairs2 wd)
  (se (first-two wd)
      (letter-pairs1 (bf wd))))

(define (letter-pairs3 wd)
  (se (first-two wd)
      (letter-pairs2 (bf wd))))
```

Pitfalls

⇒ Every recursive procedure must include two parts: one or more recursive cases, in which the recursion reduces the size of the problem, and one or more base cases, in which the result is computable without recursion. For example, our first attempt at `downup` fell into this pitfall because we had no base case.

⇒ Don't be too eager to write the recursive procedure. As we showed in the `letter-pairs` example, what looks like a generalizable pattern may not be.

Boring Exercises

11.1 Write `downup4` using only the word and sentence primitive procedures.

11.2 [8.12]* When you teach a class, people will get distracted if you say "um" too many times. Write a `count-ums` that counts the number of times "um" appears in a sentence:

---

* Exercise 8.12 in Part III asks you to solve this same problem using higher-order functions. Here we are asking you to use recursion. Whenever we pose the same problem in both parts, we'll cross-reference them in brackets as we did here. When you see the problem for the second time, you might want to consult your first solution for ideas.

```
> (count-ums
   '(today um we are going to um talk about the combining um method))
3
```

Here are some special-case `count-ums` procedures for sentences of particular lengths:

```
(define (count-ums0 sent)
  0)

(define (count-ums1 sent)
  (if (equal? 'um (first sent))
      1
      0))

(define (count-ums2 sent)
  (if (equal? 'um (first sent))
      (+ 1 (count-ums1 (bf sent)))
      (count-ums1 (bf sent))))

(define (count-ums3 sent)
  (if (equal? 'um (first sent))
      (+ 1 (count-ums2 (bf sent)))
      (count-ums2 (bf sent))))
```

Write `count-ums` recursively.

11.3 [8.13] Write a procedure `phone-unspell` that takes a spelled version of a phone number, such as `POPCORN`, and returns the real phone number, in this case `7672676`. You will need a helper procedure that translates a single letter into a digit:

```
(define (unspell-letter letter)
  (cond ((member? letter 'abc) 2)
        ((member? letter 'def) 3)
        ((member? letter 'ghi) 4)
        ((member? letter 'jkl) 5)
        ((member? letter 'mno) 6)
        ((member? letter 'prs) 7)
        ((member? letter 'tuv) 8)
        ((member? letter 'wxy) 9)
        (else 0)))
```

Here are some some special-case `phone-unspell` procedures:

```
(define (phone-unspell1 wd)
  (unspell-letter wd))

(define (phone-unspell2 wd)
  (word (unspell-letter (first wd))
        (unspell-letter (first (bf wd)))))

(define (phone-unspell3 wd)
  (word (unspell-letter (first wd))
        (unspell-letter (first (bf wd)))
        (unspell-letter (first (bf (bf wd))))))
```

Write phone-unspell recursively.

Real Exercises

Use recursion to solve these problems, not higher order functions (Chapter 8)!

11.4 Who first said "use what you have to get what you need"?

11.5 Write a procedure initials that takes a sentence as its argument and returns a sentence of the first letters in each of the sentence's words:

```
> (initials '(if i needed someone))
(I I N S)
```

11.6 Write a procedure countdown that works like this:

```
> (countdown 10)
(10 9 8 7 6 5 4 3 2 1 BLASTOFF!)

> (countdown 3)
(3 2 1 BLASTOFF!)
```

11.7 Write a procedure copies that takes a number and a word as arguments and returns a sentence containing that many copies of the given word:

```
> (copies 8 'spam)
(SPAM SPAM SPAM SPAM SPAM SPAM SPAM SPAM)
```

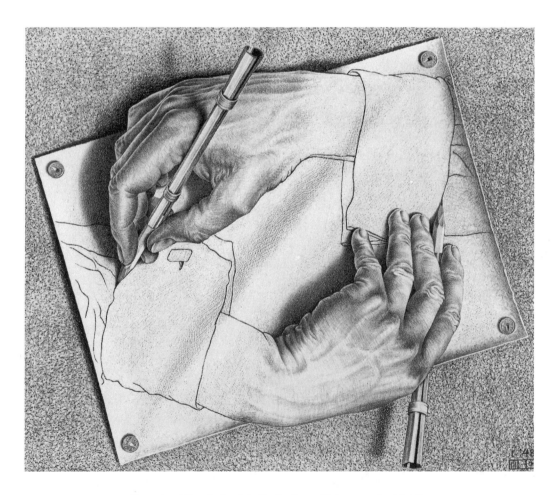

Drawing Hands, by M. C. Escher (lithograph, 1948)

12   The Leap of Faith

In the combining method, we build up to a recursive procedure by writing a number of special-case nonrecursive procedures, starting with small arguments and working toward larger ones. We find a generalizable way to use a smaller version in writing a larger one. As a result, all our procedures end up looking nearly the same, so we combine them into one procedure.

The combining method is a good way to begin thinking about recursion because each step of a solution is clearly justified by earlier steps. The sequence of events by which we get from a problem statement to a Scheme procedure is clear and straightforward. The disadvantage of the combining method, though, is that it involves a lot of drudgery, not all of which really helps toward the ultimate solution. In this chapter we're going to develop a new method called *the leap of faith* that overcomes this difficulty.

From the Combining Method to the Leap of Faith

Let's look again at the way we developed the `letter-pairs` procedure in the last chapter. We went through several steps:

- We wrote specific versions for zero-, one-, two-, and three-letter words.

- We wrote `letter-pairs4`, decided it was too complicated, and looked for a way to use `letter-pairs3` to help.

- Having rewritten `letter-pairs4`, we tried to write `letter-pairs5` using the same pattern. Since it didn't quite work, we revised the pattern.

- We generalized the pattern to write an unnumbered, recursive `letter-pairs`.

- We checked to make sure that the recursive pattern would work for two-letter and three-letter words.

- Since the pattern doesn't work for zero- or one-letter words, we made those the base cases.

Although we needed the lowest numbered procedures in order to make the entire collection of numbered procedures work, those low-numbered ones didn't contribute to the critical step of finding a generalizable pattern. Once you understand the idea of recursion, writing the individual procedures is wasted effort.

In the leap of faith method, we short-circuit this process in two ways. First, we don't bother thinking about small examples; we begin with, for example, a seven-letter word. Second, we don't use our example to write a particular numbered procedure; we write the recursive version directly.

Example: Reverse

We're going to write, using the leap of faith method, a recursive procedure to reverse the letters of a word:

```
> (reverse 'beatles)
SELTAEB
```

Is there a **reverse** of a smaller argument lurking within that return value? Yes, many of them. For example, LTA is the **reverse** of the word ATL. But it will be most helpful if we find a smaller subproblem that's only *slightly* smaller. (This idea corresponds to writing **letter-pairs7** using **letter-pairs6** in the combining method.) The closest smaller subproblem to our original problem is to find the **reverse** of a word one letter shorter than **beatles**.

```
> (reverse 'beatle)
ELTAEB
```

This result is pretty close to the answer we want for **reverse** of **beatles**. What's the relationship between ELTAEB, the answer to the smaller problem, and SELTAEB, the answer to the entire problem? There's one extra letter, S, at the beginning. Where did the extra letter come from? Obviously, it's the last letter of `beatles`.*

This may seem like a sequence of trivial observations leading nowhere. But as a result of this investigation, we can translate what we've learned directly into Scheme. In English: "the `reverse` of a word consists of its last letter followed by the `reverse` of its `butlast`." In Scheme:

```
(define (reverse wd)                    ;; unfinished
  (word (last wd)
        (reverse (bl wd))))
```

The Leap of Faith

If we think of this Scheme fragment merely as a statement of a true fact about `reverse`, it's not very remarkable. The amazing part is that this fragment is *runnable!*** It doesn't *look* runnable because it invokes itself as a helper procedure, and—if you haven't already been through the combining method—that looks as if it can't work. "How can you use `reverse` when you haven't written it yet?"

The leap of faith method is the assumption that the procedure we're in the middle of writing already works. That is, if we're thinking about writing a `reverse` procedure that can compute (`reverse 'paul`), we assume that (`reverse 'aul`) will work.

Of course it's not *really* a leap of faith, in the sense of something accepted as miraculous but not understood. The assumption is justified by our understanding of the combining method. For example, we understand that the four-letter `reverse` is relying on the three-letter version of the problem, not really on itself, so there's no circular reasoning involved. And we know that if we had to, we could write `reverse1` through `reverse3` "by hand."

The reason that our technique in this chapter may seem more mysterious than the combining method is that this time we are thinking about the problem top-down. In the combining method, we had already written `whatever3` before we even raised the question of `whatever4`. Now we start by thinking about the larger problem and assume

---

* There's also a relationship between (`reverse 'eatles`) and (`reverse 'beatles`), with the extra letter b at the end. We could take either of these subproblems as a starting point and end up with a working procedure.

** Well, almost. It needs a base case.

that we can rely on the smaller one. Again, we're entitled to that assumption because we've gone through the process from smaller to larger so many times already.

The leap of faith method, once you understand it, is faster than the combining method for writing new recursive procedures, because we can write the recursive solution immediately, without bothering with many individual cases. The reason we showed you the combining method first is that the leap of faith method seems too much like magic, or like "cheating," until you've seen several believable recursive programs. The combining method is the way to learn about recursion; the leap of faith method is the way to write recursive procedures once you've learned.

The Base Case

Of course, our definition of **reverse** isn't finished yet: As always, we need a base case. But base cases are the easy part. Base cases transform simple arguments into simple answers, and you can do that transformation in your head.

For example, what's the simplest argument to **reverse**? If you answered "a one-letter word" then pick a one-letter word and decide what the result should be:

```
> (reverse 'x)
X
```

reverse of a one-letter word should just be that same word:

```
(define (reverse wd)
  (if (= (count wd) 1)
      wd
      (word (last wd)
            (reverse (bl wd)))))
```

Example: `Factorial`

We'll use the leap of faith method to solve another problem that we haven't already solved with the combining method.

The factorial of a number n is defined as $1 \times 2 \times \cdots \times n$. So the factorial of 5 (written "5!") is $1 \times 2 \times 3 \times 4 \times 5$. Suppose you want Scheme to figure out the factorial of some large number, such as 843. You start from the definition: 843! is $1 \times 2 \times \cdots \times 842 \times 843$. Now you have to look for another factorial problem whose answer will help us find the answer to 843!. You might notice that 2!, that is, 1×2, is part of 843!, but that doesn't help very much because there's no simple relationship between 2! and 843!. A more fruitful observation would be that 842! is $1 \times \cdots \times 842$—that is, all but the last number in the product we're trying to compute. So $843! = 843 \times 842!$. In general, $n!$ is $n \times (n-1)!$. We can embody this idea in a Scheme procedure:

```
(define (factorial n)                          ;; first version
  (* n (factorial (- n 1))))
```

Asking for $(n-1)!$ is the leap of faith. We're expressing an answer we don't know, 843!, in terms of another answer we don't know, 842!. But since 842! is a smaller, similar subproblem, we are confident that the same algorithm will find it.*

Remember that in the **reverse** problem we mentioned that we could have chosen either the **butfirst** or the **butlast** of the argument as the smaller subproblem? In the case of the **factorial** problem we don't have a similar choice. If we tried to subdivide the problem as

$$6! = 1 \times (2 \times 3 \times 4 \times 5 \times 6)$$

then the part in parentheses would *not* be the factorial of a smaller number.**

---

* What makes us confident? We imagine that we've worked on this problem using the combining method, so that we've written procedures like these:

```
(define (factorial1 n)
  1)

(define (factorial2 n)
  (* 2 (factorial1 (- n 1))))

(define (factorial3 n)
  (* 3 (factorial2 (- n 1))))

;; ...

(define (factorial842 n)
  (* 842 (factorial841 (- n 1))))
```

and therefore we're entitled to use those lower-numbered versions in finding the factorial of 843. We haven't actually written them, but we could have, and that's what justifies using them. The reason we can take 842! on faith is that 842 is smaller than 843; it's the smaller values that we're pretending we've already written.

** As it happens, the part in parentheses does equal the factorial of a number, 6 itself. But expressing the solution for 6 in terms of the solution for 6 doesn't lead to a recursive procedure; we have to express this solution in terms of a *smaller* one.

As the base case for `factorial`, we'll use 1! = 1.

```
(define (factorial n)
  (if (= n 1)
      1
      (* n (factorial (- n 1))))))
```

Likely Guesses for Smaller Subproblems

To make the leap of faith method work, we have to find a smaller, similar subproblem whose solution will help solve the given problem. How do we find such a smaller subproblem?

In the examples so far, we've generally found it by finding a smaller, similar *return value* within the return value we're trying to achieve. Then we worked backward from the smaller solution to figure out what smaller argument would give us that value. For example, here's how we solved the `reverse` problem:

original argument	`beatles`
desired return value	`SELTAEB`
smaller return value	`ELTAEB`
corresponding argument	`beatle`
relationship of arguments	`beatle is (bl 'beatles)`
relationship of return values	`SELTAEB is (word 's 'ELTAEB)`
Scheme expression	`(word (last arg)`
	`        (reverse (bl arg)))`

Similarly, we looked at the definition of 843! and noticed within it the factorial of a smaller number, 842.

But a smaller return value won't necessarily leap out at us in every case. If not, there are some likely guesses we can try. For example, if the problem is about integers, it makes sense to try $n - 1$ as a smaller argument. If the problem is about words or sentences, try the `butfirst` or the `butlast`. (Often, as in the `reverse` example, either will be helpful.) Once you've guessed at a smaller argument, see what the corresponding return value should be, then compare that with the original desired return value as we've described earlier.

In fact, these two argument-guessing techniques would have suggested the same subproblems that we ended up using in our two examples so far. The reason we didn't teach these techniques from the beginning is that we don't want you to think they're essential parts of the leap of faith method. These are just good guesses; they don't always work. When they don't, you have to be prepared to think more flexibly.

Example: `Downup`

Here's how we might rewrite `downup` using the leap of faith method. Start by looking at the desired return value for a medium-sized example:

```
> (downup 'paul)
(PAUL PAU PA P PA PAU PAUL)
```

Since this is a procedure whose argument is a word, we guess that the `butfirst` or the `butlast` might be helpful.

```
> (downup 'aul)
(AUL AU A AU AUL)

> (downup 'pau)
(PAU PA P PA PAU)
```

This is a case in which it matters which we choose; the solution for the `butfirst` of the original argument doesn't help, but the solution for the `butlast` is most of the solution for the original word. All we have to do is add the original word itself at the beginning and end:

```
(define (downup wd)                    ;; no base case
  (se wd (downup (bl wd)) wd))
```

As before, this is missing the base case, but by now you know how to fill that in.

Example: `Evens`

Here's a case in which mindlessly guessing `butfirst` or `butlast` doesn't lead to a very good solution. We want a procedure that takes a sentence as its argument and returns a sentence of the even-numbered words of the original sentence:

```
> (evens '(i want to hold your hand))
(WANT HOLD HAND)
```

We look at **evens** of the `butfirst` and `butlast` of this sentence:

```
> (evens '(want to hold your hand))
(TO YOUR)

> (evens '(i want to hold your))
(WANT HOLD)
```

`Butfirst` is clearly not helpful; it gives all the wrong words. `Butlast` looks promising. The relationship between **evens** of the bigger sentence and **evens** of the smaller sentence is that the last word of the larger sentence is missing from **evens** of the smaller sentence.

```
(define (losing-evens sent)                    ;; no base case
  (se (losing-evens (bl sent))
      (last sent)))
```

For a base case, we'll take the empty sentence:

```
(define (losing-evens sent)
  (if (empty? sent)
      '()
      (se (losing-evens (bl sent))
          (last sent))))

> (losing-evens '(i want to hold your hand))
(I WANT TO HOLD YOUR HAND)
```

This isn't quite right.

It's true that **evens** of (i want to hold your hand) is the same as **evens** of (i want to hold your) plus the word hand at the end. But what about **evens** of (i want to hold your)? By the reasoning we've been using, we would expect that to be **evens** of (i want to hold) plus the word your. But since the word your is the fifth word of the argument sentence, it shouldn't be part of the result at all. Here's how **evens** should work:

```
> (evens '(i want to hold your))
(WANT HOLD)

> (evens '(i want to hold))
(WANT HOLD)
```

When the sentence has an odd number of words, its `evens` is the same as the `evens` of its `butlast`.* So here's our new procedure:

```
(define (evens sent)                         ;; better version
  (cond ((empty? sent) '())
        ((odd? (count sent))
         (evens (bl sent)))
        (else (se (evens (bl sent))
                  (last sent)))))
```

This version works, but it's more complicated than necessary. What makes it complicated is that on each recursive call we switch between two kinds of problems: even-length and odd-length sentences. If we dealt with the words two at a time, each recursive call would see the same kind of problem.

Once we've decided to go through the sentence two words at a time, we can reopen the question of whether to go right-to-left or left-to-right. It will turn out that the latter gives us the simplest procedure:

```
(define (evens sent)                         ;; best version
  (if (<= (count sent) 1)
      '()
      (se (first (bf sent))
          (evens (bf (bf sent))))))
```

Since we go through the sentence two words at a time, an odd-length argument sentence always gives rise to an odd-length recursive subproblem. Therefore, it's not good enough to check for an empty sentence as the only base case. We need to treat both the empty sentence and one-word sentences as base cases.

Simplifying Base Cases

The leap of faith is mostly about recursive cases, not base cases. In the examples in this chapter, we've picked base cases without talking about them much. How do you pick a base case?

---

* It may feel strange that in the case of an odd-length sentence, the answer to the recursive subproblem is the same as the answer to the original problem, rather than a smaller answer. But remember that it's the argument, not the return value, that has to get smaller in each recursive step.

In general, we recommend using the smallest possible base case argument, because that usually leads to the simplest procedures. For example, consider using the empty word, empty sentence, or zero instead of one-letter words, one-word sentences, or one.

How can you go about finding the simplest possible base case? Our first example in this chapter was `reverse`. We arbitrarily chose to use one-letter words as the base case:

```
(define (reverse wd)
  (if (= (count wd) 1)
      wd
      (word (last wd)
            (reverse (bl wd))))))
```

Suppose we want to consider whether a smaller base case would work. One approach is to pick an argument that would be handled by the current base case, and see what would happen if we tried to let the recursive step handle it instead. (To go along with this experiment, we pick a smaller base case, since the original base case should now be handled by the recursive step.) In this example, we pick a one-letter word, let's say m, and use that as the value of `wd` in the expression

```
(word (last wd)
      (reverse (bl wd)))
```

The result is

```
(word (last 'm)
      (reverse (bl 'm)))
```

which is the same as

```
(word 'm
      (reverse ""))
```

We want this to have as its value the word M. This will work out provided that (`reverse ""`) has the empty word as its value. So we could rewrite the procedure this way:

```
(define (reverse wd)
  (if (empty? wd)
      ""
      (word (last word)
            (reverse (bl word))))))
```

We were led to this empty-word base case by working downward from the needs of the one-letter case. However, it's also important to ensure that the return value used for the empty word is the correct value, not only to make the recursion work, but for an empty word in its own right. That is, we have to convince ourselves that (`reverse ""`) should return an empty word. But it should; the `reverse` of any word is a word containing the same letters the original word. If the original has no letters, the `reverse` must have no letters also. This exemplifies a general principle: Although we choose a base case argument for the sake of the recursive step, we must choose the corresponding return value for the sake of the argument itself, not just for the sake of the recursion.

We'll try the base case reduction technique on `downup`:

```
(define (downup wd)
  (if (= (count wd) 1)
      (se wd)
      (se wd (downup (bl wd)) wd)))
```

If we want to use the empty word as the base case, instead of one-letter words, then we have to ensure that the recursive case can return a correct answer for a one-letter word. The behavior we want is

```
> (downup 'a)
(A)
```

But if we substitute `'a` for `wd` in the recursive-case expression we get

```
(se 'a (downup "") 'a)
```

which will have two copies of the word `A` in its value no matter what value we give to `downup` of the empty word. We can't avoid treating one-letter words as a base case.

In writing `factorial`, we used 1 as the base case.

```
(define (factorial n)
  (if (= n 1)
      1
      (* n (factorial (- n 1)))))
```

Our principle of base case reduction suggests that we try for 0. To do this, we substitute 1 for `n` in the recursive case expression:

```
(* 1 (factorial 0))
```

We'd like this to have the value 1; this will be true only if we define 0! = 1. Now we can say

```
(define (factorial n)
  (if (= n 0)
      1
      (* n (factorial (- n 1)))))
```

In this case, the new procedure is no simpler than the previous version. Its only advantage is that it handles a case, 0!, that mathematicians find useful.

Here's another example in which we can't reduce the base case to an empty word. In Chapter 11 we used the combining method to write letter-pairs:

```
(define (letter-pairs wd)
  (if (<= (count wd) 1)
      '()
      (se (first-two wd)
          (letter-pairs (bf wd)))))

(define (first-two wd)
  (word (first wd) (first (bf wd))))
```

It might occur to you that one-letter words could be handled by the recursive case, and the base case could then handle only the empty word. But if you try to evaluate the expression for the recursive case as applied to a one-letter word, you find that

```
(first-two 'a)
```

is equivalent to

```
(word (first 'a) (first (bf 'a)))
```

which is an error. There is no second letter of a one-letter word. As soon as you see the expression (first (bf wd)) within this program, you know that one-letter words must be part of the base case. The same kind of reasoning can be used in many problems; the base case must handle anything that's too small to fit the needs of the recursive case.

Pitfalls

⇒ One possible pitfall is a recursive case that doesn't make progress, that is, one that doesn't reduce the size of the problem in the recursive call. For example, let's say we're trying to write the procedure **down** that works this way:

```
> (down 'town)
(TOWN TOW TO T)
```

Here's an incorrect attempt:

```
(define (down wd)                              ;; wrong!
  (if (empty? wd)
      '()
      (se wd (down (first wd))))))
```

The recursive call looks as if it reduces the size of the problem, but try it with an actual example. What's **first** of the word **splat**? What's **first** of that result? What's **first** of *that* result?

⇒ A pitfall that sounds unlikely in the abstract but is actually surprisingly common is to try to do the second step of the procedure "by hand" instead of trusting the recursion to do it. For example, here's another attempt at that **down** procedure:

```
(define (down wd)                              ;; incomplete
  (se wd ...))
```

You know the first word in the result has to be the argument word. Then what? The next thing is the same word with its last letter missing:

```
(define (down wd)                              ;; wrong!
  (se wd (bl wd) ...))
```

Instead of taking care of the entire rest of the problem with a recursive call, it's tempting to take only one more step, figuring out how to include the second word of the required solution. But that approach won't get you to a general recursive solution. Just take the first step and then trust the recursion for the rest:

```
(define (down wd)
  (if (empty? wd)
      '()
      (se wd (down (bl wd)))))
```

⇒ The value returned in the base case of your procedure must be in the range of the function you are representing. If your function is supposed to return a number, it must return a number all the time, even in the base case. You can use this idea to help you check the correctness of the base case expression.

For example, in downup, the base case returns (se wd) for the base case argument of a one-letter word. How did we think to enclose the word in a sentence? We know that in the recursive cases downup always returns a sentence, so that suggests to us that it must return a sentence in the base case also.

⇒ If your base case doesn't make sense in its own right, it probably means that you're trying to compensate for a mistake in the recursive case.

For example, suppose you've fallen into the pitfall of trying to handle the second word of a sentence by hand, and you've written the following procedure:

```
(define (square-sent sent)                      ;; wrong
  (if (empty? sent)
      '()
      (se (square (first sent))
          (square (first (bf sent)))
          (square-sent (bf sent)))))

> (square-sent '(2 3))
ERROR: Invalid argument to FIRST:  ()
```

After some experimentation, you find that you can get this example to work by changing the base case:

```
(define (square-sent sent)                      ;; still wrong
  (if (= (count sent) 1)
      '()
      (se (square (first sent))
          (square (first (bf sent)))
          (square-sent (bf sent)))))

> (square-sent '(2 3))
(4 9)
```

The trouble is that the base case doesn't make sense on its own:

```
> (square-sent '(7))
()
```

In fact, this procedure doesn't work for any sentences of length other than two. The moral is that it doesn't work to correct an error in the recursive case by introducing an absurd base case.

Boring Exercises

12.1 Here is a definition of a procedure that returns the sum of the numbers in its argument sentence:

```
(define (addup nums)
  (if (empty? (bf nums))
      (first nums)
      (+ (first nums) (addup (bf nums)))))
```

Although this works, it could be simplified by changing the base case. Do that.

12.2 Fix the bug in the following definition:

```
(define (acronym sent)                          ;; wrong
  (if (= (count sent) 1)
      (first sent)
      (word (first (first sent))
            (acronym (bf sent)))))
```

12.3 Can we reduce the `factorial` base case argument from 0 to `-1`? If so, show the resulting procedure. If not, why not?

12.4 Here's the definition of a function f:

$$f(sent) = \begin{cases} sent, & \text{if } sent \text{ is empty;} \\ \texttt{sentence}(f(\texttt{butfirst}(sent)), \texttt{first}(sent)), & \text{otherwise.} \end{cases}$$

Implement f as a Scheme procedure. What does f do?

Real Exercises

Solve all of the following problems with recursive procedures. If you've read Part III, do not use any higher-order functions such as every, keep, *or* accumulate.

12.5 [8.8] Write an `exaggerate` procedure which exaggerates sentences:

```
> (exaggerate '(i ate 3 potstickers))
(I ATE 6 POTSTICKERS)

> (exaggerate '(the chow fun is good here))
(THE CHOW FUN IS GREAT HERE)
```

It should double all the numbers in the sentence, and it should replace "good" with "great," "bad" with "terrible," and anything else you can think of.

12.6 [8.11] Write a GPA procedure. It should take a sentence of grades as its argument and return the corresponding grade point average:

```
> (gpa '(A A+ B+ B))
3.67
```

Hint: write a helper procedure `base-grade` that takes a grade as argument and returns 0, 1, 2, 3, or 4, and another helper procedure `grade-modifier` that returns −.33, 0, or .33, depending on whether the grade has a minus, a plus, or neither.

12.7 Write a procedure `spell-number` that spells out the digits of a number:

```
> (spell-number 1971)
(ONE NINE SEVEN ONE)
```

Use this helper procedure:

```
(define (spell-digit digit)
  (item (+ 1 digit)
        '(zero one two three four five six seven eight nine)))
```

12.8 Write a procedure `numbers` that takes a sentence as its argument and returns another sentence containing only the numbers in the argument:

```
> (numbers '(76 trombones and 110 cornets))
(76 110)
```

12.9 Write a procedure `real-words` that takes a sentence as argument and returns all the "real" words of the sentence, using the same rule as the `real-word?` procedure from Chapter 1.

12.10 Write a procedure `remove` that takes a word and a sentence as arguments and returns the same sentence, but with all copies of the given word removed:

```
> (remove 'the '(the song love of the loved by the beatles))
(SONG LOVE OF LOVED BY BEATLES)
```

12.11 Write the procedure `count`, which returns the number of words in a sentence or the number of letters in a word.

12.12 Write a procedure `arabic` which converts Roman numerals into Arabic numerals:

```
> (arabic 'MCMLXXI)
1971

> (arabic 'MLXVI)
1066
```

You will probably find the `roman-value` procedure from Chapter 6 helpful. Don't forget that a letter can *reduce* the overall value if the letter that comes after it has a larger value, such as the `C` in `MCM`.

12.13 Write a new version of the `describe-time` procedure from Exercise 6.14. Instead of returning a decimal number, it should behave like this:

```
> (describe-time 22222)
(6 HOURS 10 MINUTES 22 SECONDS)

> (describe-time 4967189641)
(1 CENTURIES 57 YEARS 20 WEEKS 6 DAYS 8 HOURS 54 MINUTES 1 SECONDS)
```

Can you make the program smart about saying `1 CENTURY` instead of `1 CENTURIES`?

What's the base case?

13   How Recursion Works

The last two chapters were about how to write recursive procedures. This chapter is about how to *believe in* recursive procedures, and about understanding the process by which Scheme carries them out.

Little People and Recursion

The crowning achievement of the little-people model is explaining recursion. Remember that every time you call a procedure, a little person is hired to compute the result. If you want to know (+ 2 (+ 3 4)), there are two separate plus specialists involved.

When we used the combining method, it was probably clear that it's okay for downup3 to invoke downup2, and for downup2 to invoke downup1. But it probably felt like magic when we combined these numbered procedures into a single downup procedure that calls *itself*. You may have thought, "How can downup do all the different tasks at once without getting confused?" The little-people model answers this question by showing that tasks are done by procedure *invocations*, not by procedures. Each little person handles one task, even though several little people are carrying out the same procedure. The procedure is just a set of instructions; someone has to carry out the instructions.

So what happens when we want to know (downup 'smile)? We hire Donna, a downup specialist, and she substitutes smile for wd in the body of downup, leaving her with

```
(if (= (count 'smile) 1)
    (se 'smile)
    (se 'smile (downup (bl 'smile)) 'smile)))
```

We'll leave out the details about hiring the `if`, `=`, `count`, and `bl` specialists in this example, so Donna ends up with

```
(se 'smile (downup 'smil) 'smile)
```

In order to evaluate this, Donna needs to know (`downup 'smil`). She hires David, another `downup` specialist, and waits for his answer.

David's `wd` is `smil`. He substitutes `smil` for `wd` in the body of `downup`, and *he* gets

```
(if (= (count 'smil) 1)
    (se 'smil)
    (se 'smil (downup (bl 'smil)) 'smil)))
```

After some uninteresting work, David has

```
(se 'smil (downup 'smi) 'smil)
```

and he hires Dennis to compute (`downup 'smi`). There are now three little people, all in the middle of some `downup` computation, and each of them is working on a different word.

Dennis substitutes `smi` for `wd`, and ends up with

```
(se 'smi (downup 'sm) 'smi)
```

He hires Derek to compute (`downup 'sm`). Derek needs to compute

```
(se 'sm (downup 's) 'sm)
```

Derek hires Dexter to find `downup` of `s`. Now we have to think carefully about the substitution again. Dexter substitutes his actual argument, `s`, for his formal parameter `wd`, and ends up with

```
(if (= (count 's) 1)
    (se 's)
    (se 's (downup (bl 's)) 's)))
```

`Count` of `s` *is* 1. So Dexter hires Simi, a `sentence` specialist, who returns (`s`). Dexter returns the same answer to Derek.

Derek, you will recall, is trying to compute

```
(se 'sm (downup 's) 'sm)
```

and now he knows the value of (`downup 's`). So he hires Savita to compute

```
(se 'sm '(s) 'sm)
```

and the answer is (`sm s sm`). Derek returns this answer to Dennis. By the way, do you remember what question Derek was hired to answer? Dennis wanted to know (`downup 'sm`). The answer Derek gave him was (`sm s sm`), which *is* downup of sm. Pretty neat, huh?

Dennis hires Sigrid to compute

```
(se 'smi '(sm s sm) 'smi)
```

and returns (`smi sm s sm smi`) to David. His answer is the correct value of (`downup 'smi`). David returns

```
(smil smi sm s sm smi smil)
```

to Donna, who has been waiting all this time to evaluate

```
(se 'smile (downup 'smil) 'smile)
```

Her waiting microseconds are over. She hires a `sentence` specialist and returns

```
(smile smil smi sm s sm smi smil smile)
```

If you have a group of friends whose names all start with "D," you can try this out yourselves. The rules of the game are pretty simple. Remember that each one of you can have only one single value for wd. Also, only one of you is in charge of the game at any point. When you hire somebody, that new person is in charge of the game until he or she tells you the answer to his or her question. If some of you have names that don't start with "D," you can be specialists in `sentence` or `butlast` or something. Play hard, play fair, nobody hurt.

Tracing

The little-people model explains recursion very well, as long as you're willing to focus your attention on the job of one little person, taking the next little person's subtask as a "black box" that you assume is carried out correctly. Your willingness to make that assumption is a necessary step in becoming truly comfortable with recursive programming.

Still, some people are very accustomed to a *sequential* model of computing. In that model, there's only one computer, not a lot of little people, and that one computer has to carry out one step at a time. If you're one of those people, you may find it hard to take the subtasks on faith. You want to know exactly what happens when! There's nothing wrong with such healthy scientific skepticism about recursion.

If you're a sequential thinker, you can *trace* procedures to get detailed information about the sequence of events.* But if you're happy with the way we've been talking about recursion up to now, and if you find that this section doesn't contribute to your understanding of recursion, don't worry about it. Our experience shows that this way of thinking helps some people but not everybody.** Before we get to recursive procedures,

---

* Unfortunately, `trace` isn't part of the Scheme standard, so it doesn't behave the same way in every version of Scheme.

** Even if tracing doesn't help you with recursion, you'll find that it's a useful technique in debugging any procedure.

let's just trace some nonrecursive ones:

```
(define (double wd) (word wd wd))

> (trace double)
> (double 'frozen)
(double frozen)
frozenfrozen
FROZENFROZEN
```

The argument to `trace` specifies a procedure. When you invoke `trace`, that procedure becomes "traced"; this means that every time you invoke the procedure, Scheme will print out the name of the procedure and the actual arguments. When the procedure returns a value, Scheme will print that value.*

Tracing isn't very interesting if we're just invoking a traced procedure once. But look what happens when we trace a procedure that we're using more than once:

```
> (double (double (double 'yum)))
(double yum)
yumyum
(double yumyum)
yumyumyumyum
(double yumyumyumyum)
yumyumyumyumyumyumyumyum

YUMYUMYUMYUMYUMYUMYUMYUM
```

This time, there were three separate invocations of `double`, and we saw each one as it happened. First we `double`d `yum`, and the answer was `yumyum`. Then we `double`d `yumyum`, and so on. Finally, after we invoked `double` for the last time, its result was printed by the read-eval-print loop.

When you're finished investigating a procedure, you can turn off tracing by invoking `untrace` with the procedure as argument:

```
> (untrace double)
```

---

* In this example the return value was printed twice, because the procedure we traced was invoked directly at the Scheme prompt. Its return value would have been printed once anyway, just because that's what Scheme always does. It was printed another time because of the tracing. In this book we've printed the trace-specific output in smaller type and lower-case to help you understand which is what, but of course on the actual computer you're on your own.

Let's try tracing a recursive procedure:

```
(define (downup wd)
  (if (= (count wd) 1)
      (se wd)
      (se wd (downup (bl wd)) wd)))
```

```
> (trace downup)

> (downup 'trace)
(downup trace)
|  (downup trac)
|  |  (downup tra)
|  |  |  (downup tr)
|  |  |  |  (downup t)
|  |  |  |  (t)
|  |  |  (tr t tr)
|  |  (tra tr t tr tra)
|  (trac tra tr t tr tra trac)
(trace trac tra tr t tr tra trac trace)
(TRACE TRAC TRA TR T TR TRA TRAC TRACE)
```

When a procedure calls itself recursively, depending on the phase of the moon,* Scheme may indent the trace display to show the levels of procedure calling, and draw a line of vertical bars ("|") from a procedure's invocation to its return value below. This is so you can look at a procedure invocation and see what value it returned, or vice versa.

How does the trace help us understand what is going on in the recursion? First, by reading the trace results from top to bottom, you can see the actual sequence of events when the computer is carrying out your Scheme program. For example, you can see that we start trying to figure out (downup 'trace); the first thing printed is the line that says we're starting that computation. But, before we get a result from that, four more downup computations have to begin. The one that begins last finishes first, returning (t); then another one returns a value; the one that started first is the last to return.

You can also read the trace horizontally instead of vertically, focusing on the levels of indentation. If you do this, then instead of a sequence of independent events (such-and-

---

* That's computer science slang for "depending on a number of factors that I consider too complicated to bother explaining" or "depending on a number of factors that I don't understand myself." Some computer systems automatically print the phase of the moon on program listings as an aid for programmers with "POM-dependent" programs. What we meant in this case is that it depends both on your version of Scheme and on the exact form of your recursive procedure.

such starts, such-and-such returns a value) you see the *inclusion* of processes within other ones. The smallest `downup` invocation is entirely inside the next-smallest one, and so on. The initial invocation of `downup` includes all of the others.

Perhaps you're thinking that `downup`'s pattern of inclusion is the only one possible for recursive procedures. That is, perhaps you're thinking that every invocation includes exactly one smaller invocation, and *that* one includes a yet-smaller one, and so on. But actually the pattern can be more complicated. Here's an example. The *Fibonacci numbers* are a sequence of numbers in which the first two numbers are 1 and each number after that is the sum of the two before it:

$$1, 1, 2, 3, 5, 8, 13, 21, 34, 55, \ldots$$

(They're named after Leonardo Pisano. You'd think they'd be called "Pisano numbers," but Leonardo had a kind of alias, Leonardo Fibonacci, just to confuse people.) Here's a procedure to compute the nth Fibonacci number:

```
(define (fib n)
  (if (<= n 2)
      1
      (+ (fib (- n 1))
         (fib (- n 2))))))
```

Here's a trace of computing the fourth Fibonacci number:

```
> (fib 4)
(fib 4)
|   (fib 2)
|   1
|   (fib 3)
|   |   (fib 1)
|   |   1
|   |   (fib 2)
|   |   1
|   2
3
3
```

(By the way, this trace demonstrates that in the dialect of Scheme we used, the argument subexpressions of the + expression in `fib` are evaluated from right to left, because the smaller `fib` arguments come before the larger ones in the trace.)

As you can see, we still have invocations within other invocations, but the pattern is not as simple as in the `downup` case. If you're having trouble making sense of this pattern, go back to thinking about the problem in terms of little people; who hires whom?

Pitfalls

⇒ Whenever you catch yourself using the words "go back" or "goes back" in describing how some procedure works, bite your tongue. A recursive invocation isn't a going back; it's a separate process. The model behind "go back" is that the same little person starts over again at the beginning of the procedure body. What actually happens is that a new little person carries out the same procedure. It's an important difference because when the second little person finishes, the first may still have more work to do.

For example, when we used little people to show the working of `downup`, Dennis computes the result (`smi sm s sm smi`) and returns that value to David; at that point, David still has work to do before returning his own result to Donna.

⇒ The `trace` mechanism doesn't work for special forms. For example, you can't say

```
(trace or)
```

although you can, and often will, trace primitive procedures that aren't special forms.

Boring Exercises

13.1 Trace the `explode` procedure from page 183 and invoke

```
(explode 'ape)
```

How many recursive calls were there? What were the arguments to each recursive call? Turn in a transcript showing the `trace` listing.

13.2 How many `pigl`-specialist little people are involved in evaluating the following expression?

```
(pigl 'throughout)
```

What are their arguments and return values, and to whom does each give her result?

13.3 Here is our first version of `downup` from Chapter 11. It doesn't work because it has no base case.

```
(define (downup wd)
  (se wd (downup (bl wd)) wd))
```

```
> (downup 'toe)
ERROR: Invalid argument to BUTLAST: ""
```

Explain what goes wrong to generate that error. In particular, why does Scheme try to take the `butlast` of an empty word?

13.4 Here is a Scheme procedure that never finishes its job:

```
(define (forever n)
  (if (= n 0)
      1
      (+ 1 (forever n))))
```

Explain why it doesn't give any result. (If you try to trace it, make sure you know how to make your version of Scheme stop what it's doing and give you another prompt.)

Real Exercises

13.5 It may seem strange that there is one little person per *invocation* of a procedure, instead of just one little person per procedure. For certain problems, the person-per-procedure model would work fine.

Consider, for example, this invocation of `pigl`:

```
> (pigl 'prawn)
AWNPRAY
```

Suppose there were only one `pigl` specialist in the computer, named Patricia. Alonzo hires Patricia and gives her the argument `prawn`. She sees that it doesn't begin with a vowel, so she moves the first letter to the end, gets `rawnp`, and tries to `pigl` that. Again, it doesn't begin with a vowel, so she moves another letter to the end and gets `awnpr`. That *does* begin with a vowel, so she adds an `ay`, returning `awnpray` to Alonzo.

Nevertheless, this revised little-people model doesn't always work. Show how it fails to explain what happens in the evaluation of

```
(downup 'smile)
```

13.6 As part of computing (`factorial 6`), Scheme computes (`factorial 2`) and gets the answer 2. After Scheme gets that answer, how does it know what to do next?

14 Common Patterns in Recursive Procedures

There are two ideas about how to solve programming problems.* One idea is that programmers work mostly by recognizing categories of problems that come up repeatedly and remembering the solution that worked last time; therefore, programming students should learn a lot of program *patterns,* or *templates,* and fill in the blanks for each specific problem. Another idea is that there are a few powerful principles in programming, and that if a learner understands the principles, they can be applied to *any* problem, even one that doesn't fit a familiar pattern.

Research suggests that an expert programmer, like an expert at any skill, *does* work mainly by recognizing patterns. Nevertheless, we lean toward the powerful-principle idea. The expert's memory is not full of arbitrary patterns; it's full of *meaningful* patterns, because the expert has gone through the process of struggling to reason out how each procedure works and how to write new procedures.

Still, we think it's worth pointing out a few patterns that are so common that you'll have seen several examples of each before you finish this book. Once you learn these patterns, you can write similar procedures almost automatically. But there's an irony in learning patterns: In Scheme, once you've identified a pattern, you can write a general-purpose procedure that handles all such cases without writing individual procedures for each situation. Then you don't have to use the pattern any more! Chapter 8 presents several general pattern-handling procedures, called *higher-order* procedures. In this chapter we'll consider the patterns corresponding to those higher-order procedures, and we'll use the names of those procedures to name the patterns.

---

* That's because there are two kinds of people: those who think there are two kinds of people, and those who don't.

What's the point of learning patterns if you can use higher-order procedures instead? There are at least two points. The first, as you'll see very soon, is that some problems *almost* follow one of the patterns; in that case, you can't use the corresponding higher-order procedure, which works only for problems that *exactly* follow the pattern. But you can use your understanding of the pattern to help with these related problems. The second point is that in Chapter 19 we'll show how the higher-order functions are themselves implemented using these recursive patterns.

This chapter isn't an official list of all important patterns; as you gain programming experience, you'll certainly add more patterns to your repertoire.

The **Every** Pattern

Here's a procedure to square every number in a sentence of numbers:

```
(define (square-sent sent)
  (if (empty? sent)
      '()
      (se (square (first sent))
          (square-sent (bf sent)))))
```

Here's a procedure to translate every word of a sentence into Pig Latin:

```
(define (pigl-sent sent)
  (if (empty? sent)
      '()
      (se (pigl (first sent))
          (pigl-sent (bf sent)))))
```

The pattern here is pretty clear. Our recursive case will do something straightforward to the `first` of the sentence, such as `square`ing it or `pigl`ing it, and we'll combine that with the result of a recursive call on the `butfirst` of the sentence.

The `letter-pairs` procedure that we wrote in Chapter 11 is an example of a procedure that follows the **every** pattern pretty closely, but not exactly. The difference is that `letter-pairs` looks at its argument sentence two words at a time.

```
(define (letter-pairs wd)
  (if (= (count wd) 1)
      '()
      (se (word (first wd) (first (bf wd)))
          (letter-pairs (bf wd)))))
```

Compare this with the earlier definition of `square-sent`. The recursive case still uses `se` to combine one part of the result with a recursive call based on the `butfirst` of the argument, but here both the first letter and the second letter of the argument contribute to the first word of the result. That's why the base case also has to be different; the recursive case requires at least two letters, so the base case is a one-letter word.*

Let's solve a slightly different problem. This time, we want to break the word down into *non-overlapping* pairs of letters, like this:

```
> (disjoint-pairs 'tripoli)          ;; the new problem
(TR IP OL I)

> (letter-pairs 'tripoli)            ;; compare the old one
(TR RI IP PO OL LI)
```

The main difference between these two functions is that in `disjoint-pairs` we eliminate two letters at once in the recursive call. A second difference is that we have to deal with the special case of odd-length words.

```
(define (disjoint-pairs wd)
  (cond ((empty? wd) '())
        ((= (count wd) 1) (se wd))
        (else (se (word (first wd) (first (bf wd)))
                  (disjoint-pairs (bf (bf wd)))))))
```

The **Keep** Pattern

In the **every** pattern, we collect the results of transforming each element of a word or sentence into something else. This time we'll consider a different kind of problem: choosing some of the elements and forgetting about the others. First, here is a procedure to select the three-letter words from a sentence:

```
(define (keep-three-letter-words sent)
  (cond ((empty? sent) '())
        ((= (count (first sent)) 3)
         (se (first sent) (keep-three-letter-words (bf sent))))
        (else (keep-three-letter-words (bf sent)))))
```

---

* If you've read Chapter 8, you know that you could implement `square-sent` and `pigl-sent` without recursion, using the **every** higher order function. But try using **every** to implement `letter-pairs`; you'll find that you can't quite make it work.

```
> (keep-three-letter-words '(one two three four five six seven))
(ONE TWO SIX)
```

Next, here is a procedure to select the vowels from a word:

```
(define (keep-vowels wd)
  (cond ((empty? wd) "")
        ((vowel? (first wd))
         (word (first wd) (keep-vowels (bf wd))))
        (else (keep-vowels (bf wd)))))

> (keep-vowels 'napoleon)
AOEO
```

Let's look at the differences between the **every** pattern and the **keep** pattern. First of all, the **keep** procedures have three possible outcomes, instead of just two as in most **every**-like procedures. In the **every** pattern, we only have to distinguish between the base case and the recursive case. In the **keep** pattern, there is still a base case, but there are *two* recursive cases; we have to decide whether or not to keep the first available element in the return value. When we do keep an element, we keep the element itself, not some function of the element.

As with the **every** pattern, there are situations that follow the **keep** pattern only approximately. Suppose we want to look for doubled letters within a word:

```
> (doubles 'bookkeeper)
OOKKEE

> (doubles 'mississippi)
SSSSPP
```

This isn't a pure **keep** pattern example because we can't decide whether to keep the first letter by looking at that letter alone; we have to examine two at a time. But we can write a procedure using more or less the same pattern:

```
(define (doubles wd)
  (cond ((= (count wd) 1) "")
        ((equal? (first wd) (first (bf wd)))
         (word (first wd) (first (bf wd)) (doubles (bf (bf wd)))))
        (else (doubles (bf wd)))))
```

As in the **evens** example of Chapter 12, the base case of **doubles** is unusual, and one of the recursive calls chops off two letters at once in forming the smaller subproblem.

But the structure of the `cond` with a base case clause, a clause for keeping letters, and a clause for rejecting letters is maintained.

The `Accumulate` Pattern

Here are two recursive procedures for functions that combine all of the elements of the argument into a single result:

```
(define (addup nums)
  (if (empty? nums)
      0
      (+ (first nums) (addup (bf nums)))))

(define (scrunch-words sent)
  (if (empty? sent)
      ""
      (word (first sent) (scrunch-words (bf sent)))))

> (addup '(8 3 6 1 10))
28

> (scrunch-words '(ack now ledge able))
ACKNOWLEDGEABLE
```

What's the pattern? We're using some combiner (`+` or `word`) to connect the word we're up to with the result of the recursive call. The base case tests for an empty argument, but the base case return value must be the identity element of the combiner function.

If there is no identity element for the combiner, as in the case of `max`, we modify the pattern slightly:*

```
(define (sent-max sent)
  (if (= (count sent) 1)
      (first sent)
      (max (first sent)
           (sent-max (bf sent)))))
```

---

* Of course, if your version of Scheme has $-\infty$, you can use it as the return value for an empty sentence, instead of changing the pattern.

Combining Patterns

```
(define (add-numbers sent)
  (cond ((empty? sent) 0)
        ((number? (first sent))
         (+ (first sent) (add-numbers (bf sent))))
        (else (add-numbers (bf sent)))))

> (add-numbers '(if 6 were 9))
15
```

This procedure combines aspects of keep with aspects of accumulate. We want to do two things at once: get rid of the words that aren't numbers and compute the *sum* of those that are numbers. (A simple keep would construct a sentence of them.) Add-numbers looks exactly like the keep pattern, except that there's a funny combiner and a funny base case, which look more like accumulate.*

Here's an example that combines every and keep. We want a procedure that takes a sentence as its argument and translates every word of the sentence into Pig Latin, but leaves out words that have no vowels, because the Pig Latin translator doesn't work for such words. The procedure safe-pigl will be like a keep pattern in that it keeps only words that contain vowels, but like an every in that the result contains transformed versions of the selected words, rather than the words themselves.

```
(define (safe-pigl sent)
  (cond ((empty? sent) '())
        ((has-vowel? (first sent))
         (se (pigl (first sent)) (safe-pigl (bf sent))))
        (else (safe-pigl (bf sent)))))

(define (has-vowel? wd)
  (not (empty? (keep-vowels wd))))
```

---

* Here's the higher-order function version, from Chapter 8:

```
(define (add-numbers sent)
  (accumulate + (keep number? sent)))
```

The higher-order function version is more self-documenting and easier to write. The recursive version, however, is slightly more efficient, because it avoids building up a sentence as an intermediate value only to discard it in the final result. If we were writing this program for our own use, we'd probably choose the higher-order function version; but if we were dealing with sentences of length 10,000 instead of length 10, we'd pay more attention to efficiency.

```
> (safe-pigl '(my pet fly is named xyzzy))
(ETPAY ISAY AMEDNAY)
```

Finally, here's an example that combines all three patterns. In Chapter 1 we wrote (using higher-order procedures) the `acronym` procedure, which selects the "real" words of a sentence (the `keep` pattern), takes the first letter of each word (the `every` pattern), and combines these initial letters into a single word (the `accumulate` pattern). In a recursive procedure we can carry out all three steps at once:

```
(define (acronym sent)
  (cond ((empty? sent) "")
        ((real-word? (first sent))
         (word (first (first sent))
               (acronym (bf sent))))
        (else (acronym (bf sent)))))
```

Don't become obsessed with trying to make every recursive problem fit one of the three patterns we've shown here. As we said at the beginning of the chapter, what's most important is that you understand the principles of recursion in general, and understand how versatile recursion is. The patterns are just special cases that happen to come up fairly often.

Helper Procedures

Let's say we want a procedure `every-nth` that takes a number *n* and a sentence as arguments and selects every *n*th word from the sentence.

```
> (every-nth 3 '(with a little help from my friends))
(LITTLE MY)
```

We get in trouble if we try to write this in the obvious way, as a sort of `keep` pattern.

```
(define (every-nth n sent)                        ;; wrong!
  (cond ((empty? sent) '())
        ((= n 1)
         (se (first sent) (every-nth n (bf sent))))
        (else (every-nth (- n 1) (bf sent)))))
```

The problem is with the **n** that's in boldface. We're thinking that it's going to be the n of the *original* invocation of `every-nth`, that is, 3. But in fact, we've already counted n down so that in this invocation its value is 1. (Check out the first half of the same `cond` clause.) This procedure will correctly skip the first two words but will keep all the words after that point. That's because we're trying to remember two different numbers: the number we should always skip between kept words, and the number of words we still need to skip this time.

If we're trying to remember two numbers, we need two names for them. The way to achieve this is to have our official `every-nth` procedure call a helper procedure that takes an extra argument and does the real work:

```
(define (every-nth n sent)
  (every-nth-helper n n sent))

(define (every-nth-helper interval remaining sent)
  (cond ((empty? sent) '())
        ((= remaining 1)
         (se (first sent)
             (every-nth-helper interval interval (bf sent))))
        (else (every-nth-helper interval (- remaining 1) (bf sent)))))
```

This procedure always calls itself recursively with the same value of `interval`, but with a different value of `remaining` each time. `Remaining` keeps getting smaller by one in each recursive call until it equals 1. On that call, a word is kept for the return value, and we call `every-nth-helper` recursively with the value of `interval`, that is, the *original* value of n, as the new `remaining`. If you like, you can think of this combination of an *initialization* procedure and a *helper* procedure as another pattern for your collection.

How to Use Recursive Patterns

One way in which recursive patterns can be useful is if you think of them as templates with empty slots to fill in for a particular problem. Here are template versions of the `every`, `keep`, and `accumulate` patterns as applied to sentences:

```
(define (every-something sent)
  (if (empty? sent)
      '()
      (se (_____ (first sent))
          (every-something (bf sent)))))

(define (keep-if-something sent)
  (cond ((empty? sent) '())
        ((_____? (first sent))
         (se (first sent) (keep-if-something (bf sent))))
        (else (keep-if-something (bf sent)))))
```

```
(define (accumulate-somehow sent)
  (if (empty? sent)

      _____
      (_____ (first sent)
                   (accumulate-somehow (bf sent)))))
```

Suppose you're trying to write a procedure `first-number` that takes a sentence as its argument and returns the first number in that sentence, but returns the word `no-number` if there are no numbers in the argument. The first step is to make a guess about which pattern will be most useful. In this case the program should start with an entire sentence and select a portion of that sentence, namely one word. Therefore, we start with the `keep` pattern.

```
(define (first-number sent)                  ;; first guess
  (cond ((empty? sent) '())
        ((_____ (first sent))
         (se (first sent) (first-number (bf sent))))
        (else (first-number (bf sent)))))
```

The next step is to fill in the blank. Obviously, since we're looking for a number, `number?` goes in the blank.

The trouble is that this procedure returns *all* the numbers in the given sentence. Now our job is to see how the pattern must be modified to do what we want. The overall structure of the pattern is a `cond` with three clauses; we'll consider each clause separately.

What should the procedure return if `sent` is empty? In that case, there is no first number in the sentence, so it should return `no-number`:

```
((empty? sent) 'no-number)
```

What if the first word of the sentence is a number? The program should return just that number, ignoring the rest of the sentence:

```
((number? (first sent)) (first sent))
```

What if the first word of the sentence isn't a number? The procedure must make a recursive call for the `butfirst`, and whatever that recursive call returns is the answer. So the `else` clause does not have to be changed.

Here's the whole procedure:

```
(define (first-number sent)
  (cond ((empty? sent) 'no-number)
        ((number? (first sent)) (first sent))
        (else (first-number (bf sent)))))
```

After filling in the blank in the `keep` pattern, we solved this problem by focusing on the details of the procedure definition. We examined each piece of the definition to decide what changes were necessary. Instead, we could have focused on the *behavior* of the procedure. We would have found two ways in which the program didn't do what it was supposed to do: For an argument sentence containing numbers, it would return all of the numbers instead of just one of them. For a sentence without numbers, it would return the empty sentence instead of `no-number`. We would then have finished the job by *debugging* the procedure to fix each of these problems. The final result would have been the same.

Problems That Don't Follow Patterns

We want to write the procedure `sent-before?`, which takes two sentences as arguments and returns `#t` if the first comes alphabetically before the second. The general idea is to compare the sentences word by word. If the first words are different, then whichever is alphabetically earlier determines which sentence comes before the other. If the first words are equal, we go on to compare the second words.*

```
> (sent-before? '(hold me tight) '(sun king))
#T

> (sent-before? '(lovely rita) '(love you to))
#F

> (sent-before? '(strawberry fields forever)
                '(strawberry fields usually))
#T
```

Does this problem follow any of the patterns we've seen? It's not an `every`, because the result isn't a sentence in which each word is a transformed version of a word in the arguments. It's not a `keep`, because the result isn't a subset of the words in the arguments. And it's not exactly an `accumulate`. We do end up with a single true or false result, rather than a sentence full of results. But in a typical `accumulate` problem,

---

* Dictionaries use a different ordering rule, in which the sentences are treated as if they were single words, with the spaces removed. By the dictionary rule, "a c" is treated as if it were "ac" and comes after "ab"; by our rule, "a c" comes before "ab" because we compare the first words ("a" and "ab").

every word of the argument contributes to the solution. In this case only one word from each sentence determines the overall result.

On the other hand, this problem does have something in common with the keep pattern: We know that on each invocation there will be three possibilities. We might reach a base case (an empty sentence); if not, the first words of the argument sentences might or might not be relevant to the solution.

We'll have a structure similar to the usual keep pattern, except that there's no se involved; if we find unequal words, the problem is solved without further recursion. Also, we have two arguments, and either of them might be empty.

```
(define (sent-before? sent1 sent2)
  (cond ((empty? sent1) #t)
        ((empty? sent2) #f)
        ((before? (first sent1) (first sent2)) #t)
        ((before? (first sent2) (first sent1)) #f)
        (else (sent-before? (bf sent1) (bf sent2)))))
```

Although thinking about the keep pattern helped us to work out this solution, the result really doesn't look much like a keep. We had to invent most of the details by thinking about this particular problem, not by thinking about the pattern.

In the next chapter we'll look at examples of recursive procedures that are quite different from any of these patterns. Remember, the patterns are a shortcut for many common problems, but don't learn the shortcut at the expense of the general technique.

Pitfalls

Review the pitfalls from Chapter 12; they're still relevant.

⇒ How do you test for the base case? Most of the examples in this chapter have used empty?, and it's easy to fall into the habit of using that test without thinking. But, for example, if the argument is a number, that's probably the wrong test. Even when the argument is a sentence or a non-numeric word, it may not be empty in the base case, as in the Pig Latin example.

⇒   A serious pitfall is failing to recognize a situation in which you need an extra variable and therefore need a helper procedure. If at each step you need the entire original argument as well as the argument that's getting closer to the base case, you probably need a helper procedure. For example, write a procedure `pairs` that takes a word as argument and returns a sentence of all possible two-letter words made of letters from the argument word, allowing duplicates, like this:

```
> (pairs 'toy)
(TT TO TY OT OO OY YT YO YY)
```

⇒   A simple pitfall, when using a helper procedure, is to write a recursive call in the helper that calls the main procedure instead of calling the helper. (For example, what would have happened if we'd had `every-nth-helper` invoke `every-nth` instead of invoking itself?)

⇒   Some recursive procedures with more than one argument require more than one base case. But some don't. One pitfall is to leave out a necessary base case; another is to include something that looks like a base case but doesn't fit the structure of the program.

For example, the reason `sent-before?` needs two base cases is that on each recursive call, both `sent1` and `sent2` get smaller. Either sentence might run out first, and the procedure should return different values in those two cases.

On the other hand, Exercise 11.7 asked you to write a procedure that has two arguments but needs only one base case:

```
(define (copies num wd)
  (if (= num 0)
      '()
      (se wd (copies (- num 1) wd))))
```

In this example, the `wd` argument *doesn't* get smaller from one invocation to the next. It would be silly to test for (`empty? wd`).

A noteworthy intermediate case is `every-nth-helper`. It does have two `cond` clauses that check for two different arguments reaching their smallest allowable values, but the `remaining` clause isn't a base case. If `remaining` has the value 1, the procedure still invokes itself recursively.

The only general principle we can offer is that you have to think about what base cases are appropriate, not just routinely copy whatever worked last time.

Exercises

Classify each of these problems as a pattern (`every`, `keep`, or `accumulate`), if possible, and then write the procedure recursively. In some cases we've given an example of invoking the procedure we want you to write, instead of describing it.

14.1

```
> (remove-once 'morning '(good morning good morning))
(GOOD GOOD MORNING)
```

(It's okay if your solution removes the other MORNING instead, as long as it removes only one of them.)

14.2

```
> (up 'town)
(T TO TOW TOWN)
```

14.3

```
> (remdup '(ob la di ob la da))          ;; remove duplicates
(OB LA DI DA)
```

(It's okay if your procedure returns (DI OB LA DA) instead, as long as it removes all but one instance of each duplicated word.)

14.4

```
> (odds '(i lost my little girl))
(I MY GIRL)
```

14.5 [8.7] Write a procedure `letter-count` that takes a sentence as its argument and returns the total number of letters in the sentence:

```
> (letter-count '(fixing a hole))
11
```

14.6 Write `member?`.

14.7 Write `differences`, which takes a sentence of numbers as its argument and returns a sentence containing the differences between adjacent elements. (The length of the returned sentence is one less than that of the argument.)

```
> (differences '(4 23 9 87 6 12))
(19 -14 78 -81 6)
```

14.8 Write `expand`, which takes a sentence as its argument. It returns a sentence similar to the argument, except that if a number appears in the argument, then the return value contains that many copies of the following word:

```
> (expand '(4 calling birds 3 french hens))
(CALLING CALLING CALLING CALLING BIRDS FRENCH FRENCH FRENCH HENS)

> (expand '(the 7 samurai))
(THE SAMURAI SAMURAI SAMURAI SAMURAI SAMURAI SAMURAI SAMURAI)
```

14.9 Write a procedure called `location` that takes two arguments, a word and a sentence. It should return a number indicating where in the sentence that word can be found. If the word isn't in the sentence, return `#f`. If the word appears more than once, return the location of the first appearance.

```
> (location 'me '(you never give me your money))
4
```

14.10 Write the procedure `count-adjacent-duplicates` that takes a sentence as an argument and returns the number of words in the sentence that are immediately followed by the same word:

```
> (count-adjacent-duplicates '(y a b b a d a b b a d o o))
3

> (count-adjacent-duplicates '(yeah yeah yeah))
2
```

14.11 Write the procedure `remove-adjacent-duplicates` that takes a sentence as argument and returns the same sentence but with any word that's immediately followed by the same word removed:

```
> (remove-adjacent-duplicates '(y a b b a d a b b a d o o))
(Y A B A D A B A D O)

> (remove-adjacent-duplicates '(yeah yeah yeah))
(YEAH)
```

14.12 Write a procedure `progressive-squares?` that takes a sentence of numbers as its argument. It should return `#t` if each number (other than the first) is the square of the number before it:

```
> (progressive-squares? '(3 9 81 6561))
#T

> (progressive-squares? '(25 36 49 64))
#F
```

14.13 What does the `pigl` procedure from Chapter 11 do if you invoke it with a word like "frzzmlpt" that has no vowels? Fix it so that it returns "frzzmlptay."

14.14 Write a predicate `same-shape?` that takes two sentences as arguments. It should return `#t` if two conditions are met: The two sentences must have the same number of words, and each word of the first sentence must have the same number of letters as the word in the corresponding position in the second sentence.

```
> (same-shape? '(the fool on the hill) '(you like me too much))
#T

> (same-shape? '(the fool on the hill) '(and your bird can sing))
#F
```

14.15 Write `merge`, a procedure that takes two sentences of numbers as arguments. Each sentence must consist of numbers in increasing order. `Merge` should return a single sentence containing all of the numbers, in order. (We'll use this in the next chapter as part of a sorting algorithm.)

```
> (merge '(4 7 18 40 99) '(3 6 9 12 24 36 50))
(3 4 6 7 9 12 18 24 36 40 50 99)
```

14.16 Write a procedure `syllables` that takes a word as its argument and returns the number of syllables in the word, counted according to the following rule: the number of syllables is the number of vowels, except that a group of consecutive vowels counts as one. For example, in the word "soaring," the group "oa" represents one syllable and the vowel "i" represents a second one.

Be sure to choose test cases that expose likely failures of your procedure. For example, what if the word ends with a vowel? What if it ends with two vowels in a row? What if it has more than two consecutive vowels?

(Of course this rule isn't good enough. It doesn't deal with things like silent "e"s that don't create a syllable ("like"), consecutive vowels that don't form a diphthong ("cooperate"), letters like "y" that are vowels only sometimes, etc. If you get bored, see whether you can teach the program to recognize some of these special cases.)

Project: Spelling Names of Huge Numbers

Write a procedure `number-name` that takes a positive integer argument and returns a sentence containing that number spelled out in words:

```
> (number-name 5513345)
(FIVE MILLION FIVE HUNDRED THIRTEEN THOUSAND THREE HUNDRED FORTY FIVE)

> (number-name (factorial 20))
(TWO QUINTILLION FOUR HUNDRED THIRTY TWO QUADRILLION NINE HUNDRED TWO
 TRILLION EIGHT BILLION ONE HUNDRED SEVENTY SIX MILLION SIX HUNDRED
 FORTY THOUSAND)
```

There are some special cases you will need to consider:

- Numbers in which some particular digit is zero
- Numbers like 1,000,529 in which an entire group of three digits is zero.
- Numbers in the teens.

Here are two hints. First, split the number into groups of three digits, going from right to left. Also, use the sentence

```
'(thousand million billion trillion quadrillion quintillion
  sextillion septillion octillion nonillion decillion)
```

You can write this bottom-up or top-down. To work bottom-up, pick a subtask and get that working before you tackle the overall structure of the problem. For example, write a procedure that returns the word FIFTEEN given the argument 15.

To work top-down, start by writing `number-name`, freely assuming the existence of whatever helper procedures you like. You can begin debugging by writing *stub* procedures that fit into the overall program but don't really do their job correctly. For example, as an intermediate stage you might end up with a program that works like this:

```
> (number-name 1428425)                          ;; intermediate version
(1 MILLION 428 THOUSAND 425)
```

Zoom in on some parts of a fractal and you'll see a miniature version of the whole thing.

15 Advanced Recursion

By now you've had a good deal of experience with straightforward recursive problems, and we hope you feel comfortable with them. In this chapter, we present some more challenging problems. But the same leap of faith method that we used for easier problems is still our basic approach.

Example: `Sort`

First we'll consider the example of sorting a sentence. The argument will be any sentence; our procedure will return a sentence with the same words in alphabetical order.

```
> (sort '(i wanna be your man))
(BE I MAN WANNA YOUR)
```

We'll use the `before?` primitive to decide if one word comes before another word alphabetically:

```
> (before? 'starr 'best)
#F
```

How are we going to think about this problem recursively? Suppose that we're given a sentence to sort. A relatively easy subproblem is to find the word that ought to come first in the sorted sentence; we'll write `earliest-word` later to do this.

Once we've found that word, we just need to put it in front of the sorted version of the rest of the sentence. This is our leap of faith: We're going to assume that we can already sort this smaller sentence. The algorithm we've described is called *selection* sort.

Another subproblem is to find the "rest of the sentence"—all the words except for the earliest. But in Exercise 14.1 you wrote a function `remove-once` that takes a word and a sentence and returns the sentence with that word removed. (We don't want to use `remove`, which removes all copies of the word, because our argument sentence might include the same word twice.)

Let's say in Scheme what we've figured out so far:

```
(define (sort sent)                            ;; unfinished
  (se (earliest-word sent)
      (sort (remove-once (earliest-word sent) sent))))
```

We need to add a base case. The smallest sentence is ( ), which is already sorted.

```
(define (sort sent)
  (if (empty? sent)
      '()
      (se (earliest-word sent)
          (sort (remove-once (earliest-word sent) sent)))))
```

We have one unfinished task: finding the earliest word of the argument.

```
(define (earliest-word sent)
  (earliest-helper (first sent) (bf sent)))

(define (earliest-helper so-far rest)
  (cond ((empty? rest) so-far)
        ((before? so-far (first rest))
         (earliest-helper so-far (bf rest)))
        (else (earliest-helper (first rest) (bf rest)))))*
```

For your convenience, here's `remove-once`:

```
(define (remove-once wd sent)
  (cond ((empty? sent) '())
        ((equal? wd (first sent)) (bf sent))
        (else (se (first sent) (remove-once wd (bf sent))))))
```

---

* If you've read Part III, you might instead want to use `accumulate` for this purpose:

```
(define earliest-word sent)
  (accumulate (lambda (wd1 wd2) (if (before? wd1 wd2) wd1 wd2))
              sent))
```

Example: From–Binary

We want to take a word of ones and zeros, representing a binary number, and compute the numeric value that it represents. Each binary digit (or *bit*) corresponds to a power of two, just as ordinary decimal digits represent powers of ten. So the binary number 1101 represents $(1 \times 8) + (1 \times 4) + (0 \times 2) + (1 \times 1) = 13$. We want to be able to say

```
> (from-binary 1101)
13

> (from-binary 111)
7
```

Where is the smaller, similar subproblem? Probably the most obvious thing to try is our usual trick of dividing the argument into its `first` and its `butfirst`. Suppose we divide the binary number `1101` that way. We make the leap of faith by assuming that we can translate the butfirst, `101`, into its binary value 5. What do we have to add for the leftmost 1? It contributes 8 to the total, because it's three bits away from the right end of the number, so it must be multiplied by 2^3. We could write this idea as follows:

```
(define (from-binary bits)                     ;; incomplete
  (+ (* (first bits) (expt 2 (count (bf bits))))
     (from-binary (bf bits))))
```

That is, we multiply the `first` bit by a power of two depending on the number of bits remaining, then we add that to the result of the recursive call.

As usual, we have written the algorithm for the recursive case before figuring out the base case. But it's pretty easy; a number with no bits (an empty word) has the value zero.*

```
(define (from-binary bits)
  (if (empty? bits)
      0
      (+ (* (first bits) (expt 2 (count (bf bits))))
         (from-binary (bf bits)))))
```

Although this procedure is correct, it's worth noting that a more efficient version can be written by dissecting the number from right to left. As you'll see, we can then avoid the calls to `expt`, which are expensive because we have to do more multiplication than should be necessary.

---

* A more straightforward base case would be a one-bit number, but we've reduced that to this more elegant base case, following the principle we discussed on page 197.

Suppose we want to find the value of the binary number `1101`. The `butlast` of this number, `110`, has the value six. To get the value of the entire number, we double the six (because `1100` would have the value 12, just as in ordinary decimal numbers 430 is ten times 43) and then add the rightmost bit to get 13. Here's the new version:

```
(define (from-binary bits)
  (if (empty? bits)
      0
      (+ (* (from-binary (bl bits)) 2)
         (last bits))))
```

This version may look a little unusual. We usually combine the value returned by the recursive call with some function of the current element. This time, we are combining the current element itself with a function of the recursive return value. You may want to trace this procedure to see how the intermediate return values contribute to the final result.

Example: `Mergesort`

Let's go back to the problem of sorting a sentence. It turns out that sorting one element at a time, as in selection sort, isn't the fastest possible approach. One of the fastest sorting algorithms is called *mergesort,* and it works like this: In order to mergesort a sentence, divide the sentence into two equal halves and recursively sort each half. Then take the two sorted subsentences and *merge* them together, that is, create one long sorted sentence that contains all the words of the two halves. The base case is that an empty sentence or a one-word sentence is already sorted.

```
(define (mergesort sent)
  (if (<= (count sent) 1)
      sent
      (merge (mergesort (one-half sent))
             (mergesort (other-half sent)))))
```

The leap of faith here is the idea that we can magically `mergesort` the halves of the sentence. If you try to trace this through step by step, or wonder exactly what happens at what time, then this algorithm may be very confusing. But if you just *believe* that the recursive calls will do exactly the right thing, then it's much easier to understand this program. The key point is that if the two smaller pieces have already been sorted, it's pretty easy to merge them while keeping the result in order.

We still need some helper procedures. You wrote `merge` in Exercise 14.15. It uses the following technique: Compare the first words of the two sentences. Let's say the first word of the sentence on the left is smaller. Then the first word of the return value is the first word of the sentence on the left. The rest of the return value comes from recursively merging the `butfirst` of the left sentence with the entire right sentence. (It's precisely the opposite of this if the first word of the other sentence is smaller.)

```
(define (merge left right)
  (cond ((empty? left) right)
        ((empty? right) left)
        ((before? (first left) (first right))
         (se (first left) (merge (bf left) right)))
        (else (se (first right) (merge left (bf right)))))))
```

Now we have to write `one-half` and `other-half`. One of the easiest ways to do this is to have `one-half` return the elements in odd-numbered positions, and have `other-half` return the elements in even-numbered positions. These are the same as the procedures `odds` (from Exercise 14.4) and `evens` (from Chapter 12).

```
(define (one-half sent)
  (if (<= (count sent) 1)
      sent
      (se (first sent) (one-half (bf (bf sent))))))

(define (other-half sent)
  (if (<= (count sent) 1)
      '()
      (se (first (bf sent)) (other-half (bf (bf sent))))))
```

Example: Subsets

We're now going to attack a much harder problem. We want to know all the subsets of the letters of a word—that is, words that can be formed from the original word by crossing out some (maybe zero) of the letters. For example, if we start with a short word like `rat`, the subsets are `r`, `a`, `t`, `ra`, `rt`, `at`, `rat`, and the empty word (`""`). As the word gets longer, the number of subsets gets bigger very quickly.*

As with many problems about words, we'll try assuming that we can find the subsets of the `butfirst` of our word. In other words, we're hoping to find a solution that will include an expression like

```
(subsets (bf wd))
```

---

* Try writing down all the subsets of a five-letter word if you don't believe us.

Let's actually take a four-letter word and look at its subsets. We'll pick `brat`, because we already know the subsets of its `butfirst`. Here are the subsets of `brat`:

```
"" b r a t br ba bt ra rt at bra brt bat rat brat
```

You might notice that many of these subsets are also subsets of `rat`. In fact, if you think about it, *all* of the subsets of `rat` are also subsets of `brat`. So the words in (`subsets 'rat`) are some of the words we need for (`subsets 'brat`).

Let's separate those out and look at the ones left over:

```
rat subsets:    ""  r   a   t   ra  rt   at   rat
others:         b  br  ba  bt  bra brt  bat  brat
```

Right about now you're probably thinking, "They've pulled a rabbit out of a hat, the way my math teacher always does." The words that aren't subsets of `rat` all start with `b`, followed by something that *is* a subset of `rat`. You may be thinking that you never would have thought of that yourself. But we're just following the method: Look at the smaller case and see how it fits into the original problem. It's not so different from what happened with `downup`.

Now all we have to do is figure out how to say in Scheme, "Put a `b` in front of every word in this sentence." This is a straightforward example of the **every** pattern:

```
(define (prepend-every letter sent)
  (if (empty? sent)
      '()
      (se (word letter (first sent))
          (prepend-every letter (bf sent)))))
```

The way we'll use this in (`subsets 'brat`) is

```
(prepend-every 'b (subsets 'rat))
```

Of course in the general case we won't have `b` and `rat` in our program, but instead will refer to the formal parameter:

```
(define (subsets wd)                        ;; first version
  (se (subsets (bf wd))
      (prepend-every (first wd) (subsets (bf wd)))))
```

We still need a base case. By now you're accustomed to the idea of using an empty word as the base case. It may be strange to think of the empty word as a set in the first place, let alone to try to find its subsets. But a set of zero elements is a perfectly good set, and it's the smallest one possible.

The empty set has only one subset, the empty set itself. What should `subsets` of the empty word return? It's easy to make a mistake here and return the empty word itself. But we want `subsets` to return a sentence, containing all the subsets, and we should stick with returning a sentence even in the simple case.* (This mistake would come from not thinking about the *range* of our function, which is sentences. This is why we put so much effort into learning about domains and ranges in Chapter 2.) So we'll return a sentence containing one (empty) word to represent the one subset.

```
(define (subsets wd)                        ;; second version
  (if (empty? wd)
      (se "")
      (se (subsets (bf wd))
          (prepend-every (first wd) (subsets (bf wd))))))
```

This program is entirely correct. Because it uses two identical recursive calls, however, it's a lot slower than necessary. We can use `let` to do the recursive subproblem only once:**

```
(define (subsets wd)
  (if (empty? wd)
      (se "")
      (let ((smaller (subsets (bf wd))))
        (se smaller
            (prepend-every (first wd) smaller)))))
```

Pitfalls

⇒ We've already mentioned the need to be careful about the value returned in the base case. The `subsets` procedure is particularly error-prone because the correct value, a sentence containing the empty word, is quite unusual. An empty subset isn't the same as no subsets at all!

⇒ Sometimes you write a recursive procedure with a correct recursive case and a reasonable base case, but the program still doesn't work. The trouble may be that the base case doesn't quite catch all of the ways in which the problem can get smaller. A

---

* We discussed this point in a pitfall in Chapter 12.

** How come we're worrying about efficiency all of a sudden? We really *did* pull this out of a hat. The thing is, it's a *lot* slower without the `let`. Adding one letter to the length of a word doubles the time required to find its subsets; adding 10 letters multiplies the time by about 1000.

second base case may be needed. For example, in `mergesort`, why did we write the following line?

```
(<= (count sent) 1)
```

This tests for two base cases, empty sentences and one-word sentences, whereas in most other examples the base case is just an empty sentence. Suppose the base case test were (`empty? sent`) and suppose we invoke `mergesort` with a one-word sentence, (`test`). We would end up trying to compute the expression

```
(merge (mergesort (one-half '(test)))
       (mergesort (other-half '(test))))
```

If you look back at the definitions of `one-half` and `other-half`, you'll see that this is equivalent to

```
(merge (mergesort '(test)) (mergesort '()))
```

The first argument to `merge` is the same expression we started with! Here is a situation in which the problem doesn't get smaller in a recursive call. Although we've been trying to avoid complicated base cases, in this situation a straightforward base case isn't enough. To avoid an infinite recursion, we must have two base cases.

Another example is the `fib` procedure from Chapter 13. Suppose it were defined like this:

```
(define (fib n)                          ;; wrong!
  (if (= n 1)
      1
      (+ (fib (- n 1))
         (fib (- n 2)))))
```

It would be easy to make this mistake, because everybody knows that in a recursion dealing with numbers, the base case is the smallest possible number. But in `fib`, each computation depends on *two* smaller values, and we discover that we need two base cases.

⇒ The technique of recursion is often used to do something repetitively, but don't get the idea that the word "recursion" *means* repetition. Recursion is a technique in which a procedure invokes itself. We do use recursion to solve repetitive problems, but don't confuse the method with the ends it achieves. In particular, if you've programmed in other languages that have special-purpose looping mechanisms (the ones with names like `for` and `while`), those aren't recursive. Conversely, not every recursive procedure carries out a repetition.

Exercises

15.1 Write a procedure `to-binary`:

```
> (to-binary 9)
1001

> (to-binary 23)
10111
```

15.2 A "palindrome" is a sentence that reads the same backward as forward. Write a predicate `palindrome?` that takes a sentence as argument and decides whether it is a palindrome. For example:

```
> (palindrome? '(flee to me remote elf))
#T

> (palindrome? '(flee to me remote control))
#F
```

Do not reverse any words or sentences in your solution.

15.3 Write a procedure `substrings` that takes a word as its argument. It should return a sentence containing all of the substrings of the argument. A *substring* is a subset whose letters come consecutively in the original word. For example, the word `bat` is a subset, but *not* a substring, of `brat`.

15.4 Write a predicate procedure `substring?` that takes two words as arguments and returns `#t` if and only if the first word is a substring of the second. (See Exercise 15.3 for the definition of a substring.)

Be careful about cases in which you encounter a "false start," like this:

```
> (substring? 'ssip 'mississippi)
#T
```

and also about subsets that don't appear as consecutive letters in the second word:

```
> (substring? 'misip 'mississippi)
#F
```

15.5 Suppose you have a phone number, such as 223-5766, and you'd like to figure out a clever way to spell it in letters for your friends to remember. Each digit corresponds to three possible letters. For example, the digit 2 corresponds to the letters A, B, and C. Write a procedure that takes a number as argument and returns a sentence of all the possible spellings:

```
> (phone-spell 2235766)
(AADJPMM AADJPMN ... CCFLSOO)
```

(We're not showing you all 2187 words in this sentence.) You may assume there are no zeros or ones in the number, since those don't have letters.

Hint: This problem has a lot in common with the subsets example.

15.6 Let's say a gladiator kills a roach. If we want to talk about the roach, we say "the roach the gladiator killed." But if we want to talk about the gladiator, we say "the gladiator that killed the roach."

People are pretty good at understanding even rather long sentences as long as they're straightforward: "This is the farmer who kept the cock that waked the priest that married the man that kissed the maiden that milked the cow that tossed the dog that worried the cat that killed the rat that ate the malt that lay in the house that Jack built." But even a short *nested* sentence is confusing: "This is the rat the cat the dog worried killed." Which rat was that?

Write a procedure `unscramble` that takes a nested sentence as argument and returns a straightforward sentence about the same cast of characters:

```
> (unscramble '(this is the roach the gladiator killed))
(THIS IS THE GLADIATOR THAT KILLED THE ROACH)

> (unscramble '(this is the rat the cat the dog the boy the
                 girl saw owned chased bit))
(THIS IS THE GIRL THAT SAW THE BOY THAT OWNED THE DOG THAT
     CHASED THE CAT THAT BIT THE RAT)
```

You may assume that the argument has exactly the structure of these examples, with no special cases like "that lay *in* the house" or "that *Jack* built."

Project: Scoring Poker Hands

The idea of this project is to invent a procedure `poker-value` that works like this:

```
> (poker-value '(h4 s4 c6 s6 c4))
(FULL HOUSE - FOURS OVER SIXES)

> (poker-value '(h7 s3 c5 c4 d6))
(SEVEN-HIGH STRAIGHT)

> (poker-value '(dq d10 dj da dk))
(ROYAL FLUSH - DIAMONDS)

> (poker-value '(da d6 d3 c9 h6))
(PAIR OF SIXES)
```

As you can see, we are representing cards and hands just as in the Bridge project, except that poker hands have only five cards.*

Here are the various kinds of poker hands, in decreasing order of value:

- Royal flush: ten, jack, queen, king, and ace, all of the same suit
- Straight flush: five cards of sequential rank, all of the same suit
- Four of a kind: four cards of the same rank
- Full house: three cards of the same rank, and two of a second rank
- Flush: five cards of the same suit, not sequential rank
- Straight: five cards of sequential rank, not all of the same suit
- Three of a kind: three cards of the same rank, no other matches

---

* Later on we'll think about seven-card variants of poker.

- Two pair: two pairs of cards, of two different ranks
- Pair: two cards of the same rank, no other matches
- Nothing: none of the above

An ace can be the lowest card of a straight (ace, 2, 3, 4, 5) or the highest card of a straight (ten, jack, queen, king, ace), but a straight can't "wrap around"; a hand with queen, king, ace, 2, 3 would be worthless (unless it's a flush).

Notice that most of the hand categories are either entirely about the ranks of the cards (pairs, straight, full house, etc.) or entirely about the suits (flush). It's a good idea to begin your program by separating the rank information and the suit information. To check for a straight flush or royal flush, you'll have to consider both kinds of information.

In what form do you want the suit information? Really, all you need is a true or false value indicating whether or not the hand is a flush, because there aren't any poker categories like "three of one suit and two of another."

What about ranks? There are two kinds of hand categories involving ranks: the ones about equal ranks (pairs, full house) and the ones about sequential ranks (straight). You might therefore want the rank information in two forms. A sentence containing all of the ranks in the hand, in sorted order, will make it easier to find a straight. (You still have to be careful about aces.)

For the equal-rank categories, what you want is some data structure that will let you ask questions like "are there three cards of the same rank in this hand?" We ended up using a representation like this:

```
> (compute-ranks '(q 3 4 3 4))
(ONE Q TWO 3 TWO 4)
```

One slightly tricky aspect of this solution is that we spelled out the numbers of cards, one to four, instead of using the more obvious (1 Q 2 3 2 4). The reason, as you can probably tell just by looking at the latter version, is that it would lead to confusion between the names of the ranks, most of which are digits, and the numbers of occurrences, which are also digits. More specifically, by spelling out the numbers of occurrences, we can use member? to ask easily if there is a three-of-a-kind rank in the hand.

You may find it easier to begin by writing a version that returns only the name of a category, such as three of a kind, and only after you get that to work, revise it to give more specific results such as three sixes.

Extra Work for Hotshots

In some versions of poker, each player gets seven cards and can choose any five of the seven to make a hand. How would it change your program if the argument were a sentence of seven cards? (For example, in five-card poker there is only one possible category for a hand, but in seven-card you have to pick the best category that can be made from your cards.) Fix your program so that it works for both five-card and seven-card hands.

Another possible modification to the program is to allow for playing with "wild" cards. If you play with "threes wild," it means that if there is a three in your hand you're allowed to pretend it's whatever card you like. For this modification, your program will require a second argument indicating which cards are wild. (When you play with wild cards, there's the possibility of having five of a kind. This beats a straight flush.)

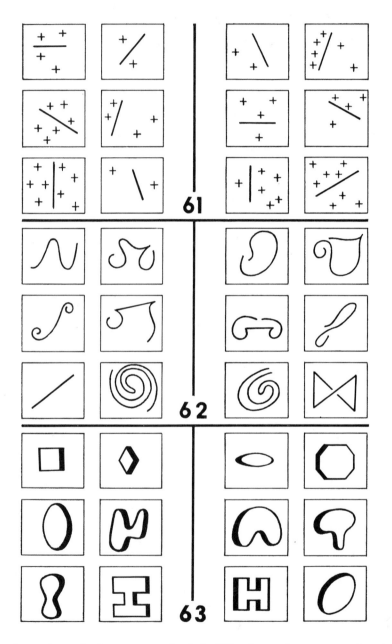

In each set, how do the ones on the left differ from the ones on the right?

16   Example: Pattern Matcher

It's time for another extended example in which we use the Scheme tools we've been learning to accomplish something practical. We'll start by describing how the program will work before we talk about how to implement it.

You can load our program into Scheme by typing

```
(load "match.scm")
```

Problem Description

A *pattern matcher* is a commonly used procedure whose job is to compare a sentence to a range of possibilities. An example may make this clear:

```
> (match '(* me *) '(love me do))
#T

> (match '(* me *) '(please please me))
#T

> (match '(* me *) '(in my life))
#F
```

The first argument, (* me *), is a *pattern*. In the pattern, each asterisk (*) means "any number of words, including no words at all." So the entire pattern matches any sentence that contains the word "me" anywhere within it. You can think of match as a more general form of equal? in the sense that it compares two sentences and tells us whether they're the same, but with a broader meaning of "the same."

Our pattern matcher will accept patterns more complicated than this first example. There are four *special characters* that indicate unspecified parts of a pattern, depending on the number of words that should be allowed:

? At most one word.
! Exactly one word.
& At least one word.
* Any number of words.

These characters are meant to be somewhat mnemonic. The question mark means "maybe there's a word." The exclamation point means "precisely one word!" (And it's vertical, just like the digit 1, sort of.) The ampersand, which ordinarily means "and," indicates that we're matching a word and maybe more. The asterisk doesn't have any mnemonic value, but it's what everyone uses for a general matching indicator anyway.

We can give a *name* to the collection of words that match an unspecified part of a pattern by including in the pattern a word that starts with one of the four special characters and continues with the name. If the match succeeds, `match` will return a sentence containing these names and the corresponding values from the sentence:

```
> (match '(*start me *end) '(love me do))
(START LOVE ! END DO !)

> (match '(*start me *end) '(please please me))
(START PLEASE PLEASE ! END !)

> (match '(mean mr mustard) '(mean mr mustard))
()

> (match '(*start me *end) '(in my life))
FAILED
```

In these examples, you see that `match` doesn't really return #t or #f; the earlier set of examples showed a simplified picture. In the first of the new examples, the special pattern word `*start` is allowed to match any number of words, as indicated by the asterisk. In this case it turned out to match the single word "love." `Match` returns a result that tells us which words of the sentence match the named special words in the pattern. (We'll call one of these special pattern words a *placeholder*.) The exclamation points in the returned value are needed to separate one match from another. (In the second example, the name `end` was matched by an empty set of words.) In the third example, the match was successful, but since there were no placeholders the returned sentence was empty. If the match is unsuccessful, `match` returns the word `failed`.*

If the same placeholder name appears more than once in the pattern, then it must be matched by the same word(s) in the sentence each time:

```
> (match '(!twice !other !twice) '(cry baby cry))
(TWICE CRY ! OTHER BABY !)

> (match '(!twice !other !twice) '(please please me))
FAILED
```

Some patterns might be matchable in more than one way. For example, the invocation

```
> (match '(*front *back) '(your mother should know))
```

might return any of five different correct answers:

```
(FRONT YOUR MOTHER SHOULD KNOW ! BACK !)
(FRONT YOUR MOTHER SHOULD ! BACK KNOW !)
(FRONT YOUR MOTHER ! BACK SHOULD KNOW !)
(FRONT YOUR ! BACK MOTHER SHOULD KNOW !)
(FRONT ! BACK YOUR MOTHER SHOULD KNOW !)
```

We arbitrarily decide that in such cases the first placeholder should match as many words as possible, so in this case `match` will actually return the first of these answers.

Before continuing, you might want to look at the first batch of exercises at the end of this chapter, which are about using the pattern matcher. (The rest of the exercises are about the implementation, which we'll discuss next.)

Implementation: When Are Two Sentences Equal?

Our approach to implementation will be to start with something we already know how

---

* Why not return the sentence if successful or `#f` otherwise? That would be fine in most versions of Scheme, but as we mentioned earlier, the empty sentence `()` is the same as the false value `#f` in some dialects. In those Schemes, a successfully matched pattern with no named placeholders, for which the program should return an empty sentence, would be indistinguishable from an unmatched pattern.

to write: a predicate that tests whether two sentences are exactly equal. We will add capabilities one at a time until we reach our goal.

Suppose that Scheme's primitive `equal?` function worked only for words and not for sentences. We could write an equality tester for sentences, like this:

```
(define (sent-equal? sent1 sent2)
  (cond ((empty? sent1)
         (empty? sent2))
        ((empty? sent2) #f)
        ((equal? (first sent1) (first sent2))
         (sent-equal? (bf sent1) (bf sent2)))
        (else #f)))
```

Two sentences are equal if each word in the first sentence is equal to the corresponding word in the second. They're unequal if one sentence runs out of words before the other.

Why are we choosing to accept Scheme's primitive word comparison but rewrite the sentence comparison? In our pattern matcher, a placeholder in the pattern corresponds to a group of words in the sentence. There is no kind of placeholder that matches only part of a word. (It would be possible to implement such placeholders, but we've chosen not to.) Therefore, we will never need to ask whether a word is "almost equal" to another word.

When Are Two Sentences Nearly Equal?

Pattern matching is just a more general form of this `sent-equal?` procedure. Let's write a very simple pattern matcher that knows only about the "!" special character and doesn't let us name the words that match the exclamation points in the pattern. We'll call this one `match?` with a question mark because it returns just true or false.

```
(define (match? pattern sent)                 ;; first version: ! only
  (cond ((empty? pattern)
         (empty? sent))
        ((empty? sent) #f)
        ((equal? (first pattern) '!)
         (match? (bf pattern) (bf sent)))
        ((equal? (first pattern) (first sent))
         (match? (bf pattern) (bf sent)))
        (else #f)))
```

This program is exactly the same as `sent-equal?`, except for the highlighted `cond` clause. We are still comparing each word of the pattern with the corresponding word of the sentence, but now an exclamation mark in the pattern matches *any* word in the sentence. (If `first` of `pattern` is an exclamation mark, we don't even look at `first` of `sent`.)

Our strategy in the next several sections will be to expand the pattern matcher by implementing the remaining special characters, then finally adding the ability to name the placeholders. For now, when we say something like "the * placeholder," we mean the placeholder consisting of the asterisk alone. Later, after we add named placeholders, the same procedures will implement any placeholder that begins with an asterisk.

Matching with Alternatives

The `!` matching is not much harder than `sent-equal?`, because it's still the case that one word of the pattern must match one word of the sentence. When we introduce the `?` option, the structure of the program must be more complicated, because a question mark in the pattern might or might not be paired up with a word in the sentence. In other words, the pattern and the sentence might match without being the same length.

```
(define (match? pattern sent)                    ;; second version: ! and ?
  (cond ((empty? pattern)
         (empty? sent))
        ((equal? (first pattern) '?)
         (if (empty? sent)
             (match? (bf pattern) '())
             (or (match? (bf pattern) (bf sent))
                 (match? (bf pattern) sent))))
        ((empty? sent) #f)
        ((equal? (first pattern) '!)
         (match? (bf pattern) (bf sent)))
        ((equal? (first pattern) (first sent))
         (match? (bf pattern) (bf sent)))
        (else #f)))
```

Note that the new `cond` clause comes *before* the check to see if `sent` is empty. That's because `sent` might be empty and a pattern of (?) would still match it. But if the sentence is empty, we know that the question mark doesn't match a word, so we just have to make sure that the `butfirst` of the pattern contains nothing but question marks. (We don't have a predicate named `all-question-marks?`; instead, we use `match?` recursively to make this test.)

In general, a question mark in the pattern has to match either one word or zero words in the sentence. How do we decide? Our rule is that each placeholder should match as many words as possible, so we prefer to match one word if we can. But allowing the question mark to match a word might prevent the rest of the pattern from matching the rest of the sentence.

Compare these two examples:

```
> (match? '(? please me) '(please please me))
#T

> (match? '(? please me) '(please me))
#T
```

In the first case, the first thing in the pattern is a question mark and the first thing in the sentence is "please," and they match. That leaves "please me" in the pattern to match "please me" in the sentence.

In the second case, we again have a question mark as the first thing in the pattern and "please" as the first thing in the sentence. But this time, we had better not use up the "please" in the sentence, because that will only leave "me" to match "please me." In this case the question mark has to match no words.

To you, these examples probably look obvious. That's because you're a human being, and you can take in the entire pattern and the entire sentence all at once. Scheme isn't as smart as you are; it has to compare words one pair at a time. To Scheme, the processing of both examples begins with question mark as the first word of the pattern and "please" as the first word of the sentence. The pattern matcher has to consider both cases.

How does the procedure consider both cases? Look at the invocation of or by the match? procedure. There are two alternatives; if either turns out true, the match succeeds. One is that we try to match the question mark with the first word of the sentence just as we matched ! in our earlier example—by making a recursive call on the butfirsts of the pattern and sentence. If that returns true, then the question mark matches the first word.

The second alternative that can make the match succeed is a recursive call to match? on the butfirst of the pattern and the *entire* sentence; this corresponds to matching the ? against nothing.*

Let's trace `match?` so that you can see how these two cases are handled differently by the program.

```
> (trace match?)
> (match? '(? please me) '(please please me))
(match? (? please me) (please please me))
| (match? (please me) (please me))          Try matching ? with please.
| | (match? (me) (me))
| | | (match? () ())
| | | #t
| | #t                                       It works!
| #t
#t
#T
```

```
> (match? '(? please me) '(please me))
(match? (? please me) (please me))
| (match? (please me) (me))                  Try matching ? with please.
| #f                                         It doesn't work.
| (match? (please me) (please me))           This time, match ? with nothing.
| | (match? (me) (me))
| | | (match? () ())
| | | #t
| | #t
| #t
#t
#T
```

Backtracking

The program structure that allows for two alternative routes to success has more profound implications than you may think at first.

When `match?` sees a question mark in the pattern, it has to decide whether or not to "use up" a word of the sentence by matching it with the question mark. You might wonder, "How does the question mark decide whether to take a word?" The answer is that the decision isn't made "by the question mark"; there's nothing about the particular

---

* Actually, since `or` is a special form, Scheme avoids the need to try the second alternative if the first one succeeds.

word that the question mark might match that helps with the decision! Instead, the decision depends on matching what comes to the right of the question mark.

Compare this situation with the `keep` recursive pattern. There, too, the procedure makes a decision about the first word of a sentence, and each alternative leads to a recursive call for the `butfirst`:

```
(cond ((empty? sent) '())
      ((some-test? (first sent))
       (se (first sent) (recursive-call (bf sent))))
      (else (recursive-call (bf sent)))))
```

The difference is that in the `keep` pattern the choice between alternatives *can* be made just by looking at the immediate situation—the single word that might or might not be chosen; the decision doesn't depend on anything in the rest of the problem. As a result, the choice has already been made before any recursive call happens. Therefore, only one of the recursive calls is actually made, to make choices about the remaining words in the sentence.

In `match?`, by contrast, any particular invocation can't make its choice until it knows the result of a recursive invocation. The result from the recursive call determines the choice made by the caller.

Here's a model that might help you think about this kind of recursion. `Match?` sees a question mark in the pattern. It makes a *tentative* decision that this question mark should match the first word of the sentence, and it uses a recursive invocation to see whether that decision allows the rest of the problem to be solved. If so, the tentative choice was correct. If not, `match?` tries an alternative decision that the question mark doesn't match a word. This alternative is still tentative; another recursive call is needed to see if the rest of the pattern can succeed. If not, the overall match fails.

This structure is called *backtracking*.

What if there are two question marks in the pattern? Then there are *four* ways to match the overall pattern. Both question marks can match a word, or only the first question mark, or only the second, or neither. A pattern with several placeholders leads to even more alternatives. A pattern with three question marks will have eight alternatives. (All three match words, the first two do but the third doesn't, and so on.) A pattern with 10 question marks will have 1024 alternatives. How can `match?` try all these alternatives? The procedure seems to make only one two-way choice; how can it accomplish a four-way or many-way decision?

The secret is the same as the usual secret of recursion: Most of the work is done in recursive calls. We take a leap of faith that recursive invocations will take care of the decisions concerning question marks later in the pattern. Think about it using the backtracking model. Let's suppose there are 10 question marks in the pattern. When `match?` encounters the leftmost question mark, it makes a tentative decision to match the question mark with a word of the sentence. To test whether this choice can work, `match?` invokes itself recursively on a pattern with nine question marks. By the leap of faith, the recursive invocation will examine 512 ways to match question marks with words—half of the total number. If one of these 512 works, we're finished. If not, the original `match?` invocation changes its tentative choice, deciding instead *not* to match its question mark (the leftmost one) with a word of the sentence. Another recursive call is made based on that decision, and that recursive call checks out the remaining 512 possibilities.

By the way, the program doesn't always have to try all of the different combinations of question marks matching or not matching words separately. For example, if the problem is

```
(match? '(a b ? ? ? ?) '(x y z w p q))
```

then the very first comparison discovers that `a` is different from `x`, so none of the 16 possible arrangements about question marks matching or not matching words will make a difference.

Here are some traced examples involving patterns with two question marks, to show how the result of backtracking depends on the individual problem.

```
> (match? '(? ? foo) '(bar foo))
(match? (? ? foo) (bar foo))
|   (match? (? foo) (foo))
|   |   (match? (foo) ())
|   |   #f
|   |   (match? (foo) (foo))
|   |   |   (match? () ())
|   |   |   #t
|   |   #t
|   #t
#t
#T
```

In this first example, the first question mark tries to match the word `bar`, but it can't tell whether or not that match will succeed until the recursive call returns. In the recursive call, the second question mark tries to match the word `foo`, and fails. Then the second question mark tries again, this time matching nothing, and succeeds. Therefore, the first question mark can report success; it never has to try a recursive call in which it doesn't match a word.

In our second example, each question mark will have to try both alternatives, matching and then not matching a word, before the overall match succeeds.

```
> (match? '(? ? foo bar) '(foo bar))
(match? (? ? foo bar) (foo bar))
| (match? (? foo bar) (bar))
| | (match? (foo bar) ())
| | #f
| | (match? (foo bar) (bar))
| | #f
| #f
| (match? (? foo bar) (foo bar))
| | (match? (foo bar) (bar))
| | #f
| | (match? (foo bar) (foo bar))
| | | (match? (bar) (bar))
| | | | (match? () ())
| | | | #t
| | | #t
| | #t
| #t
#t
#T
```

The first question mark tries to match the word foo in the sentence, leaving the pattern (? foo bar) to match (bar). The second question mark will try both matching and not matching a word, but neither succeeds. Therefore, the first question mark tries again, this time not matching a word. The second question mark first tries matching foo, and when that fails, tries not matching anything. This last attempt is successful.

In the previous example, every question mark's first attempt failed. The following example illustrates the opposite case, in which every question mark's first attempt succeeds.

```
> (match? '(? ? baz) '(foo bar baz))
(match? (? ? baz) (foo bar baz))
|   (match? (? baz) (bar baz))
|   |   (match? (baz) (baz))
|   |   |   (match? () ())
|   |   |   #t
|   |   #t
|   #t
#t
#t
```

The first question mark matches foo; the second matches bar.

If the sentence is shorter than the pattern, we may end up trying to match a pattern against an empty sentence. This is much easier than the general problem, because there aren't two alternatives; a question mark has no word in the sentence to match.

```
> (match? '(? ? foo) '())
(match? (? ? foo) ())
|   (match? (? foo) ())
|   |   (match? (foo) ())
|   |   #f
|   #f
#f
#f
```

Each question mark knows right away that it had better not try to match a word, so we never have to backtrack.

Matching Several Words

The next placeholder we'll implement is *. The order in which we're implementing these placeholders was chosen so that each new version increases the variability in the number of words a placeholder can match. The ! placeholder was very easy because it always matches exactly one word; it's hardly different at all from a non-placeholder in the pattern. Implementing ? was more complicated because there were two alternatives to consider. But for *, we might match any number of words, up to the entire rest of the sentence.

Our strategy will be a generalization of the ? strategy: Start with a "greedy" match, and then, if a recursive call tells us that the remaining part of the sentence can't match the rest of the pattern, try a less greedy match.

The difference between ? and * is that ? allows only two possible match lengths, zero and one. Therefore, these two cases can be checked with two explicit subexpressions of an or expression. In the more general case of *, any length is possible, so we can't check every possibility separately. Instead, as in any problem of unknown size, we use recursion. First we try the longest possible match; if that fails because the rest of the pattern can't be matched, a recursive call tries the next-longest match. If we get all the way down to an empty match for the * and still can't match the rest of the pattern, then we return #f.

```
(define (match? pattern sent)                    ;; third version: !, ?, and *
  (cond ((empty? pattern)
         (empty? sent))
        ((equal? (first pattern) '?)
         (if (empty? sent)
             (match? (bf pattern) '())
             (or (match? (bf pattern) (bf sent))
                 (match? (bf pattern) sent))))
        ((equal? (first pattern) '*)
         (*-longest-match (bf pattern) sent))
        ((empty? sent) #f)
        ((equal? (first pattern) '!)
         (match? (bf pattern) (bf sent)))
        ((equal? (first pattern) (first sent))
         (match? (bf pattern) (bf sent)))
        (else #f)))

(define (*-longest-match pattern-rest sent)
  (*-lm-helper pattern-rest sent '()))

(define (*-lm-helper pattern-rest sent-matched sent-unmatched)
  (cond ((match? pattern-rest sent-unmatched) #t)
        ((empty? sent-matched) #f)
        (else (*-lm-helper pattern-rest
                           (bl sent-matched)
                           (se (last sent-matched) sent-unmatched)))))
```

If an asterisk is found in the pattern, match? invokes *-longest-match, which carries out this backtracking approach.

The real work is done by *-lm-helper, which has three arguments. The first argument is the still-to-be-matched part of the pattern, following the * placeholder that we're trying to match now. Sent-matched is the part of the sentence that we're considering as a candidate to match the * placeholder. Sent-unmatched is the remainder of the sentence, following the words in `sent-matched`; it must match `pattern-rest`.

Since we're trying to find the longest possible match, `*-longest-match` chooses the entire sentence as the first attempt for `sent-matched`. Since `sent-matched` is using up the entire sentence, the initial value of `sent-unmatched` is empty. The only job of `*-longest-match` is to invoke `*-lm-helper` with these initial arguments. On each recursive invocation, `*-lm-helper` shortens `sent-matched` by one word and accordingly lengthens `sent-unmatched`.

Here's an example in which the `*` placeholder tries to match four words, then three words, and finally succeeds with two words:

```
> (trace match? *-longest-match *-lm-helper)

> (match? '(* days night) '(a hard days night))
(match? (* days night) (a hard days night))
 | (*-longest-match (days night) (a hard days night))
 | | (*-lm-helper (days night) (a hard days night) ())
 | | | (match? (days night) ())
 | | | #f
 | | | (*-lm-helper (days night) (a hard days) (night))
 | | | | (match? (days night) (night))
 | | | | #f
 | | | | (*-lm-helper (days night) (a hard) (days night))
 | | | | | (match? (days night) (days night))
 | | | | | | (match? (night) (night))
 | | | | | | | (match? () ())
 | | | | | | | #t
 | | | | | | #t
 | | | | | #t
 | | | | #t
 | | | #t
 | | #t
 | #t
#t
#t
```

Combining the Placeholders

We have one remaining placeholder, `&`, which is much like `*` except that it fails unless it can match at least one word. We could, therefore, write a `&-longest-match` that would be identical to `*-longest-match` except for the base case of its helper procedure. If `sent-matched` is empty, the result is `#f` even if it would be possible to match the rest of the pattern against the rest of the sentence. (All we have to do is exchange the first two clauses of the cond.)

```
(define (&-longest-match pattern-rest sent)
  (&-lm-helper pattern-rest sent '()))

(define (&-lm-helper pattern-rest sent-matched sent-unmatched)
  (cond ((empty? sent-matched) #f)
        ((match? pattern-rest sent-unmatched) #t)
        (else (&-lm-helper pattern-rest
                           (bl sent-matched)
                           (se (last sent-matched) sent-unmatched)))))
```

When two procedures are so similar, that's a clue that perhaps they could be combined into one. We could look at the bodies of these two procedures to find a way to combine them textually. But instead, let's step back and think about the meanings of the placeholders.

The reason that the procedures *-longest-match and &-longest-match are so similar is that the two placeholders have almost identical meanings. * means "match as many words as possible"; & means "match as many words as possible, but at least one." Once we're thinking in these terms, it's plausible to think of ? as meaning "match as many words as possible, but at most one." In fact, although this is a stretch, we can also describe ! similarly: "Match as many words as possible, but at least one, and at most one."

Placeholder	Minimum size	Maximum size
*	0	no limit
&	1	no limit
?	0	1
!	1	1

We'll take advantage of this newly understood similarity to simplify the program by using a single algorithm for all placeholders.

How do we generalize *-longest-match and &-longest-match to handle all four cases? There are two kinds of generalization involved. We'll write a procedure longest-match that will have the same arguments as *-longest-match, plus two others, one for for the minimum size of the matched text and one for the maximum.

We'll specify the minimum size with a formal parameter `min`. (The corresponding argument will always be 0 or 1.) `Longest-match` will pass the value of `min` down to `lm-helper`, which will use it to reject potential matches that are too short.

Unfortunately, we can't use a number to specify the maximum size, because for `*` and `&` there is no maximum. Instead, `longest-match` has a formal parameter `max-one?` whose value is `#t` only for `?` and `!`.

Our earlier, special-case versions of `longest-match` were written for `*` and `&`, the placeholders for which `max-one?` will be false. For those placeholders, the new `longest-match` will be just like the earlier versions. Our next task is to generalize `longest-match` so that it can handle the `#t` cases.

Think about the meaning of the `sent-matched` and `sent-unmatched` parameters in the `lm-helper` procedures. `Sent-matched` means "the longest part of the sentence that this placeholder is still allowed to match," while `sent-unmatched` contains whatever portion of the sentence has already been disqualified from being matched by the placeholder.

Consider the behavior of `*-longest-match` when an asterisk is at the beginning of a pattern that we're trying to match against a seven-word sentence. Initially, `sent-matched` is the entire seven-word sentence, and `sent-unmatched` is empty. Then, supposing that doesn't work, `sent-matched` is a six-word sentence, while `sent-unmatched` contains the remaining word. This continues as long as no match succeeds until, near the end of `longest-match`'s job, `sent-matched` is a one-word sentence and `sent-unmatched` contains six words. At this point, the longest possible match for the asterisk is a single word.

This situation is where we want to *start* in the case of the `?` and `!` placeholders. So when we're trying to match one of these placeholders, our initialization procedure won't use the entire sentence as the initial value of `sent-matched`; rather, the initial value of `sent-matched` will be a one-word sentence, and `sent-unmatched` will contain the rest of the sentence.

```
(define (longest-match pattern-rest sent min max-one?)  ;; first version
  (cond ((empty? sent)
         (and (= min 0) (match? pattern-rest sent)))
        (max-one?
         (lm-helper pattern-rest (se (first sent)) (bf sent) min))
        (else (lm-helper pattern-rest sent '() min))))
```

```
(define (lm-helper pattern-rest sent-matched sent-unmatched min)
  (cond ((< (length sent-matched) min) #f)
        ((match? pattern-rest sent-unmatched) #t)
        ((empty? sent-matched) #f)
        (else (lm-helper pattern-rest
                         (bl sent-matched)
                         (se (last sent-matched) sent-unmatched)
                         min)))))
```

Now we can rewrite match? to use longest-match. Match? will delegate the handling of all placeholders to a subprocedure match-special that will invoke longest-match with the correct values for min and max-one? according to the table.

```
(define (match? pattern sent)                    ;; fourth version
  (cond ((empty? pattern)
         (empty? sent))
        ((special? (first pattern))
         (match-special (first pattern) (bf pattern) sent))
        ((empty? sent) #f)
        ((equal? (first pattern) (first sent))
         (match? (bf pattern) (bf sent)))
        (else #f)))

(define (special? wd)                            ;; first version
  (member? wd '(* & ? !)))

(define (match-special placeholder pattern-rest sent)  ;; first version
  (cond ((equal? placeholder '?)
         (longest-match pattern-rest sent 0 #t))
        ((equal? placeholder '!)
         (longest-match pattern-rest sent 1 #t))
        ((equal? placeholder '*)
         (longest-match pattern-rest sent 0 #f))
        ((equal? placeholder '&)
         (longest-match pattern-rest sent 1 #f))))
```

Naming the Matched Text

So far we've worked out how to match the four kinds of placeholders and return a true or false value indicating whether a match is possible. Our program is almost finished; all we need to make it useful is the facility that will let us find out *which* words in the sentence matched each placeholder in the pattern.

We don't have to change the overall structure of the program in order to make this work. But most of the procedures in the pattern matcher will have to be given an additional argument, the database of placeholder names and values that have been matched so far.* The formal parameter `known-values` will hold this database. Its value will be a sentence containing placeholder names followed by the corresponding words and an exclamation point to separate the entries, as in the examples earlier in the chapter. When we begin the search for a match, we use an empty sentence as the initial `known-values`:

```
(define (match pattern sent)
  (match-using-known-values pattern sent '()))

(define (match-using-known-values pattern sent known-values)
  ...)
```

As `match-using-known-values` matches the beginning of a pattern with the beginning of a sentence, it invokes itself recursively with an expanded `known-values` containing each newly matched placeholder. For example, in evaluating

```
(match '(!twice !other !twice) '(cry baby cry))
```

the program will call `match-using-known-values` four times:

pattern	sent	known-values
(!twice !other !twice)	(cry baby cry)	()
(!other !twice)	(baby cry)	(twice cry !)
(!twice)	(cry)	(twice cry ! other baby !)
()	()	(twice cry ! other baby !)

In the first invocation, we try to match `!twice` against some part of the sentence.

---

* The word *database* has two possible meanings in computer science, a broad meaning and a narrow one. The broad meaning, which we're using here, is a repository of information to which the program periodically adds new items for later retrieval. The narrow meaning is a collection of information that's manipulated by a *database program,* which provides facilities for adding new information, modifying existing entries, selecting entries that match some specified criterion, and so on. We'll see a database program near the end of the book.

Since ! matches exactly one word, the only possibility is to match the word `cry`. The recursive invocation, therefore, is made with the first words of the pattern and sentence removed, but with the match between `twice` and `cry` added to the database.

Similarly, the second invocation matches `!other` with `baby` and causes a third invocation with shortened pattern and sentence but a longer database.

The third invocation is a little different because the pattern contains the placeholder `!twice`, but the name `twice` is already in the database. Therefore, this placeholder can't match whatever word happens to be available; it must match the same word that it matched before. (Our program will have to check for this situation.) Luckily, the sentence does indeed contain the word `cry` at this position.

The final invocation reaches the base case of the recursion, because the pattern is empty. The value that `match-using-known-values` returns is the database in this invocation.

The Final Version

We're now ready to show you the final version of the program. The program structure is much like what you've seen before; the main difference is the database of placeholder names and values. The program must add entries to this database and must look for database entries that were added earlier. Here are the three most important procedures and how they are changed from the earlier version to implement this capability:

- `match-using-known-values`, essentially the same as what was formerly named `match?` except for bookkeeping details.
- `match-special`, similar to the old version, except that it must recognize the case of a placeholder whose name has already been seen. In this case, the placeholder can match only the same words that it matched before.
- `longest-match` and `lm-helper`, also similar to the old versions, except that they have the additional job of adding to the database the name and value of any placeholder that they match.

Here are the modified procedures. Compare them to the previous versions.

```
(define (match pattern sent)
  (match-using-known-values pattern sent '()))
```

```
(define (match-using-known-values pattern sent known-values)
  (cond ((empty? pattern)
         (if (empty? sent) known-values 'failed))
        ((special? (first pattern))
         (let ((placeholder (first pattern)))
           (match-special (first placeholder)
                          (bf placeholder)
                          (bf pattern)
                          sent
                          known-values)))
        ((empty? sent) 'failed)
        ((equal? (first pattern) (first sent))
         (match-using-known-values (bf pattern) (bf sent) known-values))
        (else 'failed)))

(define (match-special howmany name pattern-rest sent known-values)
  (let ((old-value (lookup name known-values)))
    (cond ((not (equal? old-value 'no-value))
           (if (length-ok? old-value howmany)
               (already-known-match
                 old-value pattern-rest sent known-values)
               'failed))
          ((equal? howmany '?)
           (longest-match name pattern-rest sent 0 #t known-values))
          ((equal? howmany '!)
           (longest-match name pattern-rest sent 1 #t known-values))
          ((equal? howmany '*)
           (longest-match name pattern-rest sent 0 #f known-values))
          ((equal? howmany '&)
           (longest-match name pattern-rest sent 1 #f known-values)))))

(define (longest-match name pattern-rest sent min max-one? known-values)
  (cond ((empty? sent)
         (if (= min 0)
             (match-using-known-values pattern-rest
                                       sent
                                       (add name '() known-values))
             'failed))
        (max-one?
         (lm-helper name pattern-rest (se (first sent))
                    (bf sent) min known-values))
        (else (lm-helper name pattern-rest
                         sent '() min known-values))))
```

```
(define (lm-helper name pattern-rest
                   sent-matched sent-unmatched min known-values)
  (if (< (length sent-matched) min)
      'failed
      (let ((tentative-result (match-using-known-values
                               pattern-rest
                               sent-unmatched
                               (add name sent-matched known-values))))
        (cond ((not (equal? tentative-result 'failed)) tentative-result)
              ((empty? sent-matched) 'failed)
              (else (lm-helper name
                               pattern-rest
                               (bl sent-matched)
                               (se (last sent-matched) sent-unmatched)
                               min
                               known-values))))))
```

We haven't listed all of the minor procedures that these procedures invoke. A complete listing is at the end of the chapter, but we hope that you have enough confidence about the overall program structure to be able to assume these small details will work. In the next few paragraphs we discuss some of the ways in which the procedures shown here differ from the earlier versions.

In the invocation of match-special we found it convenient to split the placeholder into its first character, the one that tells how many words can be matched, and the butfirst, which is the name of the placeholder.

What happens if match-special finds that the name is already in the database? In this situation, we don't have to try multiple possibilities for the number of words to match (the usual job of longest-match); the placeholder must match exactly the words that it matched before. In this situation, three things must be true in order for the match to succeed: (1) The first words of the sent argument must match the old value stored in the database. (2) The partial pattern that remains after this placeholder must match the rest of the sent. (3) The old value must be consistent with the number of words permitted by the howmany part of the placeholder. For example, if the pattern is

(*stuff and !stuff)

and the database says that the placeholder *stuff was matched by three words from the sentence, then the second placeholder !stuff can't possibly be matched because it accepts only one word. This third condition is actually checked first, by length-ok?, and if we pass that hurdle, the other two conditions are checked by already-known-match.

The only significant change to `longest-match` is that it invokes `add` to compute an expanded database with the newly found match added, and it uses the resulting database as an argument to `match-using-known-values`.

Abstract Data Types

As you know, a database of known values is represented in this program as a sentence in which the entries are separated by exclamation points. Where is this representation accomplished in the program you've seen? There's nothing like

```
... (sentence old-known-values name value '!) ...
```

anywhere in the procedures we've shown. Instead, the program makes reference to the database of known values through two procedure calls:

```
(lookup name known-values)                    ; in match-special
(add name matched known-values)               ; in longest-match
```

Only the procedures `lookup` and `add` manipulate the database of known values:

```
(define (lookup name known-values)
  (cond ((empty? known-values) 'no-value)
        ((equal? (first known-values) name)
         (get-value (bf known-values)))
        (else (lookup name (skip-value known-values)))))

(define (get-value stuff)
  (if (equal? (first stuff) '!)
      '()
      (se (first stuff) (get-value (bf stuff)))))

(define (skip-value stuff)
  (if (equal? (first stuff) '!)
      (bf stuff)
      (skip-value (bf stuff))))

(define (add name value known-values)
  (if (empty? name)
      known-values
      (se known-values name value '!)))
```

These procedures are full of small details. For example, it's a little tricky to extract the part of a sentence from a name to the next exclamation point. It's convenient that we could write the more important procedures, such as `longest-match`, without filling them with these details. As far as `longest-match` knows, `lookup` and `add` could be Scheme primitive procedures. In effect we've created a new data type, with `add` as its constructor and `lookup` as its selector.

Types such as these, that are invented by a programmer and aren't part of the Scheme language itself, are called *abstract data types*. Creating an abstract data type means drawing a barrier between an idea about some kind of information we want to model in a program and the particular mechanism that we use to represent the information. In this case, the information is a collection of name-value associations, and the particular mechanism is a sentence with exclamation points and so on. The pattern matcher doesn't think of the database as a sentence. For example, it would be silly to translate the database into Pig Latin or find its acronym.

Just as we distinguish the *primitive* procedures that Scheme knows all along from the *compound* procedures that the Scheme programmer defines, we could use the names "primitive data type" for types such as numbers and Booleans that are built into Scheme and "compound data type" for ones that the programmer invents by defining selectors and constructors. But "compound data type" is a bit of a pun, because it also suggests a data type built out of smaller pieces, just as a compound expression is built of smaller expressions. Perhaps that's why the name "abstract data type" has become generally accepted. It's connected to the idea of abstraction that we introduced earlier, because in order to create an abstract data type, we must specify the selectors and constructors and give names to those patterns of computation.

Backtracking and `Known-Values`

What happens to the database in cases that require backtracking, where a particular recursive call might be "on the wrong track"? Let's trace `match-using-known-values` and see what happens. (We'll use the little-people model to discuss this example, and so we're annotating each invocation in the trace with the name of its little person.)

```
> (trace match-using-known-values)
> (match '(*start me *end) '(love me do))
(match-using-known-values (*start me *end) (love me do) ())          Martha
|  (match-using-known-values (me *end) () (start love me do !))       Mercutio
|  failed
|  (match-using-known-values (me *end) (do) (start love me !))        Masayuki
|  failed
|  (match-using-known-values (me *end) (me do) (start love !))        Mohammad
|  |  (match-using-known-values (*end) (do) (start love !))           Mae
|  |  |  (match-using-known-values () () (start love ! end do !))     Merlin
|  |  |  (start love ! end do !)
|  |  (start love ! end do !)
|  (start love ! end do !)
(start love ! end do !)
(START LOVE ! END DO !)
```

Martha, the first little person shown, has an empty `known-values`. She makes three attempts to match `*start` with parts of the sentence. In each case, a little person is hired with the provisional match in his or her `known-values`. (Actually, Martha does not directly hire Mercutio and the others. Martha hires a `match-special` little person, who in turn hires a `longest-match` specialist, who hires an `lm-helper` specialist, who hires Mercutio. But that added complexity isn't important for the point we're focusing on right now, namely, how backtracking can work. Pretend Martha hires Mercutio.)

If you don't use the little-people model, but instead think about the program as if there were just one `known-values` variable, then the backtracking can indeed be very mysterious. Once a provisional match is added to the database, how is it ever removed? The answer is that it doesn't work that way. There isn't a "the" database. Instead, each little person has a separate database. If an attempted match fails, the little person who reports the failure just stops working. For example, Martha hires Mercutio to attempt a match in which the name `start` has the value `love me do`. Mercutio is unable to complete the match, and reports failure. It is Martha, not Mercutio, who then hires Masayuki to try another value for `start`. Martha's database hasn't changed, so Martha gives Masayuki a database that reflects the new trial value but not the old one.

Not every hiring of a little person starts from an empty database. When a match is partially successful, the continuation of the same attempt must benefit from the work that's already been done. So, for example, when Mohammad hires Mae, and when Mae hires Merlin, each of them passes on an extended database, not an empty one. Specifically, Mae gives Merlin the new match of the name `end` with the value `do`, but also the match of `start` with `love` that she was given by Mohammad.

So as you can see, we don't have to do anything special to keep track of our database when we backtrack; the structure of the recursion takes care of everything for free.

How We Wrote It

For explanatory purposes we've chosen to present the pieces of this program in a different order from the one in which we actually wrote them. We *did* implement the easy placeholders (! and ?) before the harder ones. But our program had provision for a database of names from the beginning.

There is no "right" way to approach a programming problem. Our particular approach was determined partly by our past experience. Each of us had written similar programs before, and we had preconceived ideas about the easy and hard parts. You might well start at a different point. For example, here is an elegant small program we'd both been shown by friends:

```
(define (match? pattern sent)
  (cond ((empty? pattern) (empty? sent))
        ((empty? sent)
         (and (equal? (first pattern) '*) (match? (bf pattern) sent)))
        ((equal? (first pattern) '*)
         (or (match? pattern (bf sent))
             (match? (bf pattern) sent)))
        (else (and (equal? (first pattern) (first sent))
                   (match? (bf pattern) (bf sent))))))
```

What's appealing about this is the funny symmetry of taking the `butfirst` of the pattern *or* of the sentence. That's not something you'd naturally think of, probably, but once you've worked out how it can work, it affects your preconceptions when you set out to write a pattern matcher yourself.

Based on that inspiration, we might well have started with the hard cases (such as *), with the idea that once they're in place, the easy cases won't change the program structure much.

Complete Program Listing

```
(define (match pattern sent)
  (match-using-known-values pattern sent '()))
```

```
(define (match-using-known-values pattern sent known-values)
  (cond ((empty? pattern)
         (if (empty? sent) known-values 'failed))
        ((special? (first pattern))
         (let ((placeholder (first pattern)))
           (match-special (first placeholder)
                          (bf placeholder)
                          (bf pattern)
                          sent
                          known-values)))
        ((empty? sent) 'failed)
        ((equal? (first pattern) (first sent))
         (match-using-known-values (bf pattern) (bf sent) known-values))
        (else 'failed)))

(define (special? wd)
  (member? (first wd) '(* & ? !)))

(define (match-special howmany name pattern-rest sent known-values)
  (let ((old-value (lookup name known-values)))
    (cond ((not (equal? old-value 'no-value))
           (if (length-ok? old-value howmany)
               (already-known-match
                 old-value pattern-rest sent known-values)
               'failed))
          ((equal? howmany '?)
           (longest-match name pattern-rest sent 0 #t known-values))
          ((equal? howmany '!)
           (longest-match name pattern-rest sent 1 #t known-values))
          ((equal? howmany '*)
           (longest-match name pattern-rest sent 0 #f known-values))
          ((equal? howmany '&)
           (longest-match name pattern-rest sent 1 #f known-values)))))

(define (length-ok? value howmany)
  (cond ((empty? value) (member? howmany '(? *)))
        ((not (empty? (bf value))) (member? howmany '(* &)))
        (else #t)))

(define (already-known-match value pattern-rest sent known-values)
  (let ((unmatched (chop-leading-substring value sent)))
    (if (not (equal? unmatched 'failed))
        (match-using-known-values pattern-rest unmatched known-values)
        'failed)))
```

```
(define (chop-leading-substring value sent)
  (cond ((empty? value) sent)
        ((empty? sent) 'failed)
        ((equal? (first value) (first sent))
         (chop-leading-substring (bf value) (bf sent)))
        (else 'failed)))

(define (longest-match name pattern-rest sent min max-one? known-values)
  (cond ((empty? sent)
         (if (= min 0)
             (match-using-known-values pattern-rest
                                       sent
                                       (add name '() known-values))
             'failed))
        (max-one?
         (lm-helper name pattern-rest (se (first sent))
                    (bf sent) min known-values))
        (else (lm-helper name pattern-rest
                         sent '() min known-values))))

(define (lm-helper name pattern-rest
                   sent-matched sent-unmatched min known-values)
  (if (< (length sent-matched) min)
      'failed
      (let ((tentative-result (match-using-known-values
                               pattern-rest
                               sent-unmatched
                               (add name sent-matched known-values))))
        (cond ((not (equal? tentative-result 'failed)) tentative-result)
              ((empty? sent-matched) 'failed)
              (else (lm-helper name
                               pattern-rest
                               (bl sent-matched)
                               (se (last sent-matched) sent-unmatched)
                               min
                               known-values))))))

;;; Known values database abstract data type

(define (lookup name known-values)
  (cond ((empty? known-values) 'no-value)
        ((equal? (first known-values) name)
         (get-value (bf known-values)))
        (else (lookup name (skip-value known-values)))))
```

```
(define (get-value stuff)
  (if (equal? (first stuff) '!)
      '()
      (se (first stuff) (get-value (bf stuff)))))

(define (skip-value stuff)
  (if (equal? (first stuff) '!)
      (bf stuff)
      (skip-value (bf stuff))))

(define (add name value known-values)
  (if (empty? name)
      known-values
      (se known-values name value '!)))
```

Exercises about Using the Pattern Matcher

16.1 Design and test a pattern that matches any sentence containing the word C three times (not necessarily next to each other).

16.2 Design and test a pattern that matches a sentence consisting of two copies of a smaller sentence, such as (a b a b).

16.3 Design and test a pattern that matches any sentence of no more than three words.

16.4 Design and test a pattern that matches any sentence of at least three words.

16.5 Show sentences of length 2, 3, and 4 that match the pattern

(*x *y *y *x)

For each length, if no sentence can match the pattern, explain why not.

16.6 Show sentences of length 2, 3, and 4 that match the pattern

(*x *y &y &x)

For each length, if no sentence can match the pattern, explain why not.

16.7 List *all* the sentences of length 6 or less, starting with a b a, that match the pattern

(*x *y *y *x)

Exercises about Implementation

16.8 Explain how `longest-match` handles an empty sentence.

16.9 Suppose the first `cond` clause in `match-using-known-values` were

```
((empty? pattern) known-values)
```

Give an example of a pattern and sentence for which the modified program would give a different result from the original.

16.10 What happens if the sentence argument—not the pattern—contains the word `*` somewhere?

16.11 For each of the following examples, how many `match-using-known-values` little people are required?

```
(match '(from me to you) '(from me to you))
(match '(*x *y *x) '(a b c a b))
(match '(*x *y *z) '(a b c a b))
(match '(*x hey *y bulldog *z) '(a hey b bulldog c))
(match '(*x a b c d e f) '(a b c d e f))
(match '(a b c d e f *x) '(a b c d e f))
```

In general, what can you say about the characteristics that make a pattern easy or hard to match?

16.12 Show a pattern with the following two properties: (1) It has at least two placeholders. (2) When you match it against any sentence, every invocation of `lookup` returns `no-value`.

16.13 Show a pattern and a sentence that can be used as arguments to `match` so that `lookup` returns (`the beatles`) at some point during the match.

16.14 Our program can still match patterns with unnamed placeholders. How would it affect the operation of the program if these unnamed placeholders were added to the database? What part of the program keeps them from being added?

16.15 Why don't `get-value` and `skip-value` check for an empty argument as the base case?

16.16 Why didn't we write the first `cond` clause in `length-ok?` as the following?

```
((and (empty? value) (member? howmany '(? *))) #t)
```

16.17 Where in the program is the initial empty database of known values established?

16.18 For the case of matching a placeholder name that's already been matched in this pattern, we said on page 268 that three conditions must be checked. For each of the three, give a pattern and sentence that the program would incorrectly match if the condition were not checked.

16.19 What will the following example do?

```
(match '(?x is *y !x) '(! is an exclamation point !))
```

Can you suggest a way to fix this problem?

16.20 Modify the pattern matcher so that a placeholder of the form `*15x` is like `*x` except that it can be matched only by exactly 15 words.

```
> (match '(*3front *back) '(your mother should know))
(FRONT YOUR MOTHER SHOULD ! BACK KNOW !)
```

16.21 Modify the pattern matcher so that a + placeholder (with or without a name attached) matches only a number:

```
> (match '(*front +middle *back) '(four score and 7 years ago))
(FRONT FOUR SCORE AND ! MIDDLE 7 ! BACK YEARS AGO !)
```

The + placeholder is otherwise like !—it must match exactly one word.

16.22 Does your favorite text editor or word processor have a search command that allows you to search for patterns rather than only specific strings of characters? Look into this and compare your editor's capabilities with that of our pattern matcher.

Part V
Abstraction

We've really been talking about abstraction all along. Whenever you find yourself performing several similar computations, such as

```
> (sentence 'she (word 'run 's))
(SHE RUNS)

> (sentence 'she (word 'walk 's))
(SHE WALKS)

> (sentence 'she (word 'program 's))
(SHE PROGRAMS)
```

and you capture the similarity in a procedure

```
(define (third-person verb)
  (sentence 'she (word verb 's)))
```

you're *abstracting* the pattern of the computation by expressing it in a form that leaves out the particular verb in any one instance.

In the preface we said that our approach to computer science is to teach you to think in larger chunks, so that you can fit larger problems in your mind at once; "abstraction" is the technical name for that chunking process.

In this part of the book we take a closer look at two specific kinds of abstraction. One is *data abstraction,* which means the invention of new data types. The other is the implementation of *higher-order functions,* an important category of the same process abstraction of which `third-person` is a trivial example.

Until now we've used words and sentences as though they were part of the natural order of things. Now we'll discover that Scheme sentences exist only in our minds and take shape through the use of constructors and selectors (`sentence`, `first`, and so on) that we wrote. The implementation of sentences is based on a more fundamental data type called *lists*. Then we'll see how lists can be used to invent another in-our-minds data type, *trees*. (The technical term for an invented data type is an *abstract* data type.)

You already know how higher-order functions can express many computational processes in a very compact form. Now we focus our attention on the higher-order *procedures* that implement those functions, exploring the mechanics by which we create these process abstractions.

17   Lists

Suppose we're using Scheme to model an ice cream shop. We'll certainly need to know all the flavors that are available:

```
(vanilla ginger strawberry lychee raspberry mocha)
```

For example, here's a procedure that models the behavior of the salesperson when you place an order:

```
(define (order flavor)
  (if (member? flavor
               '(vanilla ginger strawberry lychee raspberry mocha))
      '(coming right up!)
      (se '(sorry we have no) flavor)))
```

But what happens if we want to sell a flavor like "root beer fudge ripple" or "ultra chocolate"? We can't just put those words into a sentence of flavors, or our program will think that each word is a separate flavor. Beer ice cream doesn't sound very appealing.

What we need is a way to express a collection of items, each of which is itself a collection, like this:

```
(vanilla (ultra chocolate) (heath bar crunch) ginger (cherry garcia))
```

This is meant to represent five flavors, two of which are named by single words, and the other three of which are named by sentences.

Luckily for us, Scheme provides exactly this capability. The data structure we're using in this example is called a *list*. The difference between a sentence and a list is that the elements of a sentence must be words, whereas the elements of a list can be anything at all: words, #t, procedures, or other lists. (A list that's an element of another list is called a *sublist*. We'll use the name *structured* list for a list that includes sublists.)

Another way to think about the difference between sentences and lists is that the definition of "list" is self-referential, because a list can include lists as elements. The definition of "sentence" is not self-referential, because the elements of a sentence must be words. We'll see that the self-referential nature of recursive procedures is vitally important in coping with lists.

Another example in which lists could be helpful is the pattern matcher. We used sentences to hold `known-values` databases, such as this one:

```
(FRONT YOUR MOTHER ! BACK SHOULD KNOW !)
```

This would be both easier for you to read and easier for programs to manipulate if we used list structure to indicate the grouping instead of exclamation points:

```
((FRONT (YOUR MOTHER)) (BACK (SHOULD KNOW)))
```

We remarked when we introduced sentences that they're a feature we added to Scheme just for the sake of this book. Lists, by contrast, are at the core of what Lisp has been about from its beginning. (In fact the name "Lisp" stands for "LISt Processing.")

Selectors and Constructors

When we introduced words and sentences we had to provide ways to take them apart, such as `first`, and ways to put them together, such as `sentence`. Now we'll tell you about the selectors and constructors for lists.

The function to select the first element of a list is called `car`.* The function to select the portion of a list containing all but the first element is called `cdr`, which is

---

* Don't even try to figure out a sensible reason for this name. It's a leftover bit of history from the first computer on which Lisp was implemented. It stands for "contents of address register" (at least that's what all the books say, although it's really the address *portion* of the accumulator register). `Cdr`, coming up in the next sentence, stands for "contents of decrement register." The names seem silly in the Lisp context, but that's because the Lisp people used these register components in ways the computer designers didn't intend. Anyway, this is all very interesting to history buffs but irrelevant to our purposes. We're just showing off that one of us is actually old enough to remember these antique computers first-hand.

pronounced "could-er." These are analogous to `first` and `butfirst` for words and sentences.

Of course, we can't extract pieces of a list that's empty, so we need a predicate that will check for an empty list. It's called `null?` and it returns `#t` for the empty list, `#f` for anything else. This is the list equivalent of `empty?` for words and sentences.

There are two constructors for lists. The function `list` takes any number of arguments and returns a list with those arguments as its elements.

```
> (list (+ 2 3) 'squash (= 2 2) (list 4 5) remainder 'zucchini)
(5 SQUASH #T (4 5) #<PROCEDURE> ZUCCHINI)
```

The other constructor, `cons`, is used when you already have a list and you want to add one new element. `Cons` takes two arguments, an element and a list (in that order), and returns a new list whose `car` is the first argument and whose `cdr` is the second.

```
> (cons 'for '(no one))
(FOR NO ONE)

> (cons 'julia '())
(JULIA)
```

There is also a function that combines the elements of two or more lists into a larger list:

```
> (append '(get back) '(the word))
(GET BACK THE WORD)
```

It's important that you understand how `list`, `cons`, and `append` differ from each other:

```
> (list '(i am) '(the walrus))
((I AM) (THE WALRUS))

> (cons '(i am) '(the walrus))
((I AM) THE WALRUS)

> (append '(i am) '(the walrus))
(I AM THE WALRUS)
```

When `list` is invoked with two arguments, it considers them to be two proposed elements for a new two-element list. `List` doesn't care whether the arguments are themselves lists, words, or anything else; it just creates a new list whose elements are the arguments. In this case, it ends up with a list of two lists.

`Cons` requires that its second argument be a list.* `Cons` will extend that list to form a new list, one element longer than the original; the first element of the resulting list comes from the first argument to `cons`. In other words, when you pass `cons` two arguments, you get back a list whose `car` is the first argument to `cons` and whose `cdr` is the second argument.

Thus, in this example, the three elements of the returned list consist of the first argument as one single element, followed by *the elements of* the second argument (in this case, two words). (You may be wondering why anyone would want to use such a strange constructor instead of `list`. The answer has to do with recursive procedures, but hang on for a few paragraphs and we'll show you an example, which will help more than any explanation we could give in English.)

Finally, `append` of two arguments uses the elements of *both* arguments as elements of its return value.

Pictorially, `list` creates a list whose elements are the arguments:

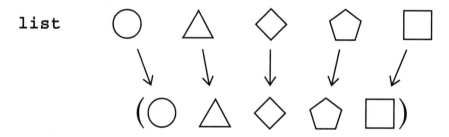

`Cons` creates an extension of its second argument with one new element:

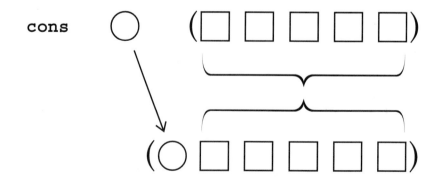

---

* This is not the whole story. See the "pitfalls" section for a slightly expanded version.

`Append` creates a list whose elements are the *elements of* the arguments, which must be lists:

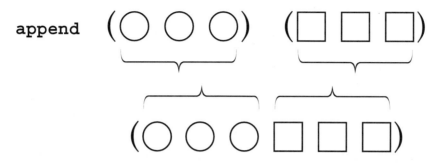

Programming with Lists

```
(define (praise flavors)
  (if (null? flavors)
      '()
      (cons (se (car flavors) '(is delicious))
            (praise (cdr flavors)))))
```

```
> (praise '(ginger (ultra chocolate) lychee (rum raisin)))
((GINGER IS DELICIOUS) (ULTRA CHOCOLATE IS DELICIOUS)
 (LYCHEE IS DELICIOUS) (RUM RAISIN IS DELICIOUS))
```

In this example our result is a *list of sentences.* That is, the result is a list that includes smaller lists as elements, but each of these smaller lists is a sentence, in which only words are allowed. That's why we used the constructor `cons` for the overall list, but `se` for each sentence within the list.

This is the example worth a thousand words that we promised, to show why `cons` is useful. `List` wouldn't work in this situation. You can use `list` only when you know exactly how many elements will be in your complete list. Here, we are writing a procedure that works for any number of elements, so we recursively build up the list, one element at a time.

In the following example we take advantage of structured lists to produce a translation dictionary. The entire dictionary is a list; each element of the dictionary, a single translation, is a two-element list; and in some cases a translation may involve a phrase rather than a single word, so we can get three deep in lists.

```
(define (translate wd)
  (lookup wd '((window fenetre) (book livre) (computer ordinateur)
               (house maison) (closed ferme) (pate pate) (liver foie)
               (faith foi) (weekend (fin de semaine))
               ((practical joke) attrape) (pal copain))))

(define (lookup wd dictionary)
  (cond ((null? dictionary) '(parlez-vous anglais?))
        ((equal? wd (car (car dictionary)))
         (car (cdr (car dictionary))))
        (else (lookup wd (cdr dictionary)))))

> (translate 'computer)
ORDINATEUR

> (translate '(practical joke))
ATTRAPE

> (translate 'recursion)
(PARLEZ-VOUS ANGLAIS?)
```

By the way, this example will help us explain why those ridiculous names `car` and `cdr` haven't died out. In this not-so-hard program we find ourselves saying

```
(car (cdr (car dictionary)))
```

to refer to the French part of the first translation in the dictionary. Let's go through that slowly. (`Car dictionary`) gives us the first element of the dictionary, one English-French pairing. `Cdr` of that first element is a one-element list, that is, all but the English word that's the first element of the pairing. What we want isn't the one-element list but rather its only element, the French word, which is its `car`.

This `car` of `cdr` of `car` business is pretty lengthy and awkward. But Scheme gives us a way to say it succinctly:

```
(cadar dictionary)
```

In general, we're allowed to use names like `cddadr` up to four deep in As and Ds. That one means

```
(cdr (cdr (car (cdr something))))
```

or in other words, take the `cdr` of the `cdr` of the `car` of the `cdr` of its argument. Notice that the order of letters A and D follows the order in which you'd write the procedure names, but (as always) the procedure that's invoked first is the one on the right. Don't make the mistake of reading `cadr` as meaning "first take the `car` and then take the `cdr`." It means "take the `car` of the `cdr`."

The most commonly used of these abbreviations are `cadr`, which selects the second element of a list; `caddr`, which selects the third element; and `cadddr`, which selects the fourth.

The Truth about Sentences

You've probably noticed that it's hard to distinguish between a sentence (which *must* be made up of words) and a list that *happens* to have words as its elements.

The fact is, sentences *are* lists. You could take `car` of a sentence, for example, and it'd work fine. Sentences are an abstract data type represented by lists. We created the sentence ADT by writing special selectors and constructors that provide a different way of using the same underlying machinery—a different interface, a different metaphor, a different point of view.

How does our sentence point of view differ from the built-in Scheme point of view using lists? There are three differences:

- A sentence can contain only words, not sublists.
- Sentence selectors are symmetrical front-to-back.
- Sentences and words have the same selectors.

All of these differences fit a common theme: Words and sentences are meant to represent English text. The three differences reflect three characteristics of English text: First, text is made of sequences of words, not complicated structures with sublists. Second, in manipulating text (for example, finding the plural of a noun) we need to look at the end of a word or sentence as often as at the beginning. Third, since words and sentences work together so closely, it makes sense to use the same tools with both. By contrast, from Scheme's ordinary point of view, an English sentence is just one particular case of a much more general data structure, whereas a symbol* is something entirely different.

---

* As we said in Chapter 5, "symbol" is the official name for words that are neither strings nor numbers.

The constructors and selectors for sentences reflect these three differences. For example, it so happens that Scheme represents lists in a way that makes it easy to find the first element, but harder to find the last one. That's reflected in the fact that there are no primitive selectors for lists equivalent to `last` and `butlast` for sentences. But we want `last` and `butlast` to be a part of the sentence package, so we have to write them in terms of the "real" Scheme list selectors. (In the versions presented here, we are ignoring the issue of applying the selectors to words.)

```
(define (first sent)                              ;;; just for sentences
  (car sent))

(define (last sent)
  (if (null? (cdr sent))
      (car sent)
      (last (cdr sent))))

(define (butfirst sent)
  (cdr sent))

(define (butlast sent)
  (if (null? (cdr sent))
      '()
      (cons (car sent) (butlast (cdr sent)))))
```

If you look "behind the curtain" at the implementation, `last` is a lot more complicated than `first`. But from the point of view of a sentence user, they're equally simple.

In Chapter 16 we used the pattern matcher's known-values database to introduce the idea of abstract data types. In that example, the most important contribution of the ADT was to isolate the details of the implementation, so that the higher-level procedures could invoke `lookup` and `add` without the clutter of looking for exclamation points. We did hint, though, that the ADT represents a shift in how the programmer thinks about the sentences that are used to represent databases; we don't take the acronym of a database, even though the database *is* a sentence and so it would be possible to apply the `acronym` procedure to it. Now, in thinking about sentences, this idea of shift in viewpoint is more central. Although sentences are represented as lists, they behave much like words, which are represented quite differently.* Our sentence mechanism highlights the *uses* of sentences, rather than the implementation.

---

* We implemented words by combining three data types that are primitive in Scheme: strings, symbols, and numbers.

Higher-Order Functions

The higher-order functions that we've used until now work only for words and sentences. But the *idea* of higher-order functions applies perfectly well to structured lists. The official list versions of `every`, `keep`, and `accumulate` are called `map`, `filter`, and `reduce`.

Map takes two arguments, a function and a list, and returns a list containing the result of applying the function to each element of the list.

```
> (map square '(9 8 7 6))
(81 64 49 36)

> (map (lambda (x) (se x x)) '(rocky raccoon))
((ROCKY ROCKY) (RACCOON RACCOON))

> (every (lambda (x) (se x x)) '(rocky raccoon))
(ROCKY ROCKY RACCOON RACCOON)

> (map car '((john lennon) (paul mccartney)
              (george harrison) (ringo starr)))
(JOHN PAUL GEORGE RINGO)

> (map even? '(9 8 7 6))
(#F #T #F #T)

> (map (lambda (x) (word x x)) 'rain)
ERROR -- INVALID ARGUMENT TO MAP: RAIN
```

The word "map" may seem strange for this function, but it comes from the mathematical study of functions, in which they talk about a *mapping* of the domain into the range. In this terminology, one talks about "mapping a function over a set" (a set of argument values, that is), and Lispians have taken over the same vocabulary, except that we talk about mapping over lists instead of mapping over sets. In any case, `map` is a genuine Scheme primitive, so it's the official grownup way to talk about an `every`-like higher-order function, and you'd better learn to like it.

Filter also takes a function and a list as arguments; it returns a list containing only those elements of the argument list for which the function returns a true value. This is the same as `keep`, except that the elements of the argument list may be sublists, and their structure is preserved in the result.

```
> (filter (lambda (flavor) (member? 'swirl flavor))
          '((rum raisin) (root beer swirl) (rocky road) (fudge swirl)))
((ROOT BEER SWIRL) (FUDGE SWIRL))

> (filter word? '((ultra chocolate) ginger lychee (raspberry sherbet)))
(GINGER LYCHEE)

> (filter (lambda (nums) (= (car nums) (cadr nums)))
          '((2 3) (4 4) (5 6) (7 8) (9 9)))
((4 4) (9 9))
```

Filter probably makes sense to you as a name; the metaphor of the air filter that allows air through but doesn't allow dirt, and so on, evokes something that passes some data and blocks other data. The only problem with the name is that it doesn't tell you whether the elements for which the predicate function returns #t are filtered in or filtered out. But you're already used to keep, and filter works the same way. Filter is not a standard Scheme primitive, but it's a universal convention; everyone defines it the same way we do.

Reduce is just like accumulate except that it works only on lists, not on words. Neither is a built-in Scheme primitive; both names are seen in the literature. (The name "reduce" is official in the languages APL and Common Lisp, which do include this higher-order function as a primitive.)

```
> (reduce * '(4 5 6))
120

> (reduce (lambda (list1 list2) (list (+ (car list1) (car list2))
                                       (+ (cadr list1) (cadr list2))))
          '((1 2) (30 40) (500 600)))
(531 642)
```

Other Primitives for Lists

The list? predicate returns #t if its argument is a list, #f otherwise.

The predicate equal?, which we've discussed earlier as applied to words and sentences, also works for structured lists.

The predicate member?, which we used in one of the examples above, isn't a true Scheme primitive, but part of the word and sentence package. (You can tell because it "takes apart" a word to look at its letters separately, something that Scheme doesn't ordinarily do.) Scheme does have a member primitive without the question mark that's like `member?` except for two differences: Its second argument must be a list (but can be a structured list); and instead of returning `#t` it returns the portion of the argument list starting with the element equal to the first argument. This will be clearer with an example:

```
> (member 'd '(a b c d e f g))
(D E F G)

> (member 'h '(a b c d e f g))
#F
```

This is the main example in Scheme of the semipredicate idea that we mentioned earlier in passing. It doesn't have a question mark in its name because it returns values other than `#t` and `#f`, but it works as a predicate because any non-`#f` value is considered true.

The only word-and-sentence functions that we haven't already mentioned are `item` and `count`. The list equivalent of `item` is called `list-ref` (short for "reference"); it's different in that it counts items from zero instead of from one and takes its arguments in the other order:

```
> (list-ref '(happiness is a warm gun) 3)
WARM
```

The list equivalent of `count` is called `length`, and it's exactly the same except that it doesn't work on words.

Association Lists

An example earlier in this chapter was about translating from English to French. This involved searching for an entry in a list by comparing the first element of each entry with the information we were looking for. A list of names and corresponding values is called an *association list,* or an *a-list.* The Scheme primitive `assoc` looks up a name in an a-list:

```
> (assoc 'george
         '((john lennon) (paul mccartney)
           (george harrison) (ringo starr)))
(GEORGE HARRISON)

> (assoc 'x '((i 1) (v 5) (x 10) (l 50) (c 100) (d 500) (m 1000)))
(X 10)

> (assoc 'ringo '((mick jagger) (keith richards) (brian jones)
                  (charlie watts) (bill wyman)))
#F
```

```
(define dictionary
  '((window fenetre) (book livre) (computer ordinateur)
    (house maison) (closed ferme) (pate pate) (liver foie)
    (faith foi) (weekend (fin de semaine))
    ((practical joke) attrape) (pal copain)))

(define (translate wd)
  (let ((record (assoc wd dictionary)))
    (if record
        (cadr record)
        '(parlez-vous anglais?))))
```

Assoc returns #f if it can't find the entry you're looking for in your association list. Our translate procedure checks for that possibility before using cadr to extract the French translation, which is the second element of an entry.

Functions That Take Variable Numbers of Arguments

In the beginning of this book we told you about some Scheme procedures that can take any number of arguments, but you haven't yet learned how to write such procedures for yourself, because Scheme's mechanism for writing these procedures requires the use of lists.

Here's a procedure that takes one or more numbers as arguments and returns true if these numbers are in increasing order:

```
(define (increasing? number . rest-of-numbers)
  (cond ((null? rest-of-numbers) #t)
        ((> (car rest-of-numbers) number)
         (apply increasing? rest-of-numbers))
        (else #f)))
```

```
> (increasing? 4 12 82)
#T

> (increasing? 12 4 82 107)
#F
```

The first novelty to notice in this program is the dot in the first line. In listing the formal parameters of a procedure, you can use a dot just before the last parameter to mean that that parameter (rest-of-numbers in this case) represents any number of arguments, including zero. The value that will be associated with this parameter when the procedure is invoked will be a list whose elements are the actual argument values.

In this example, you must invoke `increasing?` with at least one argument; that argument will be associated with the parameter `number`. If there are no more arguments, `rest-of-numbers` will be the empty list. But if there are more arguments, `rest-of-numbers` will be a list of their values. (In fact, these two cases are the same: `Rest-of-numbers` will be a list of all the remaining arguments, and if there are no such arguments, `rest-of-numbers` is a list with no elements.)

The other novelty in this example is the procedure `apply`. It takes two arguments, a procedure and a list. `Apply` invokes the given procedure with the elements of the given list as its arguments, and returns whatever value the procedure returns. Therefore, the following two expressions are equivalent:

```
(+ 3 4 5)
(apply + '(3 4 5))
```

We use `apply` in `increasing?` because we don't know how many arguments we'll need in its recursive invocation. We can't just say

```
(increasing? rest-of-numbers)
```

because that would give `increasing?` a list as its single argument, and it doesn't take lists as arguments—it takes numbers. We want *the numbers in the list* to be the arguments.

We've used the name `rest-of-numbers` as the formal parameter to suggest "the rest of the arguments," but that's not just an idea we made up. A parameter that follows a dot and therefore represents a variable number of arguments is called a *rest parameter*.

Here's a table showing the values of `number` and `rest-of-numbers` in the recursive invocations of `increasing?` for the example

```
(increasing? 3 5 8 20 6 43 72)
```

number	rest-of-numbers
3	(5 8 20 6 43 72)
5	(8 20 6 43 72)
8	(20 6 43 72)
20	(6 43 72) (returns false at this point)

In the `increasing?` example we've used one formal parameter before the dot, but you may use any number of such parameters, including zero. The number of formal parameters before the dot determines the *minimum* number of arguments that must be used when your procedure is invoked. There can be only one formal parameter *after* the dot.

Recursion on Arbitrary Structured Lists

Let's pretend we've stored this entire book in a gigantic Scheme list structure. It's a list of chapters. Each chapter is a list of sections. Each section is a list of paragraphs. Each paragraph is a list of sentences, which are themselves lists of words.

Now we want to know how many times the word "mathematicians" appears in the book. We could do it the incredibly boring way:

```
(define (appearances-in-book wd book)
  (reduce + (map (lambda (chapter) (appearances-in-chapter wd chapter))
                 book)))

(define (appearances-in-chapter wd chapter)
  (reduce + (map (lambda (section) (appearances-in-section wd section))
                 chapter)))

(define (appearances-in-section wd section)
  (reduce + (map (lambda (paragraph)
                   (appearances-in-paragraph wd paragraph))
                 section)))

(define (appearances-in-paragraph wd paragraph)
  (reduce + (map (lambda (sent) (appearances-in-sentence wd sent))
                 paragraph)))

(define (appearances-in-sentence given-word sent)
  (length (filter (lambda (sent-word) (equal? sent-word given-word))
                  sent)))
```

but that *would* be incredibly boring.

What we're going to do is similar to the reasoning we used in developing the idea of recursion in Chapter 11. There, we wrote a family of procedures named `downup1`, `downup2`, and so on; we then noticed that most of these procedures looked almost identical, and "collapsed" them into a single recursive procedure. In the same spirit, notice that all the `appearances-in-` procedures are very similar. We can make them even more similar by rewriting the last one:

```
(define (appearances-in-sentence wd sent)
  (reduce + (map (lambda (wd2) (appearances-in-word wd wd2))
                 sent)))

(define (appearances-in-word wd wd2)
  (if (equal? wd wd2) 1 0))
```

Now, just as before, we want to write a single procedure that combines all of these.

What's the base case? Books, chapters, sections, paragraphs, and sentences are all lists of smaller units. It's only when we get down to individual words that we have to do something different:

```
(define (deep-appearances wd structure)
  (if (word? structure)
      (if (equal? structure wd) 1 0)
      (reduce +
              (map (lambda (sublist) (deep-appearances wd sublist))
                   structure))))

> (deep-appearances
   'the
   '(((the man) in ((the) moon)) ate (the) potstickers))
3

> (deep-appearances 'n '(lambda (n) (if (= n 0) 1 (* n (f (- n 1)))))))
4

> (deep-appearances 'mathematicians the-book-structure)
7
```

This is quite different from the recursive situations we've seen before. What looks like a recursive call from `deep-appearances` to itself is actually inside an anonymous procedure that will be called *repeatedly* by `map`. `Deep-appearances` doesn't just call itself once in the recursive case; it uses `map` to call itself for each element of `structure`. Each of those calls returns a number; `map` returns a list of those numbers. What we want is the sum of those numbers, and that's what `reduce` will give us.

This explains why `deep-appearances` must accept words as well as lists as the `structure` argument. Consider a case like

```
(deep-appearances 'foo '((a) b))
```

Since `structure` has two elements, `map` will call `deep-appearances` twice. One of these calls uses the list `(a)` as the second argument, but the other call uses the word `b` as the second argument.

Of course, if `structure` is a word, we can't make recursive calls for its elements; that's why words are the base case for this recursion. What should `deep-appearances` return for a word? If it's the word we're looking for, that counts as one appearance. If not, it counts as no appearances.

You're accustomed to seeing the empty list as the base case in a recursive list processing procedure. Also, you're accustomed to thinking of the base case as the end of a *complete* problem; you've gone through all of the elements of a list, and there are no more elements to find. In most problems, there is only one recursive invocation that turns out to be a base case. But in using `deep-appearances`, there are *many* invocations for base cases—one for every word in the list structure. Reaching a base case doesn't mean that we've reached the end of the entire structure! You might want to trace a short example to help you understand the sequence of events.

Although there's no official name for a structure made of lists of lists of ... of lists, there *is* a common convention for naming procedures that deal with these structures; that's why we've called this procedure `deep-appearances`. The word "deep" indicates that this procedure is just like a procedure to look for the number of appearances of a word in a list, except that it looks "all the way down" into the sub-sub-· · ·-sublists instead of just looking at the elements of the top-level list.

This version of `deep-appearances`, in which higher-order procedures are used to deal with the sublists of a list, is a common programming style. But for some problems, there's another way to organize the same basic program without higher-order procedures. This other organization leads to very compact, but rather tricky, programs. It's also a widely used style, so we want you to be able to recognize it.

Here's the idea. We deal with the base case—words—just as before. But for lists we do what we often do in trying to simplify a list problem: We divide the list into its first element (its `car`) and all the rest of its elements (its `cdr`). But in this case, the resulting program is a little tricky. Ordinarily, a recursive program for lists makes a recursive call for the `cdr`, which is a list of the same kind as the whole argument, but does something non-recursive for the `car`, which is just one element of that list. This time, the `car` of the kind of structured list-of-lists we're exploring may itself be a list-of-lists! So we make a recursive call for it, as well:

```
(define (deep-appearances wd structure)
  (cond ((equal? wd structure) 1)          ; base case: desired word
        ((word? structure) 0)              ; base case: other word
        ((null? structure) 0)              ; base case: empty list
        (else (+ (deep-appearances wd (car structure))
                 (deep-appearances wd (cdr structure))))))
```

This procedure has two different kinds of base case. The first two cond clauses are similar to the base case in the previous version of deep-appearances; they deal with a "structure" consisting of a single word. If the structure is the word we're looking for, then the word appears once in it. If the structure is some other word, then the word appears zero times. The third clause is more like the base case of an ordinary list recursion; it deals with an empty list, in which case the word appears zero times in it. (This still may not be the end of the entire structure used as the argument to the top-level invocation, but may instead be merely the end of a sublist within that structure.)

If we reach the else clause, then the structure is neither a word nor an empty list. It must, therefore, be a non-empty list, with a car and a cdr. The number of appearances in the entire structure of the word we're looking for is equal to the number of appearances in the car plus the number in the cdr.

In deep-appearances the desired result is a single number. What if we want to build a new list-of-lists structure? Having used car and cdr to disassemble a structure, we can use cons to build a new one. For example, we'll translate our entire book into Pig Latin:

```
(define (deep-pigl structure)
  (cond ((word? structure) (pigl structure))
        ((null? structure) '())
        (else (cons (deep-pigl (car structure))
                    (deep-pigl (cdr structure))))))

> (deep-pigl '((this is (a structure of (words)) with)
               (a (peculiar) shape)))
((ISTHAY ISAY (AAY UCTURESTRAY OFAY (ORDSWAY)) ITHWAY)
 (AAY (ECULIARPAY) APESHAY))
```

Compare deep-pigl with an every-pattern list recursion such as praise on page 285. Both look like

```
(cons (something (car argument)) (something (cdr argument)))
```

And yet these procedures are profoundly different. `Praise` is a simple left-to-right walk through the elements of a sequence; `deep-pigl` dives in and out of sublists. The difference is a result of the fact that `praise` does one recursive call, for the `cdr`, while `deep-pigl` does two, for the `car` as well as the `cdr`. The pattern exhibited by `deep-pigl` is called `car-cdr` recursion. (Another name for it is "tree recursion," for a reason we'll see in the next chapter.)

Pitfalls

⇒ Just as we mentioned about the names `word` and `sentence`, resist the temptation to use `list` as a formal parameter. We use `lst` instead, but other alternatives are capital `L` or `seq` (for "sequence").

⇒ The list constructor `cons` does not treat its two arguments equivalently. The second one must be the list you're trying to extend. There is no equally easy way to extend a list on the right (although you can put the new element into a one-element list and use `append`). If you get the arguments backward, you're likely to get funny-looking results that aren't lists, such as

```
((3 . 2) . 1)
```

The result you get when you `cons` onto something that isn't a list is called a *pair.* It's sometimes called a "dotted pair" because of what it looks like when printed:

```
> (cons 'a 'b)
(A . B)
```

It's just the printed representation that's dotted, however; the dot isn't part of the pair any more than the parentheses around a list are elements of the list. Lists are made of pairs; that's why `cons` can construct lists. But we're not going to talk about any pairs that *aren't* part of lists, so you don't have to think about them at all, except to know that if dots appear in your results you're `cons`ing backward.

⇒ Don't get confused between lists and sentences. Sentences have no internal structure; the good aspect of this is that it's hard to make mistakes about building the structure, but the bad aspect is that you might need such a structure. You can have lists whose elements are sentences, but it's confusing if you think of the same structure sometimes as a list and sometimes as a sentence.

⇒   In reading someone else's program, it's easy not to notice that a procedure is making two recursive calls instead of just one. If you notice only the recursive call for the `cdr`, you might think you're looking at a sequential recursion.

⇒   If you're writing a procedure whose argument is a list-of-lists, it may feel funny to let it also accept a word as the argument value. People therefore sometimes insist on a list as the argument, leading to an overly complicated base case. If your base case test says

```
(word? (car structure))
```

then think about whether you'd have a better-organized program if the base case were

```
(word? structure)
```

⇒   Remember that in a deep-structure recursion you may need two base cases, one for reaching an element that isn't a sublist, and the other for an empty list, with no elements at all. (Our `deep-appearances` procedure is an example.) Don't forget the empty-list case.

Boring Exercises

17.1   What will Scheme print in response to each of the following expressions? Try to figure it out in your head before you try it on the computer.

```
> (car '(Rod Chris Colin Hugh Paul))

> (cadr '(Rod Chris Colin Hugh Paul))

> (cdr '(Rod Chris Colin Hugh Paul))

> (car 'Rod)

> (cons '(Rod Argent) '(Chris White))

> (append '(Rod Argent) '(Chris White))

> (list '(Rod Argent) '(Chris White))

> (caadr '((Rod Argent) (Chris White)
           (Colin Blunstone) (Hugh Grundy) (Paul Atkinson)))
```

```
> (assoc 'Colin '((Rod Argent) (Chris White)
                  (Colin Blunstone) (Hugh Grundy) (Paul Atkinson)))

> (assoc 'Argent '((Rod Argent) (Chris White)
                   (Colin Blunstone) (Hugh Grundy) (Paul Atkinson)))
```

17.2   For each of the following examples, write a procedure of two arguments that, when applied to the sample arguments, returns the sample result. Your procedures may not include any quoted data.

```
> (f1 '(a b c) '(d e f))
((B C D))

> (f2 '(a b c) '(d e f))
((B C) E)

> (f3 '(a b c) '(d e f))
(A B C A B C)

> (f4 '(a b c) '(d e f))
((A D) (B C E F))
```

17.3   Describe the value returned by this invocation of **map**:

```
> (map (lambda (x) (lambda (y) (+ x y))) '(1 2 3 4))
```

Real Exercises

17.4   Describe the result of calling the following procedure with a list as its argument. (See if you can figure it out before you try it.)

```
(define (mystery lst)
  (mystery-helper lst '()))

(define (mystery-helper lst other)
  (if (null? lst)
      other
      (mystery-helper (cdr lst) (cons (car lst) other))))
```

17.5 Here's a procedure that takes two numbers as arguments and returns whichever number is larger:

```
(define (max2 a b)
  (if (> b a) b a))
```

Use `max2` to implement `max`, a procedure that takes one or more numeric arguments and returns the largest of them.

17.6 Implement `append` using `car`, `cdr`, and `cons`. (Note: The built-in `append` can take any number of arguments. First write a version that accepts only two arguments. Then, optionally, try to write a version that takes any number.)

17.7 `Append` may remind you of `sentence`. They're similar, except that `append` works only with lists as arguments, whereas `sentence` will accept words as well as lists. Implement `sentence` using `append`. (Note: The built-in `sentence` can take any number of arguments. First write a version that accepts only two arguments. Then, optionally, try to write a version that takes any number. Also, you don't have to worry about the error checking that the real `sentence` does.)

17.8 Write `member`.

17.9 Write `list-ref`.

17.10 Write `length`.

17.11 Write `before-in-list?`, which takes a list and two elements of the list. It should return #t if the second argument appears in the list argument before the third argument:

```
> (before-in-list? '(back in the ussr) 'in 'ussr)
#T

> (before-in-list? '(back in the ussr) 'the 'back)
#F
```

The procedure should also return `#f` if either of the supposed elements doesn't appear at all.

17.12 Write a procedure called `flatten` that takes as its argument a list, possibly including sublists, but whose ultimate building blocks are words (not Booleans or procedures). It should return a sentence containing all the words of the list, in the order in which they appear in the original:

```
> (flatten '(((a b) c (d e)) (f g) ((((h))) (i j) k)))
(A B C D E F G H I J K)
```

17.13 Here is a procedure that counts the number of words anywhere within a structured list:

```
(define (deep-count lst)
  (cond ((null? lst) 0)
        ((word? (car lst)) (+ 1 (deep-count (cdr lst))))
        (else (+ (deep-count (car lst))
                 (deep-count (cdr lst))))))
```

Although this procedure works, it's more complicated than necessary. Simplify it.

17.14 Write a procedure `branch` that takes as arguments a list of numbers and a nested list structure. It should be the list-of-lists equivalent of `item`, like this:

```
> (branch '(3) '((a b) (c d) (e f) (g h)))
(E F)

> (branch '(3 2) '((a b) (c d) (e f) (g h)))
F

> (branch '(2 3 1 2) '((a b) ((c d) (e f) ((g h) (i j)) k) (l m)))
H
```

In the last example above, the second element of the list is

```
((C D) (E F) ((G H) (I J)) K)
```

The third element of that smaller list is `((G H) (I J))`; the first element of that is `(G H)`; and the second element of *that* is just `H`.

17.15 Modify the pattern matcher to represent the `known-values` database as a list of two-element lists, as we suggested at the beginning of this chapter.

17.16 Write a predicate `valid-infix?` that takes a list as argument and returns `#t` if and only if the list is a legitimate infix arithmetic expression (alternating operands and operators, with parentheses—that is, sublists—allowed for grouping).

```
> (valid-infix? '(4 + 3 * (5 - 2)))
#T

> (valid-infix? '(4 + 3 * (5 2)))
#F
```

Apple Tree in Blossom, Piet Mondrian (1912)

18   Trees

The big advantage of full-featured lists over sentences is their ability to represent *structure* in our data by means of sublists. In this chapter we'll look at examples in which we use lists and sublists to represent two-dimensional information structures. The kinds of structures we'll consider are called *trees* because they resemble trees in nature:

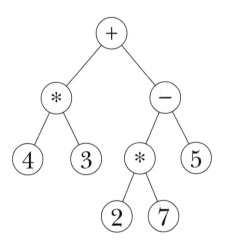

The components of a tree are called *nodes*. At the top is the *root node* of the tree; in the interior of the diagram there are *branch nodes;* at the bottom are the *leaf nodes*, from which no further branches extend.

We're going to begin by considering a tree as an abstract data type, without thinking about how lists are used to represent trees. For example, we'll construct trees using a procedure named `make-node`, as if that were a Scheme primitive. About halfway through the chapter, we'll explore the relationship between trees and lists.

Example: The World

Here is a tree that represents the world:

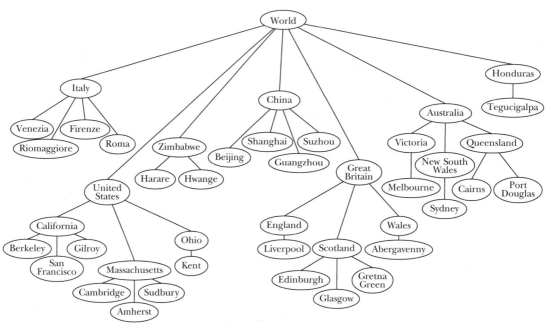

Each node in the tree represents some region of the world. Consider the node labeled "Great Britain." There are two parts to this node: The obvious part is the label itself, the name "Great Britain." But the regions of the world that are included within Great Britain—that is, the nodes that are attached beneath Great Britain in the figure—are also part of this node.

We say that every node has a *datum* and zero or more *children*. For the moment, let's just say that the datum can be either a word or a sentence. The children, if any, are themselves trees. Notice that this definition is recursive—a tree is made up of trees. (What's the base case?)

This family metaphor is also part of the terminology of trees.* We say that a node is the *parent* of another node, or that two nodes are *siblings*. In more advanced treatments, you even hear things like "grandparent" and "cousin," but we won't get into that.

---

* Contrariwise, the tree metaphor is also part of the terminology of families.

What happens when you prune an actual tree by cutting off a branch? The cut-off part is essentially a tree in itself, with a smaller trunk and fewer branches. The metaphor isn't perfect because the cut-off part doesn't have roots, but still, we can stick the end in the ground and hope that the cut-off end will take root as a new tree.

It's the same with a country in our example; each country is a branch node of the entire world tree, but also a tree in itself. Depending on how you think about it, Great Britain can be either a component of the entire world or a collection of smaller locations. So the branch node that represents Great Britain is the root node of a *subtree* of the entire tree.

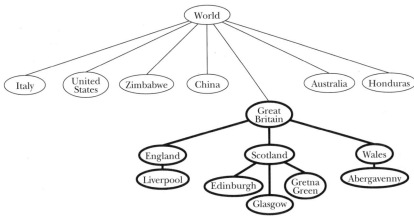

What is a node? It might seem natural to think of a node as being just the information in one of the circles in the diagram—that is, to think of a node as including only its datum. In that way of thinking, each node would be separate from every other node, just as the words in a sentence are all separate elements. However, it will be more useful to think of a node as a structure that includes everything below that circle also: the datum and the children. So when we think of the node for Great Britain, we're thinking not only of the name "Great Britain," but also of everything *in* Great Britain. From this perspective, the root node of a tree includes the entire tree. We might as well say that the node *is* the tree.

The constructor for a tree is actually the constructor for one node, its root node. Our constructor for trees is therefore called make-node. It takes two arguments: the datum and a (possibly empty) list of children. As the following example shows, constructing what we think of as one tree requires the construction of many such nodes.

```
(define world-tree                              ;; painful-to-type version
  (make-node
   'world
   (list (make-node
          'italy
          (list (make-node 'venezia '())
                (make-node 'riomaggiore '())
                (make-node 'firenze '())
                (make-node 'roma '())))
         (make-node
          '(united states)
          (list (make-node 'california
                           (list (make-node 'berkeley '())
                                 (make-node '(san francisco) '())
                                 (make-node 'gilroy '())))
                (make-node 'massachusetts
                           (list (make-node 'cambridge '())
                                 (make-node 'amherst '())
                                 (make-node 'sudbury '())))))))))
```

You'll notice that we haven't defined all of the places shown in the figure. That's because we got tired of doing all this typing; we're going to invent some abbreviations later. For now, we'll take time out to show you the selectors for trees.

```
> (datum world-tree)
WORLD

> (datum (car (children world-tree)))
ITALY

> (datum (car (children (cadr (children world-tree)))))
CALIFORNIA

> (datum (car (children (car (children
                              (cadr (children world-tree)))))))
BERKELEY
```

Datum of a tree node returns the datum of that node. Children of a node returns a list of the children of the node. (A list of trees is called a *forest*.)

Here are some abbreviations to help us construct the world tree with less typing. Unlike make-node, datum, and children, which are intended to work on trees in general, these abbreviations were designed with the world tree specifically in mind:

```
(define (leaf datum)
  (make-node datum '()))

(define (cities name-list)
  (map leaf name-list))
```

With these abbreviations the world tree is somewhat easier to define:

```
(define world-tree
  (make-node
   'world
   (list (make-node
           'italy
           (cities '(venezia riomaggiore firenze roma)))
         (make-node
          '(united states)
          (list (make-node
                  'california
                  (cities '(berkeley (san francisco) gilroy)))
                (make-node
                 'massachusetts
                 (cities '(cambridge amherst sudbury)))
                (make-node 'ohio (cities '(kent)))))
         (make-node 'zimbabwe (cities '(harare hwange)))
         (make-node 'china
                    (cities '(beijing shanghai guangzhou suzhou)))
         (make-node
          '(great britain)
          (list
           (make-node 'england (cities '(liverpool)))
           (make-node 'scotland
                      (cities '(edinburgh glasgow (gretna green))))
           (make-node 'wales (cities '(abergavenny)))))
         (make-node
          'australia
          (list
           (make-node 'victoria (cities '(melbourne)))
           (make-node '(new south wales) (cities '(sydney)))
           (make-node 'queensland
                      (cities '(cairns (port douglas))))))
         (make-node 'honduras (cities '(tegucigalpa))))))
```

How Big Is My Tree?

Now that we have the tree, how many cities are there in our world?

```
(define (count-leaves tree)
  (if (leaf? tree)
      1
      (reduce + (map count-leaves (children tree)))))

(define (leaf? node)
  (null? (children node)))

> (count-leaves world-tree)
27
```

At first glance, this may seem like a simple case of recursion, with `count-leaves` calling `count-leaves`. But since what looks like a single recursive call is really a call to `map`, it is equivalent to *several* recursive calls, one for each child of the given tree node.

Mutual Recursion

In Chapter 14 we wrote recursive procedures that were equivalent to using higher-order functions. Let's do the same for `count-leaves`.

```
(define (count-leaves tree)
  (if (leaf? tree)
      1
      (count-leaves-in-forest (children tree))))

(define (count-leaves-in-forest forest)
  (if (null? forest)
      0
      (+ (count-leaves (car forest))
         (count-leaves-in-forest (cdr forest)))))
```

Note that `count-leaves` calls `count-leaves-in-forest`, and `count-leaves-in-forest` calls `count-leaves`. This pattern is called *mutual recursion*.

Mutual recursion is often a useful technique for dealing with trees. In the typical recursion we've seen before this chapter, we've moved sequentially through a list or sentence, with each recursive call taking us one step to the right. In the following paragraphs we present three different models to help you think about how the shape of a tree gives rise to a mutual recursion.

In the first model, we're going to think of `count-leaves` as an initialization procedure, and `count-leaves-in-forest` as its helper procedure. Suppose we want to count the leaves of a tree. Unless the argument is a very shallow* tree, this will involve counting the leaves of all of the children of that tree. What we want is a straightforward sequential recursion over the list of children. But we're given the wrong argument: the tree itself, not its list of children. So we need an initialization procedure, `count-leaves`, whose job is to extract the list of children and invoke a helper procedure, `count-leaves-in-forest`, with that list as argument.

The helper procedure follows the usual sequential list pattern: Do something to the `car` of the list, and recursively handle the `cdr` of the list. Now, what do we have to do to the `car`? In the usual sequential recursion, the `car` of the list is something simple, such as a word. What's special about trees is that here the `car` is itself a tree, just like the entire data structure we started with. Therefore, we must invoke a procedure whose domain is trees: `count-leaves`.

This model is built on two ideas. One is the idea of the domain of a function; the reason we need two procedures is that we need one that takes a tree as its argument and one that takes a list of trees as its argument. The other idea is the leap of faith; we assume that the invocation of `count-leaves` within `count-leaves-in-forest` will correctly handle each child without tracing the exact sequence of events.

The second model is easier to state but less rigorous. Because of the two-dimensional nature of trees, in order to visit every node we have to be able to move in two different directions. From a given node we have to be able to move *down* to its children, but from each child we must be able to move *across* to its next sibling.

The job of `count-leaves-in-forest` is to move from left to right through a list of children. (It does this using the more familiar kind of recursion, in which it invokes itself directly.) The downward motion happens in `count-leaves`, which moves down one level by invoking `children`. How does the program move down more than one level? At each level, `count-leaves` is invoked recursively from `count-leaves-in-forest`.

The third model is also based on the two-dimensional nature of trees. Imagine for a moment that each node in the tree has at most one child. In that case, `count-leaves` could move from the root down to the single leaf with a structure very similar to the actual procedure, but carrying out a sequential recursion:

---

* You probably think of trees as being short or tall. But since our trees are upside-down, the convention is to call them shallow or deep.

```
(define (count-leaf tree)
  (if (leaf? tree)
      1
      (count-leaf (child tree))))
```

The trouble with this, of course, is that at each downward step there isn't a single "next" node. Instead of a single path from the root to the leaf, there are multiple paths from the root to many leaves. To make our idea of downward motion through sequential recursion work in a real tree, at each level we must "clone" `count-leaves` as many times as there are children. `Count-leaves-in-forest` is the factory that manufactures the clones. It hires one `count-leaves` little person for each child and accumulates their results.

The key point in recursion on trees is that each child of a tree is itself a perfectly good tree. This recursiveness in the nature of trees gives rise to a very recursive structure for programs that use trees. The reason we say "very" recursive is that each invocation of `count-leaves` causes not just one but several recursive invocations, one for each child, by way of `count-leaves-in-forest`.

In fact, we use the name *tree recursion* for any situation in which a procedure invocation results in more than one recursive call, even if there isn't an argument that's a tree. The computation of Fibonacci numbers from Chapter 13 is an example of a tree recursion with no tree. The `car-cdr` recursions in Chapter 17 are also tree recursions; any structured list-of-lists has a somewhat tree-like, two-dimensional character even though it doesn't use the formal mechanisms we're exploring in this chapter. The `cdr` recursion is a "horizontal" one, moving from one element to another within the same list; the `car` recursion is a "vertical" one, exploring a sublist of the given list.

Searching for a Datum in the Tree

Procedures that explore trees aren't always as simple as `count-leaves`. We started with that example because we could write it using higher-order functions, so that you'd understand the structure of the problem before we had to take on the complexity of mutual recursion. But many tree problems don't quite fit our higher-order functions.

For example, let's write a predicate `in-tree?` that takes the name of a place and a tree as arguments and tells whether or not that place is in the tree. It *is* possible to make it work with `filter`:

```
(define (in-tree? place tree)
  (or (equal? place (datum tree))
      (not (null? (filter (lambda (subtree) (in-tree? place subtree))
                          (children tree))))))
```

This awkward construction, however, also performs unnecessary computation. If the place we're looking for happens to be in the first child of a node, `filter` will nevertheless look in all the other children as well. We can do better by replacing the use of `filter` with a mutual recursion:

```
(define (in-tree? place tree)
  (or (equal? place (datum tree))
      (in-forest? place (children tree))))

(define (in-forest? place forest)
  (if (null? forest)
      #f
      (or (in-tree? place (car forest))
          (in-forest? place (cdr forest)))))

> (in-tree? 'abergavenny world-tree)
#T

> (in-tree? 'abbenay world-tree)
#F

> (in-tree? 'venezia (cadr (children world-tree)))
#F
```

Although any mutual recursion is a little tricky to read, the structure of this program does fit the way we'd describe the algorithm in English. A place is in a tree if one of two conditions holds: the place is the datum at the root of the tree, or the place is (recursively) in one of the child trees of this tree. That's what `in-tree?` says. As for `in-forest?`, it says that a place is in one of a group of trees if the place is in the first tree, or if it's in one of the remaining trees.

Locating a Datum in the Tree

Our next project is similar to the previous one, but a little more intricate. We'd like to be able to locate a city and find out all of the larger regions that enclose the city. For example, we want to say

```
> (locate 'berkeley world-tree)
(WORLD (UNITED STATES) CALIFORNIA BERKELEY)
```

Instead of just getting a yes-or-no answer about whether a city is in the tree, we now want to find out *where* it is.

The algorithm is recursive: To look for Berkeley within the world, we need to be able to look for Berkeley within any subtree. The `world` node has several children (countries). `Locate` recursively asks each of those children to find a path to Berkeley. All but one of the children return #f, because they can't find Berkeley within their territory. But the (united states) node returns

```
((UNITED STATES) CALIFORNIA BERKELEY)
```

To make a complete path, we just prepend the name of the current node, `world`, to this path. What happens when `locate` tries to look for Berkeley in Australia? Since all of Australia's children return #f, there is no path to Berkeley from Australia, so `locate` returns #f.

```
(define (locate city tree)
  (if (equal? city (datum tree))
      (list city)
      (let ((subpath (locate-in-forest city (children tree))))
        (if subpath
            (cons (datum tree) subpath)
            #f))))

(define (locate-in-forest city forest)
  (if (null? forest)
      #f
      (or (locate city (car forest))
          (locate-in-forest city (cdr forest)))))
```

Compare the structure of `locate` with that of `in-tree?`. The helper procedures `in-forest?` and `locate-in-forest` are almost identical. The main procedures look different, because `locate` has a harder job, but both of them check for two possibilities: The city might be the datum of the argument node, or it might belong to one of the child trees.

Representing Trees as Lists

We've done a lot with trees, but we haven't yet talked about the way Scheme stores trees internally. How do `make-node`, `datum`, and `children` work? It turns out to be very convenient to represent trees in terms of lists.

```
(define (make-node datum children)
  (cons datum children))
```

```
(define (datum node)
  (car node))

(define (children node)
  (cdr node))
```

In other words, a tree is a list whose first element is the datum and whose remaining elements are subtrees.

```
> world-tree
(WORLD
   (ITALY (VENEZIA) (RIOMAGGIORE) (FIRENZE) (ROMA))
   ((UNITED STATES)
    (CALIFORNIA (BERKELEY) ((SAN FRANCISCO)) (GILROY))
    (MASSACHUSETTS (CAMBRIDGE) (AMHERST) (SUDBURY))
    (OHIO (KENT)))
   (ZIMBABWE (HARARE) (HWANGE))
   (CHINA (BEIJING) (SHANGHAI) (GUANGSZHOU) (SUZHOW))
   ((GREAT BRITAIN)
    (ENGLAND (LIVERPOOL))
    (SCOTLAND (EDINBURGH) (GLASGOW) ((GRETNA GREEN)))
    (WALES (ABERGAVENNY)))
   (AUSTRALIA
    (VICTORIA (MELBOURNE))
    ((NEW SOUTH WALES) (SYDNEY))
    (QUEENSLAND (CAIRNS) ((PORT DOUGLAS))))
   (HONDURAS (TEGUCIGALPA)))

> (car (children world-tree))
(ITALY (VENEZIA) (RIOMAGGIORE) (FIRENZE) (ROMA))
```

Ordinarily, however, we're not going to print out trees in their entirety. As in the locate example, we'll extract just some subset of the information and put it in a more readable form.

Abstract Data Types

The procedures make-node, datum, and children define an abstract data type for trees. Using this ADT, we were able to write several useful procedures to manipulate trees before pinning down exactly how a tree is represented as a Scheme list.

Although it would be possible to refer to the parts of a node by using car and cdr directly, your programs will be more readable if you use the ADT-specific selectors and constructors. Consider this example:

```
(in-tree? 'venezia (caddr world-tree))
```

What does `caddr` mean in this context? Is the `caddr` of a tree a datum? A child? A forest? Of course you could work it out by careful reasoning, but the form in which we presented this example originally was much clearer:

```
(in-tree? 'venezia (cadr (children world-tree)))
```

Even better would be

```
(in-tree? 'venezia (list-ref (children world-tree) 1))
```

Using the appropriate selectors and constructors is called *respecting* the data abstraction. Failing to use the appropriate selectors and constructors is called a *data abstraction violation*.

Since we wrote the selectors and constructor for trees ourselves, we could have defined them to use some different representation:

```
(define (make-node datum children)
  (list 'the 'node 'with 'datum datum 'and 'children children))

(define (datum node) (list-ref node 4))

(define (children node) (list-ref node 7))

> (make-node 'italy (cities '(venezia riomaggiore firenze roma)))
(THE NODE WITH DATUM ITALY AND CHILDREN
    ((THE NODE WITH DATUM VENEZIA AND CHILDREN ())
     (THE NODE WITH DATUM RIOMAGGIORE AND CHILDREN ())
     (THE NODE WITH DATUM FIRENZE AND CHILDREN ())
     (THE NODE WITH DATUM ROMA AND CHILDREN ())))
```

You might expect that this change in the representation would require changes to all the procedures we wrote earlier, such as `count-leaves`. But in fact, those procedures would continue to work perfectly because they don't see the representation. (They respect the data abstraction.) As long as `datum` and `children` find the right information, it doesn't matter how the trees are stored. All that matters is that the constructors and selectors have to be compatible with each other.

On the other hand, the example in this section in which we violated the data abstraction by using `caddr` to find the second child of `world-tree` would fail if we changed the representation. Many cases like this one, in which formerly working programs failed after a change in representation, led programmers to use such moralistic terms as "respecting" and "violating" data abstractions.*

An Advanced Example: Parsing Arithmetic Expressions

Consider the notation for arithmetic expressions. Scheme uses *prefix* notation: (+ 3 4). By contrast, people who aren't Scheme programmers generally represent arithmetic computations using an *infix* notation, in which the function symbol goes between two arguments: $3 + 4$.

Our goal in this section is to translate an infix arithmetic expression into a tree representing the computation. This translation process is called *parsing* the expression. For example, we'll turn the expression

$$4 + 3 \times 7 - 5 / (3 + 4) + 6$$

into the tree

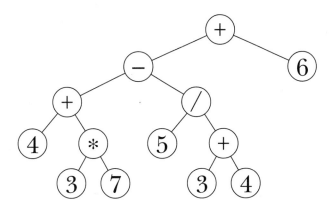

---

* Another example of a data abstraction violation is in Chapter 16. When `match` creates an empty known-values database, we didn't use a constructor. Instead, we merely used a quoted empty sentence:

```
(define (match pattern sent)
  (match-using-known-values pattern sent '()))
```

The point of using a tree is that it's going to be very easy to perform the computation once we have it in tree form. In the original infix form, it's hard to know what to do first, because there are *precedence* rules that determine an implicit grouping: Multiplication and division come before addition and subtraction; operations with the same precedence are done from left to right. Our sample expression is equivalent to

$$(((4 + (3 \times 7)) - (5/(3 + 4))) + 6)$$

In the tree representation, it's easy to see that the operations nearer the leaves are done first; the root node is the last operation, because it depends on the results of lower-level operations.

Our program will take as its argument an infix arithmetic expression in the form of a list:

```
> (parse '(4 + 3 * 7 - 5 / (3 + 4) + 6))
```

Each element of the list must be one of three things: a number; one of the four symbols +, -, *, or /; or a sublist (such as the three-element list (3 + 4) in this example) satisfying the same rule. (You can imagine that we're implementing a pocket calculator. If we were implementing a computer programming language, then we'd also accept variable names as operands. But we're not bothering with that complication because it doesn't really affect the part of the problem about turning the expression into a tree.)

What makes this problem tricky is that we can't put the list elements into the tree as soon as we see them. For example, the first three elements of our sample list are 4, +, and 3. It's tempting to build a subtree of those three elements:

But if you compare this picture with the earlier picture of the correct tree, you'll see that the second argument to this + invocation isn't the number 3, but rather the subexpression 3 * 7.

By this reasoning you might think that we have to examine the entire expression before we can start building the tree. But in fact we can sometimes build a subtree with confidence. For example, when we see the minus sign in our sample expression, we can tell that the subexpression 3 * 7 that comes before it is complete, because * has higher precedence than − does.

Here's the plan. The program will examine its argument from left to right. Since the program can't finish processing each list element right away, it has to maintain information about the elements that have been examined but not entirely processed. It's going to be easier to maintain that information in two parts: one list for still-pending operations and another for still-pending operands. Here are the first steps in parsing our sample expression; the program examines the elements of the argument, putting numbers onto the operand list and operation symbols onto the operation list:*

Remaining Expression	Operations	Operands
4+3*7−5/(3+4)+6	()	()
+3*7−5/(3+4)+6	()	(④)
3*7−5/(3+4)+6	(+)	(④)
*7−5/(3+4)+6	(+)	(③ ④)

At this point, the program is looking at the * operator in the infix expression. If this newly seen operator had lower precedence than the + that's already at the head of the list of operations, then it would be time to carry out the + operation by creating a tree with + at the root and the first two operands in the list as its children. Instead, since * has higher precedence than +, the program isn't ready to create a subtree but must instead add the * to its operation list.

7−5/(3+4)+6	(* +)	(③ ④)
−5/(3+4)+6	(* +)	(⑦ ③ ④)

This time, the newly seen − operation has lower precedence than the * at the head of the operation list. Therefore, it's time for the program to *handle* the * operator, by

---

* Actually, as we'll see shortly, the elements of the operand list are trees, so what we put in the operand list is a one-node tree whose datum is the number.

making a subtree containing that operator and the first two elements of the operand list. This new subtree becomes the new first element of the operand list.

$$-5/(3+4)+6 \qquad (+) \qquad \left(\underset{3 \quad 7}{*} \quad 4 \right)$$

Because the program decided to handle the waiting * operator, it still hasn't moved the − operator from the infix expression to the operator list. Now the program must compare − with the + at the head of the list. These two operators have the same precedence. Since we want to carry out same-precedence operators from left to right, it's time to handle the + operator.

$$-5/(3+4)+6 \qquad () \qquad \left(\underset{4 \quad \underset{3 \quad 7}{*}}{+} \right)$$

Finally the program can move the − operator onto the operator list. The next several steps are similar to ones we've already seen.

$$5/(3+4)+6 \qquad (-) \qquad \left(\underset{4 \quad \underset{3 \quad 7}{*}}{+} \right)$$

$$/(3+4)+6 \qquad (-) \qquad \left(5 \quad \underset{4 \quad \underset{3 \quad 7}{*}}{+} \right)$$

$$(3+4)+6 \qquad (/\ -) \qquad \left(5 \quad \underset{4 \quad \underset{3 \quad 7}{*}}{+} \right)$$

This is a new situation: The first unseen element of the infix expression is neither a number nor an operator, but a sublist. We recursively `parse` this subexpression, adding the resulting tree to the operand list.

Then we proceed as before, processing the / because it has higher precedence than the +, then the − because it has the same priority as the +, and so on.

Once the program has examined every element of the infix expression, the operators remaining on the operator list must be handled. In this case there is only one such operator. Once the operators have all been handled, there should be one element remaining on the operand list; that element is the desired tree for the entire original expression.

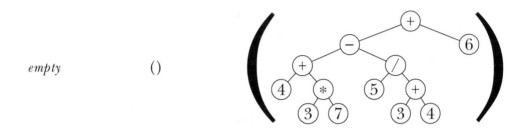

empty   ()

The following program implements this algorithm. It works only for correctly formed infix expressions; if given an argument like (3 + *), it'll give an incorrect result or a Scheme error.

```
(define (parse expr)
  (parse-helper expr '() '()))

(define (parse-helper expr operators operands)
  (cond ((null? expr)
         (if (null? operators)
             (car operands)
             (handle-op '() operators operands)))
        ((number? (car expr))
         (parse-helper (cdr expr)
                       operators
                       (cons (make-node (car expr) '()) operands)))
        ((list? (car expr))
         (parse-helper (cdr expr)
                       operators
                       (cons (parse (car expr)) operands)))
        (else (if (or (null? operators)
                      (> (precedence (car expr))
                         (precedence (car operators))))
                  (parse-helper (cdr expr)
                                (cons (car expr) operators)
                                operands)
                  (handle-op expr operators operands)))))
```

```
(define (handle-op expr operators operands)
  (parse-helper expr
                (cdr operators)
                (cons (make-node (car operators)
                                 (list (cadr operands) (car operands)))
                      (cddr operands))))

(define (precedence oper)
  (if (member? oper '(+ -)) 1 2))
```

We promised that after building the tree it would be easy to compute the value of the expression. Here is the program to do that:

```
(define (compute tree)
  (if (number? (datum tree))
      (datum tree)
      ((function-named-by (datum tree))
       (compute (car (children tree)))
       (compute (cadr (children tree))))))

(define (function-named-by oper)
  (cond ((equal? oper '+) +)
        ((equal? oper '-) -)
        ((equal? oper '*) *)
        ((equal? oper '/) /)
        (else (error "no such operator as" oper))))

> (compute (parse '(4 + 3 * 7 - 5 / (3 + 4) + 6)))
30.285714285714
```

Pitfalls

⇒ A leaf node is a perfectly good actual argument to a tree procedure, even though the picture of a leaf node doesn't look treeish because there aren't any branches. A common mistake is to make the base case of the recursion be a node whose children are leaves, instead of a node that's a leaf itself.

⇒ The value returned by `children` is not a tree, but a forest. It's therefore not a suitable actual argument to a procedure that expects a tree.

Exercises

18.1 What does

```
((SAN FRANCISCO))
```

mean in the printout of `world-tree`? Why two sets of parentheses?

18.2 Suppose we change the definition of the tree constructor so that it uses `list` instead of `cons`:

```
(define (make-node datum children)
  (list datum children))
```

How do we have to change the selectors so that everything still works?

18.3 Write `depth`, a procedure that takes a tree as argument and returns the largest number of nodes connected through parent-child links. That is, a leaf node has depth 1; a tree in which all the children of the root node are leaves has depth 2. Our world tree has depth 4 (because the longest path from the root to a leaf is, for example, world, country, state, city).

18.4 Write `count-nodes`, a procedure that takes a tree as argument and returns the total number of nodes in the tree. (Earlier we counted the number of *leaf* nodes.)

18.5 Write `prune`, a procedure that takes a tree as argument and returns a copy of the tree, but with all the leaf nodes of the original tree removed. (If the argument to `prune` is a one-node tree, in which the root node has no children, then `prune` should return `#f` because the result of removing the root node wouldn't be a tree.)

18.6 Write a program `parse-scheme` that parses a Scheme arithmetic expression into the same kind of tree that `parse` produces for infix expressions. Assume that all procedure invocations in the Scheme expression have two arguments.

The resulting tree should be a valid argument to `compute`:

```
> (compute (parse-scheme '(* (+ 4 3) 2)))
14
```

(You can solve this problem without the restriction to two-argument invocations if you rewrite `compute` so that it doesn't assume every branch node has two children.)

19   Implementing Higher-Order Functions

This chapter is about writing *higher-order procedures*—that is, procedures that implement higher-order functions. We are going to study the implementation of **every**, **keep**, and so on.

Really there are no new techniques involved. You know how to write recursive procedures that follow the **every** pattern, the **keep** pattern, and so on; it's a small additional step to generalize those patterns. The truly important point made in this chapter is that you aren't limited to a fixed set of higher-order functions. If you feel a need for a new one, you can implement it.

Generalizing Patterns

In Chapter 14, we showed you the procedures **square-sent** and **pigl-sent**, which follow the **every** pattern of recursion. In order to write the general tool, **every** itself, we have to *generalize the pattern* that those two have in common.

Before we get to writing higher-order procedures, let's look at a simpler case of generalizing patterns.

Suppose we want to find out the areas of several different kinds of shapes, given one linear dimension. A straightforward way would be to do it like this:

```
(define pi 3.141592654)

(define (square-area r) (* r r))

(define (circle-area r) (* pi r r))

(define (sphere-area r) (* 4 pi r r))
```

```
(define (hexagon-area r) (* (sqrt 3) 1.5 r r))

> (square-area 6)
36

> (circle-area 5)
78.53981635
```

This works fine, but it's somewhat tedious to define all four of these procedures, given that they're so similar. Each one returns the square of its argument times some constant factor; the only difference is the constant factor.

We want to generalize the pattern that these four procedures exhibit. Each of these procedures has a particular constant factor built in to its definition. What we'd like instead is one single procedure that lets you choose a constant factor when you invoke it. This new procedure will take a second argument besides the linear dimension **r** (the radius or side): a **shape** argument whose value is the desired constant factor.

```
(define (area shape r) (* shape r r))
(define square 1)
(define circle pi)
(define sphere (* 4 pi))
(define hexagon (* (sqrt 3) 1.5))

> (area sphere 7)
615.752160184
```

What's the point? We started with several procedures. Then we found that they had certain points of similarity and certain differences. In order to write a single procedure that generalizes the points of similarity, we had to use an additional argument for each point of difference. (In this example, there was only one point of difference.)

In fact, *every* procedure with arguments is a generalization in the same way. Even **square-area**, which we presented as the special case to be generalized, is more general than these procedures:

```
(define (area-of-square-of-side-5)
  (* 5 5))

(define (area-of-square-of-side-6)
  (* 6 6))
```

These may seem too trivial to be taken seriously. Indeed, nobody would write such procedures. But it's possible to take the area of a particular size square without using a procedure at all, and then later discover that you need to deal with squares of several sizes.

This idea of using a procedure to generalize a pattern is part of the larger idea of abstraction that we've been discussing throughout the book. We notice an algorithm that we need to use repeatedly, and so we separate the algorithm from any particular data values and give it a name.

The idea of generalization may seem obvious in the example about areas of squares. But when we apply the same idea to generalizing over a function, rather than merely generalizing over a number, we gain the enormous expressive power of higher-order functions.

The **Every** Pattern Revisited

Here again is the **every** template:

```
(define (every-something sent)
  (if (empty? sent)
      '()
      (se (_____ (first sent))
          (every-something (bf sent)))))
```

You've been writing **every**-like procedures by filling in the blank with a specific function. To generalize the pattern, we'll use the trick of adding an argument, as we discussed in the last section.

```
(define (every fn sent)
  (if (empty? sent)
      '()
      (se (fn (first sent))
          (every fn (bf sent)))))
```

This is hardly any work at all for something that seemed as mysterious as **every** probably did when you first saw it.

Recall that **every** will also work if you pass it a word as its second argument. The version shown here does indeed work for words, because **first** and **butfirst** work for words. So probably "**stuff**" would be a better formal parameter than "**sent**." (The result from `every` is always a sentence, because `sentence` is used to construct the result.)

The Difference between `Map` and `Every`

Here's the definition of the `map` procedure:

```
(define (map fn lst)
  (if (null? lst)
      '()
      (cons (fn (car lst))
            (map fn (cdr lst)))))
```

The structure here is identical to that of `every`; the only difference is that we use `cons`, `car`, and `cdr` instead of `se`, `first`, and `butfirst`.

One implication of this is that you can't use `map` with a word, since it's an error to take the `car` of a word. When is it advantageous to use `map` instead of `every`? Suppose you're using `map` with a structured list, like this:

```
> (map (lambda (flavor) (se flavor '(is great)))
       '(ginger (ultra chocolate) pumpkin (rum raisin)))
((GINGER IS GREAT) (ULTRA CHOCOLATE IS GREAT)
 (PUMPKIN IS GREAT) (RUM RAISIN IS GREAT))

> (every (lambda (flavor) (se flavor '(is great)))
         '(ginger (ultra chocolate) pumpkin (rum raisin)))
(GINGER IS GREAT ULTRA CHOCOLATE IS GREAT PUMPKIN IS GREAT
 RUM RAISIN IS GREAT)
```

Why does `map` preserve the structure of the sublists while `every` doesn't? Map uses `cons` to combine the elements of the result, whereas `every` uses `sentence`:

```
> (cons '(pumpkin is great)
        (cons '(rum raisin is great)
              '()))
((PUMPKIN IS GREAT) (RUM RAISIN IS GREAT))

> (se '(pumpkin is great)
      (se '(rum raisin is great)
          '()))
(PUMPKIN IS GREAT RUM RAISIN IS GREAT)
```

Filter

Here's the implementation of `filter`:

```
(define (filter pred lst)
  (cond ((null? lst) '())
        ((pred (car lst))
         (cons (car lst) (filter pred (cdr lst))))
        (else (filter pred (cdr lst)))))
```

Like `map`, this uses `cons` as the constructor so that it will work properly on structured lists. We're leaving the definition of `keep`, the version for words and sentences, as an exercise.

(Aside from the difference between lists and sentences, this is just like the `keep` template on page 224.)

Accumulate and Reduce

Here are the examples of the `accumulate` pattern that we showed you before:

```
(define (addup nums)
  (if (empty? nums)
      0
      (+ (first nums) (addup (bf nums)))))

(define (scrunch-words sent)
  (if (empty? sent)
      ""
      (word (first sent) (scrunch-words (bf sent)))))
```

What are the similarities and differences? There are *two* important differences between these procedures: the combiners (+ versus `word`) and the values returned in the base cases (zero versus the empty word). According to what we said about generalizing patterns, you might expect that we'd need two extra arguments. You'd invoke `three-arg-accumulate` like this:

```
> (three-arg-accumulate + 0 '(6 7 8))
21

> (three-arg-accumulate word "" '(come together))
COMETOGETHER
```

But we've actually defined `accumulate` and `reduce` so that only two arguments are required, the procedure and the sentence or list. We thought it would be too much trouble to have to provide the identity element all the time. How did we manage to avoid it?

The trick is that in our `reduce` and `accumulate` the base case is a one-element argument, rather than an empty argument. When we're down to one element in the argument, we just return that element:

```
(define (accumulate combiner stuff)              ;; first version
  (if (empty? (bf stuff))
      (first stuff)
      (combiner (first stuff)
                (accumulate combiner (bf stuff)))))
```

This version is a simplification of the one we actually provide. What happens if `stuff` is empty? This version blows up, since it tries to take the `butfirst` of `stuff` immediately. Our final version has a specific check for empty arguments:

```
(define (accumulate combiner stuff)
  (cond ((not (empty? stuff)) (real-accumulate combiner stuff))
        ((member combiner (list + * word se append))
         (combiner))
        (else (error
               "Can't accumulate empty input with that combiner"))))

(define (real-accumulate combiner stuff)
  (if (empty? (bf stuff))
      (first stuff)
      (combiner (first stuff) (real-accumulate combiner (bf stuff)))))
```

This version works just like the earlier version as long as `stuff` isn't empty. (`Reduce` is the same, except that it uses `null?`, `car`, and `cdr`.)

As we mentioned in Chapter 8, many of Scheme's primitive procedures return their identity element when invoked with no arguments. We can take advantage of this; if `accumulate` is invoked with an empty second argument and one of the procedures `+`, `*`, `word`, `sentence`, `append` or `list`, we invoke the combiner with no arguments to produce the return value.

On the other hand, if `accumulate`'s combiner argument is something like `(lambda (x y) (word x '- y))` or `max`, then there's nothing `accumulate` can return, so we give an error message. (But it's a more descriptive error message than the first version; what message do you get when you call that first version with an empty second argument?)

It's somewhat of a kludge that we have to include in our procedure a list of the functions that can be called without arguments. What we'd like to do is invoke the combiner and find out if that causes an error, but Scheme doesn't provide a mechanism for causing errors on purpose and recovering from them. (Some dialects of Lisp do have that capability.)

Robustness

Instead of providing a special error message for empty-argument cases that `accumulate` can't handle, we could have just let it blow up:

```
(define (accumulate combiner stuff)          ;; non-robust version
  (if (not (empty? stuff))
      (real-accumulate combiner stuff)
      (combiner)))
```

Some questions about programming have clear right and wrong answers—if your program doesn't work, it's wrong! But the decision about whether to include the extra check for a procedure that's usable with an empty argument is a matter of judgment.

Here is the reasoning in favor of this simpler version: In either version, the user who tries to evaluate an expression like

```
(accumulate max '())
```

is going to get an error message. In the longer version we've spent both our own programming effort and a little of the computer's time on every invocation just to give a *different* error message from the one that Scheme would have given anyway. What's the point?

Here is the reasoning in favor of the longer version: In practice, the empty-argument situation isn't going to arise because someone uses a quoted empty sentence; instead the second argument to `accumulate` will be some expression whose value happens to be empty under certain conditions. The user will then have to debug the program that caused those conditions. Debugging is hard; we should make it easier for the user, if we can, by giving an error message that points clearly to the problem.

A program that behaves politely when given incorrect input is called *robust*. It's not always a matter of better or worse error messages. For example, a program that reads input from a human user might offer the chance to try again if some input value is incorrect. A robust program will also be alert for hardware problems, such as running out of space on a disk, or getting garbled information over a telephone connection to another machine because of noise on the line.

It's possible to pay either too little or too much attention to program robustness. If you're a professional programmer, your employer will expect your programs to survive errors that are likely to happen. On the other hand, your programs will be hard to read and debug if the error checking swamps the real work! As a student, unless you are specifically asked to "bulletproof" your program, don't answer exam questions by writing procedures like this one:

```
(define (even? num)                            ;; silly example
  (cond ((not (number? num)) (error "Not a number."))
        ((not (integer? num)) (error "Not an integer."))
        ((< num 0) (error "Argument must be positive."))
        (else (= (remainder num 2) 0))))
```

In the case of `accumulate`, we decided to be extra robust because we were writing a procedure for use in a beginning programming course. If we were writing this tool just for our own use, we might have chosen the non-robust version. Deciding how robust a program will be is a matter of taste.

Higher-Order Functions for Structured Lists

We've given you a fairly standard set of higher-order functions, but there's no law that says these are the only ones. Any time you notice yourself writing what feels like the same procedure over again, but with different details, consider inventing a higher-order function.

For example, here's a procedure we defined in Chapter 17.

```
(define (deep-pigl structure)
  (cond ((word? structure) (pigl structure))
        ((null? structure) '())
        (else (cons (deep-pigl (car structure))
                    (deep-pigl (cdr structure))))))
```

This procedure converts every word in a structured list to Pig Latin. Suppose we have a structure full of numbers and we want to compute all of their squares. We could write a specific procedure **deep-square**, but instead, we'll write a higher-order procedure:

```
(define (deep-map f structure)
  (cond ((word? structure) (f structure))
        ((null? structure) '())
        (else (cons (deep-map f (car structure))
                    (deep-map f (cdr structure))))))
```

The Zero-Trip Do Loop

The first programming language that provided a level of abstraction over the instructions understood directly by computer hardware was Fortran, a language that is still widely used today despite the advances in programming language design since then. Fortran remains popular because of the enormous number of useful programs that have already been written in it; if an improvement is needed, it's easier to modify the Fortran program than to start again in some more modern language.

Fortran includes a control mechanism called do, a sort of higher-order procedure that carries out a computation repeatedly, as **every** does. But instead of carrying out the computation once for each element of a given collection of data (like the sentence argument to **every**), do performs a computation once for each integer in a range specified by its endpoints. "For every number between 4 and 16, do such-and-such."

What if you specify endpoints such that the starting value is greater than the ending value? In the first implementation of Fortran, nobody thought very hard about this question, and they happened to implement do in such a way that if you specified a backward range, the computation was done once, for the given starting value, before Fortran noticed that it was past the ending value.

Twenty years later, a bunch of computer scientists argued that this behavior was wrong—that a do loop with its starting value greater than its ending value should not carry out its computation at all. This proposal for a "zero-trip do loop" was strongly opposed by Fortran old-timers, not because of any principle but because of all the thousands of Fortran programs that had been written to rely on the one-trip behavior.

The point of this story is that the Fortran users had to debate the issue so heatedly because they are stuck with only the control mechanisms that are built into the language. Fortran doesn't have the idea of function as data, so Fortran programmers can't write their own higher-order procedures. But you, using the techniques of this chapter, can create precisely the control mechanism that you need for whatever problem you happen to be working on.

Pitfalls

⇒ The most crucial point in inventing a higher-order function is to make sure that the pattern you have in mind really does generalize. For example, if you want to write a higher-order function for structured data, what is the base case? Will you use the tree abstract data type, or will you use `car`/`cdr` recursion?

⇒ When you generalize a pattern by adding a new argument (typically a procedure), be sure you add it to the recursive invocation(s) as well as to the formal parameter list!

Boring Exercises

19.1   What happens if you say the following?

```
(every cdr '((john lennon) (paul mccartney)
             (george harrison) (ringo starr)))
```

How is this different from using `map`, and why? How about `cadr` instead of `cdr`?

Real Exercises

19.2   Write `keep`. Don't forget that `keep` has to return a sentence if its second argument is a sentence, and a word if its second argument is a word.

(Hint: it might be useful to write a `combine` procedure that uses either `word` or `sentence` depending on the types of its arguments.)

19.3   Write the three-argument version of `accumulate` that we described.

```
> (three-arg-accumulate + 0 '(4 5 6))
15

> (three-arg-accumulate + 0 '())
0
```

```
> (three-arg-accumulate cons '() '(a b c d e))
(A B C D E)
```

19.4 Our `accumulate` combines elements from right to left. That is,

```
(accumulate - '(2 3 4 5))
```

computes $2-(3-(4-5))$. Write `left-accumulate`, which will compute $((2-3)-4)-5$ instead. (The result will be the same for an operation such as `+`, for which grouping order doesn't matter, but will be different for `-`.)

19.5 Rewrite the `true-for-all?` procedure from Exercise 8.10. Do not use `every`, `keep`, or `accumulate`.

19.6 Write a procedure `true-for-any-pair?` that takes a predicate and a sentence as arguments. The predicate must accept two words as its arguments. Your procedure should return `#t` if the argument predicate will return true for any two adjacent words in the sentence:

```
> (true-for-any-pair? equal? '(a b c b a))
#F

> (true-for-any-pair? equal? '(a b c c d))
#T

> (true-for-any-pair? < '(20 16 5 8 6))        ;; 5 is less than 8
#T
```

19.7 Write a procedure `true-for-all-pairs?` that takes a predicate and a sentence as arguments. The predicate must accept two words as its arguments. Your procedure should return `#t` if the argument predicate will return true for *every* two adjacent words in the sentence:

```
> (true-for-all-pairs? equal? '(a b c c d))
#F

> (true-for-all-pairs? equal? '(a a a a a))
#T

> (true-for-all-pairs? < '(20 16 5 8 6))
#F
```

```
> (true-for-all-pairs? < '(3 7 19 22 43))
#T
```

19.8 Rewrite `true-for-all-pairs?` (Exercise 19.7) using `true-for-any-pair?` (Exercise 19.6) as a helper procedure. Don't use recursion in solving this problem (except for the recursion you've already used to write `true-for-any-pair?`). Hint: You'll find the `not` procedure helpful.

19.9 Rewrite either of the sort procedures from Chapter 15 to take two arguments, a list and a predicate. It should sort the elements of that list according to the given predicate:

```
> (sort '(4 23 7 5 16 3) <)
(3 4 5 7 16 23)

> (sort '(4 23 7 5 16 3) >)
(23 16 7 5 4 3)

> (sort '(john paul george ringo) before?)
(GEORGE JOHN PAUL RINGO)
```

19.10 Write `tree-map`, analogous to our `deep-map`, but for trees, using the `datum` and `children` selectors.

19.11 Write `repeated`. (This is a hard exercise!)

19.12 Write `tree-reduce`. You may assume that the combiner argument can be invoked with no arguments.

```
> (tree-reduce
   +
   (make-node 3 (list (make-node 4 '())
                      (make-node 7 '())
                      (make-node 2 (list (make-node 3 '())
                                         (make-node 8 '()))))))
27
```

19.13 Write `deep-reduce`, similar to `tree-reduce`, but for structured lists:

```
> (deep-reduce word '(r ((a (m b) (l)) (e (r)))))
RAMBLER
```

Part VI
Sequential Programming

The three big ideas in this part are *effect, sequence,* and *state.*

Until now, we've been doing functional programming, where the focus is on functions and their return values. Invoking a function is like asking a question: "What's two plus two?" In this part of the book we're going to talk about giving commands to the computer as well as asking it questions. That is, we'll invoke procedures that tell Scheme to *do* something, such as `wash-the-dishes`. (Unfortunately, the Scheme standard leaves out this primitive.) Instead of merely computing a value, such a procedure has an *effect,* an action that changes something.

Once we're thinking about actions, it's very natural to consider a *sequence* of actions. First cooking dinner, then eating, and then washing the dishes is one sequence. First eating, then washing the dishes, and then cooking is a much less sensible sequence.

Although these ideas of sequence and effect are coming near the end of our book, they're the ideas with which almost every introduction to programming begins. Most books compare a program to a recipe or a sequence of instructions, along the lines of

```
to go-to-work
  get-dressed
  eat-breakfast
  catch-the-bus
```

This sequential programming style is simple and natural, and it does a good job of modeling computations in which the problem concerns a sequence of events. If you're writing an airline reservation system, a sequential program with `reserve-seat` and `issue-ticket` commands makes sense. But if you want to know the acronym of a phrase, that's not inherently sequential, and a question-asking approach is best.

Some actions that Scheme can take affect the "outside" world, such as printing something on the computer screen. But Scheme can also carry out internal actions, invisible outside the computer, but changing the environment in which Scheme itself carries out computations. Defining a new variable with `define` is an example; before the definition, Scheme wouldn't understand what that name means, but once the definition has been made, the name can be used in evaluating later expressions. Scheme's knowledge about the leftover effects of past computations is called its *state*. The third big idea in this part of the book is that we can write programs that maintain state information and use it to determine their results.

Like sequence, the notion of state contradicts functional programming. Earlier in the book, we emphasized that every time a function is invoked with the same arguments, it must return the same value. But a procedure whose returned value depends on state—on the past history of the computation—might return a different value on each invocation, even with identical arguments.

We'll explore several situations in which effects, sequence, and state are useful:

- Interactive, question-and-answer programs that involve keyboard input while the computation is in progress;

- Programs that must read and write long-term data file storage;

- Computations that *model* an actual sequence of events in time and use the state of the program to model information about the state of the simulated events.

After introducing Scheme's mechanisms for sequential programming, we'll use those mechanisms to implement versions of two commonly used types of business computer applications, a spreadsheet and a database program.

20   Input and Output

In the tic-tac-toe project in Chapter 10, we didn't write a complete game program. We wrote a *function* that took a board position and **x** or **o** as arguments, returning the next move. We noted at the time that a complete game program would also need to carry on a *conversation* with the user. Instead of computing and returning one single value, a conversational program must carry out a sequence of events in time, reading information from the keyboard and displaying other information on the screen.

Before we complete the tic-tac-toe project, we'll start by exploring Scheme's mechanisms for interactive programming.

Printing

Up until now, we've never told Scheme to print anything. The programs we've written have computed values and returned them; we've relied on the read-eval-print loop to print these values.*

But let's say we want to write a program to print out all of the words to "99 Bottles of Beer on the Wall." We could implement a function to produce a humongous *list* of the lines of the song, like this:

```
(define (bottles n)
  (if (= n 0)
      '()
      (append (verse n)
              (bottles (- n 1)))))
```

---

* The only exception is that we've used `trace`, which prints messages about the progress of a computation.

```
(define (verse n)
  (list (cons n '(bottles of beer on the wall))
        (cons n '(bottles of beer))
        '(if one of those bottles should happen to fall)
        (cons (- n 1) '(bottles of beer on the wall))
        '()))

> (bottles 3)
((3 BOTTLES OF BEER ON THE WALL)
 (3 BOTTLES OF BEER)
 (IF ONE OF THOSE BOTTLES SHOULD HAPPEN TO FALL)
 (2 BOTTLES OF BEER ON THE WALL)
 ()
 (2 BOTTLES OF BEER ON THE WALL)
 (2 BOTTLES OF BEER)
 (IF ONE OF THOSE BOTTLES SHOULD HAPPEN TO FALL)
 (1 BOTTLES OF BEER ON THE WALL)
 ()
 (1 BOTTLES OF BEER ON THE WALL)
 (1 BOTTLES OF BEER)
 (IF ONE OF THOSE BOTTLES SHOULD HAPPEN TO FALL)
 (0 BOTTLES OF BEER ON THE WALL)
 ())
```

The problem is that we don't want a list. All we want is to print out the lines of the song; storing them in a data structure is unnecessary and inefficient. Also, some versions of Scheme would print the above list like this:

```
((3 BOTTLES OF BEER ON THE WALL) (3 BOTTLES OF BEER) (IF ONE OF
 THOSE BOTTLES SHOULD HAPPEN TO FALL) (2 BOTTLES OF BEER ON THE
 WALL) () (2 BOTTLES OF BEER ON THE WALL) (2 BOTTLES OF BEER) (IF
 ONE OF THOSE BOTTLES SHOULD HAPPEN TO FALL) (1 BOTTLES OF BEER ON
 THE WALL) () (1 BOTTLES OF BEER ON THE WALL) (1 BOTTLES OF BEER)
 (IF ONE OF THOSE BOTTLES SHOULD HAPPEN TO FALL) (0 BOTTLES OF BEER
 ON THE WALL) ())
```

or even all on one line. We can't rely on Scheme's mechanism for printing lists if we want to be sure of a particular arrangement on the screen.

Instead we'll write a program to *print* a verse, rather than return it in a list:

```
(define (bottles n)
  (if (= n 0)
      'burp
      (begin (verse n)
             (bottles (- n 1)))))
```

```
(define (verse n)
  (show (cons n '(bottles of beer on the wall)))
  (show (cons n '(bottles of beer)))
  (show '(if one of those bottles should happen to fall))
  (show (cons (- n 1) '(bottles of beer on the wall)))
  (show '()))

> (bottles 3)
(3 BOTTLES OF BEER ON THE WALL)
(3 BOTTLES OF BEER)
(IF ONE OF THOSE BOTTLES SHOULD HAPPEN TO FALL)
(2 BOTTLES OF BEER ON THE WALL)
()
(2 BOTTLES OF BEER ON THE WALL)
(2 BOTTLES OF BEER)
(IF ONE OF THOSE BOTTLES SHOULD HAPPEN TO FALL)
(1 BOTTLES OF BEER ON THE WALL)
()
(1 BOTTLES OF BEER ON THE WALL)
(1 BOTTLES OF BEER)
(IF ONE OF THOSE BOTTLES SHOULD HAPPEN TO FALL)
(0 BOTTLES OF BEER ON THE WALL)
()
BURP
```

Notice that Scheme doesn't print an outer set of parentheses. Each line was printed separately; there isn't one big list containing all of them.*

Why was "burp" printed at the end? Just because we're printing things explicitly doesn't mean that the read-eval-print loop stops functioning. We typed the expression (bottles 3). In the course of evaluating that expression, Scheme printed several lines for us. But the *value* of the expression was the word burp, because that's what bottles returned.

Side Effects and Sequencing

How does our program work? There are two new ideas here: *side effects* and *sequencing*.

Until now, whenever we've invoked a procedure, our only goal has been to get a return value. The procedures we've used compute and return a value, and do nothing else. Show is different. Although every Scheme procedure returns a value, the Scheme

---

* We know that it's still not as beautiful as can be, because of the capital letters and parentheses, but we'll get to that later.

language standard doesn't specify what value the printing procedures should return.* Instead, we are interested in their side effects. In other words, we invoke show because we want it to *do* something, namely, print its argument on the screen.

What exactly do we mean by "side effect"? The kinds of procedures that we've used before this chapter can compute values, invoke helper procedures, provide arguments to the helper procedures, and return a value. There may be a lot of activity going on within the procedure, but the procedure affects the world outside of itself only by returning a value that some other procedure might use. Show affects the world outside of itself by putting something on the screen. After show has finished its work, someone who looks at the screen can tell that show was used.**

Here's an example to illustrate the difference between values and effects:

```
(define (effect x)
  (show x)
  'done)

(define (value x)
  x)

> (effect '(oh! darling))
(OH! DARLING)
DONE

> (value '(oh! darling))
(OH! DARLING)

> (bf (effect '(oh! darling)))
(OH! DARLING)
ONE
```

---

 * Suppose show returns #f in your version of Scheme. Then you might see

```
> (show 7)
7
#F
```

But since the return value is unspecified, we try to write programs in such a way that we never use show's return value as the return value from our procedures. That's why we return values like burp.

** The term *side* effect is based on the idea that a procedure may have a useful return value as its main purpose and may also have an effect "on the side." It's a misnomer to talk about the side effect of show, since the effect is its main purpose. But nobody ever says "side return value"!

```
> (bf (value '(oh! darling)))
(DARLING)

> (define (lots-of-effect x)
    (effect x)
    (effect x)
    (effect x))

> (define (lots-of-value x)
    (value x)
    (value x)
    (value x))

> (lots-of-effect '(oh! darling))
(OH! DARLING)
(OH! DARLING)
(OH! DARLING)
DONE

> (lots-of-value '(oh! darling))
(OH! DARLING)
```

This example also demonstrates the second new idea, sequencing: Each of `effect`, `lots-of-effect`, and `lots-of-value` contains more than one expression in its body. When you invoke such a procedure, Scheme evaluates all the expressions in the body, in order, and returns the value of the last one.* This also works in the body of a `let`, which is really the body of a procedure, and in each clause of a `cond`.**

---

* In Chapter 4, we said that the body of a procedure was always one single expression. We lied. But as long as you don't use any procedures with side effects, it doesn't do you any good to evaluate more than one expression in a body.

** For example:

```
> (cond ((< 4 0)
         (show '(how interesting))
         (show '(4 is less than zero?))
         #f)
        ((> 4 0)
         (show '(more reasonable))
         (show '(4 really is more than zero))
         'value)
        (else
         (show '(you mean 4=0?))
         #f))
(MORE REASONABLE)
(4 REALLY IS MORE THAN ZERO)
VALUE
```

When we invoked `lots-of-value`, Scheme invoked `value` three times; it discarded the values returned by the first two invocations, and returned the value from the third invocation. Similarly, when we invoked `lots-of-effect`, Scheme invoked `effect` three times and returned the value from the third invocation. But each invocation of `effect` caused its argument to be printed by invoking `show`.

The **Begin** Special Form

The `lots-of-effect` procedure accomplished sequencing by having more than one expression in its body. This works fine if the sequence of events that you want to perform is the entire body of a procedure. But in `bottles` we wanted to include a sequence as one of the alternatives in an `if` construction. We couldn't just say

```
(define (bottles n)                              ;; wrong
  (if (= n 0)
      '()
      (verse n)
      (bottles (- n 1))))
```

because `if` must have exactly three arguments. Otherwise, how would `if` know whether we meant `(verse n)` to be the second expression in the true case, or the first expression in the false case?

Instead, to turn the sequence of expressions into a single expression, we use the special form `begin`. It takes any number of arguments, evaluates them from left to right, and returns the value of the last one.

```
(define bottles n)
  (if (= n 0)
      'burp
      (begin (verse n)
             (bottles (- n 1)))))
```

(One way to think about sequences in procedure bodies is that every procedure body has an invisible `begin` surrounding it.)

This Isn't Functional Programming

Sequencing and side effects are radical departures from the idea of functional programming. In fact, we'd like to reserve the name *function* for something that computes and returns one value, with no side effects. "Procedure" is the general term for the thing that `lambda` returns—an embodiment of an algorithm. If the algorithm is the kind that computes and returns a single value without side effects, then we say that the procedure implements a function.*

There is a certain kind of sequencing even in functional programming. If you say

```
(* (+ 3 4) (- 92 15))
```

it's clear that the addition has to happen before the multiplication, because the result of the addition provides one of the arguments to the multiplication. What's new in the sequential programming style is the *emphasis* on sequence, and the fact that the expressions in the sequence are *independent* instead of contributing values to each other. In this multiplication problem, for example, we don't care whether the addition happens before or after the subtraction. If the addition and subtraction were in a sequence, we'd be using them for independent purposes:

```
(begin
 (show (+ 3 4))
 (show (- 92 15)))
```

This is what we mean by being independent. Neither expression helps in computing the other. And the order matters because we can see the order in which the results are printed.

Not Moving to the Next Line

Each invocation of `show` prints a separate line. What if we want a program that prints several things on the same line, like this:

```
> (begin (show-addition 3 4)
         (show-addition 6 8)
         'done)
3+4=7
6+8=14
DONE
```

---

* Sometimes people sloppily say that the procedure *is* a function. In fact, you may hear people be *really* sloppy and call a non-functional procedure a function!

We use `display`, which doesn't move to the next line after printing its argument:

```
(define (show-addition x y)
  (display x)
  (display '+)
  (display y)
  (display '=)
  (show (+ x y)))
```

(The last one is a `show` because we *do* want to start a new line after it.)

What if you just want to print a blank line? You use `newline`:

```
(define (verse n)
  (show (cons n '(bottles of beer on the wall)))
  (show (cons n '(bottles of beer)))
  (show '(if one of those bottles should happen to fall))
  (show (cons (- n 1) '(bottles of beer on the wall)))
  (newline))                               ; replaces (show '())
```

In fact, `show` isn't an official Scheme primitive; we wrote it in terms of `display` and `newline`.

Strings

Throughout the book we've occasionally used strings, that is, words enclosed in double-quote marks so that Scheme will permit the use of punctuation or other unusual characters. Strings also preserve the case of letters, so they can be used to beautify our song even more. Since *any* character can be in a string, including spaces, the easiest thing to do in this case is to treat all the letters, spaces, and punctuation characters of each line of the song as one long word. (If we wanted to be able to compute functions of the individual words in each line, that wouldn't be such a good idea.)

```
(define (verse n)
  (display n)
  (show " bottles of beer on the wall,")
  (display n)
  (show " bottles of beer.")
  (show "If one of those bottles should happen to fall,")
  (display (- n 1))
  (show " bottles of beer on the wall.")
  (newline))
```

```
> (verse 6)
6 bottles of beer on the wall,
6 bottles of beer.
If one of those bottles should happen to fall,
5 bottles of beer on the wall.

#F                                      ; or whatever is returned by (newline)
```

It's strange to think of " bottles of beer on the wall," as a single word. But the rule is that anything inside double quotes counts as a single word. It doesn't have to be an English word.

A Higher-Order Procedure for Sequencing

Sometimes we want to print each element of a list separately:

```
(define (show-list lst)
  (if (null? lst)
      'done
      (begin (show (car lst))
             (show-list (cdr lst)))))

> (show-list '((dig a pony) (doctor robert) (for you blue)))
(DIG A PONY)
(DOCTOR ROBERT)
(FOR YOU BLUE)
DONE
```

Like other patterns of computation involving lists, this one can be abstracted into a higher-order procedure. (We can't call it a "higher-order function" because this one is for computations with side effects.) The procedure for-each is part of standard Scheme:

```
> (for-each show '((mean mr mustard) (no reply) (tell me why)))
(MEAN MR MUSTARD)
(NO REPLY)
(TELL ME WHY)
```

The value returned by for-each is unspecified.

Why couldn't we just use map for this purpose? There are two reasons. One is just an efficiency issue: Map constructs a list containing the values returned by each of its sub-computations; in this example, it would be a list of three instances of the unspecified value returned by show. But we aren't going to use that list for anything, so there's no point in constructing it. The second reason is more serious. In functional programming, the order of evaluation of subexpressions is unspecified. For example, when we evaluate the expression

```
(- (+ 4 5) (* 6 7))
```

we don't know whether the addition or the multiplication happens first. Similarly, the
order in which map computes the results for each element is unspecified. That's okay
as long as the ultimately returned list of results is in the right order. But when we are
using side effects, we *do* care about the order of evaluation. In this case, we want to make
sure that the elements of the argument list are printed from left to right. For-each
guarantees this ordering.

Tic-Tac-Toe Revisited

We're working up toward playing a game of tic-tac-toe against the computer. But as a first
step, let's have the computer play against itself. What we already have is ttt, a *strategy*
function: one that takes a board position as argument (and also a letter x or o) and
returns the chosen next move. In order to play a game of tic-tac-toe, we need two players;
to make it more interesting, each should have its own strategy. So we'll write another
one, quickly, that just moves in the first empty square it sees:

```
(define (stupid-ttt position letter)
  (location '_ position))

(define (location letter word)
  (if (equal? letter (first word))
      1
      (+ 1 (location letter (bf word))))))
```

Now we can write a program that takes two strategies as arguments and actually plays
a game between them.

```
(define (play-ttt x-strat o-strat)
  (play-ttt-helper x-strat o-strat '_____ 'x))

(define (play-ttt-helper x-strat o-strat position whose-turn)
  (cond ((already-won? position (opponent whose-turn))
         (list (opponent whose-turn) 'wins!))
        ((tie-game? position) '(tie game))
        (else (let ((square (if (equal? whose-turn 'x)
                                (x-strat position 'x)
                                (o-strat position 'o))))
                (play-ttt-helper x-strat
                                 o-strat
                                 (add-move square whose-turn position)
                                 (opponent whose-turn))))))
```

We use a helper procedure because we need to keep track of two pieces of information besides the strategy procedures: the current board position and whose turn it is (x or o). The helper procedure is invoked recursively for each move. First it checks whether the game is already over (won or tied).* If not, the helper procedure invokes the current player's strategy procedure, which returns the square number for the next move. For the recursive call, the arguments are the same two strategies, the new position after the move, and the letter for the other player.

We still need `add-move`, the procedure that takes a square and an old position as arguments and returns the new position.

```
(define (add-move square letter position)
  (if (= square 1)
      (word letter (bf position))
      (word (first position)
            (add-move (- square 1) letter (bf position)))))

> (play-ttt ttt stupid-ttt)
(X WINS!)

> (play-ttt stupid-ttt ttt)
(O WINS!)
```

Accepting User Input

The work we did in the last section was purely functional. We didn't print anything (except the ultimate return value, as always) and we didn't have to read information from a human player, because there wasn't one.

You might expect that the structure of an *interactive* game program would be very different, with a top-level procedure full of sequential operations. But the fact is that we hardly have to change anything to turn this into an interactive game. All we need is a

---

* You wrote the procedures `already-won?` and `tie-game?` in Exercises 10.1 and 10.2:

```
(define (already-won? position who)
  (member? (word who who who)  (find-triples position)))

(define (tie-game? position)
  (not (member? '_ position)))
```

new "strategy" procedure that asks the user where to move, instead of computing a move based on built-in rules.

```
(define (ask-user position letter)
  (print-position position)
  (display letter)
  (display "'s move: ")
  (read))

(define (print-position position)                ;; first version
  (show position))
```

(Ultimately we're going to want a beautiful two-dimensional display of the current position, but we don't want to get distracted by that just now. That's why we've written a trivial temporary version.)

```
> (play-ttt ttt ask-user)
____X____
O'S MOVE: 1
O___XX___
O'S MOVE: 4
O__OXXX__
O'S MOVE: 3
OXOOXXX__
O'S MOVE: 8
(TIE GAME)
```

What the user typed is just the single digits shown in boldface at the ends of the lines.

What's new here is that we invoke the procedure **read**. It waits for you to type a Scheme expression, and returns that expression. Don't be confused: Read does *not* evaluate what you type. It returns exactly the same expression that you type:

```
(define (echo)
  (display "What? ")
  (let ((expr (read)))
    (if (equal? expr 'stop)
        'okay
        (begin
         (show expr)
         (echo)))))
```

```
> (echo)
What? hello
HELLO
What? (+ 2 3)
(+ 2 3)
What? (first (glass onion))
(FIRST (GLASS ONION))
What? stop
OKAY
```

Aesthetic Board Display

Here's our beautiful position printer:

```
(define (print-position position)
  (print-row (subword position 1 3))
  (show "-+-+-")
  (print-row (subword position 4 6))
  (show "-+-+-")
  (print-row (subword position 7 9))
  (newline))

(define (print-row row)
  (maybe-display (first row))
  (display "|")
  (maybe-display (first (bf row)))
  (display "|")
  (maybe-display (last row))
  (newline))

(define (maybe-display letter)
  (if (not (equal? letter '_))
      (display letter)
      (display " ")))

(define (subword wd start end)
  ((repeated bf (- start 1))
   ((repeated bl (- (count wd) end))
    wd)))*
```

---

* Alternate version:

```
(define (subword wd start end)
  (cond ((> start 1) (subword (bf wd) (- start 1) (- end 1)))
        ((< end (count wd)) (subword (bl wd) start end))
        (else wd)))
```

You can take your choice, depending on which you think is easier, recursion or higher-order functions.

Here's how it works:

```
> (print-position '_x_oo__xx)
 |x|
-+-+-
o|o|
-+-+-
 |x|x
```

Reading and Writing Normal Text

The `read` procedure works fine as long as what you type looks like a Lisp program. That is, it reads one expression at a time. In the tic-tac-toe program the user types a single number, which is a Scheme expression, so `read` works fine. But what if we want to read more than one word?

```
(define (music-critic)                       ;; first version
  (show "What's your favorite Beatles song?")
  (let ((song (read)))
    (show (se "I like" song "too."))))

> (music-critic)
What's your favorite Beatles song?
She Loves You
(I like SHE too.)
```

If the user had typed the song title in parentheses, then it would have been a single Scheme expression and `read` would have accepted it. But we don't want the users of our program to have to be typing parentheses all the time.

Scheme also lets you read one character at a time. This allows you to read any text, with no constraints on its format. The disadvantage is that you find yourself putting a lot of effort into minor details. We've provided a procedure `read-line` that reads one line of input and returns a sentence. The words in that sentence will contain any punctuation characters that appear on the line, including parentheses, which are not interpreted as sublist delimiters by `read-line`. `Read-line` also preserves the case of letters.

```
(define (music-critic)                       ;; second version
  (read-line)   ; See explanation on next page.
  (show "What's your favorite Beatles song?")
  (let ((song (read-line)))
    (show (se "I like" song "too."))))
```

```
> (music-critic)
What's your favorite Beatles song?
She Loves You
(I like She Loves You too.)
```

Why do we call read-line and ignore its result at the beginning of music-critic? It has to do with the interaction between read-line and read. Read treats what you type as a sequence of Scheme expressions; each invocation of read reads one of them. Read pays no attention to formatting details, such as several consecutive spaces or line breaks. If, for example, you type several expressions on the same line, it will take several invocations of read to read them all.

By contrast, read-line treats what you type as a sequence of lines, reading one line per invocation, so it does pay attention to line breaks.

Either of these ways to read input is sensible in itself, but if you mix the two, by invoking read sometimes and read-line sometimes in the same program, the results can be confusing. Suppose you type a line containing an expression and your program invokes read to read it. Since there might have been another expression on the line, read doesn't advance to the next line until you ask for the next expression. So if you now invoke read-line, thinking that it will read another line from the keyboard, it will instead return an empty list, because what it sees is an empty line—what's left after read uses up the expression you typed.

You may be thinking, "But music-critic doesn't call read!" That's true, but Scheme itself used read to read the expression that you used to invoke music-critic. So the first invocation of read-line is needed to skip over the spurious empty line.

Our solution works only if music-critic is invoked directly at a Scheme prompt. If music-critic were a subprocedure of some larger program that has already called read-line before calling music-critic, the extra read-line in music-critic would really read and ignore a useful line of text.

If you write a procedure using read-line that will sometimes be called directly and sometimes be used as a subprocedure, you can't include an extra read-line call in it. Instead, when you call your procedure directly from the Scheme prompt, you must say

```
> (begin (read-line) (my-procedure))
```

Another technical detail about read-line is that since it preserves the capitalization of words, its result may include strings, which will be shown in quotation marks if you return the value rather than showing it:

```
(define (music-critic-return)
  (read-line)
  (show "What's your favorite Beatles song?")
  (let ((song (read-line)))
    (se "I like" song "too.")))

> (music-critic-return)
What's your favorite Beatles song?
She Loves You
("I like" "She" "Loves" "You" "too.")
```

We have also provided show-line, which takes a sentence as argument. It prints the sentence without surrounding parentheses, followed by a newline. (Actually, it takes any list as argument; it prints all the parentheses except for the outer ones.)

```
(define (music-critic)
  (read-line)
  (show "What's your favorite Beatles song?")
  (let ((song (read-line)))
    (show-line (se "I like" song "too."))))

> (music-critic)
What's your favorite Beatles song?
She Loves You
I like She Loves You too.
```

The difference between show and show-line isn't crucial. It's just a matter of a pair of parentheses. The point is that read-line and show-line go together. Read-line reads a bunch of disconnected words and combines them into a sentence. Show-line takes a sentence and prints it as if it were a bunch of disconnected words. Later, when we read and write files in Chapter 22, this ability to print in the same form in which we read will be important.

Formatted Text

We've been concentrating on the use of sequential programming with explicit printing instructions for the sake of conversational programs. Another common application of sequential printing is to display tabular information, such as columns of numbers. The difficulty is to get the numbers to line up so that corresponding digits are in the same position, even when the numbers have very widely separated values. The align function can be used to convert a number to a printable word with a fixed number of positions before and after the decimal point:

```
(define (square-root-table nums)
  (if (null? nums)
      'done
      (begin (display (align (car nums) 7 1))
             (show (align (sqrt (car nums)) 10 5))
             (square-root-table (cdr nums)))))
```

```
> (square-root-table '(7 8 9 10 20 98 99 100 101 1234 56789))
    7.0    2.64575
    8.0    2.82843
    9.0    3.00000
   10.0    3.16228
   20.0    4.47214
   98.0    9.89949
   99.0    9.94987
  100.0   10.00000
  101.0   10.04988
 1234.0   35.12834
56789.0 238.30443
DONE
```

Align takes three arguments. The first is the value to be displayed. The second is the width of the column in which it will be displayed; the returned value will be a word with that many characters in it. The third argument is the number of digits that should be displayed to the right of the decimal point. (If this number is zero, then no decimal point will be displayed.) The width must be great enough to include all the digits, as well as the decimal point and minus sign, if any.

As the program example above indicates, `align` does not print anything. It's a function that returns a value suitable for printing with `display` or `show`.

What if the number is too big to fit in the available space?

```
> (align 12345679 4 0)
"123+"
```

Align returns a word containing the first few digits, as many as fit, ending with a plus sign to indicate that part of the value is missing.

Align can also be used to include non-numeric text in columns. If the first argument is not a number, then only two arguments are needed; the second is the column width.

In this case `align` returns a word with extra spaces at the right, if necessary, so that the argument word will appear at the left in its column:

```
(define (name-table names)
  (if (null? names)
      'done
      (begin (display (align (cadar names) 11))
             (show (caar names))
             (name-table (cdr names)))))

> (name-table '((john lennon) (paul mccartney)
                (george harrison) (ringo starr)))
LENNON     JOHN
MCCARTNEY  PAUL
HARRISON   GEORGE
STARR      RINGO
DONE
```

As with numbers, if a non-numeric word won't fit in the allowed space, `align` returns a partial word ending with a plus sign.

This `align` function is not part of standard Scheme. Most programming languages, including some versions of Scheme, offer much more elaborate formatting capabilities with many alternate ways to represent both numbers and general text. Our version is a minimal capability to show the flavor and to meet the needs of projects in this book.

Sequential Programming and Order of Evaluation

Our expanded tic-tac-toe program includes both functional and sequential parts. The program computes its strategy functionally but uses sequences of commands to control the *user interface* by alternately printing information to the screen and reading information from the keyboard.

By adding sequential programming to our toolkit, we've increased our ability to write interactive programs. But there is a cost that goes along with this benefit: We now have to pay more attention to the order of events than we did in purely functional programs.

The obvious concern about order of events is that sequences of `show` expressions must come in the order in which we want them to appear, and `read` expressions must fit into the sequence properly so that the user is asked for the right information at the right time.

But there is another, less obvious issue about order of events. When the evaluation of expressions can have side effects in addition to returning values, the order of evaluation of argument subexpressions becomes important. Here's an example to show what we mean. Suppose we type the expression

```
(list (+ 3 4) (- 10 2))
```

The answer, of course, is `(7 8)`. It doesn't matter whether Scheme computes the seven first (left to right) or the eight first (right to left). But here's a similar example in which it *does* matter:

```
(define (show-and-return x)
  (show x)
  x)

> (list (show-and-return (+ 3 4)) (show-and-return (- 10 2)))
8
7
(7 8)
```

The value that's ultimately returned, in this example, is the same as before. But the two numeric values that go into the list are also printed separately, so we can see which is computed first. (We've shown the case of right-to-left computation; your Scheme might be different.)

Suppose you want to make sure that the seven prints first, regardless of which order your Scheme uses. You could do this:

```
> (let ((left (show-and-return (+ 3 4))))
    (list left (show-and-return (- 10 2))))
7
8
(7 8)
```

The expression in the body of a `let` can't be evaluated until the `let` variables (such as `left`) have had their values computed.

It's hard to imagine a practical use for the artificial `show-and-return` procedure, but a similar situation arises whenever we use `read`. Suppose we want to write a procedure to ask a person for his or her full name, returning a two-element list containing the first and last name. A natural mistake to make would be to write this procedure:

```
(define (ask-for-name)                              ;; wrong
  (show "Please type your first name, then your last name:")
  (list (read) (read)))

> (ask-for-name)
Please type your first name, then your last name:
John
Lennon
(LENNON JOHN)
```

What went wrong? We happen to be using a version of Scheme that evaluates argument subexpressions from right to left. Therefore, the word John was read by the rightmost call to read, which provided the second argument to list. The best solution is to use let as we did above:

```
(define (ask-for-name)
  (show "Please type your first name, then your last name:")
  (let ((first-name (read)))
    (list first-name (read))))
```

Even this example looks artificially simple, because of the two invocations of read that are visibly right next to each other in the erroneous version. But look at play-ttt-helper. The word read doesn't appear in its body at all. But when we invoke it using ask-user as the strategy procedure for x, the expression

```
(x-strat position 'x)
```

hides an invocation of read. The structure of play-ttt-helper includes a let that controls the timing of that read. (As it turns out, in this particular case we could have gotten away with writing the program without let. The hidden invocation of read is the only subexpression with a side effect, so there aren't two effects that might get out of order. But we had to think carefully about the program to be sure of that.)

Pitfalls

⇒ It's easy to get confused about what is printed explicitly by your program and what is printed by Scheme's read-eval-print loop. Until now, *all* printing was of the second kind. Here's an example that doesn't do anything very interesting but will help make the point clear:

```
(define (name)
  (display "MATT ")
  'wright)

> (name)
MATT WRIGHT
```

At first glance it looks as if putting the word "Matt" inside a call to `display` is unnecessary. After all, the word `wright` is printed even without using `display`. But watch this:

```
> (bf (name))
MATT RIGHT
```

Every time you invoke `name`, whether or not as the entire expression used at a Scheme prompt, the word `MATT` is printed. But the word `wright` is *returned*, and may or may not be printed depending on the context in which `name` is invoked.

⇒ A sequence of expressions returns the value of the *last* expression. If that isn't what you want, you must remember the value you want to return using `let`:

```
(let ((result (compute-this-first)))
  (begin
    (compute-this-second)
    (compute-this-third)
    result))
```

⇒ Don't forget that the first call to `read-line`, or any call to `read-line` after a call to `read`, will probably read the empty line that `read` left behind.

⇒ Sometimes you want to use what the user typed more than once in your program. But don't forget that `read` has an effect as well as a return value. Don't try to read the same expression twice:

```
(define (ask-question question)                    ;; wrong
  (show question)
  (cond ((equal? (read) 'yes) #t)
        ((equal? (read) 'no) #f)
        (else (show "Please answer yes or no.")
              (ask-question question))))
```

If the answer is **yes**, this procedure will work fine. But if not, the second invocation of `read` will read a second expression, not test the same expression again as intended. To avoid this problem, invoke `read` only once for each expression you want to read, and use `let` to remember the result:

```
(define (ask-question question)
  (show question)
  (let ((answer (read)))
    (cond ((equal? answer 'yes) #t)
          ((equal? answer 'no) #f)
          (else (show "Please answer yes or no.")
                (ask-question question)))))
```

Boring Exercises

20.1 What happens when we evaluate the following expression? What is printed, and what is the return value? Try to figure it out in your head before you try it on the computer.

```
(cond ((= 2 3) (show '(lady madonna)) '(i call your name))
      ((< 2 3) (show '(the night before)) '(hello little girl))
      (else '(p.s. i love you)))
```

20.2 What does `newline` return in your version of Scheme?

20.3 Define `show` in terms of `newline` and `display`.

Real Exercises

20.4 Write a program that carries on a conversation like the following example. What the user types is in boldface.

```
> (converse)
Hello, I'm the computer.  What's your name? Brian Harvey
Hi, Brian.  How are you? I'm fine.
Glad to hear it.
```

20.5 Our `name-table` procedure uses a fixed width for the column containing the last names of the people in the argument list. Suppose that instead of liking British-invasion music you are into late romantic Russian composers:

```
> (name-table '((piotr tchaikovsky) (nicolay rimsky-korsakov)
                 (sergei rachmaninov) (modest musorgsky)))
```

Alternatively, perhaps you like jazz:

```
> (name-table '((bill evans) (paul motian) (scott lefaro)))
```

Modify `name-table` so that it figures out the longest last name in its argument list, adds two for spaces, and uses that number as the width of the first column.

20.6 The procedure `ask-user` isn't robust. What happens if you type something that isn't a number, or isn't between 1 and 9? Modify it to check that what the user types is a number between 1 and 9. If not, it should print a message and ask the user to try again.

20.7 Another problem with `ask-user` is that it allows a user to request a square that isn't free. If the user does this, what happens? Fix `ask-user` to ensure that this can't happen.

20.8 At the end of the game, if the computer wins or ties, you never find out which square it chose for its final move. Modify the program to correct this. (Notice that this exercise requires you to make `play-ttt-helper` non-functional.)

20.9 The way we invoke the game program isn't very user-friendly. Write a procedure `game` that asks you whether you wish to play x or o, then starts a game. (By definition, x plays first.) Then write a procedure `games` that allows you to keep playing repeatedly. It can ask "do you want to play again?" after each game. (Make sure that the outcome of each game is still reported, and that the user can choose whether to play x or o before each game.)

Once you see how it works, it's not so mysterious.

21   Example: The `Functions` Program

In Chapter 2 you used a program called `functions` to explore some of Scheme's primitive functions. Now we're going to go back to that program from the other point of view: instead of using the program to learn about functions, we're going to look at how the program works as an example of programming with input and output.

The Main Loop

The `functions` program is an infinite loop similar to Scheme's read-eval-print loop. It reads in a function name and some arguments, prints the result of applying that function to those arguments, and then does the whole thing over again.

There are some complexities, though. The `functions` program keeps asking you for arguments until it has enough. This means that the `read` portion of the loop has to read a function name, figure out how many arguments that procedure takes, and then ask for the right number of arguments. On the other hand, each argument is an implicitly quoted datum rather than an expression to be evaluated; the `functions` evaluator avoids the recursive complexity of arbitrary subexpressions within expressions. (That's why we wrote it: to focus attention on one function invocation at a time, rather than on the composition of functions.) Here's the main loop:

```
(define (functions-loop)
  (let ((fn-name (get-fn)))
    (if (equal? fn-name 'exit)
        "Thanks for using FUNCTIONS!"
        (let ((args (get-args (arg-count fn-name))))
          (if (not (in-domain? args fn-name))
              (show "Argument(s) not in domain.")
              (show-answer (apply (scheme-procedure fn-name) args)))
          (functions-loop)))))
```

This invokes a lot of helper procedures. `Arg-count` takes the name of a procedure as its argument and returns the number of arguments that the given procedure takes. `In-domain?` takes a list and the name of a procedure as arguments; it returns `#t` if the elements of the list are valid arguments to the given procedure. `Scheme-procedure` takes a name as its argument and returns the Scheme procedure with the given name. We'll get back to these helpers later.

The other helper procedures are the ones that do the input and output. The actual versions are more complicated because of error checking; we'll show them to you later.

```
(define (get-fn)                        ;; first version
  (display "Function: ")
  (read))

(define (get-args n)
  (if (= n 0)
      '()
      (let ((first (get-arg)))
        (cons first (get-args (- n 1)))))))

(define (get-arg)                       ;; first version
  (display "Argument: ")
  (read))

(define (show-answer answer)
  (newline)
  (display "The result is: ")
  (if (not answer)
      (show "#F")
      (show answer))
  (newline))
```

(That weird `if` expression in `show-answer` is needed because in some old versions of Scheme the empty list means the same as `#f`. We wanted to avoid raising this issue in Chapter 2, so we just made sure that false values always printed as `#F`.)

The Difference between a Procedure and Its Name

You may be wondering why we didn't just say

```
(show-answer (apply fn-name args))
```

in the definition of `functions-loop`. Remember that the value of the variable `fn-name` comes from `get-fn`, which invokes `read`. Suppose you said

```
(define x (read))
```

and then typed

```
(+ 2 3)
```

The value of `x` would be the three element list `(+ 2 3)`, not the number five.

Similarly, if you type "butfirst," then read will return the *word* `butfirst`, not the procedure of that name. So we need a way to turn the name of a function into the procedure itself.

The Association List of Functions

We accomplish this by creating a huge association list that contains all of the functions the program knows about. Given a word, such as `butfirst`, we need to know three things:

- The Scheme procedure with that name (in this case, the `butfirst` procedure).

- The number of arguments required by the given procedure (one).*

- The types of arguments required by the given procedure (one word or sentence, which must not be empty).

We need to know the number of arguments the procedure requires because the program prompts the user individually for each argument; it has to know how many to ask for. Also, it needs to know the domain of each function so it can complain if the arguments you give it are not in the domain.**

This means that each entry in the association list is a list of four elements:

---

* Some Scheme procedures can accept any number of arguments, but for the purposes of the `functions` program we restrict these procedures to their most usual case, such as two arguments for +.

** Scheme would complain all by itself, of course, but would then stop running the `functions` program. We want to catch the error before Scheme does, so that after seeing the error message you're still in `functions`. As we mentioned in Chapter 19, a program meant for beginners, such as the readers of Chapter 2, should be especially robust.

```
(define *the-functions*                          ;; partial listing
  (list (list '* * 2 (lambda (x y) (and (number? x) (number? y))))
        (list '+ + 2 (lambda (x y) (and (number? x) (number? y))))
        (list 'and (lambda (x y) (and x y)) 2
                   (lambda (x y) (and (boolean? x) (boolean? y))))
        (list 'equal? equal? 2 (lambda (x y) #t))
        (list 'even? even? 1 integer?)
        (list 'word word 2 (lambda (x y) (and (word? x) (word? y))))))
```

The real list is much longer, of course, but you get the idea.* It's a convention in Scheme programming that names of global variables used throughout a program are surrounded by *asterisks* to distinguish them from parameters of procedures.

Here are the selector procedures for looking up information in this a-list:

```
(define (scheme-procedure fn-name)
  (cadr (assoc fn-name *the-functions*)))

(define (arg-count fn-name)
  (caddr (assoc fn-name *the-functions*)))

(define (type-predicate fn-name)
  (cadddr (assoc fn-name *the-functions*)))
```

Domain Checking

Note that we represent the domain of a procedure by another procedure.** Each

---

* Since and is a special form, we can't just say

```
(list 'and and 2 (lambda (x y) (and (boolean? x) (boolean? y))))
```

That's because special forms can't be elements of lists. Instead, we have to create a normal procedure that can be put in a list but computes the same function as and:

```
(lambda (x y) (and x y))
```

We can get away with this because in the functions program we don't care about argument evaluation, so it doesn't matter that and is a special form. We do the same thing for if and or.

** The domain of a procedure is a set, and sets are generally represented in programs as lists. You might think that we'd have to store, for example, a list of all the legal arguments to butfirst. But that would be impossible, since that list would have to be infinitely large. Instead, we can take advantage of the fact that the only use we make of this set is membership testing, that is, finding out whether a particular argument is in a function's domain.

domain-checking procedure, or *type predicate,* takes the same arguments as the procedure whose domain it checks. For example, the type predicate for + is

```
(lambda (x y) (and (number? x) (number? y)))
```

The type predicate returns #t if its arguments are valid and #f otherwise. So in the case of +, any two numbers are valid inputs, but any other types of arguments aren't.

Here's the `in-domain?` predicate:

```
(define (in-domain? args fn-name)
  (apply (type-predicate fn-name) args))
```

Of course, certain type predicates are applicable to more than one procedure. It would be silly to type

```
(lambda (x y) (and (number? x) (number? y)))
```

for +, −, =, and so on. Instead, we give this function a name:

```
(define (two-numbers? x y)
  (and (number? x) (number? y)))
```

We then refer to the type predicate by name in the a-list:

```
(define *the-functions*                         ;; partial listing, revised
  (list (list '* * 2 two-numbers?)
        (list '+ + 2 two-numbers?)
        (list 'and (lambda (x y) (and x y)) 2
                (lambda (x y) (and (boolean? x) (boolean? y))))
        (list 'equal? equal? 2 (lambda (x y) #t))
        (list 'even? even? 1 integer?)
        (list 'word word 2 (lambda (x y) (and (word? x) (word? y))))))
```

Some of the type predicates are more complicated. For example, here's the one for the `member?` and `appearances` functions:

```
(define (member-types-ok? small big)
  (and (word? small)
       (or (sentence? big) (and (word? big) (= (count small) 1)))))
```

`Item` also has a complicated domain:

```
(lambda (n stuff)
  (and (integer? n) (> n 0)
       (word-or-sent? stuff) (<= n (count stuff)))))
```

This invokes `word-or-sent?`, which is itself the type predicate for the `count` procedure:

```
(define (word-or-sent? x)
  (or (word? x) (sentence? x)))
```

On the other hand, some are less complicated. `Equal?` will accept any two arguments, so its type predicate is just

```
(lambda (x y) #t)
```

The complete listing at the end of the chapter shows the details of all these procedures. Note that the `functions` program has a more restricted idea of domain than Scheme does. For example, in Scheme

```
(and 6 #t)
```

returns `#t` and does not generate an error. But in the `functions` program the argument 6 is considered out of the domain.*

If you don't like math, just ignore the domain predicates for the mathematical primitives; they involve facts about the domains of math functions that we don't expect you to know.**

---

* Why did we choose to restrict the domain? We were trying to make the point that invoking a procedure makes sense only with appropriate arguments; that point is obscured by the complicating fact that Scheme interprets any non-#f value as true. In the `functions` program, where composition of functions is not allowed, there's no benefit to Scheme's more permissive rule.

** A reason that we restricted the domains of some mathematical functions is to protect ourselves from the fact that some version of Scheme support complex numbers while others do not. We wanted to write one version of `functions` that would work in either case; sometimes the easiest way to avoid possible problems was to restrict some function's domain.

Intentionally Confusing a Function with Its Name

Earlier we made a big deal about the difference between a procedure and its name, to make sure you wouldn't think you can apply the *word* butfirst to arguments. But the functions program completely hides this distinction from the user:

```
Function: count
Argument: butlast

The result is: 7

Function: every
Argument: butlast
Argument: (helter skelter)

The result is: (HELTE SKELTE)
```

When we give butlast as an argument to count, it's as if we'd said

```
(count 'butlast)
```

In other words, it's taken as a word. But when we give butlast as an argument to every, it's as if we'd said

```
(every butlast '(helter skelter))
```

How can we treat some arguments as quoted and others not? The way this works is that *everything* is considered a word or a sentence by the functions program. The higher-order functions every and keep are actually represented in the functions implementation by Scheme procedures that take the *name* of a function as an argument, instead of a procedure itself as the ordinary versions do:

```
(define (named-every fn-name list)
  (every (scheme-procedure fn-name) list))

(define (named-keep fn-name list)
  (keep (scheme-procedure fn-name) list))

> (every first '(another girl))
(A G)
> (named-every 'first '(another girl))
(A G)
> (every 'first '(another girl))
ERROR: ATTEMPT TO APPLY NON-PROCEDURE FIRST
```

This illustration hides a subtle point. When we invoked `named-every` at a Scheme prompt, we had to quote the word `first` that we used as its argument. But when you run the `functions` program, you don't quote anything. The point is that `functions` provides an evaluator that uses a different notation from Scheme's notation. It may be clearer if we show an interaction with an imaginary version of `functions` that *does* use Scheme notation:

```
Function: first
Non-Automatically-Quoted-Argument: 'datum

The result is: D

Function: first
Non-Automatically-Quoted-Argument: datum

ERROR: THE VARIABLE DATUM IS UNBOUND.
```

We didn't want to raise the issue of quoting at that early point in the book, so we wrote `functions` so that *every* argument is automatically quoted. Well, if that's the case, it's true even when we're invoking `every`. If you say

```
Function: every
Argument: first
...
```

then by the rules of the `functions` program, that argument is the quoted word `first`. So `named-every`, the procedure that pretends to be `every` in the `functions` world, has to "un-quote" that argument by looking up the corresponding procedure.

More on Higher-Order Functions

One of the higher-order functions that you can use in the `functions` program is called `number-of-arguments`. It takes a procedure (actually the name of a procedure, as we've just been saying) as argument and returns the number of arguments that that procedure accepts. This example is unusual because there's no such function in Scheme. (It would be complicated to define, for one thing, because some Scheme procedures can accept a variable number of arguments. What should `number-of-arguments` return for such a procedure?)

The implementation of `number-of-arguments` makes use of the same a-list of functions that the `functions` evaluator itself uses. Since the `functions` program needs to know the number of arguments for every procedure anyway, it's hardly any extra effort to make that information available to the user. We just add an entry to the a-list:

```
(list 'number-of-arguments arg-count 1 valid-fn-name?)
```

The type predicate merely has to check that the argument is found in the a-list of functions:

```
(define (valid-fn-name? name)
  (assoc name *the-functions*))
```

The type checking for the arguments to **every** and **keep** is unusually complicated because what's allowed as the second argument (the collection of data) depends on which function is used as the first argument. For example, it's illegal to compute

```
(every square '(think for yourself))
```

even though either of those two arguments would be allowable if we changed the other one:

```
> (every square '(3 4 5))
(9 16 25)

> (every first '(think for yourself))
(T F Y)
```

The type-checking procedures for **every** and **keep** use a common subprocedure. The one for **every** is

```
(lambda (fn stuff)
  (hof-types-ok? fn stuff word-or-sent?))
```

and the one for **keep** is

```
(lambda (fn stuff)
  (hof-types-ok? fn stuff boolean?))
```

The third argument specifies what types of results **fn** must return when applied to the elements of **stuff**.

```
(define (hof-types-ok? fn-name stuff range-predicate)
  (and (valid-fn-name? fn-name)
       (= 1 (arg-count fn-name))
       (word-or-sent? stuff)
       (empty? (keep (lambda (element)
                       (not ((type-predicate fn-name) element)))
                     stuff))
       (null? (filter (lambda (element)
                        (not (range-predicate element)))
                      (map (scheme-procedure fn-name)
                           (every (lambda (x) x) stuff))))))
```

This says that the function being used as the first argument must be a one-argument function (so you can't say, for example, **every** of word and something); also, *each element* of the second argument must be an acceptable argument to that function. (If you **keep** the unacceptable arguments, you get nothing.) Finally, each invocation of the given function on an element of **stuff** must return an object of the appropriate type: words or sentences for **every**, true or false for **keep**.*

More Robustness

The program we've shown you so far works fine, as long as the user never makes a mistake. Because this program was written for absolute novices, we wanted to bend over backward to catch any kind of strange input they might give us.

Using **read** to accept user input has a number of disadvantages:

- If the user enters an empty line, **read** continues waiting silently for input.

- If the user types an unmatched open parenthesis, **read** continues reading forever.

- If the user types two expressions on a line, the second one will be taken as a response to the question the **functions** program hasn't asked yet.

---

* That last argument to **and** is complicated. The reason we use **map** instead of **every** is that the results of the invocations of **fn** might not be words or sentences, so **every** wouldn't accept them. But **map** has its own limitation: It won't accept a word as the **stuff** argument. So we use **every** to turn **stuff** into a sentence—which, as you know, is really a list—and that's guaranteed to be acceptable to **map**. (This is an example of a situation in which respecting a data abstraction would be too horrible to contemplate.)

We solve all these problems by using `read-line` to read exactly one line, even if it's empty or ill-formed, and then checking explicitly for possible errors.

`Read-line` treats parentheses no differently from any other character. That's an advantage if the user enters mismatched or inappropriately nested parentheses. However, if the user correctly enters a sentence as an argument to some function, `read-line` will include the initial open parenthesis as the first character of the first word, and the final close parenthesis as the last character of the last word. `Get-arg` must correct for these extra characters.

Similarly, `read-line` treats number signs (#) like any other character, so it doesn't recognize #t and #f as special values. Instead it reads them as the strings "#t" and "#f". `Get-arg` calls `booleanize` to convert those strings into Boolean values.

```
(define (get-arg)
  (display "Argument: ")
  (let ((line (read-line)))
    (cond ((empty? line)
           (show "Please type an argument!")
           (get-arg))
          ((and (equal? "(" (first (first line)))
                (equal? ")" (last (last line))))
           (let ((sent (remove-first-paren (remove-last-paren line))))
             (if (any-parens? sent)
                 (begin (show "Sentences can't have parentheses inside.")
                        (get-arg))
                 (map booleanize sent))))
          ((any-parens? line)
           (show "Bad parentheses")
           (get-arg))
          ((empty? (bf line)) (booleanize (first line)))
          (else (show "You typed more than one argument!  Try again.")
                (get-arg)))))
```

`Get-arg` invokes `any-parens?`, `remove-first-paren`, `remove-last-paren`, and `booleanize`, whose meanings should be obvious from their names. You can look up their definitions in the complete listing at the end of this chapter.

`Get-fn` is simpler than `get-arg`, because there's no issue about parentheses, but it's still much more complicated than the original version, because of error checking.

```
(define (get-fn)
  (display "Function: ")
  (let ((line (read-line)))
    (cond ((empty? line)
           (show "Please type a function!")
           (get-fn))
          ((not (= (count line) 1))
           (show "You typed more than one thing!  Try again.")
           (get-fn))
          ((not (valid-fn-name? (first line)))
           (show "Sorry, that's not a function.")
           (get-fn))
          (else (first line)))))
```

This version of get-fn uses valid-fn-name? (which you've already seen) to ensure that what the user types is the name of a function we know about.

There's a problem with using read-line. As we mentioned in a pitfall in Chapter 20, reading some input with read and then reading the next input with read-line results in read-line returning an empty line left over by read. Although the functions program doesn't use read, Scheme itself used read to read the (functions) expression that started the program. Therefore, get-fn's first attempt to read a function name will see an empty line. To fix this problem, the functions procedure has an extra invocation of read-line:

```
(define (functions)
  (read-line)
  (show "Welcome to the FUNCTIONS program.")
  (functions-loop))
```

Complete Program Listing

```
;;; The functions program

(define (functions)
  ;; (read-line)
  (show "Welcome to the FUNCTIONS program.")
  (functions-loop))
```

```scheme
(define (functions-loop)
  (let ((fn-name (get-fn)))
    (if (equal? fn-name 'exit)
        "Thanks for using FUNCTIONS!"
        (let ((args (get-args (arg-count fn-name))))
          (if (not (in-domain? args fn-name))
              (show "Argument(s) not in domain.")
              (show-answer (apply (scheme-function fn-name) args)))
          (functions-loop)))))

(define (get-fn)
  (display "Function: ")
  (let ((line (read-line)))
    (cond ((empty? line)
           (show "Please type a function!")
           (get-fn))
          ((not (= (count line) 1))
           (show "You typed more than one thing!  Try again.")
           (get-fn))
          ((not (valid-fn-name? (first line)))
           (show "Sorry, that's not a function.")
           (get-fn))
          (else (first line)))))

(define (get-arg)
  (display "Argument: ")
  (let ((line (read-line)))
    (cond ((empty? line)
           (show "Please type an argument!")
           (get-arg))
          ((and (equal? "(" (first (first line)))
                (equal? ")" (last (last line))))
           (let ((sent (remove-first-paren (remove-last-paren line))))
             (if (any-parens? sent)
                 (begin
                  (show "Sentences can't have parentheses inside.")
                  (get-arg))
                 (map booleanize sent))))
          ((any-parens? line)
           (show "Bad parentheses")
           (get-arg))
          ((empty? (bf line)) (booleanize (first line)))
          (else (show "You typed more than one argument!  Try again.")
                (get-arg)))))
```

```
(define (get-args n)
  (if (= n 0)
      '()
      (let ((first (get-arg)))
        (cons first (get-args (- n 1))))))

(define (any-parens? line)
  (let ((letters (accumulate word line)))
    (or (member? "(" letters)
        (member? ")" letters))))

(define (remove-first-paren line)
  (if (equal? (first line) "(")
      (bf line)
      (se (bf (first line)) (bf line))))

(define (remove-last-paren line)
  (if (equal? (last line) ")")
      (bl line)
      (se (bl line) (bl (last line)))))

(define (booleanize x)
  (cond ((equal? x "#t") #t)
        ((equal? x "#f") #f)
        (else x)))

(define (show-answer answer)
  (newline)
  (display "The result is: ")
  (if (not answer)
      (show "#F")
      (show answer))
  (newline))

(define (scheme-function fn-name)
  (cadr (assoc fn-name *the-functions*)))

(define (arg-count fn-name)
  (caddr (assoc fn-name *the-functions*)))

(define (type-predicate fn-name)
  (cadddr (assoc fn-name *the-functions*)))

(define (in-domain? args fn-name)
  (apply (type-predicate fn-name) args))
```

```
;; Type predicates

(define (word-or-sent? x)
  (or (word? x) (sentence? x)))

(define (not-empty? x)
  (and (word-or-sent? x) (not (empty? x))))

(define (two-numbers? x y)
  (and (number? x) (number? y)))

(define (two-reals? x y)
  (and (real? x) (real? y)))

(define (two-integers? x y)
  (and (integer? x) (integer? y)))

(define (can-divide? x y)
  (and (number? x) (number? y) (not (= y 0))))

(define (dividable-integers? x y)
  (and (two-integers? x y) (not (= y 0))))

(define (trig-range? x)
  (and (number? x) (<= (abs x) 1)))

(define (hof-types-ok? fn-name stuff range-predicate)
  (and (valid-fn-name? fn-name)
       (= 1 (arg-count fn-name))
       (word-or-sent? stuff)
       (empty? (keep (lambda (element)
                       (not ((type-predicate fn-name) element)))
                     stuff))
       (null? (filter (lambda (element)
                        (not (range-predicate element)))
                      (map (scheme-function fn-name)
                           (every (lambda (x) x) stuff))))))

(define (member-types-ok? small big)
  (and (word? small)
       (or (sentence? big) (and (word? big) (= (count small) 1)))))
```

```
;; Names of functions as functions

(define (named-every fn-name list)
  (every (scheme-function fn-name) list))

(define (named-keep fn-name list)
  (keep (scheme-function fn-name) list))

(define (valid-fn-name? name)
  (assoc name *the-functions*))


;; The list itself

(define *the-functions*
  (list (list '* * 2 two-numbers?)
        (list '+ + 2 two-numbers?)
        (list '- - 2 two-numbers?)
        (list '/ / 2 can-divide?)
        (list '< < 2 two-reals?)
        (list '<= <= 2 two-reals?)
        (list '= = 2 two-numbers?)
        (list '> > 2 two-reals?)
        (list '>= >= 2 two-reals?)
        (list 'abs abs 1 real?)
        (list 'acos acos 1 trig-range?)
        (list 'and (lambda (x y) (and x y)) 2
              (lambda (x y) (and (boolean? x) (boolean? y)))))
        (list 'appearances appearances 2 member-types-ok?)
        (list 'asin asin 1 trig-range?)
        (list 'atan atan 1 number?)
        (list 'bf bf 1 not-empty?)
        (list 'bl bl 1 not-empty?)
        (list 'butfirst butfirst 1 not-empty?)
        (list 'butlast butlast 1 not-empty?)
        (list 'ceiling ceiling 1 real?)
        (list 'cos cos 1 number?)
        (list 'count count 1 word-or-sent?)
        (list 'equal? equal? 2 (lambda (x y) #t))
        (list 'even? even? 1 integer?)
        (list 'every named-every 2
              (lambda (fn stuff)
                (hof-types-ok? fn stuff word-or-sent?)))
        (list 'exit '() 0 '())
           ; in case user applies number-of-arguments to exit
        (list 'exp exp 1 number?)
```

```
(list 'expt expt 2
      (lambda (x y)
        (and (number? x) (number? y)
             (or (not (real? x)) (>= x 0) (integer? y)))))
(list 'first first 1 not-empty?)
(list 'floor floor 1 real?)
(list 'gcd gcd 2 two-integers?)
(list 'if (lambda (pred yes no) (if pred yes no)) 3
      (lambda (pred yes no) (boolean? pred)))
(list 'item item 2
      (lambda (n stuff)
        (and (integer? n) (> n 0)
             (word-or-sent? stuff) (<= n (count stuff)))))
(list 'keep named-keep 2
      (lambda (fn stuff)
        (hof-types-ok? fn stuff boolean?)))
(list 'last last 1 not-empty?)
(list 'lcm lcm 2 two-integers?)
(list 'log log 1 (lambda (x) (and (number? x) (not (= x 0)))))
(list 'max max 2 two-reals?)
(list 'member? member? 2 member-types-ok?)
(list 'min min 2 two-reals?)
(list 'modulo modulo 2 dividable-integers?)
(list 'not not 1 boolean?)
(list 'number-of-arguments arg-count 1 valid-fn-name?)
(list 'odd? odd? 1 integer?)
(list 'or (lambda (x y) (or x y)) 2
      (lambda (x y) (and (boolean? x) (boolean? y))))
(list 'quotient quotient 2 dividable-integers?)
(list 'random random 1 (lambda (x) (and (integer? x) (> x 0))))
(list 'remainder remainder 2 dividable-integers?)
(list 'round round 1 real?)
(list 'se se 2
      (lambda (x y) (and (word-or-sent? x) (word-or-sent? y))))
(list 'sentence sentence 2
      (lambda (x y) (and (word-or-sent? x) (word-or-sent? y))))
(list 'sentence? sentence? 1 (lambda (x) #t))
(list 'sin sin 1 number?)
(list 'sqrt sqrt 1 (lambda (x) (and (real? x) (>= x 0))))
(list 'tan tan 1 number?)
(list 'truncate truncate 1 real?)
(list 'vowel? (lambda (x) (member? x '(a e i o u))) 1
      (lambda (x) #t))
(list 'word word 2 (lambda (x y) (and (word? x) (word? y))))
(list 'word? word? 1 (lambda (x) #t)))
```

Exercises

21.1 The `get-args` procedure has a `let` that creates the variable `first`, and then that variable is used only once inside the body of the `let`. Why doesn't it just say the following?

```
(define (get-args n)
  (if (= n 0)
      '()
      (cons (get-arg) (get-args (- n 1))))))
```

21.2 The domain-checking function for `equal?` is

```
(lambda (x y) #t)
```

This seems silly; it's a function of two arguments that ignores both arguments and always returns `#t`. Since we know ahead of time that the answer is `#t`, why won't it work to have `equal?`'s entry in the a-list be

```
(list 'equal? equal? 2 #t)
```

21.3 Every time we want to know something about a function that the user typed in, such as its number of arguments or its domain-checking predicate, we have to do an `assoc` in `*the-functions*`. That's inefficient. Instead, rewrite the program so that `get-fn` returns a function's entry from the a-list, instead of just its name. Then rename the variable `fn-name` to `fn-entry` in the `functions-loop` procedure, and rewrite the selectors `scheme-procedure`, `arg-count`, and so on, so that they don't invoke `assoc`.

21.4 Currently, the program always gives the message "argument(s) not in domain" when you try to apply a function to bad arguments. Modify the program so that each record in `*the-functions*` also contains a specific out-of-domain message like "both arguments must be numbers," then modify `functions` to look up and print this error message along with "argument(s) not in domain."

21.5   Modify the program so that it prompts for the arguments this way:

```
Function: if
First Argument: #t
Second Argument: paperback
Third Argument: writer

The result is: PAPERBACK
```

but if there's only one argument, the program shouldn't say `First`:

```
Function: sqrt
Argument: 36

The result is 6
```

21.6   The `assoc` procedure might return `#f` instead of an a-list record. How come it's okay for `arg-count` to take the `caddr` of `assoc`'s return value if (`caddr #f`) is an error?

21.7   Why is the domain-checking predicate for the `word?` function

```
(lambda (x) #t)
```

instead of the following procedure?

```
(lambda (x) (word? x))
```

21.8   What is the value of the following Scheme expression?

```
(functions)
```

21.9   We said in the recursion chapters that every recursive procedure has to have a base case and a recursive case, and that the recursive case has to somehow reduce the size of the problem, getting closer to the base case. How does the recursive call in `get-fn` reduce the size of the problem?

22   Files

We learned in Chapter 20 how to read from the keyboard and write to the screen. The same procedures (`read`, `read-line`, `display`, `show`, `show-line`, and `newline`) can also be used to read and write data files on the disk.

Ports

Imagine a complicated program that reads a little bit of data at a time from a lot of different files. For example, soon we will write a program to merge two files the way we merged two sentences in `mergesort` in Chapter 15. In order to make this work, each invocation of `read` must specify which file to read from this time. Similarly, we might want to direct output among several files.

Each of the input/output procedures can take an extra argument to specify a file:

```
(show '(across the universe) file1)
(show-line '(penny lane) file2)
(read file3)
```

What are `file1` and so on? You might think that the natural thing would be for them to be words, that is, the names of files.

It happens not to work that way. Instead, before you can use a file, you have to *open* it. If you want to read a file, the system has to check that the file exists. If you want to write a file, the system has to create a new, empty file. The Scheme procedures that open a file return a *port*, which is what Scheme uses to remember the file you opened. Ports are useful only as arguments to the input/output procedures. Here's an example:

```
> (let ((port (open-output-file "songs")))
    (show '(all my loving) port)
    (show '(ticket to ride) port)
    (show '(martha my dear) port)
    (close-output-port port))
```

(Close-output-port, like define, has an unspecified return value that we're not going to include in the examples.)

We've created a file named songs and put three expressions, each on its own line, in that file. Notice that nothing appeared on the screen when we called show. Because we used a port argument to show, the output went into the file. Here's what's in the file:

```
(ALL MY LOVING)
(TICKET TO RIDE)
(MARTHA MY DEAR)
```

The example illustrates two more details about using files that we haven't mentioned before: First, the name of a file must be given in double-quote marks. Second, when you're finished using a file, you have to *close* the port associated with it. (This is very important. On some systems, if you forget to close the port, the file disappears.)

The file is now permanent. If we were to exit from Scheme, we could read the file in a word processor or any other program. But let's read it using Scheme:

```
(define in (open-input-file "songs"))

> (read in)
(ALL MY LOVING)

> (read in)
(TICKET TO RIDE)

> (read in)
(MARTHA MY DEAR)

> (close-input-port in)
```

(In this illustration, we've used a global variable to hold the port because we wanted to show the results of reading the file step by step. In a real program, we'd generally use a let structure like the one we used to write the file. Now that we've closed the port, the variable in contains a port that can no longer be used.)

Writing Files for People to Read

A file full of sentences in parentheses is a natural representation for information that will be used by a Scheme program, but it may seem awkward if the file will be read by human beings. We could use `show-line` instead of `show` to create a file, still with one song title per line, but without the parentheses:

```
> (let ((port (open-output-file "songs2")))
    (show-line '(all my loving) port)
    (show-line '(ticket to ride) port)
    (show-line '(martha my dear) port)
    (close-output-port port))
```

The file `songs2` will contain

```
ALL MY LOVING
TICKET TO RIDE
MARTHA MY DEAR
```

What should we do if we want to read this file back into Scheme? We must read the file a line at a time, with `read-line`. In effect, `read-line` treats the breaks between lines as if they were parentheses:

```
(define in (open-input-file "songs2"))

> (read-line in)
(ALL MY LOVING)

> (close-input-port in)
```

(Notice that we don't have to read the entire file before closing the port. If we open the file again later, we start over again from the beginning.)

As far as Scheme is concerned, the result of writing the file with `show-line` and reading it with `read-line` was the same as that of writing it with `show` and reading it with `read`. The difference is that without parentheses the file itself is more "user-friendly" for someone who reads it outside of Scheme.*

---

* Another difference, not apparent in this example, is that `show` and `read` can handle structured lists. `Show-line` can print a structured list, leaving off only the outermost parentheses, but `read-line` will treat any parentheses in the file as ordinary characters; it always returns a sentence.

Using a File as a Database

It's not very interesting merely to read the file line by line. Instead, let's use it as a very small database in which we can look up songs by number. (For only three songs, it would be more realistic and more convenient to keep them in a list and look them up with `list-ref`. Pretend that this file has 3000 songs, too many for you to want to keep them all at once in your computer's memory.)

```
(define (get-song n)
  (let ((port (open-input-file "songs2")))
    (skip-songs (- n 1) port)
    (let ((answer (read-line port)))
      (close-input-port port)
      answer)))

(define (skip-songs n port)
  (if (= n 0)
      'done
      (begin (read-line port)
             (skip-songs (- n 1) port))))

> (get-song 2)
(TICKET TO RIDE)
```

When we invoke `read-line` in `skip-songs`, we pay no attention to the value it returns. Remember that the values of all but the last expression in a sequence are discarded. `Read` and `read-line` are the first procedures we've seen that have both a useful return value and a useful side effect—moving forward in the file.

`Skip-songs` returns the word `done` when it's finished. We don't do anything with that return value, and there's no particular reason why we chose that word. But every Scheme procedure has to return *something*, and this was as good as anything.

What if we asked for a song number greater than three? In other words, what if we read beyond the end of the file? In that case, `read` will return a special value called an *end-of-file object*. The only useful thing to do with that value is to test for it. Our next sample program reads an entire file and prints it to the screen:

```
(define (print-file name)
  (let ((port (open-input-file name)))
    (print-file-helper port)
    (close-input-port port)
    'done))
```

```
(define (print-file-helper port)                ;; first version
  (let ((stuff (read-line port)))
    (if (eof-object? stuff)
        'done
        (begin (show-line stuff)
               (print-file-helper port)))))

> (print-file "songs")
ALL MY LOVING
TICKET TO RIDE
MARTHA MY DEAR
DONE
```

Did you notice that each recursive call in `print-file-helper` has exactly the same argument as the one before? How does the problem get smaller? (Up to now, recursive calls have involved something like the `butfirst` of an old argument, or one less than an old number.) When we're reading a file, the sense in which the problem gets smaller at each invocation is that we're getting closer to the end of the file. You don't `butfirst` the port; reading it makes the unread portion of the file smaller as a side effect.

Transforming the Lines of a File

Often we want to transform a file one line at a time. That is, we want to copy lines from an input file to an output file, but instead of copying the lines exactly, we want each output line to be a *function* of the corresponding input line. Here are some examples: We have a file full of text and we want to *justify* the output so that every line is exactly the same length, as in a book. We have a file of students' names and grades, and we want a summary with the students' total and average scores. We have a file with people's first and last names, and we want to rearrange them to be last-name-first.

We'll write a procedure `file-map`, analogous to `map` but for files. It will take three arguments: The first will be a procedure whose domain and range are sentences; the second will be the name of the input file; the third will be the name of the output file.

Of course, this isn't exactly like the way `map` works—if it were exactly analogous, it would take only two arguments, the procedure and the *contents* of a file. But one of the important features of files is that they let us handle amounts of information that are too big to fit all at once in the computer's memory. Another feature is that once we write a file, it's there permanently, until we erase it. So instead of having a `file-map` *function* that returns the contents of the new file, we have a procedure that writes its result to the disk.

```
(define (file-map fn inname outname)
  (let ((inport (open-input-file inname))
        (outport (open-output-file outname)))
    (file-map-helper fn inport outport)
    (close-input-port inport)
    (close-output-port outport)
    'done))

(define (file-map-helper fn inport outport)
  (let ((line (read-line inport)))
    (if (eof-object? line)
        'done
        (begin (show-line (fn line) outport)
               (file-map-helper fn inport outport)))))
```

Compare this program with the earlier **print-file** example. The two are almost identical. One difference is that now the output goes to a file instead of to the screen; the other is that we apply the function **fn** to each line before doing the output. But that small change vastly increases the generality of our program. We've performed our usual trick of generalizing a pattern by adding a procedure argument, and instead of a program that carries out one specific task (printing the contents of a file), we have a tool that can be used to create many programs.

We'll start with an easy example: putting the last name first in a file full of names. That is, if we start with an input file named **dddbmt** that contains

```
David Harmon
Trevor Davies
John Dymond
Michael Wilson
Ian Amey
```

we want the output file to contain

```
Harmon, David
Davies, Trevor
Dymond, John
Wilson, Michael
Amey, Ian
```

Since we are using **file-map** to handle our progress through the file, all we have to write is a procedure that takes a sentence (one name) as its argument and returns the same name but with the last word moved to the front and with a comma added:

```
(define (lastfirst name)
  (se (word (last name) ",") (bl name)))
```

We use butlast rather than first in case someone in the file has a middle name.

To use this procedure we call file-map like this:

```
> (file-map lastfirst "dddbmt" "dddbmt-reversed")
DONE
```

Although you don't see the results on the screen, you can

```
> (print-file "dddbmt-reversed")
```

to see that we got the results we wanted.

Our next example is averaging grades. Suppose the file grades contains this text:

```
John 88 92 100 75 95
Paul 90 91 85 80 91
George 85 87 90 72 96
Ringo 95 84 88 87 87
```

The output we want is:

```
John total: 450 average: 90
Paul total: 437 average: 87.4
George total: 430 average: 86
Ringo total: 441 average: 88.2
```

Here's the program:

```
(define (process-grades line)
  (se (first line)
      "total:"
      (accumulate + (bf line))
      "average:"
      (/ (accumulate + (bf line))
         (count (bf line)))))
```

```
> (file-map process-grades "grades" "results")
```

As before, you can

```
> (print-file "results")
```

to see that we got the results we wanted.

Justifying Text

Many word-processing programs *justify* text; that is, they insert extra space between words so that every line reaches exactly to the right margin. We can do that using `file-map`.

Let's suppose we have a file `r5rs`, written in some text editor, that looks like this:

```
Programming languages should be designed not by
piling feature on top of feature, but by
removing the weaknesses and restrictions that
make additional features appear necessary.
Scheme demonstrates that a very small number of
rules for forming expressions, with no
restrictions on how they are composed, suffice
to form a practical and efficient programming
language that is flexible enough to support most
of the major programming paradigms in use today.
```

(This is the first paragraph of the *Revised⁵ Report on the Algorithmic Language Scheme*, edited by William Clinger and Jonathan Rees.)

Here is what the result should be if we justify our `r5rs` text:

```
Programming languages should be  designed  not   by
piling  feature  on  top  of   feature,   but   by
removing  the  weaknesses  and  restrictions  that
make    additional    features    appear   necessary.
Scheme demonstrates that a very  small   number   of
rules    for    forming    expressions,   with   no
restrictions on how  they  are  composed,  suffice
to form  a  practical  and  efficient  programming
language that is flexible enough to  support  most
of the major programming paradigms in  use  today.
```

The tricky part is that ordinarily we don't control the spaces that appear when a sentence is printed. We just make sure the words are right, and we get one space between words automatically. The solution used in this program is that each line of the output file is constructed as a single long word, including space characters that we place explicitly within it. (Since `show-line` requires a sentence as its argument, our procedure will actually return a one-word sentence. In the following program, `pad` constructs the word, and `justify` makes a one-word sentence containing it.)

This program, although short, is much harder to understand than most of our short examples. There is no big new idea involved; instead, there are a number of unexciting but necessary details. How many spaces between words? Do some words get more space than others? The program structure is messy because the problem itself is messy. Although it will be hard to read and understand, this program is a more realistic example of input/output programming than the cleanly structured examples we've shown until now.

Justify takes two arguments, the line of text (a sentence) and a number indicating the desired width (how many characters). Here's the algorithm: First the program computes the total number of characters the sentence would take up without adding extras. That's the job of char-count, which adds up the lengths of all the words, and adds to that the $n-1$ spaces between words. Extra-spaces subtracts that length from the desired line width to get the number of extra spaces we need.

The hard part of the job is done by pad. It's invoked with three arguments: the part of the line not yet processed, the number of opportunities there are to insert extra spaces in that part of the line (that is, the number of words minus one), and the number of extra spaces that the program still needs to insert. The number of extra spaces to insert *this time* is the integer quotient of the number pad wants to insert and the number of chances it'll have. That is, if there are five words on the line, there are four places where pad can insert extra space. If it needs to insert nine spaces altogether, then it should insert 9/4 or two spaces at the first opportunity. (Are you worried about the remainder? It will turn out that pad doesn't lose any spaces because it takes the quotient over again for each word break. The base case is that the number of remaining word breaks (the divisor) is one, so there will be no remainder, and all the leftover extra spaces will be inserted at the last word break.)

```
(define (justify line width)
  (if (< (count line) 2)
      line
      (se (pad line
               (- (count line) 1)
               (extra-spaces width (char-count line))))))

(define (char-count line)
  (+ (accumulate + (every count line))    ; letters within words
     (- (count line) 1)))                 ; plus spaces between words

(define (extra-spaces width chars)
  (if (> chars width)
      0                                    ; none if already too wide
      (- width chars)))
```

```
(define (pad line chances needed)
  (if (= chances 0)                            ; only one word in line
      (first line)
      (let ((extra (quotient needed chances)))
        (word (first line)
              (spaces (+ extra 1))
              (pad (bf line) (- chances 1) (- needed extra)))))))

(define (spaces n)
  (if (= n 0)
      ""
      (word " " (spaces (- n 1)))))
```

Because `justify` takes two arguments, we have to decide what line width we want to give it. Here's how to make each line take 50 characters:

```
> (file-map (lambda (sent) (justify sent 50)) "r5rs" "r5rs-just")
```

Preserving Spacing of Text from Files

If we try to print the file `r5rs-just` from the previous section using `print-file`, it'll look exactly like `r5rs`. That's because `read-line` doesn't preserve consecutive spaces in the lines that it reads. `Read-line` cares only where each word (consisting of non-space characters) begins and ends; it pays no attention to how many spaces come between any two words. The lines

```
All     My          Loving
```

and

```
All My Loving
```

are the same, as far as `read-line` tells you.

For situations in which we do care about spacing, we have another way to read a line from a file. The procedure `read-string` reads all of the characters on a line, returning a single word that contains all of them, spaces included:*

---

* Like all the input and output primitives, `read-string` can be invoked with or without a port argument.

```
> (define inport (open-input-file "r5rs-just"))

> (read-string inport)
"Programming languages should be  designed  not  by"

> (read-string inport)
"piling  feature  on  top  of    feature,    but   by"

> (close-input-port inport)
```

We can use **read-string** to rewrite **print-file** so that it makes an exact copy of the input file:

```
(define (print-file-helper port)
  (let ((stuff (read-string port)))
    (if (eof-object? stuff)
        'done
        (begin (show stuff)
               (print-file-helper port)))))
```

(We only had to change the helper procedure.)

Merging Two Files

Suppose you have two files of people's names. Each file has been sorted in alphabetical order. You want to combine them to form a single file, still in order. (If this sounds unrealistic, it isn't. Programs that sort very large amounts of information can't always fit it all in memory at once, so they read in as much as fits, sort it, and write a file. Then they read and sort another chunk. At the end of this process, the program is left with several sorted partial files, and it has to merge those files to get the overall result.)

The algorithm for merging files is exactly the same as the one we used for merging sentences in the **mergesort** program of Chapter 15. The only difference is that the items to be sorted come from reading ports instead of from **first**ing a sentence.

```
(define (filemerge file1 file2 outfile)
  (let ((p1 (open-input-file file1))
        (p2 (open-input-file file2))
        (outp (open-output-file outfile)))
    (filemerge-helper p1 p2 outp (read-string p1) (read-string p2))
    (close-output-port outp)
    (close-input-port p1)
    (close-input-port p2)
    'done))
```

```
(define (filemerge-helper p1 p2 outp line1 line2)
  (cond ((eof-object? line1) (merge-copy line2 p2 outp))
        ((eof-object? line2) (merge-copy line1 p1 outp))
        ((before? line1 line2)
         (show line1 outp)
         (filemerge-helper p1 p2 outp (read-string p1) line2))
        (else (show line2 outp)
              (filemerge-helper p1 p2 outp line1 (read-string p2)))))

(define (merge-copy line inp outp)
  (if (eof-object? line)
      #f
      (begin (show line outp)
             (merge-copy (read-string inp) inp outp))))
```

You might think, comparing `filemerge-helper` with such earlier examples as
`print-file-helper` and `file-map-helper`, that it would make more sense for
`filemerge-helper` to take just the three ports as arguments and work like this:

```
(define (filemerge-helper p1 p2 outp)            ;; wrong
  (let ((line1 (read-string p1))
        (line2 (read-string p2)))
    (cond ((eof-object? line1) (merge-copy p2 outp))
          ((eof-object? line2) (merge-copy p1 outp))
          ((before? line1 line2)
           (show line1 outp)
           (filemerge-helper p1 p2 outp))
          (else (show line2 outp)
                (filemerge-helper p1 p2 outp)))))
```

Unfortunately, this won't work. Suppose that the first line of `file2` comes before
the first line of `file1`. This program correctly writes the first line of `file2` to the output
file, as we expect. But what about the first line of `file1`? Since we called `read-string`
on `file1`, we've "gobbled"* that line, but we're not yet ready to write it to the output.

In each invocation of `filemerge-helper`, only one line is written to the output
file, so unless we want to lose information, we'd better read only one line. This means
that we can't call `read-string` twice on each recursive call. One of the lines has to be
handed down from one invocation to the next. (That is, it has to be an argument to the

---

* Computer programmers really talk this way.

recursive call.) Since we don't know in advance *which* line to keep, the easiest solution is to hand down both lines.

Therefore, `filemerge-helper` also takes as arguments the first line of each file that hasn't yet been written to the output. When we first call `filemerge-helper` from `filemerge`, we read the first line of each file to provide the initial values of these arguments. Then, on each recursive call, `filemerge-helper` calls `read-string` only once.

Writing Files for Scheme to Read

You may be thinking that the three file-reading procedures we've shown, `read`, `read-line`, and `read-string`, have been getting better and better. `Read` ignores case and forces you to have parentheses in your file. `Read-line` fixes those problems, but it loses spacing information. `Read-string` can read anything and always gets it right.

But there's a cost to the generality of `read-string`; it can read any file, but it loses *structure* information. For example, when we processed a file of people's names with `file-map`, we used this function:

```
(define (lastfirst name)
  (se (word (last name) ",") (bl name)))
```

It's easy to break a name into its components if you have the name in the form of a sentence, with the words separated already. But if we had read each line with `read-string`, `last` of a line would have been the last letter, not the last name.

The `lastfirst` example illustrates why you might want to use `read-line` rather than `read-string`: `Read-line` "understands" spaces. Here's an example in which the even more structured `read` is appropriate. We have a file of Beatles songs and the albums on which they appear:

```
((love me do) (please please me))
((do you want to know a secret?) (please please me))
((think for yourself) (rubber soul))
((your mother should know) (magical mystery tour))
```

Each line of this file contains two pieces of information: a song title and an album title. If each line contained only the words of the two titles, as in

```
love me do please please me
```

how would we know where the song title stops and the album title starts? The natural way to represent this grouping information is to use the mechanism Scheme provides for grouping, namely, list structure.

If we use `read-line` to read the file, we'll lose the list structure; it will return a sentence containing words like `"((love"`. `Read`, however, will do what we want.

How did we create this file in the first place? We just used one `show` per line of the file, like this:

```
> (show '((love me do) (please please me)) port)
```

But what about the movie soundtracks? We're going to have to come to terms with the apostrophe in "A Hard Day's Night."

The straightforward solution is to put `day's` in a string:

```
(show '((and i love her) (a hard "day's" night)) port)
```

The corresponding line in the file will look like this:

```
((AND I LOVE HER) (A HARD day's NIGHT))
```

This result is actually even worse than it looks, because when we try to `read` the line back, the `'s` will be expanded into `(quote s)` in most versions of Scheme. Using a string made it possible for us to get an apostrophe into Scheme. If the word `day's` were inside quotation marks in the file, then `read` would understand our intentions.

Why aren't there double quotes in the file? All of the printing procedures we've seen so far assume that whatever you're printing is intended to be read by people. Therefore, they try to minimize distracting notation such as double-quote marks. But, as we've discovered, if you're writing a file to be read by Scheme, then you do want enough notation so that Scheme can tell what the original object was.

`Write` is a printing procedure just like `display`, except that it includes quote marks around strings:*

---

* There are other kinds of data that `write` prints differently from `display`, but we don't use them in this book. The general rule is that `display` formats the output for human readers, while `write` ensures that Scheme can reread the information unambiguously. `Show` and `show-line` are extensions that we wrote using `display`. We could have written `show-in-write-format`, for example, but happened not to need it.

```
> (write '(a hard "day's" night))
(A HARD "day's" NIGHT)
```

Once we're using strings, and since we're not extracting individual words from the titles, we might as well represent each title as one string:

```
> (write '("And I Love Her" "A Hard Day's Night") port)
```

Pitfalls

⇒ One pitfall crucial to avoid when using files is that if there is an error in your program, it might blow up and return you to the Scheme prompt without closing the open files. If you fix the program and try to run it again, you may get a message like "file busy" because the operating system of your computer may not allow you to open the same file on two ports at once. Even worse, if you exit from Scheme without closing all your ports, on some computers you may find that you have unreadable files thereafter.

To help cope with this problem, we've provided a procedure `close-all-ports` that can be invoked to close every port that you've opened since starting Scheme. This procedure works only in our modified Scheme, but it can help you out of trouble while you're learning.

⇒ Be sure you don't open or close a file within a recursive procedure, if you intend to do it only once. That's why most of the programs in this chapter have the structure of a procedure that opens files, calls a recursive helper, and then closes the files.

⇒ As we explained in the `filemerge` example, you can't read the same line twice. Be sure your program remembers each line in a variable as long as it's needed.

Exercises

22.1 Write a `concatenate` procedure that takes two arguments: a list of names of input files, and one name for an output file. The procedure should copy all of the input files, in order, into the output file.

22.2 Write a procedure to count the number of lines in a file. It should take the filename as argument and return the number.

22.3 Write a procedure to count the number of words in a file. It should take the filename as argument and return the number.

22.4 Write a procedure to count the number of characters in a file, including space characters. It should take the filename as argument and return the number.

22.5 Write a procedure that copies an input file to an output file but eliminates multiple consecutive copies of the same line. That is, if the input file contains the lines

```
John Lennon
Paul McCartney
Paul McCartney
George Harrison


Paul McCartney
Ringo Starr
```

then the output file should contain

```
John Lennon
Paul McCartney
George Harrison

Paul McCartney
Ringo Starr
```

22.6 Write a `lookup` procedure that takes as arguments a filename and a word. The procedure should print (on the screen, not into another file) only those lines from the input file that include the chosen word.

22.7 Write a `page` procedure that takes a filename as argument and prints the file a screenful at a time. Assume that a screen can fit 24 lines; your procedure should print 23 lines of the file and then a prompt message, and then wait for the user to enter a (probably empty) line. It should then print the most recent line from the file again (so that the user will see some overlap between screenfuls) and 22 more lines, and so on until the file ends.

22.8 A common operation in a database program is to *join* two databases, that is, to create a new database combining the information from the two given ones. There has to be some piece of information in common between the two databases. For example, suppose we have a class roster database in which each record includes a student's name, student ID number, and computer account name, like this:

```
((john alec entwistle) 04397 john)
((keith moon) 09382 kmoon)
((peter townshend) 10428 pete)
((roger daltrey) 01025 roger)
```

We also have a grade database in which each student's grades are stored according to computer account name:

```
(john 87 90 76 68 95)
(kmoon 80 88 95 77 89)
(pete 100 92 80 65 72)
(roger 85 96 83 62 74)
```

We want to create a combined database like this:

```
((john alec entwistle) 04397 john 87 90 76 68 95)
((keith moon) 09382 kmoon 80 88 95 77 89)
((peter townshend) 10428 pete 100 92 80 65 72)
((roger daltrey) 01025 roger 85 96 83 62 74)
```

in which the information from the roster and grade databases has been combined for each account name.

Write a program `join` that takes five arguments: two input filenames, two numbers indicating the position of the item within each record that should overlap between the files, and an output filename. For our example, we'd say

```
> (join "class-roster" "grades" 3 1 "combined-file")
```

In our example, both files are in alphabetical order of computer account name, the account name is a word, and the same account name never appears more than once in each file. In general, you may assume that these conditions hold for the item that the two files have in common. Your program should *not* assume that every item in one file also appears in the other. A line should be written in the output file only for the items that do appear in both files.

A row of boxes

23   Vectors

So far all the programs we've written in this book have had no memory of the past history of the computation. We invoke a function with certain arguments, and we get back a value that depends only on those arguments. Compare this with the operation of Scheme itself:

```
> (foo 3)
ERROR: FOO HAS NO VALUE

> (define (foo x)
    (word x x))

> (foo 3)
33
```

Scheme *remembers* that you have defined `foo`, so its response to the very same expression is different the second time. Scheme maintains a record of certain results of its past interaction with you; in particular, Scheme remembers the global variables that you have defined. This record is called its *state*.

Most of the programs that people use routinely are full of state; your text editor, for example, remembers all the characters in your file. In this chapter you will learn how to write programs with state.

The Indy 500

The Indianapolis 500 is an annual 500-mile automobile race, famous among people who like that sort of thing. It's held at the Indianapolis Motor Speedway, a racetrack in Indianapolis, Indiana. (Indiana is better known as the home of Dan Friedman, the coauthor of some good books about Scheme.) The racetrack is $2\frac{1}{2}$ miles long, so, as you might imagine, the racers have to complete 200 laps in order to finish the race. This means that someone has to keep track of how many laps each car has completed so far.

Let's write a program to help this person keep count. Each car has a number, and the count person will invoke the procedure `lap` with that number as argument every time a car completes a lap. The procedure will return the number of laps that that car has completed altogether:

```
> (lap 87)
1

> (lap 64)
1

> (lap 17)
1

> (lap 64)
2

> (lap 64)
3
```

(Car 64 managed to complete three laps before the other cars completed two because the others had flat tires.) Note that we typed the expression (`lap 64`) three times and got three different answers. `Lap` isn't a function! A function has to return the same answer whenever it's invoked with the same arguments.

Vectors

The point of this chapter is to show how procedures like `lap` can be written. To accomplish this, we're going to use a data structure called a *vector*. (You may have seen something similar in other programming languages under the name "array.")

A vector is, in effect, a row of boxes into which values can be put. Each vector has a fixed number of boxes; when you create a vector, you have to say how many boxes you want. Once a vector is created, there are two things you can do with it: You can put a new value into a box (replacing any old value that might have been there), or you can examine the value in a box. The boxes are numbered, starting with zero.

```
> (define v (make-vector 5))
```

```
> (vector-set! v 0 'shoe)

> (vector-set! v 3 'bread)

> (vector-set! v 2 '(savoy truffle))

> (vector-ref v 3)
BREAD
```

There are several details to note here. When we invoke `make-vector` we give it one argument, the number of boxes we want the vector to have. (In this example, there are five boxes, numbered 0 through 4. There is no box 5.) When we create the vector, there is nothing in any of the boxes.*

We put things in boxes using the `vector-set!` procedure. The exclamation point in its name, indicates that this is a *mutator*—a procedure that changes the value of some previously created data structure. The exclamation point is pronounced "bang," as in "vector set bang." (Scheme actually has several such mutators, including mutators for lists, but this is the only one we'll use in this book. A procedure that modifies its argument is also called *destructive*.) The arguments to `vector-set!` are the vector, the number of the box (the *index*), and the desired new value. Like `define`, `vector-set!` returns an unspecified value.

We examine the contents of a box using `vector-ref`, which takes two arguments, the vector and an index. `Vector-ref` is similar to `list-ref`, except that it operates on vectors instead of lists.

We can change the contents of a box that already has something in it.

```
> (vector-set! v 3 'jewel)

> (vector-ref v 3)
JEWEL
```

The old value of box 3, `bread`, is no longer there. It's been replaced by the new value.

```
> (vector-set! v 1 741)
```

---

* The Scheme standard says that the initial contents of the boxes is "unspecified." That means that the result depends on the particular version of Scheme you're using. It's a bad idea to try to examine the contents of a box before putting something in it.

```
> (vector-set! v 4 #t)

> v
#(SHOE 741 (SAVOY TRUFFLE) JEWEL #T)
```

Once the vector is completely full, we can print its value. Scheme prints vectors in a format like that of lists, except that there is a number sign (#) before the open parenthesis. If you ever have need for a constant vector (one that you're not going to mutate), you can quote it using the same notation:

```
> (vector-ref '#(a b c d) 2)
C
```

Using Vectors in Programs

To implement our `lap` procedure, we'll keep its state information, the lap counts, in a vector. We'll use the car number as the index into the vector. It's not enough to create the vector; we have to make sure that each box has a zero as its initial value.

```
(define *lap-vector* (make-vector 100))

(define (initialize-lap-vector index)
  (if (< index 0)
      'done
      (begin (vector-set! *lap-vector* index 0)
             (initialize-lap-vector (- index 1)))))

> (initialize-lap-vector 99)
DONE
```

We've created a global variable whose value is the vector. We used a recursive procedure to put a zero into each box of the vector.* Note that the vector is of length 100, but its largest index is 99. Also, the base case of the recursion is that the index is less than zero, not equal to zero as in many earlier examples. That's because zero is a valid index.

---

* In some versions of Scheme, `make-vector` can take an optional argument specifying an initial value to put in every box. In those versions, we could just say

```
(define *lap-vector* (make-vector 100 0))
```

without having to use the initialization procedure.

Now that we have the vector, we can write `lap`.

```
(define (lap car-number)
  (vector-set! *lap-vector*
               car-number
               (+ (vector-ref *lap-vector* car-number) 1))
  (vector-ref *lap-vector* car-number))
```

Remember that a procedure body can include more than one expression. When the procedure is invoked, the expressions will be evaluated in order. The value returned by the procedure is the value of the last expression (in this case, the second one).

Lap has both a return value and a side effect. The job of the first expression is to carry out that side effect, that is, to add 1 to the lap count for the specified car. The second expression looks at the value we just put in a box to determine the return value.

Non-Functional Procedures and State

We remarked earlier that `lap` isn't a function because invoking it twice with the same argument doesn't return the same value both times.*

It's not a coincidence that `lap` also violates functional programming by maintaining state information. Any procedure whose return value is not a function of its arguments (that is, whose return value is not always the same for any particular arguments) must depend on knowledge of what has happened in the past. After all, computers don't pull results out of the air; if the result of a computation doesn't depend entirely on the arguments we give, then it must depend on some other information available to the program.

Suppose somebody asks you, "Car 54 has just completed a lap; how many has it completed in all?" You can't answer that question with only the information in the question itself; you have to remember earlier events in the race. By contrast, if someone asks you, "What's the plural of 'book'?" what has happened in the past doesn't matter at all.

The connection between non-functional procedures and state also applies to non-functional Scheme primitives. The `read` procedure, for example, returns different results when you invoke it repeatedly with the same argument because it remembers how

---

* That's what we mean by "non-functional," not that it doesn't work!

far it's gotten in the file. That's why the argument is a port instead of a file name: A port is an abstract data type that includes, among other things, this piece of state. (If you're reading from the keyboard, the state is in the person doing the typing.)

A more surprising example is the `random` procedure that you met in Chapter 2. Random isn't a function because it doesn't always return the same value when called with the same argument. How does `random` compute its result? Some versions of `random` compute a number that's based on the current time (in tiny units like milliseconds so you don't get the same answer from two calls in quick succession). How does your computer know the time? Every so often some procedure (or some hardware device) adds 1 to a remembered value, the number of milliseconds since midnight. That's state, and `random` relies on it.

The most commonly used algorithm for random numbers is a little trickier; each time you invoke `random`, the result is a function of *the result from the last time you invoked it*. (The procedure is pretty complicated; typically the old number is multiplied by some large, carefully chosen constant, and only the middle digits of the product are kept.) Each time you invoke `random`, the returned value is stashed away somehow so that the next invocation can remember it. That's state too.

Just because a procedure remembers something doesn't necessarily make it stateful. *Every* procedure remembers the arguments with which it was invoked, while it's running. Otherwise the arguments wouldn't be able to affect the computation. A procedure whose result depends only on its arguments (the ones used in the current invocation) is functional. The procedure is non-functional if it depends on something outside of its current arguments. It's that sort of "long-term" memory that we consider to be state.

In particular, a procedure that uses `let` isn't stateful merely because the body of the `let` remembers the values of the variables created by the `let`. Once `let` returns a value, the variables that it created no longer exist. You couldn't use `let`, for example, to carry out the kind of remembering that `random` needs. `Let` doesn't remember a value *between* invocations, just during a single invocation.

Shuffling a Deck

One of the advantages of the vector data structure is that it allows elements to be rearranged. As an example, we'll create and shuffle a deck of cards.

We'll start with a procedure `card-list` that returns a list of all the cards, in standard order:

```
(define (card-list)
  (reduce append
          (map (lambda (suit) (map (lambda (rank) (word suit rank))
                                   '(a 2 3 4 5 6 7 8 9 10 j q k)))
               '(h s d c))))

> (card-list)
(HA H2 H3 H4 H5 H6 H7 H8 H9 H10 HJ HQ HK
 SA S2 S3 S4 S5 S6 S7 S8 S9 S10 SJ SQ SK
 DA D2 D3 D4 D5 D6 D7 D8 D9 D10 DJ DQ DK
 CA C2 C3 C4 C5 C6 C7 C8 C9 C10 CJ CQ CK)
```

In writing `card-list`, we need `reduce append` because the result from the outer invocation of `map` is a list of lists: `((HA H2 ...) (SA ...) ...)`.*

Each time we want a new deck of cards, we start with this list of 52 cards, copy the list into a vector, and shuffle that vector. We'll use the Scheme primitive `list->vector`, which takes a list as argument and returns a vector of the same length, with the boxes initialized to the corresponding elements of the list. (There is also a procedure `vector->list` that does the reverse. The characters `->` in these function names are

---

* We could get around this problem in a different way:

```
(define (card-list)
  (every (lambda (suit) (every (lambda (rank) (word suit rank))
                               '(a 2 3 4 5 6 7 8 9 10 j q k)))
         '(h s d c)))
```

In this version, we're taking advantage of the fact that our sentence data type was defined in a way that prevents the creation of sublists. A sentence of cards is a good representation for the deck. However, with this approach we are mixing up the list and sentence data types, because later we're going to invoke `list->vector` with this deck of cards as its argument. If we use sentence tools such as `every` to create the deck, then the procedure `card-list` should really be called `card-sentence`.

What difference does it make? The `every` version works fine, as long as sentences are implemented as lists, so that `list->vector` can be applied to a sentence. But the point about abstract data types such as sentences is to avoid making assumptions about their implementation. If for some reason we decided to change the internal representation of sentences, then `list->vector` could no longer be applied to a sentence. Strictly speaking, if we're going to use this trick, we need a separate conversion procedure `sentence->vector`.

Of course, if you don't mind a little typing, you can avoid this whole issue by having a quoted list of all 52 cards built into the definition of `card-list`.

meant to look like an arrow ($\rightarrow$); this is a Scheme convention for functions that convert information from one data type to another.)

```
(define (make-deck)
  (shuffle! (list->vector (card-list)) 51))

(define (shuffle! deck index)
  (if (< index 0)
      deck
      (begin (vector-swap! deck index (random (+ index 1)))
             (shuffle! deck (- index 1)))))

(define (vector-swap! vector index1 index2)
  (let ((temp (vector-ref vector index1)))
    (vector-set! vector index1 (vector-ref vector index2))
    (vector-set! vector index2 temp)))
```

Now, each time we call **make-deck**, we get a randomly shuffled vector of cards:

```
> (make-deck)
#(C4 SA C7 DA S4 D9 SQ H4 C10 D5 H9 S10 D6
  S9 CA C9 S2 H7 S5 H6 D7 HK S7 C3 C2 C6
  HJ SK CQ CJ D4 SJ D8 S8 HA C5 DK D3 HQ
  D10 H8 DJ C8 H2 H5 H3 CK S3 DQ S6 D2 H10)

> (make-deck)
#(CQ H7 D10 D5 S8 C7 H10 SQ H4 H3 D8 C9 S7
  SK DK S6 DA D4 C6 HQ D6 S2 H5 CA H2 HJ
  CK D7 H6 HA CJ C4 SJ HK SA C2 D2 S4 DQ
  S5 C10 H9 D9 C5 D3 DJ C3 S9 S3 C8 S10 H8)
```

How does the shuffling algorithm work? Conceptually it's not complicated, but there are some implementation details that make the actual procedures a little tricky. The general idea is this: We want all the cards shuffled into a random order. So we choose any card at random, and make it the first card. We're then left with a one-card-smaller deck to shuffle, and we do that by recursion. (This algorithm is similar to selection sort from Chapter 15, except that we select a random card each time instead of selecting the smallest value.)

The details that complicate this algorithm have to do with the fact that we're using a vector, in which it's easy to change the value in one particular position, but it's not easy to do what would otherwise be the most natural thing: If you had a handful of actual cards and wanted to move one of them to the front, you'd slide the other cards over to make room. There's no "sliding over" in a vector. Instead we use a trick; we happen to have an empty slot, the one from which we removed the randomly chosen card, so instead of moving several cards, we just move the one card that was originally at the front into that slot. In other words, we exchange two cards, the randomly chosen one and the one that used to be in front.

Second, there's nothing comparable to `cdr` to provide a one-card-smaller vector to the recursive invocation. Instead, we must use the entire vector and also provide an additional `index` argument, a number that keeps track of how many cards remain to be shuffled. It's simplest if each recursive invocation is responsible for the range of cards from position `0` to position `index` of the vector, and therefore the program actually moves each randomly selected card to the *end* of the remaining portion of the deck.

More Vector Tools

If you want to make a vector with only a few boxes, and you know in advance what values you want in those boxes, you can use the constructor `vector`. Like `list`, it takes any number of arguments and returns a vector containing those arguments as elements:

```
> (define beatles (vector 'john 'paul 'george 'pete))

> (vector-set! beatles 3 'ringo)

> beatles
#(JOHN PAUL GEORGE RINGO)
```

The procedure `vector-length` takes a vector as argument and returns the number of boxes in the vector.

```
> (vector-length beatles)
4
```

The predicate `equal?`, which we've used with words and lists, also accepts vectors as arguments. Two vectors are equal if they are the same size and all their corresponding elements are equal. (A list and a vector are never equal, even if their elements are equal.)

Finally, the predicate `vector?` takes anything as argument and returns #t if and only if its argument is a vector.

The Vector Pattern of Recursion

Here are two procedures that you've seen earlier in this chapter, which do something to each element of a vector:

```
(define (initialize-lap-vector index)
  (if (< index 0)
      'done
      (begin (vector-set! *lap-vector* index 0)
             (initialize-lap-vector (- index 1)))))

(define (shuffle! deck index)
  (if (< index 0)
      deck
      (begin (vector-swap! deck index (random (+ index 1)))
             (shuffle! deck (- index 1)))))
```

These procedures have a similar structure, like the similarities we found in other recursive patterns. Both of these procedures take an index as an argument, and both have

```
(< index 0)
```

as their base case. Also, both have, as their recursive case, a `begin` in which the first action does something to the vector element selected by the current index, and the second action is a recursive call with the index decreased by one. These procedures are initially called with the largest possible index value.

In some cases it's more convenient to count the index upward from zero:

```
(define (list->vector lst)
  (l->v-helper (make-vector (length lst)) lst 0))

(define (l->v-helper vec lst index)
  (if (= index (vector-length vec))
      vec
      (begin (vector-set! vec index (car lst))
             (l->v-helper vec (cdr lst) (+ index 1)))))
```

Since lists are naturally processed from left to right (using `car` and `cdr`), this program must process the vector from left to right also.

Vectors versus Lists

Since we introduced vectors to provide mutability, you may have the impression that mutability is the main difference between vectors and lists. Actually, lists are mutable too, although the issues are more complicated; that's why we haven't used list mutation in this book.

The most important difference between lists and vectors is that each kind of aggregate lends itself to a different style of programming, because some operations are faster than others in each. List programming is characterized by two operations: dividing a list into its first element and all the rest, and sticking one new element onto the front of a list. Vector programming is characterized by selecting elements in any order, from a collection whose size is set permanently when the vector is created.

To make these rather vague descriptions more concrete, here are two procedures, one of which squares every number in a list, and the other of which squares every number in a vector:

```
(define (list-square numbers)
  (if (null? numbers)
      '()
      (cons (square (car numbers))
            (list-square (cdr numbers)))))

(define (vector-square numbers)
  (vec-sq-helper (make-vector (vector-length numbers))
                 numbers
                 (- (vector-length numbers) 1)))

(define (vec-sq-helper new old index)
  (if (< index 0)
      new
      (begin (vector-set! new index (square (vector-ref old index)))
             (vec-sq-helper new old (- index 1)))))
```

In the list version, the intermediate stages of the algorithm deal with lists that are smaller than the original argument. Each recursive invocation "strips off" one element of its argument and "glues on" one extra element in its return value. In the vector version, the returned vector is created, at full size, as the first step in the algorithm; its component parts are filled in as the program proceeds.

This example can plausibly be done with either vectors or lists, so we've used it to compare the two techniques. But some algorithms fit most naturally with one kind of aggregate and would be awkward and slow using the other kind. The swapping of pairs of elements in the shuffling algorithm would be much harder using lists, while mergesort would be harder using vectors.

The best way to understand these differences in style is to know the operations that are most efficient for each kind of aggregate. In each case, there are certain operations that can be done in one small unit of time, regardless of the number of elements in the aggregate, while other operations take more time for more elements. The *constant time* operations for lists are `cons`, `car`, `cdr`, and `null?`; the ones for vectors are `vector-ref`, `vector-set!`, and `vector-length`.* And if you reread the squaring programs, you'll find that these are precisely the operations they use.

We might have used `list-ref` in the list version, but we didn't, and Scheme programmers usually don't, because we know that it would be slower. Similarly, we could implement something like `cdr` for vectors, but that would be slow, too, since it would have to make a one-smaller vector and copy the elements one at a time. There are two possible morals to this story, and they're both true: First, programmers invent and learn the algorithms that make sense for whatever data structure is available. Thus we have well-known programming patterns, such as the `filter` pattern, appropriate for lists, and different patterns appropriate for vectors. Second, programmers choose which data structure to use depending on what algorithms they need. If you want to shuffle cards, use a vector, but if you want to split the deck into a bunch of variable-size piles, lists might be more appropriate. In general, vectors are good at selecting elements in arbitrary order from a fixed-size collection; lists are good only at selecting elements strictly from left to right, but they can vary in size.

In this book, despite what we're saying here about efficiency, we've generally tried to present algorithms in the way that's easiest to understand, even when we know that there's a faster way. For example, we've shown several recursive procedures in which the base case test was

```
(= (count sent) 1)
```

If we were writing the program for practical use, rather than for a book, we would have written

```
(empty? (butfirst sent))
```

---

* Where did this information come from? Just take our word for it. In later courses you'll study how vectors and lists are implemented, and then there will be reasons.

because we know that `empty?` and `butfirst` are both constant time operations (because for sentences they're implemented as `null?` and `cdr`), while `count` takes a long time for large sentences. But the version using `count` makes the intent clearer.*

State, Sequence, and Effects

Effects, sequence, and state are three sides of the same coin.**

In Chapter 20 we explained the connection between effect (printing something on the screen) and sequence: It matters what you print first. We also noted that there's no benefit to a sequence of expressions unless those expressions produce an effect, since the values returned by all but the last expression are discarded.

In this chapter we've seen another connection. The way our vector programs maintain state information is by carrying out effects, namely, `vector-set!` invocations. Actually, *every* effect changes some kind of state; if not in Scheme's memory, then on the computer screen or in a file.

The final connection to be made is between state and sequence. Once a program maintains state, it matters whether some computation is carried out before or after another computation that changes the state. The example at the beginning of this chapter in which an expression had different results before and after defining a variable illustrates this point. As another example, if we evaluate `(lap 1)` 200 times and `(lap 2)` 200 times, the program's determination of the winner of the race depends on whether the last evaluation of `(lap 1)` comes before or after the last invocation of `(lap 2)`.

Because these three ideas are so closely connected, the names *sequential programming* (emphasizing sequence) and *imperative programming* (emphasizing effect) are both used to refer to a style of programming that uses all three. This style is in contrast with functional programming, which, as you know, uses none of them.

Although functional and sequential programming are, in a sense, opposites, it's perfectly possible to use both styles within one program, as we pointed out in the tic-tac-toe program of Chapter 20. We'll show more such hybrid programs in the following chapters.

---

* For words, it turns out, the `count` version is faster, because words behave more like vectors than like lists.

** ... to coin a phrase.

Pitfalls

⇒ Don't forget that the first element of a vector is number zero, and there is no element whose index number is equal to the length of the vector. (Although these points are equally true for lists, it doesn't often matter, because we rarely select the elements of a list by number.) In particular, in a vector recursion, if zero is the base case, then there's probably still one element left to process.

⇒ Try the following experiment:

```
> (define dessert (vector 'chocolate 'sundae))
> (define two-desserts (list dessert dessert))
> (vector-set! (car two-desserts) 1 'shake)
> two-desserts
(#(CHOCOLATE SHAKE) #(CHOCOLATE SHAKE))
```

You might have expected that after asking to change one word in **two-desserts**, the result would be

```
(#(CHOCOLATE SHAKE) #(CHOCOLATE SUNDAE))
```

However, because of the way we created **two-desserts**, both of its elements are the *same* vector. If you think of a list as a collection of things, it's strange to imagine the very same thing in two different places, but that's the situation. If you want to have two separate vectors that happen to have the same values in their elements, but are individually mutable, you'd have to say

```
> (define two-desserts (list (vector 'chocolate 'sundae)
                             (vector 'chocolate 'sundae)))
> (vector-set! (car two-desserts) 1 'shake)
> two-desserts
(#(CHOCOLATE SHAKE) #(CHOCOLATE SUNDAE))
```

Each invocation of **vector** or **make-vector** creates a new, independent vector.

Exercises

Do not solve any of the following exercises by converting a vector to a list, using list procedures, and then converting the result back to a vector.

23.1 Write a procedure `sum-vector` that takes a vector full of numbers as its argument and returns the sum of all the numbers:

```
> (sum-vector '#(6 7 8))
21
```

23.2 Some versions of Scheme provide a procedure `vector-fill!` that takes a vector and anything as its two arguments. It replaces every element of the vector with the second argument, like this:

```
> (define vec (vector 'one 'two 'three 'four))

> vec
#(one two three four)

> (vector-fill! vec 'yeah)

> vec
#(yeah yeah yeah yeah)
```

Write `vector-fill!`. (It doesn't matter what value it returns.)

23.3 Write a function `vector-append` that works just like regular `append`, but for vectors:

```
> (vector-append '#(not a) '#(second time))
#(not a second time)
```

23.4 Write `vector->list`.

23.5 Write a procedure `vector-map` that takes two arguments, a function and a vector, and returns a new vector in which each box contains the result of applying the function to the corresponding element of the argument vector.

23.6 Write a procedure `vector-map!` that takes two arguments, a function and a vector, and modifies the argument vector by replacing each element with the result of applying the function to that element. Your procedure should return the same vector.

23.7 Could you write `vector-filter`? How about `vector-filter!`? Explain the issues involved.

23.8 Modify the `lap` procedure to print "Car 34 wins!" when car 34 completes its 200th lap. (A harder but more correct modification is to print the message only if no other car has completed 200 laps.)

23.9 Write a procedure `leader` that says which car is in the lead right now.

23.10 Why doesn't this solution to Exercise 23.9 work?

```
(define (leader)
  (leader-helper 0 1))

(define (leader-helper leader index)
  (cond ((= index 100) leader)
        ((> (lap index) (lap leader))
         (leader-helper index (+ index 1)))
        (else (leader-helper leader (+ index 1)))))
```

23.11 In some restaurants, the servers use computer terminals to keep track of what each table has ordered. Every time you order more food, the server enters your order into the computer. When you're ready for the check, the computer prints your bill.

You're going to write two procedures, `order` and `bill`. `Order` takes a table number and an item as arguments and adds the cost of that item to that table's bill. `Bill` takes a table number as its argument, returns the amount owed by that table, and resets the table for the next customers. (Your `order` procedure can examine a global variable `*menu*` to find the price of each item.)

```
> (order 3 'potstickers)

> (order 3 'wor-won-ton)

> (order 5 'egg-rolls)

> (order 3 'shin-shin-special-prawns)

> (bill 3)
13.85

> (bill 5)
2.75
```

23.12 Rewrite selection sort (from Chapter 15) to sort a vector. This can be done in a way similar to the procedure for shuffling a deck: Find the smallest element of the vector and exchange it (using `vector-swap!`) with the value in the first box. Then find the smallest element not including the first box, and exchange that with the second box, and so on. For example, suppose we have a vector of numbers:

```
#(23 4 18 7 95 60)
```

Your program should transform the vector through these intermediate stages:

```
#(4 23 18 7 95 60)    ; exchange 4 with 23
#(4 7 18 23 95 60)    ; exchange 7 with 23
#(4 7 18 23 95 60)    ; exchange 18 with itself
#(4 7 18 23 95 60)    ; exchange 23 with itself
#(4 7 18 23 60 95)    ; exchange 60 with 95
```

23.13 Why doesn't this work?

```
(define (vector-swap! vector index1 index2)
  (vector-set! vector index1 (vector-ref vector index2))
  (vector-set! vector index2 (vector-ref vector index1)))
```

23.14 Implement a two-dimensional version of vectors. (We'll call one of these structures a *matrix*.) The implementation will use a vector of vectors. For example, a three-by-five matrix will be a three-element vector, in which each of the elements is a five-element vector. Here's how it should work:

```
> (define m (make-matrix 3 5))

> (matrix-set! m 2 1 '(her majesty))

> (matrix-ref m 2 1)
(HER MAJESTY)
```

23.15 Generalize Exercise 23.14 by implementing an *array* structure that can have any number of dimensions. Instead of taking two numbers as index arguments, as the matrix procedures do, the array procedures will take one argument, a *list* of numbers. The number of numbers is the number of dimensions, and it will be constant for any particular array. For example, here is a three-dimensional array ($4 \times 5 \times 6$):

```
> (define a1 (make-array '(4 5 6)))

> (array-set! a1 '(3 2 3) '(the end))
```

23.16 We want to reimplement sentences as vectors instead of lists.

(a) Write versions of `sentence`, `empty?`, `first`, `butfirst`, `last`, and `butlast` that use vectors. Your selectors need only work for sentences, not for words.

```
> (sentence 'a 'b 'c)
#(A B C)

> (butfirst (sentence 'a 'b 'c))
#(B C)
```

(You don't have to make these procedures work on lists as well as vectors!)

(b) Does the following program still work with the new implementation of sentences? If not, fix the program.

```
(define (praise stuff)
  (sentence stuff '(is good)))
```

(c) Does the following program still work with the new implementation of sentences? If not, fix the program.

```
(define (praise stuff)
  (sentence stuff 'rules!))
```

(d) Does the following program still work with the new implementation of sentences? If not, fix the program. If so, is there some optional rewriting that would improve its performance?

```
(define (item n sent)
  (if (= n 1)
      (first sent)
      (item (- n 1) (butfirst sent))))
```

(e) Does the following program still work with the new implementation of sentences? If not, fix the program. If so, is there some optional rewriting that would improve its performance?

```
(define (every fn sent)
  (if (empty? sent)
      sent
      (sentence (fn (first sent))
                (every fn (butfirst sent)))))
```

(f) In what ways does using vectors to implement sentences affect the speed of the selectors and constructor? Why do you think we chose to use lists?

	A	B	C	D	E	F
1	NAME	NUMBER	PRICE	GROSS	DISCOUNT	NET
2	Widget	40.00	1.27	50.80	0.00	50.80
3	Thingo	203.00	14.95	3034.85	15.00	2579.62
4	Computer	1.00	6500.00	6500.00	8.00	5980.00
5	Yacht	300.00	200000.00	60000000.00	0.00	60000000.00
6						
7						
8						
9	TOTALS			60009585.7		60008610.4

Spreadsheet display from Microsoft Excel

24   Example: A Spreadsheet Program

Until now, you may have felt that the programs you've been writing in Scheme don't act like other computer programs you've used. In this chapter and the next, we're going to tie together almost everything you've learned so far to write a *spreadsheet* program, just like the ones accountants use.

This chapter describes the operation of the spreadsheet program, as a user manual would. The next chapter explains how the program is implemented in Scheme.

You can load our program into Scheme by typing

```
(load "spread.scm")
```

To start the program, invoke the procedure `spreadsheet` with no arguments; to quit the spreadsheet program, type `exit`.

A spreadsheet is a program that displays information in two dimensions on the screen. It can also compute some of the information automatically. On the next page is an example of a display from our spreadsheet program. The display is a rectangle of information with six columns and 20 rows. The intersection of a row with a column is called a *cell;* for example, the cell `c4` contains the number 6500. The column letters (`a` through `f`) and row numbers are provided by the spreadsheet program, as is the information on the bottom few lines, which we'll talk about later. (The `??` at the very bottom is the spreadsheet prompt; you type commands on that line.) We typed most of the entries in the cells, using commands such as

```
(put 6500 c4)
```

```
      -----a----   -----b----   -----c----   -----d----   -----e----   -----f----
  1   NAME         NUMBER       PRICE        GROSS        DISCOUNT     NET
  2   Widget           40.00         1.27         50.80         0.00         50.80
  3   Thingo          203.00        14.95 >    3034.85<        15.00       2579.62
  4   Computer          1.00      6500.00      6500.00         8.00       5980.00
  5   Yacht           300.00    200000.00   60000000.+         0.00    60000000.+
  6
  7
  8
  9   TOTALS       60009585.+                60008610.+
 10
 11
 12
 13
 14
 15
 16
 17
 18
 19
 20
 d3:   3034.85
 (* b3 c3)
 ??
```

What's most useful about a spreadsheet is its ability to compute some of the cell values itself. For example, every number in column d is the product of the numbers in columns b and c of the same row. Instead of putting a particular number in a particular cell, we put a *formula* in all the cells of the column at once.* This implies that when we change the value of one cell, other cells will be updated automatically. For example, if we put the number 5 into cell b4, the spreadsheet will look like this:

---

* We did it by saying

```
(put (* (cell b) (cell c)) d)
```

but we aren't going to talk about the details of formulas for a while longer.

```
        -----a----    ----b----   -----c----   -----d----   -----e----   -----f----
   1   NAME          NUMBER       PRICE         GROSS       DISCOUNT     NET
   2   Widget          40.00        1.27         50.80        0.00          50.80
   3   Thingo         203.00       14.95 >     3034.85<      15.00        2579.62
   4   Computer         5.00      6500.00      32500.00       8.00       29900.00
   5   Yacht          300.00    200000.00    60000000.+       0.00     60000000.+
   6
   7
   8
   9   TOTALS      60035585.+                 60032530.+
  10
  11
  12
  13
  14
  15
  16
  17
  18
  19
  20
  d3:   3034.85
  (* b3 c3)
  ??
```

In addition to cell **b4**, the spreadsheet program has changed the values in **d4**, **f4**, **d9**, and **f9**.

One detail we haven't mentioned so far is that at any moment there is one *selected* cell. Right now cell **d3** is selected. You can tell that because of the arrowheads surrounding it in the display, like this:

```
>    3034.85<
```

Also, the lines

```
d3:   3034.85
(* b3 c3)
```

at the bottom of the screen mean that cell **d3** is selected, its value is 3034.85, and its formula is (* b3 c3).

Limitations of Our Spreadsheet

In commercial spreadsheet programs, you generally select a cell with arrow keys or by clicking on it with a mouse. The highlighted cell is typically displayed in inverse video, and there might be thin lines drawn in a grid on the screen to separate the cells.

Our program leaves all this out for two reasons. First, details like this don't add very much to what you learn from studying the program, but they take a disproportionate effort to get exactly right. Second, the facilities needed in Scheme to control screen graphics are specific to each model of computer. We couldn't write a single program that would work in all versions of Scheme. (A program that works in all versions is called *portable*.)

Similarly, our program prints an entire new screenful of information after every command. A better program would change only the parts of the screen for which the corresponding values have changed. But there is no uniform way to ask Scheme to print at a particular position on the screen; some versions of Scheme can do that, but not using standard procedures.

Also, of course, if you spend $500 on a spreadsheet program, it will have hundreds of bells and whistles, such as graphing, printing your spreadsheet on paper, changing the widths of columns, and undoing the last command you typed. But each of those is a straightforward extension. We didn't write them all because there are only two of us and we're not getting paid enough! You'll add some features as exercises.

Spreadsheet Commands

When you begin the spreadsheet program, you will see an empty grid and a prompt at the bottom of the screen.

Most spreadsheet programs are controlled using single-keystroke commands (or equivalent mouse clicks). That's another thing we can't do entirely portably in Scheme. We've tried to compromise by including one-letter command names in our program, but you do have to type the `return` or `enter` key after each command. The single-letter commands are for simple operations, such as selecting a cell one position up, down, left, or right from the previously selected cell.

For more complicated commands, such as entering values, a longer notation is obviously required. In our program we use a notation that looks very much like that of a Scheme program: A command consists of a name and some arguments, all enclosed in parentheses. However, the spreadsheet commands are *not* Scheme expressions. In particular, the arguments are not evaluated as they would be in Scheme. For example, earlier we said

```
(put 6500 c4)
```

If this were a Scheme expression, we would have had to quote the second argument:

```
(put 6500 'c4)                              ;; wrong!
```

Moving the Selection

There are four one-letter commands to move to a new selected cell:

Command Name	Meaning
f	move Forward (right)
b	move Back (left)
n	move to Next line (down)
p	move to Previous line (up)

(These command names are taken from EMACS, the industry standard text editor.)

If you want to move one step, you can just type the letter f, b, n, or p on a line by itself. If you want to move farther, you can invoke the same commands in Scheme notation, with the distance to move as an argument:

```
?? (f 4)
```

Another way to move the selection is to choose a particular cell by name. The command for this is called select:

```
(select e12)
```

The spreadsheet grid includes columns a through z and rows 1 through 30. Not all of it can fit on the screen at once. If you select a cell that's not shown on the screen, then the program will shift the entire screen display so that the rows and columns shown will include the newly selected cell.

Putting Values in Cells

As we've already seen, the `put` command is used to put a value in a particular cell. It can be used with either one or two arguments. The first (or only) argument is a value. If there is a second argument, it is the (unquoted) name of the desired cell. If not, the currently selected cell will be used.

A value can be a number or a quoted word. (As in Scheme programming, most words can be quoted using the single-quote notation `'word`, but words that include spaces, mixed-case letters, or some punctuation characters must be quoted using the double-quote string notation `"Widget"`.) However, non-numeric words are used only as labels; they can't provide values for formulas that compute values in other cells.

The program displays numbers differently from labels. If the value in a cell is a number, it is displayed at the right edge of its cell, and it is shown with two digits following the decimal point. (Look again at the screen samples earlier in this chapter.) If the value is a non-numeric word, it is displayed at the left edge of its cell.

If the value is too wide to fit in the cell (that is, more than ten characters wide), then the program prints the first nine characters followed by a plus sign (`+`) to indicate that there is more information than is visible. (If you want to see the full value in such a cell, select it and look at the bottom of the screen.)

To erase the value from a cell, you can put an empty list (`)` in it. With this one exception, lists are not allowed as cell values.

It's possible to put a value in an entire row or column, instead of just one cell. To do this, use the row number or the column letter as the second argument to `put`. Here's an example:

```
(put 'peter d)
```

This command will put the word `peter` into all the cells in column `d`. (Remember that not all the cells are visible at once, but even the invisible ones are affected. Cells `d1` through `d30` are given values by this command.)

What happens if you ask to fill an entire row or column at once, but some of the cells already have values? In this case, only the vacant cells will be affected. The only exception is that if the *value* you are using is the empty list, indicating that you want to erase old values, then the entire row or column is affected. (So if you put a formula in an entire row or column and then change your mind, you must erase the old one before you can install a new one.)

Formulas

We mentioned earlier that the value of one cell can be made to depend on the values of other cells. This, too, is done using the `put` command. The difference is that instead of putting a constant value into a cell, you can put a formula in the cell. Here's an example:

```
(put (+ b3 c5) d6)
```

This command says that the value in cell `d6` should be the sum of the values in `b3` and `c5`. The command may or may not have any immediately visible effect; it depends on whether those two cells already have values. If so, a value will immediately appear in `d6`; if not, nothing happens until you put values into `b3` and `c5`.

If you erase the value in a cell, then any cells that depend on it are also erased. For example, if you erase the value in `b3`, then the value in `d6` will disappear also.

So far we've seen only one example of a formula; it asks for the sum of two cells. Formulas, like Scheme expressions, can include invocations of functions with sub-formulas as the arguments.

```
(put (* d6 (+ b4 92)) a3)
```

The "atomic" formulas are constants (numbers or quoted words) and cell references (such as `b4` in our example).

Not every Scheme function can be used in a formula. Most important, there is no `lambda` in the spreadsheet language, so you can't invent your own functions. Also, since formulas can be based only on numbers, only the numeric functions can be used.

Although we've presented the idea of putting a formula in a cell separately from the idea of putting a value in a cell, a value is really just a particularly simple formula. The program makes no distinction internally between these two cases. (Since a constant formula doesn't depend on any other cells, its value is always displayed right away.)

We mentioned that a value can be `put` into an entire row or column at once. The same is true of formulas in general. But this capability gives rise to a slight complication. The typical situation is that each cell in the row or column should be computed using the same algorithm, but based on different values. For example, in the spreadsheet at the beginning of the chapter, every cell in column `d` is the product of a cell in column `b` and a cell in column `c`, but not the *same* cell for every row. If we used a formula like

```
(put (* b2 c2) d)
```

then every cell in column **d** would have the value `50.80`. Instead we want the equivalent of

```
(put (* b2 c2) d2)
(put (* b3 c3) d3)
(put (* b4 c4) d4)
```

and so on. The spreadsheet program meets this need by providing a notation for cells that indicates position relative to the cell being computed, rather than by name. In our case we could say

```
(put (* (cell b) (cell c)) d)
```

`Cell` can take one or two arguments. In this example we've used the one-argument version. The argument must be either a letter, to indicate a column, or a number between 1 and 30, to indicate a row. Whichever dimension (row or column) is *not* specified by the argument will be the same as that of the cell being computed. So, for example, if we are computing a value for cell **d5**, then (`cell b`) refers to cell **b5**, but (`cell 12`) would refer to cell **d12**.

The one-argument form of `cell` is adequate for many situations, but not if you want a cell to depend on one that's both in a different row and in a different column. For example, suppose you wanted to compute the change of a number across various columns, like this:

	-----a----	-----b----	-----c----	-----d----	-----e----	-----f----
1	MONTH	January	February	March	April	May
2	PRICE	70.00	74.00	79.00	76.50	81.00
3	CHANGE		4.00	5.00	-2.50	4.50

The value of cell **d3**, for example, is a function of the values of cells **d2** and **c2**.

To create this spreadsheet, we said

```
(put (- (cell 2) (cell <1 2)) 3)
```

The first appearance of `cell` asks for the value of the cell immediately above the one being calculated. (That is, it asks for the cell in row 2 of the same column.) But the one-argument notation doesn't allow us to ask for the cell above and to the left.

In the two-argument version, the first argument determines the column and the second determines the row. Each argument can take any of several forms. It can be a letter (for the column) or number (for the row), to indicate a specific column or row. It can be an asterisk (*) to indicate the same column or row as the cell being calculated. Finally, either argument can take the form <3 to indicate a cell three before the one being calculated (above or to the left, depending on whether this is the row or column argument) or >5 to indicate a cell five after this one (below or to the right).

So any of the following formulas would have let us calculate the change in this example:

```
(put (- (cell 2) (cell <1 2)) 3)

(put (- (cell 2) (cell <1 <1)) 3)

(put (- (cell * 2) (cell <1 2)) 3)

(put (- (cell * <1) (cell <1 2)) 3)

(put (- (cell <0 <1) (cell <1 <1)) 3)
```

When a formula is put into every cell in a particular row or column, it may not be immediately computable for all those cells. The value for each cell will depend on the values of the cells to which the formula refers, and some of those cells may not have values. (If a cell has a non-numeric value, that's the same as not having a value at all for this purpose.) New values are computed only for those cells for which the formula is computable. For example, cell b3 in the monthly change display has the formula (- b2 a2), but the value of cell a2 is the label PRICE, so no value is computed for b3.

Displaying Formula Values

Formulas can be used in two ways. We've seen that a formula can be associated with a cell, so that changes to one cell can automatically recompute the value of another. You can also type a formula directly to the spreadsheet prompt, in which case the value of the formula will be shown at the bottom of the screen. In a formula used in this way, cell references relative to "the cell being computed" refer instead to the selected cell.

Loading Spreadsheet Commands from a File

Sometimes you use a series of several spreadsheet commands to set up some computation.

For example, we had to use several commands such as

```
(put "Thingo" a3)
```

to set up the sample spreadsheet displays at the beginning of this chapter.

If you want to avoid retyping such a series of commands, you can put the commands in a file using a text editor. Then, in the spreadsheet program, use the command

```
(load "filename")
```

This looks just like Scheme's `load` (on purpose), but it's not the same thing; the file that it loads must contain spreadsheet commands, not Scheme expressions. It will list the commands from the file as it carries them out.

Application Programs and Abstraction

We've talked throughout this book about the importance of abstraction, the act of giving a name to some process or structure. Writing an application program can be seen as the ultimate in abstraction. The user of the program is encouraged to think in a vocabulary that reflects the tasks for which the program is used, rather than the steps by which the program does its work. Some of these names are explicitly used to control the program, either by typing commands or by selecting named choices from a menu. Our spreadsheet program, for example, uses the name `put` for the task of putting a formula into a cell. The algorithm used by the `put` command is quite complicated, but the user's picture of the command is simple. Other names are not explicitly used to control the program; instead, they give the user a *metaphor* with which to think about the work of the program. For example, in describing the operation of our spreadsheet program, we've talked about rows, columns, cells, and formulas. Introducing this vocabulary in our program *documentation* is just as much an abstraction as introducing new procedures in the program itself.

In the past we've used procedural abstraction to achieve *generalization* of an algorithm, moving from specific instances to a more universal capability, especially when we implemented the higher-order functions. If you've used application programs, though, you've probably noticed that in a different sense the abstraction in the program *loses* generality. For example, a formula in our spreadsheet program can operate only on data that are in cells. The same formula, expressed as a Scheme procedure, can get its arguments from anywhere: from reading a file, from the keyboard, from a global variable, or from the result of invoking some other procedure.

An application program doesn't have to be less general than a programming language. The best application programs are *extensible*. Broadly speaking, this means that the programmer has made it possible for the user to add capabilities to the program, or modify existing capabilities. This broad idea of extensibility can take many forms in practice. Some kinds of extensibility are more flexible than others; some are easier to use than others. Here are a few examples:

Commercial spreadsheet programs have grown in extensibility. We mentioned that our spreadsheet program allows the user to express a function only as a formula attached to a cell. Modern commercial programs allow the user to define a procedure, similar in spirit to a Scheme procedure, that can then be used in formulas.

Our program, on the other hand, is extensible in a different sense: We provide the Scheme programs that implement the spreadsheet in a form that users can read and modify. In the next chapter, in fact, you'll be asked to extend our spreadsheet. Most commercial programs are provided in a form that computers can read, but people can't. The provision of human-readable programs is an extremely flexible form of extensibility, but not necessarily an easy one, since you have to know how to program to take advantage of it.

We have written much of this book using a home computer as a remote terminal to a larger computer at work. The telecommunication program we're using, called *Zterm*, has dozens of options. We can set frivolous things like the screen color and the sound used to attract our attention; we can set serious things like the file transfer protocol used to "download" a chapter for printing at home. The program has a directory of telephone numbers for different computers we use, and we can set the technical details of the connection separately for each number. It's very easy to customize the program in all of these ways, because it uses a mouse-driven graphical interface. But the interface is inflexible. For example, although the screen can display thousands of colors, only eight are available in Zterm. More important, if we think of an entirely new feature that would require a modification to the program, there's no way we can do it. This program's extensibility is the opposite of that in our spreadsheet: It's very easy to use, but limited in flexibility.

We started by saying that the abstraction in an application program runs the risk of limiting the program's generality, but that this risk can be countered by paying attention to the goal of *extensibility*. The ultimate form of extensibility is to provide the full capabilities of a programming language to the user of the application program. This can be done by inventing a special-purpose language for one particular application, such as the *Hypertalk* language that's used only in the *Hypercard* application program. Alternatively, the application programmer can take advantage of an existing general-purpose language by making it available within the program. You'll see an example soon, in the database project, which the user controls by typing expressions at a Scheme prompt. The EMACS text editor is a better-known example that includes a Lisp interpreter.

Exercises

For each of the following exercises, the information to hand in is the sequence of spreadsheet commands you used to carry out the assignment. You will find the `load` command helpful in these exercises.

24.1 Set up a spreadsheet to keep track of the grades in a course. Each column should be an assignment; each row should be a student. The last column should add the grade points from the individual assignments. You can make predictions about your grades on future assignments and see what overall numeric grade each prediction gives you.

24.2 Make a table of tax and tip amounts for a range of possible costs at a restaurant. Column **a** should contain the pre-tax amounts, starting at 50 cents and increasing by 50 cents per row. (Do this without entering each row separately!) Column **b** should compute the tax, based on your state's tax rate. Column **c** should compute the 15% tip. Column **d** should add columns **a** through **c** to get the total cost of the meal. Column **e** should contain the same total cost, rounded up to the next whole dollar amount.

24.3 Make a spreadsheet containing the values from Pascal's triangle: Each element should be the sum of the number immediately above it and the number immediately to its left, except that all of column **a** should have the value 1, and all of row 1 should have the value 1.

They did spreadsheets by hand in the old days.

25 Implementing the Spreadsheet Program

This is a big program and you can't keep it all in your head at once. In this chapter, we'll discuss different parts of the program separately. For example, while we're talking about the screen display procedures, we'll just take the rest of the program for granted. We'll assume that we can ask for the value in a cell, and some other part of the program will ensure that we can find it out.

Our division of the program includes these parts:

- The command processor, which reads user commands and oversees their execution.

- The specific commands: cell selection commands, `load`, and `put`.

- The formula translator, which turns a formula into an *expression* by translating relative cell positions to specific cells.

- The dependency manager, which keeps track of which cells' expressions depend on which other cells.

- The expression evaluator.

- The screen printer.

- The cell management procedures, which store and retrieve cell information for the rest of the program.

The diagram on the next page shows the interconnections among these seven parts of the program by showing what information they have to provide for each other.

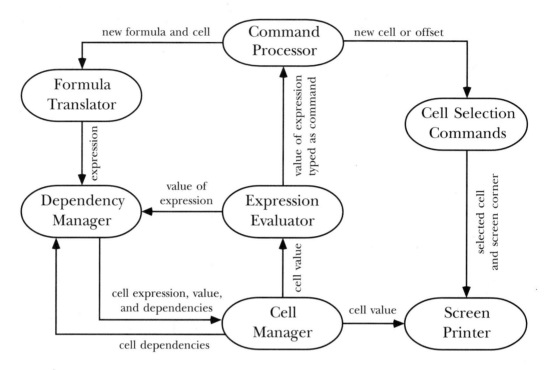

(The arrows that *aren't* in the diagram convey as much information as the ones that are. For example, since there is no arrow from the evaluator to the printer, we know that when the spreadsheet program redisplays the screen, the values printed are found directly in the data structure; no new computation of formulas is needed.)

Cells, Cell Names, and Cell IDs

The spreadsheet program does its work by manipulating cells. In this section we introduce three abstract data types having to do with cells. Before we jump into the spreadsheet procedures themselves, we must introduce these three types, which are used throughout the program.

Each cell is a data structure that contains various pieces of information, including its value and other things that we'll talk about later. Just as these cells are arranged in a two-dimensional pattern on the screen, they are kept within the program in a two-dimensional data structure: a vector of vectors.

The elements of a vector are selected by number, using `vector-ref`. Therefore, if we're looking for a particular cell, such as `c5`, what the program really wants to know is that this cell is in column 3, row 5.* If the program refers to cells by name, then there will be several occasions for it to split the word c5 into its pieces c and 5, and to convert the letter c into the number 3. These operations are fairly slow. To avoid carrying them out repeatedly, the spreadsheet program identifies cells internally using a form that's invisible to the person using the program, called a "cell ID."

Therefore, there are three different abstract data types in the program that have to do with cells: cell names, such as c5; cell IDs; and cells themselves. We've chosen to represent cell IDs as three-element lists like this one:

```
(id 3 5)
```

but you won't see much evidence of that fact within the program because we've implemented selectors and constructors for all of these three types. The representation includes the word id because one facility that the program needs is the ability to determine whether some datum is or is not a cell ID. The predicate cell-id? looks for a list whose first element is id.

The selectors for cell IDs are id-row and id-col; both take a cell ID as argument and return a number. The constructor, make-id, takes a column number (not a letter) and a row number as arguments.

When the program recognizes a cell name typed by the user, it calls cell-name->id to translate the name to an ID, and only the ID is stored for later use.

(These application-specific ADTs are similar to the database of known values in the pattern matcher, as opposed to more general-purpose ADTs like trees and sentences.)

The Command Processor

Here's the core of the command processor:

```
(define (command-loop)
  (print-screen)
  (let ((command-or-formula (read)))
    (if (equal? command-or-formula 'exit)
        "Bye!"
        (begin (process-command command-or-formula)
               (command-loop)))))
```

* The vector elements are numbered from zero, but we number rows and columns from one, subtracting one in the selector that actually extracts information from the array of cells.

This short program runs until the user types `exit`, because it invokes itself as its last step. During each invocation, it prints the current spreadsheet display, uses `read` to read a command, and carries out whatever actions that command requires. Those actions probably change something in the spreadsheet data, so the next cycle has to redisplay the modified data before accepting another command.

`Print-screen` is a large chunk of the program and will be discussed in its own section.

How does `process-command` work? It looks for the command name (a word such as `put`) in its list of known commands. The commands are kept in an association list, like this:

```
((p ...) (n ...) (b ...) (f ...) (select ...) (put ...) (load ...))
```

Each of these sublists contains two elements: the name and the procedure that carries out the command. We'll see shortly how these procedures are invoked.

Looking for the command name is a little tricky because in the spreadsheet language a command can be invoked either by typing its name inside parentheses with arguments, as in Scheme, or by typing the name alone, without parentheses, which Scheme wouldn't interpret as a request to invoke a procedure. For example, the argument to `process-command` might be a list, such as (`f 3`), or just a word, such as `f`. A third case is that the argument might not be one of these commands at all, but instead might be a formula, just like one that could be used to determine the value in a cell. `Process-command` must recognize these three cases:

```
(define (process-command command-or-formula)
  (cond ((and (list? command-or-formula)
              (command? (car command-or-formula)))
         (execute-command command-or-formula))
        ((command? command-or-formula)
         (execute-command (list command-or-formula 1)))
        (else (exhibit (ss-eval (pin-down command-or-formula
                                          (selection-cell-id)))))))
```

The `command?` predicate tells whether its argument is one of the command names in the list. As you can see, if a command name is used without parentheses, `process-command` pretends that it was given an argument of 1.

`Execute-command` looks up the command name in the list of commands, then applies the associated procedure to the arguments, if any:

```
(define (execute-command command)
  (apply (get-command (car command))
         (cdr command)))
```

The else clause in process-command, which handles the case of a formula typed instead of a command, invokes several procedures that you haven't seen yet. We'll explain them when we get to the section of the program that manipulates formulas. The only one that's used just for command processing is exhibit:

```
(define (exhibit val)
  (show val)
  (show "Type RETURN to redraw screen")
  (read-line)
  (read-line))
```

This prints a value on the screen, gives the user a chance to read it, and then, when the user is ready, returns to processing commands. (This will entail redrawing the spreadsheet display; that's why we have to wait for the user to hit return.) The reason that we invoke read-line twice is that the call to read from command-loop reads the spreadsheet formula you typed but doesn't advance to the next line. Therefore, the first read-line invocation gobbles that empty line; the second call to read-line reads the (probably empty) line that the user typed in response to the prompting message.*

Cell Selection Commands

Several commands have to do with selecting a cell. We'll show just one typical procedure, the one that carries out the p (previous row) command:

```
(define (prev-row delta)
  (let ((row (id-row (selection-cell-id))))
    (if (< (- row delta) 1)
        (error "Already at top.")
        (set-selected-row! (- row delta)))))

(define (set-selected-row! new-row)
  (select-id! (make-id (id-column (selection-cell-id)) new-row)))
```

---

* Not every version of Scheme has this behavior. If you find that you have to hit return twice after exhibiting the value of a formula, take out one of the read-line invocations.

```
(define (select-id! id)
  (set-selection-cell-id! id)
  (adjust-screen-boundaries))
```

Prev-row must ensure that the selected cell is within the legal boundaries. Since prev-row only moves upward, it has to check only that we don't go beyond row 1. (Next-row will instead check that we don't go beyond row 30 in the other direction.)

Adjust-screen-boundaries checks for the situation in which the newly selected cell, although within the bounds of the spreadsheet, is not within the portion currently visible on the screen. In that case the visible portion is shifted to include the selected cell. (The procedure is straightforward and uninteresting, so we're not showing it here. You can see it in the complete listing of the spreadsheet program at the end of this chapter.)

Selection-cell-id is a procedure that returns the cell ID of the cell that's currently selected. Similarly, set-selection-cell-id! sets the current selection. There are comparable procedures screen-corner-cell-id and set-screen-corner-cell-id! to keep track of which cell should be in the upper left corner of the screen display. There is a vector named *special-cells* that holds these two cell IDs; you can see the details in the complete program listing.

The Load Command

Loading commands from files is easy. The command-loop procedure, which carries out commands from the keyboard, repeatedly reads a command with read and invokes process-command to carry it out. To load commands from a file, we want to do exactly the same thing, except that we read from a file instead of from the keyboard:

```
(define (spreadsheet-load filename)
  (let ((port (open-input-file filename)))
    (sl-helper port)
    (close-input-port port)))

(define (sl-helper port)
  (let ((command (read port)))
    (if (eof-object? command)
        'done
        (begin (show command)
               (process-command command)
               (sl-helper port)))))
```

The **Put** Command

The put command takes two arguments, a formula and a place to put it. The second of these can specify either a single cell or an entire row or column. (If there is no second argument, then a single cell, namely the selected cell, is implied.) Put invokes put-formula-in-cell either once or several times, as needed. If only a single cell is involved, then put calls put-formula-in-cell directly. If a row or column is specified, then put uses the auxiliary procedure put-all-cells-in-row or put-all-cells-in-col as an intermediary.

```
(define (put formula . where)
  (cond ((null? where)
           (put-formula-in-cell formula (selection-cell-id)))
          ((cell-name? (car where))
           (put-formula-in-cell formula (cell-name->id (car where))))
          ((number? (car where))
           (put-all-cells-in-row formula (car where)))
          ((letter? (car where))
           (put-all-cells-in-col formula (letter->number (car where))))
          (else (error "Put it where?"))))
```

The only tricky part of this is the first line. Put can be invoked with either one or two arguments. Therefore, the dot notation is used to allow a variable number of arguments; the parameter where will have as its value not the second argument itself, but a list that either contains the second argument or is empty. Thus, if there is a second argument, put refers to it as (car where).

```
(define (put-all-cells-in-row formula row)
  (put-all-helper formula (lambda (col) (make-id col row)) 1 26))

(define (put-all-cells-in-col formula col)
  (put-all-helper formula (lambda (row) (make-id col row)) 1 30))

(define (put-all-helper formula id-maker this max)
  (if (> this max)
      'done
      (begin (try-putting formula (id-maker this))
             (put-all-helper formula id-maker (+ 1 this) max))))

(define (try-putting formula id)
  (if (or (null? (cell-value id)) (null? formula))
      (put-formula-in-cell formula id)
      'do-nothing))
```

`Put-all-cells-in-row` and `put-all-cells-in-col` invoke `put-all-helper`, which repeatedly puts the formula into a cell.* `Put-all-helper` is a typical sequential recursion: Do something for this element, and recur for the remaining elements. The difference is that "this element" means a cell ID that combines one constant index with one index that varies with each recursive call. How are those two indices combined? What differs between filling a row and filling a column is the *function* used to compute each cell ID.

The substitution model explains how the `lambda` expressions used as arguments to `put-all-helper` implement this idea. Suppose we are putting a formula into every cell in row 4. Then `put-all-cells-in-row` will be invoked with the value 4 substituted for the parameter `row`. After this substitution, the body is

```
(put-all-helper formula (lambda (col) (make-id col 4)) 1 26)
```

The `lambda` expression creates a procedure that takes a column number as argument and returns a cell ID for the cell in row 4 and that column. This is just what `put-all-helper` needs. It invokes the procedure with the varying column number as its argument to get the proper cell ID.

`Put-all-helper` doesn't directly invoke `put-formula-in-cell`. The reason is that if a particular cell already has a value, then the new formula isn't used for that

---

* We originally wrote two separate helper procedures for the two cases, like this:

```
(define (put-all-cells-in-row formula row)
  (row-helper formula 1 26 row))

(define (row-helper formula this-col max-col row)
  (if (> this-col max-col)
      'done
      (begin (try-putting formula (make-id this-col row))
             (row-helper formula (+ this-col 1) max-col row))))

(define (put-all-cells-in-col formula col)
  (column-helper formula 1 30 col))

(define (column-helper formula this-row max-row col)
  (if (> this-row max-row)
      'done
      (begin (try-putting formula (make-id col this-row))
             (column-helper formula (+ this-row 1) max-row col))))
```

but the procedures were so similar that we decided to generalize the pattern.

particular cell, unless the formula is empty. That is, you can erase an entire row or column at once, but a non-empty formula affects only cells that were empty before this command. `Try-putting` decides whether or not to put the formula into each possible cell. (In `try-putting`, the third argument to `if` could be anything; we're interested only in what happens if the condition is true.)

All that's left is, finally, to put the formula into a cell:

```
(define (put-formula-in-cell formula id)
  (put-expr (pin-down formula id) id))
```

The two new procedures seen here, `pin-down` and `put-expr`, are both large sections of the program and are described in the next two sections of this chapter.

The Formula Translator

Suppose the user has said

```
(put (* (cell b) (cell c)) d)
```

The `put` procedure puts this formula into each cell of column `d` by repeatedly calling `put-formula-in-cell`; as an example, let's concentrate on cell `d4`.

The purpose of the formula is that later we're going to use it to compute a value for `d4`. For that purpose, we will need to multiply two particular numbers together: the ones in cells `b4` and `c4`. Although the same formula applies to cell `d5`, the particular numbers multiplied together will be found in different places. So instead of storing the same general formula in every `d` cell, what we'd really like to store in `d4` is something that refers specifically to `b4` and `c4`.

We'll use the term "expression" for a formula whose cell references have been replaced by specific cell IDs. We started with the idea that we wanted to put a formula into a cell; we've refined that idea so that we now want to put an expression into the cell. This goal has two parts: We must translate the formula (as given to us by the user in the `put` command) to an expression, and we must store that expression in the cell data structure. These two subtasks are handled by `pin-down`, discussed in this section, and by `put-expr`, discussed in the next section. `Pin-down` is entirely functional; the only modification to the spreadsheet program's state in this process is carried out by `put-expr`.

We'll refer to the process of translating a formula to an expression as "pinning down" the formula; the procedure `pin-down` carries out this process. It's called "pinning down" because we start with a *general* formula and end up with a *specific* expression. `Pin-down` takes two arguments: The first is, of course, a formula; the second is the ID of the cell that will be used as the reference point for relative cell positions. In the context of the `put` command, the reference point is the cell into which we'll put the expression. But `pin-down` doesn't think about putting anything anywhere; its job is to translate a formula (containing relative cell locations) into an expression (containing only absolute cell IDs).* `Pin-down` needs a reference point as a way to understand the notation `<3`, which means "three cells before the reference point."

Let's go back to the specific example. `Put-formula-in-cell` will invoke

```
(pin-down '(* (cell b) (cell c)) 'd4)
```

and `pin-down` will return the expression

```
(* (id 2 4) (id 3 4))
```

The overall structure of this problem is tree recursive. That's because a formula can be arbitrarily complicated, with sublists of sublists, just like a Scheme expression:

```
(put (+ (* (cell b) (cell c)) (- (cell 2< 3>) 6)) f)
```

Here's `pin-down`:

```
(define (pin-down formula id)
  (cond ((cell-name? formula) (cell-name->id formula))
        ((word? formula) formula)
        ((null? formula) '())
        ((equal? (car formula) 'cell)
         (pin-down-cell (cdr formula) id))
        (else (bound-check
                (map (lambda (subformula) (pin-down subformula id))
                     formula)))))
```

The base cases of the tree recursion are specific cell names, such as `c3`; other words, such

---

* In fact, `process-command` also invokes `pin-down` when the user types a formula in place of a command. In that situation, the result doesn't go into a cell but is immediately evaluated and printed.

as numbers and procedure names, which are unaffected by `pin-down`; null formulas, which indicate that the user is erasing the contents of a cell; and sublists that start with the word `cell`. The first three of these are trivial; the fourth, which we will describe shortly, is the important case. If a formula is not one of these four base cases, then it's a compound expression. In that case, we have to pin down all of the subexpressions individually. (We basically `map pin-down` over the formula. That's what makes this process tree recursive.)

One complication is that the pinned-down formula might refer to nonexistent cells. For example, saying

```
(put (+ (cell 2< 3<) 1) d)
```

refers to cells in column **b** (two to the left of **d**) three rows above the current row. That works for a cell such as **d7**, referring to cell **b4**, but not for **d2**, which has no row that's three above it. (There is no row **-1**.) So our program must refrain from pinning down this formula for cells **d1**, **d2**, and **d3**. `Pin-down` will instead return the word `out-of-bounds` to signal this situation.

The case of a nonexistent cell is discovered by `pin-down-cell` at the base of a tree recursion. The `out-of-bounds` signal must be returned not only by the base case but by the initial invocation of `pin-down`. That's why `bound-check` is used to ensure that if any part of a formula is out of bounds, the entire formula will also be considered out of bounds:

```
(define (bound-check form)
  (if (member 'out-of-bounds form)
      'out-of-bounds
      form))
```

When a formula contains a `(cell ...)` sublist, the procedure `pin-down-cell` is invoked to translate that notation into a cell ID.

The arguments to `pin-down-cell` are a list of the "arguments" of the `cell` sublist and the reference point's cell ID. (The word "arguments" is in quotation marks because the word `cell` doesn't represent a Scheme procedure, even though the parenthesized notation looks like an invocation. In a way, the special treatment of `cell` by `pin-down` is analogous to the treatment of special forms, such as `cond`, by the Scheme evaluator.)

There can be one or two of these "arguments" to `cell`. A single argument is either a number, indicating a row, or a letter, indicating a column. Two arguments specify both a column and a row, in that order:

```
(define (pin-down-cell args reference-id)
  (cond ((null? args)
         (error "Bad cell specification: (cell)"))
        ((null? (cdr args))
         (cond ((number? (car args))         ; they chose a row
                (make-id (id-column reference-id) (car args)))
               ((letter? (car args))         ; they chose a column
                (make-id (letter->number (car args))
                         (id-row reference-id)))
               (else (error "Bad cell specification:"
                            (cons 'cell args)))))
        (else
         (let ((col (pin-down-col (car args) (id-column reference-id)))
               (row (pin-down-row (cadr args) (id-row reference-id))))
           (if (and (>= col 1) (<= col 26) (>= row 1) (<= row 30))
               (make-id col row)
               'out-of-bounds)))))
```

In the two-argument case, the job of `pin-down-col` and `pin-down-row` is to understand notations like <3 for relative rows and columns:

```
(define (pin-down-col new old)
  (cond ((equal? new '*) old)
        ((equal? (first new) '>) (+ old (bf new)))
        ((equal? (first new) '<) (- old (bf new)))
        ((letter? new) (letter->number new))
        (else (error "What column?"))))

(define (pin-down-row new old)
  (cond ((number? new) new)
        ((equal? new '*) old)
        ((equal? (first new) '>) (+ old (bf new)))
        ((equal? (first new) '<) (- old (bf new)))
        (else (error "What row?"))))
```

The Dependency Manager

The remaining part of the `put` command is `put-expr`, which actually stores the translated expression in the cell data structure. You might imagine that putting an expression into a cell would require nothing more than invoking a mutator, like this:

```
(define (put-expr expr cell)                    ;; wrong
  (set-cell-expr! cell expr))
```

The trouble is that adding an expression to a cell might have many consequences beyond the mutation itself. For example, suppose we say

```
(put (+ a3 b2) c4)
```

If cells a3 and b2 already have values, we can't just put the formula into c4; we must also compute its value and put that value into c4.

Also, once c4 has a value, that could trigger the computation of some other cell's value. If we've previously said

```
(put (+ a3 c4) b5)
```

then we're now able to compute a value for b5 because both of the cells that it depends on have values.

All this implies that what's inside a cell is more than just an expression, or even an expression and a value. Each cell needs to know which other cells it depends on for its value, and also which other cells depend on it.

Our program represents each cell as a four-element vector. Each cell includes a value, an expression, a list of *parents* (the cells that it depends on), and a list of *children* (the cells that depend on it). The latter two lists contain cell IDs. So our example cell c4 might look like this:

```
#(12
  (+ (id 1 3) (id 2 2))
  ((id 1 3) (id 2 2))
  ((id 2 5)))
```

In a simpler case, suppose we put a value into a cell that nothing depends on, by saying, for example,

```
(put 6 a1)
```

Then cell a1 would contain

```
#(6 6 () ())
```

(Remember that a value is just a very simple formula.)

There are selectors `cell-value` and so on that take a cell ID as argument, and mutators `set-cell-value!` and so on that take a cell ID and a new value as arguments.

There's also the constructor `make-cell`, but it's called only at the beginning of the program, when the 780 cells in the spreadsheet are created at once.

When a cell is given a new expression, several things change:

- The new expression becomes the cell's expression, of course.
- The cells mentioned in the expression become the parents of this cell.
- This cell becomes a child of the cells mentioned in the expression.
- If all the parents have values, the value of this cell is computed.

Some of these changes are simple, but others are complicated. For example, it's not enough to tell the cell's new parents that the cell is now their child (the third task). First we have to tell the cell's *old* parents that this cell *isn't* their child any more. That has to be done before we forget the cell's old parents.

Here is an example. (In the following tables, we represent the data structures as if cells were represented by their names, even though really their IDs are used. We've done this to make the example more readable.) Suppose that we have five cells set up like this:

cell	expression	value	parents	children
a1	20	20	()	(a2)
b1	5	5	()	(a2 b2)
c1	8	8	()	()
a2	(+ a1 b1)	25	(a1 b1)	(b2)
b2	(+ a2 b1)	30	(a2 b1)	()

If we now enter the spreadsheet command

```
(put (+ b1 c1) a2)
```

the program must first remove a2 from the children of its old parents (changes are shown in boldface):

cell	expression	value	parents	children
a1	20	20	()	**()**
b1	5	5	()	**(b2)**
c1	8	8	()	()
a2	(+ a1 b1)	25	(a1 b1)	(b2)
b2	(+ a2 b1)	30	(a2 b1)	()

Then the program can change the expression and compute a new list of parents:

```
cell  expression value  parents  children
a1    20          20     ()       ()
b1    5           5      ()       (b2)
c1    8           8      ()       ()
a2    (+ b1 c1)   25     (b1 c1)  (b2)
b2    (+ a2 b1)   30     (a2 b1)  ()
```

Next it can tell the new parents to add a2 as a child, and can compute a2's new value:

```
cell  expression value  parents  children
1     20          20     ()       ()
b1    5           5      ()       (a2 b2)
c1    8           8      ()       (a2)
a2    (+ b1 c1)   13     (b1 c1)  (b2)
b2    (+ a2 b1)   30     (a2 b1)  ()
```

Changing a2's value affects the values of all of its children, and also its grandchildren and so on (except that in this example there are no grandchildren):

```
cell  expression value  parents  children
a1    20          20     ()       ()
b1    5           5      ()       (a2 b2)
c1    8           8      ()       (a2)
a2    (+ b1 c1)   13     (b1 c1)  (b2)
b2    (+ a2 b1)   18     (a2 b1)  ()
```

Now that we've considered an example, here is the main procedure that oversees all these tasks:

```
(define (put-expr expr-or-out-of-bounds id)
  (let ((expr (if (equal? expr-or-out-of-bounds 'out-of-bounds)
                  '()
                  expr-or-out-of-bounds)))
    (for-each (lambda (old-parent)
                (set-cell-children!
                 old-parent
                 (remove id (cell-children old-parent))))
              (cell-parents id))
    (set-cell-expr! id expr)
    (set-cell-parents! id (remdup (extract-ids expr)))
    (for-each (lambda (new-parent)
                (set-cell-children!
                 new-parent
                 (cons id (cell-children new-parent))))
              (cell-parents id))
    (figure id)))
```

Remember that `put-expr`'s first argument is the return value from `pin-down`, so it might be the word `out-of-bounds` instead of an expression. In this case, we store an empty list as the expression, indicating that there is no active expression for this cell.

Within the body of the `let` there are five Scheme expressions, each of which carries out one of the tasks we've listed. The first expression tells the cell's former parents that the cell is no longer their child. The second expression stores the expression in the cell.

The third Scheme expression invokes `extract-ids` to find all the cell ids used in `expr`, removes any duplicates, and establishes those identified cells as the argument cell's parents. (You wrote `remdup` in Exercise 14.3.) For example, if the `expr` is

```
(+ (id 4 2) (* (id 1 3) (id 1 3)))
```

then `extract-ids` will return the list

```
((id 4 2) (id 1 3) (id 1 3))
```

and `remdup` of that will be

```
((id 4 2) (id 1 3))
```

The fourth expression in the `let` tells each of the new parents to consider the argument cell as its child. The fifth expression may or may not compute a new value for this cell. (As we'll see in a moment, that process is a little complicated.)

Two of these steps require closer examination. Here is the procedure used in the third step:

```
(define (extract-ids expr)
  (cond ((id? expr) (list expr))
        ((word? expr) '())
        ((null? expr) '())
        (else (append (extract-ids (car expr))
                      (extract-ids (cdr expr))))))
```

This is a tree recursion. The first three `cond` clauses are base cases; cell IDs are included in the returned list, while other words are ignored. For compound expressions, we use the trick of making recursive calls on the `car` and `cdr` of the list. We combine the results with `append` because `extract-ids` must return a flat list of cell IDs, not a cheap tree.

The fifth step in `put-expr` is complicated because, as we saw in the example, changing the value of one cell may require us to recompute the value of other cells:

```
(define (figure id)
  (cond ((null? (cell-expr id)) (setvalue id '()))
        ((all-evaluated? (cell-parents id))
         (setvalue id (ss-eval (cell-expr id))))
        (else (setvalue id '()))))

(define (all-evaluated? ids)
  (cond ((null? ids) #t)
        ((not (number? (cell-value (car ids)))) #f)
        (else (all-evaluated? (cdr ids)))))

(define (setvalue id value)
  (let ((old (cell-value id)))
    (set-cell-value! id value)
    (if (not (equal? old value))
        (for-each figure (cell-children id))
        'do-nothing)))
```

Figure is invoked for the cell whose expression we've just changed. If there is no expression (that is, if we've changed it to an empty expression or to an out-of-bounds one), then figure will remove any old value that might be left over from a previous expression. If there is an expression, then figure will compute and save a new value, but only if all of this cell's parents have numeric values. If any parent doesn't have a value, or if its value is a non-numeric label, then figure has to remove the value from this cell.

Setvalue actually puts the new value in the cell. It first looks up the old value. If the new and old values are different, then all of the children of this cell must be re-figured. This, too, is a tree recursion because there might be several children, and each of them might have several children.

We haven't yet explained how ss-eval actually computes the value from the expression. That's the subject of the next major part of the program.

The Expression Evaluator

Figure invokes ss-eval to convert a cell's expression into its value. Also, we've seen earlier that process-command uses ss-eval to evaluate an expression that the user types in response to a spreadsheet prompt. (That is, ss-eval is invoked if what the user types isn't one of the special commands recognized by process-command itself.)

The ss in ss-eval stands for "spreadsheet"; it distinguishes this procedure from `eval`, a primitive procedure that evaluates Scheme expressions. As it turns out, `ss-eval`'s algorithm is similar in many ways to that of Scheme's `eval`, although `ss-eval` is much simpler in other ways. The experience you already have with Scheme's expression evaluation will help you understand the spreadsheet's.

Scheme's evaluator takes an expression and computes the corresponding value. The expressions look quite different from the values, but there are well-defined rules (the ones we studied in Chapter 3) to translate expressions to values. In the spreadsheet language, as in Scheme, an expression can be one of three things:

- a constant expression (a number or quoted word), whose value is itself.

- a variable (a cell ID, in the case of the spreadsheet language).

- a procedure invocation enclosed in parentheses.

The spreadsheet language is simpler than Scheme for three main reasons.

- There are no special forms such as `if` or `define`.*

- The only variables, the cell IDs, are global; in Scheme, much of the complexity of evaluation has to do with variables that are local to procedures (i.e., formal parameters).

- The only procedures are primitives, so there is no need to evaluate procedure bodies.

The structure of `ss-eval` is a `cond` whose clauses handle the three types of expressions. Constants and variables are easy; invocations require recursively evaluating the arguments before the procedure can be invoked.

```
(define (ss-eval expr)
  (cond ((number? expr) expr)
        ((quoted? expr) (quoted-value expr))
        ((id? expr) (cell-value expr))
        ((invocation? expr)
         (apply (get-function (car expr))
                (map ss-eval (cdr expr))))
        (else (error "Invalid expression:" expr))))
```

---

* You can think of the `cell` notation in generalized formulas as a kind of special form, but `pin-down` has turned those into specific cell IDs before the formula is eligible for evaluation as an expression.

The value of a number is itself; the value of a quoted word is the word without the quotation mark. (Actually, by the time `ss-eval` sees a quoted word, Scheme has translated the `'abc` notation into `(quote abc)` and that's what we deal with here. Also, double-quoted strings look different to the program from single-quoted words.)

```
(define (quoted? expr)
  (or (string? expr)
      (and (list? expr) (equal? (car expr) 'quote))))

(define (quoted-value expr)
  (if (string? expr)
      expr
      (cadr expr)))
```

The third clause checks for a cell ID; the value of such an expression is the value stored in the corresponding cell.

If an expression is none of those things, it had better be a function invocation, that is, a list. In that case, `ss-eval` has to do three things: It looks up the function name in a table (as we did earlier for spreadsheet commands); it recursively evaluates all the argument subexpressions; and then it can invoke `apply` to apply the procedure to the argument values.

`Get-function` looks up a function name in the name-to-function association list and returns the corresponding Scheme procedure. Thus, only the functions included in the list can be used in spreadsheet formulas.

The entire expression evaluator, including `ss-eval` and its helper procedures, is functional. Like the formula translator, it doesn't change the state of the spreadsheet.

The Screen Printer

The procedures that print the spreadsheet on the screen are straightforward but full of details. Much of the work here goes into those details.

As we mentioned earlier, a better spreadsheet program wouldn't redraw the entire screen for each command but would change only the parts of the screen that were affected by the previous command. However, Scheme does not include a standard way to control the positioning of text on the screen, so we're stuck with this approach.

```
(define (print-screen)
  (newline)
  (newline)
  (newline)
  (show-column-labels (id-column (screen-corner-cell-id)))
  (show-rows 20
             (id-column (screen-corner-cell-id))
             (id-row (screen-corner-cell-id)))
  (display-cell-name (selection-cell-id))
  (show (cell-value (selection-cell-id)))
  (display-expression (cell-expr (selection-cell-id)))
  (newline)
  (display "?? "))
```

Screen-corner-cell-id returns the ID of the cell that should be shown in the top left corner of the display; selection-cell-id returns the ID of the selected cell.

Show-column-labels prints the first row of the display, the one with the column letters. Show-rows is a sequential recursion that prints the actual rows of the spreadsheet, starting with the row number of the screen-corner cell and continuing for 20 rows. (There are 30 rows in the entire spreadsheet, but they don't all fit on the screen at once.) The rest of the procedure displays the value and expression of the selected cell at the bottom of the screen and prompts for the next command.

Why isn't display-expression just display? Remember that the spreadsheet stores expressions in a form like

```
(+ (id 2 5) (id 6 3))
```

but the user wants to see

```
(+ b5 f3)
```

Display-expression is yet another tree recursion over expressions. Just as pin-down translates cell names into cell IDs, display-expression translates IDs back into names. (But display-expression prints as it goes along, instead of reconstructing and returning a list.) The definition of display-expression, along with the remaining details of printing, can be seen in the full program listing at the end of this chapter.

Just to give the flavor of those details, here is the part that displays the rectangular array of cell values. Show-rows is a sequential recursion in which each invocation prints an entire row. It does so by invoking `show-row`, another sequential recursion, in which each invocation prints a single cell value.

```
(define (show-rows to-go col row)
  (cond ((= to-go 0) 'done)
        (else
         (display (align row 2 0))
         (display " ")
         (show-row 6 col row)
         (newline)
         (show-rows (- to-go 1) col (+ row 1)))))

(define (show-row to-go col row)
  (cond ((= to-go 0) 'done)
        (else
            (display (if (selected-indices? col row) ">" " "))
            (display-value (cell-value-from-indices col row))
            (display (if (selected-indices? col row) "<" " "))
            (show-row (- to-go 1) (+ 1 col) row))))

(define (selected-indices? col row)
  (and (= col (id-column (selection-cell-id)))
       (= row (id-row (selection-cell-id)))))
```

Why didn't we write `show-row` in the following way?

```
(define (show-row to-go col row)                  ;; alternate version
  (cond ((= to-go 0) 'done)
        (else
         (let ((id (make-id col row)))
           (display (if (equal? id (selection-cell-id)) ">" " "))
           (display-value (cell-value id))
           (display (if (equal? id (selection-cell-id)) "<" " "))
           (show-row (- to-go 1) (+ 1 col) row)))))
```

That would have worked fine and would have been a little clearer. In fact, we did write `show-row` this way originally. But it's a little time-consuming to construct an ID, and `show-row` is called 120 times whenever `print-screen` is used. Since printing the screen was annoyingly slow, we sped things up as much as we could, even at the cost of this kludge.

The Cell Manager

The program keeps information about the current status of the spreadsheet cells in a vector called *the-spreadsheet-array*. It contains all of the 780 cells that make up the spreadsheet (30 rows of 26 columns). It's not a vector of length 780; rather, it's a vector of length 30, each of whose elements is itself a vector of length 26. In other words, each element of the spreadsheet array is a vector representing one row of the spreadsheet. (Each element of *those* vectors is one cell, which, as you recall, is represented as a vector of length four. So the spreadsheet array is a vector of vectors of vectors!)

The selectors for the parts of a cell take the cell's ID as argument and return one of the four elements of the cell vector. Each must therefore be implemented as two steps: We must find the cell vector, given its ID; and we must then select an element from the cell vector. The first step is handled by the selector cell-structure that takes a cell ID as argument:

```
(define (cell-structure id)
  (global-array-lookup (id-column id)
                       (id-row id)))

(define (global-array-lookup col row)
  (if (and (<= row 30) (<= col 26))
      (vector-ref (vector-ref *the-spreadsheet-array* (- row 1))
                  (- col 1))
      (error "Out of bounds")))
```

Global-array-lookup makes sure the desired cell exists. It also compensates for the fact that Scheme vectors begin with element number zero, while our spreadsheet begins with row and column number one. Two invocations of vector-ref are needed, one to select an entire row and the next to select a cell within that row.

Selectors and mutators for the parts of a cell are written using cell-structure:

```
(define (cell-value id)
  (vector-ref (cell-structure id) 0))

(define (set-cell-value! id val)
  (vector-set! (cell-structure id) 0 val))

(define (cell-expr id)
  (vector-ref (cell-structure id) 1))
```

```
(define (set-cell-expr! id val)
  (vector-set! (cell-structure id) 1 val))

(define (cell-parents id)
  (vector-ref (cell-structure id) 2))

(define (set-cell-parents! id val)
  (vector-set! (cell-structure id) 2 val))

(define (cell-children id)
  (vector-ref (cell-structure id) 3))

(define (set-cell-children! id val)
  (vector-set! (cell-structure id) 3 val))
```

The constructor is

```
(define (make-cell)
  (vector '() '() '() '()))
```

The spreadsheet program begins by invoking `init-array` to set up this large array. (Also, it sets the initial values of the selected cell and the screen corner.)

```
(define (spreadsheet)
  (init-array)
  (set-selection-cell-id! (make-id 1 1))
  (set-screen-corner-cell-id! (make-id 1 1))
  (command-loop))

(define *the-spreadsheet-array* (make-vector 30))

(define (init-array)
  (fill-array-with-rows 29))

(define (fill-array-with-rows n)
  (if (< n 0)
      'done
      (begin (vector-set! *the-spreadsheet-array* n (make-vector 26))
             (fill-row-with-cells
              (vector-ref *the-spreadsheet-array* n) 25)
             (fill-array-with-rows (- n 1)))))
```

```
(define (fill-row-with-cells vec n)
  (if (< n 0)
      'done
      (begin (vector-set! vec n (make-cell))
             (fill-row-with-cells vec (- n 1)))))
```

That's the end of the project, apart from some straightforward procedures such as letter->number that you can look up in the complete listing if you're interested.

Complete Program Listing

```
(define (spreadsheet)
  (init-array)
  (set-selection-cell-id! (make-id 1 1))
  (set-screen-corner-cell-id! (make-id 1 1))
  (command-loop))

(define (command-loop)
  (print-screen)
  (let ((command-or-formula (read)))
    (if (equal? command-or-formula 'exit)
        "Bye!"
        (begin (process-command command-or-formula)
               (command-loop)))))

(define (process-command command-or-formula)
  (cond ((and (list? command-or-formula)
              (command? (car command-or-formula)))
         (execute-command command-or-formula))
        ((command? command-or-formula)
         (execute-command (list command-or-formula 1)))
        (else (exhibit (ss-eval (pin-down command-or-formula
                                          (selection-cell-id)))))))

(define (execute-command command)
  (apply (get-command (car command))
         (cdr command)))

(define (exhibit val)
  (show val)
  (show "Type RETURN to redraw screen")
  (read-line)
  (read-line))
```

```
;;; Commands

;; Cell selection commands: F, B, N, P, and SELECT

(define (prev-row delta)
  (let ((row (id-row (selection-cell-id))))
    (if (< (- row delta) 1)
        (error "Already at top.")
        (set-selected-row! (- row delta)))))

(define (next-row delta)
  (let ((row (id-row (selection-cell-id))))
    (if (> (+ row delta) 30)
        (error "Already at bottom.")
        (set-selected-row! (+ row delta)))))

(define (prev-col delta)
  (let ((col (id-column (selection-cell-id))))
    (if (< (- col delta) 1)
        (error "Already at left.")
        (set-selected-column! (- col delta)))))

(define (next-col delta)
  (let ((col (id-column (selection-cell-id))))
    (if (> (+ col delta) 26)
        (error "Already at right.")
        (set-selected-column! (+ col delta)))))

(define (set-selected-row! new-row)
  (select-id! (make-id (id-column (selection-cell-id)) new-row)))

(define (set-selected-column! new-column)
  (select-id! (make-id new-column (id-row (selection-cell-id)))))

(define (select-id! id)
  (set-selection-cell-id! id)
  (adjust-screen-boundaries))

(define (select cell-name)
  (select-id! (cell-name->id cell-name)))
```

```
(define (adjust-screen-boundaries)
  (let ((row (id-row (selection-cell-id)))
        (col (id-column (selection-cell-id))))
    (if (< row (id-row (screen-corner-cell-id)))
        (set-corner-row! row)
        'do-nothing)
    (if (>= row (+ (id-row (screen-corner-cell-id)) 20))
        (set-corner-row! (- row 19))
        'do-nothing)
    (if (< col (id-column (screen-corner-cell-id)))
        (set-corner-column! col)
        'do-nothing)
    (if (>= col (+ (id-column (screen-corner-cell-id)) 6))
        (set-corner-column! (- col 5))
        'do-nothing)))

(define (set-corner-row! new-row)
  (set-screen-corner-cell-id!
   (make-id (id-column (screen-corner-cell-id)) new-row)))

(define (set-corner-column! new-column)
  (set-screen-corner-cell-id!
   (make-id new-column (id-row (screen-corner-cell-id)))))


;; LOAD

(define (spreadsheet-load filename)
  (let ((port (open-input-file filename)))
    (sl-helper port)
    (close-input-port port)))

(define (sl-helper port)
  (let ((command (read port)))
    (if (eof-object? command)
        'done
        (begin (show command)
               (process-command command)
               (sl-helper port)))))
```

```
;; PUT

(define (put formula . where)
  (cond ((null? where)
         (put-formula-in-cell formula (selection-cell-id)))
        ((cell-name? (car where))
         (put-formula-in-cell formula (cell-name->id (car where))))
        ((number? (car where))
         (put-all-cells-in-row formula (car where)))
        ((letter? (car where))
         (put-all-cells-in-col formula (letter->number (car where))))
        (else (error "Put it where?"))))

(define (put-all-cells-in-row formula row)
  (put-all-helper formula (lambda (col) (make-id col row)) 1 26))

(define (put-all-cells-in-col formula col)
  (put-all-helper formula (lambda (row) (make-id col row)) 1 30))

(define (put-all-helper formula id-maker this max)
  (if (> this max)
      'done
      (begin (try-putting formula (id-maker this))
             (put-all-helper formula id-maker (+ 1 this) max))))

(define (try-putting formula id)
  (if (or (null? (cell-value id)) (null? formula))
      (put-formula-in-cell formula id)
      'do-nothing))

(define (put-formula-in-cell formula id)
  (put-expr (pin-down formula id) id))


;;; The Association List of Commands

(define (command? name)
  (assoc name *the-commands*))

(define (get-command name)
  (let ((result (assoc name *the-commands*)))
    (if (not result)
        #f
        (cadr result))))
```

```scheme
(define *the-commands*
  (list (list 'p prev-row)
        (list 'n next-row)
        (list 'b prev-col)
        (list 'f next-col)
        (list 'select select)
        (list 'put put)
        (list 'load spreadsheet-load)))


;;; Pinning Down Formulas Into Expressions

(define (pin-down formula id)
  (cond ((cell-name? formula) (cell-name->id formula))
        ((word? formula) formula)
        ((null? formula) '())
        ((equal? (car formula) 'cell)
         (pin-down-cell (cdr formula) id))
        (else (bound-check
                (map (lambda (subformula) (pin-down subformula id))
                     formula)))))

(define (bound-check form)
  (if (member 'out-of-bounds form)
      'out-of-bounds
      form))

(define (pin-down-cell args reference-id)
  (cond ((null? args)
         (error "Bad cell specification: (cell)"))
        ((null? (cdr args))
         (cond ((number? (car args))          ; they chose a row
                (make-id (id-column reference-id) (car args)))
               ((letter? (car args))          ; they chose a column
                (make-id (letter->number (car args))
                         (id-row reference-id)))
               (else (error "Bad cell specification:"
                            (cons 'cell args)))))
        (else
         (let ((col (pin-down-col (car args) (id-column reference-id)))
               (row (pin-down-row (cadr args) (id-row reference-id))))
           (if (and (>= col 1) (<= col 26) (>= row 1) (<= row 30))
               (make-id col row)
               'out-of-bounds)))))
```

```
(define (pin-down-col new old)
  (cond ((equal? new '*) old)
        ((equal? (first new) '>) (+ old (bf new)))
        ((equal? (first new) '<) (- old (bf new)))
        ((letter? new) (letter->number new))
        (else (error "What column?"))))

(define (pin-down-row new old)
  (cond ((number? new) new)
        ((equal? new '*) old)
        ((equal? (first new) '>) (+ old (bf new)))
        ((equal? (first new) '<) (- old (bf new)))
        (else (error "What row?"))))


;;; Dependency Management

(define (put-expr expr-or-out-of-bounds id)
  (let ((expr (if (equal? expr-or-out-of-bounds 'out-of-bounds)
                  '()
                  expr-or-out-of-bounds)))
    (for-each (lambda (old-parent)
                (set-cell-children!
                 old-parent
                 (remove id (cell-children old-parent))))
              (cell-parents id))
    (set-cell-expr! id expr)
    (set-cell-parents! id (remdup (extract-ids expr)))
    (for-each (lambda (new-parent)
                (set-cell-children!
                 new-parent
                 (cons id (cell-children new-parent))))
              (cell-parents id))
    (figure id)))

(define (extract-ids expr)
  (cond ((id? expr) (list expr))
        ((word? expr) '())
        ((null? expr) '())
        (else (append (extract-ids (car expr))
                      (extract-ids (cdr expr))))))

(define (figure id)
  (cond ((null? (cell-expr id)) (setvalue id '()))
        ((all-evaluated? (cell-parents id))
         (setvalue id (ss-eval (cell-expr id))))
        (else (setvalue id '()))))
```

```
(define (all-evaluated? ids)
  (cond ((null? ids) #t)
        ((not (number? (cell-value (car ids)))) #f)
        (else (all-evaluated? (cdr ids)))))

(define (setvalue id value)
  (let ((old (cell-value id)))
    (set-cell-value! id value)
    (if (not (equal? old value))
        (for-each figure (cell-children id))
        'do-nothing)))


;;; Evaluating Expressions

(define (ss-eval expr)
  (cond ((number? expr) expr)
        ((quoted? expr) (quoted-value expr))
        ((id? expr) (cell-value expr))
        ((invocation? expr)
         (apply (get-function (car expr))
                (map ss-eval (cdr expr))))
        (else (error "Invalid expression:" expr))))

(define (quoted? expr)
  (or (string? expr)
      (and (list? expr) (equal? (car expr) 'quote))))

(define (quoted-value expr)
  (if (string? expr)
      expr
      (cadr expr)))

(define (invocation? expr)
  (list? expr))

(define (get-function name)
  (let ((result (assoc name *the-functions*)))
    (if (not result)
        (error "No such function: " name)
        (cadr result))))
```

```
(define *the-functions*
  (list (list '* *)
        (list '+ +)
        (list '- -)
        (list '/ /)
        (list 'abs abs)
        (list 'acos acos)
        (list 'asin asin)
        (list 'atan atan)
        (list 'ceiling ceiling)
        (list 'cos cos)
        (list 'count count)
        (list 'exp exp)
        (list 'expt expt)
        (list 'floor floor)
        (list 'gcd gcd)
        (list 'lcm lcm)
        (list 'log log)
        (list 'max max)
        (list 'min min)
        (list 'modulo modulo)
        (list 'quotient quotient)
        (list 'remainder remainder)
        (list 'round round)
        (list 'sin sin)
        (list 'sqrt sqrt)
        (list 'tan tan)
        (list 'truncate truncate)))

;;; Printing the Screen

(define (print-screen)
  (newline)
  (newline)
  (newline)
  (show-column-labels (id-column (screen-corner-cell-id)))
  (show-rows 20
             (id-column (screen-corner-cell-id))
             (id-row (screen-corner-cell-id)))
  (display-cell-name (selection-cell-id))
  (display ":  ")
  (show (cell-value (selection-cell-id)))
  (display-expression (cell-expr (selection-cell-id)))
  (newline)
  (display "?? "))

(define (display-cell-name id)
  (display (number->letter (id-column id)))
  (display (id-row id)))
```

```
(define (show-column-labels col-number)
  (display "  ")
  (show-label 6 col-number)
  (newline))

(define (show-label to-go this-col-number)
  (cond ((= to-go 0) '())
        (else
         (display "  -----")
         (display (number->letter this-col-number))
         (display "----")
         (show-label (- to-go 1) (+ 1 this-col-number)))))

(define (show-rows to-go col row)
  (cond ((= to-go 0) 'done)
        (else
         (display (align row 2 0))
         (display " ")
         (show-row 6 col row)
         (newline)
         (show-rows (- to-go 1) col (+ row 1)))))

(define (show-row to-go col row)
  (cond ((= to-go 0) 'done)
        (else
          (display (if (selected-indices? col row) ">" " "))
          (display-value (cell-value-from-indices col row))
          (display (if (selected-indices? col row) "<" " "))
          (show-row (- to-go 1) (+ 1 col) row))))

(define (selected-indices? col row)
  (and (= col (id-column (selection-cell-id)))
       (= row (id-row (selection-cell-id)))))

(define (display-value val)
  (display (align (if (null? val) "" val) 10 2)))

(define (display-expression expr)
  (cond ((null? expr) (display '()))
        ((quoted? expr) (display (quoted-value expr)))
        ((word? expr) (display expr))
        ((id? expr)
         (display-cell-name expr))
        (else (display-invocation expr))))
```

```
(define (display-invocation expr)
  (display "(")
  (display-expression (car expr))
  (for-each (lambda (subexpr)
              (display " ")
              (display-expression subexpr))
            (cdr expr))
  (display ")"))


;;; Abstract Data Types

;; Special cells: the selected cell and the screen corner

(define *special-cells* (make-vector 2))

(define (selection-cell-id)
  (vector-ref *special-cells* 0))

(define (set-selection-cell-id! new-id)
  (vector-set! *special-cells* 0 new-id))

(define (screen-corner-cell-id)
  (vector-ref *special-cells* 1))

(define (set-screen-corner-cell-id! new-id)
  (vector-set! *special-cells* 1 new-id))


;; Cell names

(define (cell-name? expr)
  (and (word? expr)
       (letter? (first expr))
       (number? (bf expr))))

(define (cell-name-column cell-name)
  (letter->number (first cell-name)))

(define (cell-name-row cell-name)
  (bf cell-name))
```

```
(define (cell-name->id cell-name)
  (make-id (cell-name-column cell-name)
           (cell-name-row cell-name)))

;; Cell IDs

(define (make-id col row)
  (list 'id col row))

(define (id-column id)
  (cadr id))

(define (id-row id)
  (caddr id))

(define (id? x)
  (and (list? x)
       (not (null? x))
       (equal? 'id (car x))))

;; Cells

(define (make-cell)
  (vector '() '() '() '()))

(define (cell-value id)
  (vector-ref (cell-structure id) 0))

(define (cell-value-from-indices col row)
  (vector-ref (cell-structure-from-indices col row) 0))

(define (cell-expr id)
  (vector-ref (cell-structure id) 1))

(define (cell-parents id)
  (vector-ref (cell-structure id) 2))

(define (cell-children id)
  (vector-ref (cell-structure id) 3))

(define (set-cell-value! id val)
  (vector-set! (cell-structure id) 0 val))

(define (set-cell-expr! id val)
  (vector-set! (cell-structure id) 1 val))

(define (set-cell-parents! id val)
  (vector-set! (cell-structure id) 2 val))
```

```
(define (set-cell-children! id val)
  (vector-set! (cell-structure id) 3 val))

(define (cell-structure id)
  (global-array-lookup (id-column id)
                       (id-row id)))

(define (cell-structure-from-indices col row)
  (global-array-lookup col row))

(define *the-spreadsheet-array* (make-vector 30))

(define (global-array-lookup col row)
  (if (and (<= row 30) (<= col 26))
      (vector-ref (vector-ref *the-spreadsheet-array* (- row 1))
                  (- col 1))
      (error "Out of bounds")))

(define (init-array)
  (fill-array-with-rows 29))

(define (fill-array-with-rows n)
  (if (< n 0)
      'done
      (begin (vector-set! *the-spreadsheet-array* n (make-vector 26))
             (fill-row-with-cells
              (vector-ref *the-spreadsheet-array* n) 25)
             (fill-array-with-rows (- n 1)))))

(define (fill-row-with-cells vec n)
  (if (< n 0)
      'done
      (begin (vector-set! vec n (make-cell))
             (fill-row-with-cells vec (- n 1)))))

;;; Utility Functions

(define alphabet
  '#(a b c d e f g h i j k l m n o p q r s t u v w x y z))

(define (letter? something)
  (and (word? something)
       (= 1 (count something))
       (vector-member something alphabet)))

(define (number->letter num)
  (vector-ref alphabet (- num 1)))
```

```
(define (letter->number letter)
  (+ (vector-member letter alphabet) 1))

(define (vector-member thing vector)
  (vector-member-helper thing vector 0))

(define (vector-member-helper thing vector index)
  (cond ((= index (vector-length vector)) #f)
        ((equal? thing (vector-ref vector index)) index)
        (else (vector-member-helper thing vector (+ 1 index)))))

(define (remdup lst)
  (cond ((null? lst) '())
        ((member (car lst) (cdr lst))
         (remdup (cdr lst)))
        (else (cons (car lst) (remdup (cdr lst))))))

(define (remove bad-item lst)
  (filter (lambda (item) (not (equal? item bad-item)))
          lst))
```

Exercises

25.1 The "magic numbers" 26 and 30 (and some numbers derived from them) appear many times in the text of this program. It's easy to imagine wanting more rows or columns.

Create global variables `total-cols` and `total-rows` with values 26 and 30 respectively. Then modify the spreadsheet program to refer to these variables rather than to the numbers 26 and 30 directly. When you're done, redefine `total-rows` to be 40 and see if it works.

25.2 Suggest a way to notate columns beyond `z`. What procedures would have to change to accommodate this?

25.3 Modify the program so that the spreadsheet array is kept as a single vector of 780 elements, instead of a vector of 30 vectors of 26 vectors. What procedures do you have to change to make this work? (It shouldn't be very many.)

25.4 The procedures `get-function` and `get-command` are almost identical in structure; both look for an argument in an association list. They differ, however, in their handling of the situation in which the argument is not present in the list. Why?

25.5 The reason we had to include the word `id` in each cell ID was so we would be able to distinguish a list representing a cell ID from a list of some other kind in an expression. Another way to distinguish cell IDs would be to represent them as vectors, since vectors do not otherwise appear within expressions. Change the implementation of cell IDs from three-element lists to two-element vectors:

```
> (make-id 4 2)
#(4 2)
```

Make sure the rest of the program still works.

25.6 The `put` command can be used to label a cell by using a quoted word as the "formula." How does that work? For example, how is such a formula translated into an expression? How is that expression evaluated? What if the labeled cell has children?

25.7 Add commands to move the "window" of cells displayed on the screen without changing the selected cell. (There are a lot of possible user interfaces for this feature; pick anything reasonable.)

25.8 Modify the `put` command so that after doing its work it prints

```
14 cells modified
```

(but, of course, using the actual number of cells modified instead of 14). This number may not be the entire length of a row or column because `put` doesn't change an existing formula in a cell when you ask it to set an entire row or column.

25.9 Modify the program so that each column remembers the number of digits that should be displayed after the decimal point (currently always 2). Add a command to set this value for a specified column. And, of course, modify `print-screen` to use this information.

25.10 Add an `undo` command, which causes the effect of the previous command to be nullified. That is, if the previous command was a cell selection command, `undo` will return to the previously selected cell. If the previous command was a `put`, `undo` will re-`put` the previous expressions in every affected cell. You don't need to undo `load` or `exit` commands. To do this, you'll need to modify the way the other commands work.

25.11 Add an `accumulate` procedure that can be used as a function in formulas. Instead of specifying a sequence of cells explicitly, in a formula like

```
(put (+ c2 c3 c4 c5 c6 c7) c10)
```

we want to be able to say

```
(put (accumulate + c2 c7) c10)
```

In general, the two cell names should be taken as corners of a rectangle, all of whose cells should be included, so these two commands are equivalent:

```
(put (accumulate * a3 c5) d7)
(put (* a3 b3 c3 a4 b4 c4 a5 b5 c5) d7)
```

Modify `pin-down` to convert the `accumulate` form into the corresponding spelled-out form.

25.12 Add variable-width columns to the spreadsheet. There should be a command to set the print width of a column. This may mean that the spreadsheet can display more or fewer than six columns.

Project: A Database Program

A *database* is a large file with lots of related data in it. For example, you might have a database of your local Chinese restaurants, listing their names, their addresses, and how good their potstickers are, like this:

```
Name:          Address:                  City:            Potstickers:

Cal's          1866 Euclid               Berkeley         nondescript
Hunan          924 Sansome               San Francisco    none
Mary Chung's   464 Massachusetts Avenue  Cambridge        great
Shin Shin      1715 Solano Avenue        Berkeley         awesome
TC Garden      2507 Hearst Avenue        Berkeley         doughy
Yet Wah        2140 Clement              San Francisco    fantastic
```

There are six *records* in this database, one for each restaurant. Each record contains four pieces of information; we say that the database has four *fields*.

A *database program* is a program that can create, store, modify, and examine databases. At the very least, a database program must let you create new databases, enter records, and save the database to a file. More sophisticated operations involve sorting the records in a database by a particular field, printing out the contents of the database, counting the number of records that satisfy a certain condition, taking statistics such as averages, and so on.

There are many commercial database programs available; our version will have some of the flavor of more sophisticated programs while leaving out a lot of the details.

A Sample Session with Our Database

Most database programs come with their own programming language built in. Our database program will use Scheme itself as the language; you will be able to perform database commands by invoking Scheme procedures at the Scheme prompt. Here is a sample session with our program:

```
> (load "database.scm")
#F
> (new-db "albums" '(artist title year brian-likes?))
CREATED
```

First we loaded the database program, then we created a new database called `"albums"`* with four fields.** Let's enter some data:

```
> (insert)
Value for ARTIST--> (the beatles)
Value for TITLE--> "A Hard Day's Night"
Value for YEAR--> 1964
Value for BRIAN-LIKES?--> #t
Insert another? yes
Value for ARTIST--> (the zombies)
Value for TITLE--> "Odessey and Oracle"
Value for YEAR--> 1967
Value for BRIAN-LIKES?--> #t
Insert another? y
Value for ARTIST--> (frank zappa)
Value for TITLE--> "Hot Rats"
Value for YEAR--> 1970
Value for BRIAN-LIKES?--> #f
Insert another? y
Value for ARTIST--> (the beatles)
Value for TITLE--> "Rubber Soul"
Value for YEAR--> 1965
Value for BRIAN-LIKES?--> #t
Insert another? no
INSERTED
```

(We used strings for the album titles but sentences for the artists, partly because one of the titles has an apostrophe in it, but mainly just to demonstrate that fields can contain any data type.)

---

* The double-quote marks are necessary because `albums` will be used as a filename when we save the database to a file.

** We don't need a `matt-likes?` field because Matt likes all the albums in this database.

At this point we start demonstrating features that aren't actually in the version of the program that we've provided. You will implement these features in this project. We're showing them now as if the project were finished to convey the overall flavor of how the program should work.

We can print out the information in a database, and count the number of records:*

```
> (list-db)
RECORD 1
ARTIST: (THE BEATLES)
TITLE: Rubber Soul
YEAR: 1965
BRIAN-LIKES?: #T

RECORD 2
ARTIST: (FRANK ZAPPA)
TITLE: Hot Rats
YEAR: 1970
BRIAN-LIKES?: #F

RECORD 3
ARTIST: (THE ZOMBIES)
TITLE: Odessey and Oracle
YEAR: 1967
BRIAN-LIKES?: #T

RECORD 4
ARTIST: (THE BEATLES)
TITLE: A Hard Day's Night
YEAR: 1964
BRIAN-LIKES?: #T

LISTED
> (count-db)
4
```

---

* Readers who are old enough to remember the days before compact discs may be disturbed by the ambiguity of the word "record," which could mean either a database record or a phonograph record. Luckily, in our example it doesn't matter, because each database record represents a phonograph record. But we intend the word "record" to mean a database record; we'll say "album" if we mean the musical kind.

We can insert new records into the database later on:

```
> (insert)
Value for ARTIST--> (the bill frisell band)
Value for TITLE--> "Where in the World?"
Value for YEAR--> 1991
Value for BRIAN-LIKES?--> #f
Insert another? no
INSERTED
```

We can sort the records of the database, basing the sorting order on a particular field:

```
> (sort-on 'year)
YEAR

> (list-db)
RECORD 1
ARTIST: (THE BEATLES)
TITLE: A Hard Day's Night
YEAR: 1964
BRIAN-LIKES?: #T

RECORD 2
ARTIST: (THE BEATLES)
TITLE: Rubber Soul
YEAR: 1965
BRIAN-LIKES?: #T

RECORD 3
ARTIST: (THE ZOMBIES)
TITLE: Odessey and Oracle
YEAR: 1967
BRIAN-LIKES?: #T

RECORD 4
ARTIST: (FRANK ZAPPA)
TITLE: Hot Rats
YEAR: 1970
BRIAN-LIKES?: #F
```

```
RECORD 5
ARTIST: (THE BILL FRISELL BAND)
TITLE: Where in the World?
YEAR: 1991
BRIAN-LIKES?: #F

LISTED
```

We can change the information in a record:

```
> (edit-record 1)
ARTIST: (THE BEATLES)
TITLE: A Hard Day's Night
YEAR: 1964
BRIAN-LIKES?: #T

Edit which field?  title
New value for TITLE--> "A Hard Day's Night (original soundtrack)"
ARTIST: (THE BEATLES)
TITLE: A Hard Day's Night (original soundtrack)
YEAR: 1964
BRIAN-LIKES?: #T

Edit which field?  #f
EDITED
```

(The `edit-record` procedure takes a record number as its argument. In this case, we wanted the first record. Also, the way you stop editing a record is by entering `#f` as the field name.)

Finally, we can save a database to a file and retrieve it later:

```
> (save-db)
SAVED

> (load-db "albums")
LOADED
```

How Databases Are Stored Internally

Our program will store a database as a vector of three elements: the file name associated with the database, a list of the names of the fields of the database, and a list of records in the database.

Each record of the database is itself a vector, containing values for the various fields. (So the length of a record vector depends on the number of fields in the database.)

Why is each record a vector, but the collection of records a list? Records have to be vectors because they are mutable; the edit command lets you change the value of a field for a record. But there is no command to replace an entire record with a new one, so the list of records doesn't have to be mutable.

An advantage of storing the records in a list instead of a vector is that it's easy to insert new records. If you've got a new record and a list of the old records, you simply cons the new record onto the old ones, and that's the new list. You need to mutate the vector that represents the entire database to contain this new list instead of the old one, but you don't need to mutate the list itself.

Here's the albums database we created, as it looks to Scheme:

```
#("albums"
  (ARTIST TITLE YEAR BRIAN-LIKES?)
  (#((THE BEATLES) "A Hard Day's Night (original soundtrack)" 1964 #T)
   #((THE BEATLES) "Rubber Soul" 1965 #T)
   #((THE ZOMBIES) "Odessey and Oracle" 1967 #T)
   #((FRANK ZAPPA) "Hot Rats" 1970 #F)
   #((THE BILL FRISELL BAND) "Where in the World?" 1991 #F)))
```

We'll treat databases as an abstract data type; here is how we implement it:

```
;;; The database ADT: a filename, list of fields and list of records

(define (make-db filename fields records)
  (vector filename fields records))

(define (db-filename db)
  (vector-ref db 0))

(define (db-set-filename! db filename)
  (vector-set! db 0 filename))

(define (db-fields db)
  (vector-ref db 1))

(define (db-set-fields! db fields)
  (vector-set! db 1 fields))
```

```
(define (db-records db)
  (vector-ref db 2))

(define (db-set-records! db records)
  (vector-set! db 2 records))
```

The Current Database

The database program works on one database at a time. Every command implicitly refers to the current database. Since the program might switch to a new database, it has to keep the current database in a vector that it can mutate if necessary. For now, the current database is the only state information that the program keeps, so it's stored in a vector of length one. If there is no current database (for example, when you start the database program), the value #f is stored in this vector:

```
(define current-state (vector #f))

(define (no-db?)
  (not (vector-ref current-state 0)))

(define (current-db)
  (if (no-db?)
      (error "No current database!")
      (vector-ref current-state 0)))

(define (set-current-db! db)
  (vector-set! current-state 0 db))

(define (current-fields)
  (db-fields (current-db)))
```

Implementing the Database Program Commands

Once we have the basic structure of the database program, the work consists of inventing the various database operations. Here is the new-db procedure:

```
(define (new-db filename fields)
  (set-current-db! (make-db filename fields '()))
  'created)
```

(Remember that when you first create a database there are no records in it.)

Here's the `insert` procedure:

```
(define (insert)
  (let ((new-record (get-record)))
    (db-insert new-record (current-db)))
  (if (ask "Insert another? ")
      (insert)
      'inserted))

(define (db-insert record db)
  (db-set-records! db (cons record (db-records db))))

(define (get-record)
  (get-record-loop 0
                   (make-vector (length (current-fields)))
                   (current-fields)))

(define (get-record-loop which-field record fields)
  (if (null? fields)
      record
      (begin (display "Value for ")
             (display (car fields))
             (display "--> ")
             (vector-set! record which-field (read))
             (get-record-loop (+ which-field 1) record (cdr fields)))))

(define (ask question)
  (display question)
  (let ((answer (read)))
    (cond ((equal? (first answer) 'y) #t)
          ((equal? (first answer) 'n) #f)
          (else (show "Please type Y or N.")
                (ask question)))))
```

Additions to the Program

The database program we've shown so far has the structure of a more sophisticated program, but it's missing almost every feature you'd want it to have. Some of the following additions are ones that we've demonstrated, but for which we haven't provided an implementation; others are introduced here for the first time.

In all of these additions, think about possible error conditions and how to handle them. Try to find a balance between failing even on errors that are very likely to occur and having an entirely safe program that has more error checking than actual content.

Count-db

Implement the `count-db` procedure. It should take no arguments, and it should return the number of records in the current database.

List-db

Implement the `list-db` procedure. It should take no arguments, and it should print the current database in the format shown earlier.

Edit-record

Implement `edit-record,` which takes a number between one and the number of records in the current database as its argument. It should allow the user to interactively edit the given record of the current database, as shown earlier.

Save-db and Load-db

Write `save-db` and `load-db`. `Save-db` should take no arguments and should save the current database into a file with the name that was given when the database was created. Make sure to save the field names as well as the information in the records.

`Load-db` should take one argument, the filename of the database you want to load. It should replace the current database with the one in the specified file. (Needless to say, it should expect files to be in the format that `save-db` creates.)

In order to save information to a file in a form that Scheme will be able to read back later, you will need to use the `write` procedure instead of `display` or `show`, as discussed in Chapter 22.

Clear-current-db!

The `new-db` and `load-db` procedures change the current database. `New-db` creates a new, blank database, while `load-db` reads in an old database from a file. In both cases, the program just throws out the current database. If you forgot to save it, you could lose a lot of work.

Write a procedure `clear-current-db!` that clears the current database. If there is no current database, `clear-current-db!` should do nothing. Otherwise, it should ask the user whether to save the database, and if so it should call `save-db`.

Modify `new-db` and `load-db` to invoke `clear-current-db!`.

Get

Many of the kinds of things that you would want to do to a database involve looking up the information in a record by the field name. For example, the user might want to list only the artists and titles of the album database, or sort it by year, or list only the albums that Brian likes.

But this isn't totally straightforward, since a record doesn't contain any information about names of fields. It doesn't make sense to ask what value the `price` field has in the record

```
#(SPROCKET 15 23 17 2)
```

without knowing the names of the fields of the current database and their order.

Write a procedure `get` that takes two arguments, a field name and a record, and returns the given field of the given record. It should work by looking up the field name in the list of field names of the current database.

```
> (get 'title '#((the zombies) "Odessey and Oracle" 1967 #t))
"Odessey and Oracle"
```

Get can be thought of as a selector for the record data type. To continue the implementation of a record ADT, write a constructor `blank-record` that takes no arguments and returns a record with no values in its fields. (Why doesn't `blank-record` need any arguments?) Finally, write the mutator `record-set!` that takes three arguments: a field name, a record, and a new value for the corresponding field.

Modify the rest of the database program to use this ADT instead of directly manipulating the records as vectors.

Sort

Write a `sort` command that takes a predicate as its argument and sorts the database according to that predicate. The predicate should take two records as arguments and return `#t` if the first record belongs before the second one, or `#f` otherwise. Here's an example:

```
> (sort (lambda (r1 r2) (before? (get 'title r1) (get 'title r2))))
SORTED

> (list-db)
RECORD 1
ARTIST: (THE BEATLES)
TITLE: A Hard Day's Night (original soundtrack)
YEAR: 1964
BRIAN-LIKES?: #T

RECORD 2
ARTIST: (FRANK ZAPPA)
TITLE: Hot Rats
YEAR: 1970
BRIAN-LIKES?: #F

RECORD 3
ARTIST: (THE ZOMBIES)
TITLE: Odessey and Oracle
YEAR: 1967
BRIAN-LIKES?: #T

RECORD 4
ARTIST: (THE BEATLES)
TITLE: Rubber Soul
YEAR: 1965
BRIAN-LIKES?: #T

RECORD 5
ARTIST: (THE BILL FRISELL BAND)
TITLE: Where in the World?
YEAR: 1991
BRIAN-LIKES?: #F
```

```
LISTED

> (sort (lambda (r1 r2) (< (get 'year r1) (get 'year r2))))
SORTED

> (list-db)
RECORD 1
ARTIST: (THE BEATLES)
TITLE: A Hard Day's Night (original soundtrack)
YEAR: 1964
BRIAN-LIKES?: #T

RECORD 2
ARTIST: (THE BEATLES)
TITLE: Rubber Soul
YEAR: 1965
BRIAN-LIKES?: #T

RECORD 3
ARTIST: (THE ZOMBIES)
TITLE: Odessey and Oracle
YEAR: 1967
BRIAN-LIKES?: #T

RECORD 4
ARTIST: (FRANK ZAPPA)
TITLE: Hot Rats
YEAR: 1970
BRIAN-LIKES?: #F

RECORD 5
ARTIST: (THE BILL FRISELL BAND)
TITLE: Where in the World?
YEAR: 1991
BRIAN-LIKES?: #F

LISTED
```

Note: Don't invent a sorting algorithm for this problem. You can just use one of the sorting procedures from Chapter 15 and modify it slightly to sort a list of records instead of a sentence of words.

Sort-on-by

Although `sort` is a very general-purpose tool, the way that you have to specify how to sort the database is cumbersome. Write a procedure `sort-on-by` that takes two arguments, the name of a field and a predicate. It should invoke `sort` with an appropriate predicate to achieve the desired sort. For example, you could say

```
(sort-on-by 'title before?)
```

and

```
(sort-on-by 'year <)
```

instead of the two `sort` examples we showed earlier.

Generic-before?

The next improvement is to eliminate the need to specify a predicate explicitly. Write a procedure `generic-before?` that takes two arguments of any types and returns `#t` if the first comes before the second. The meaning of "before" depends on the types of the arguments:

If the arguments are numbers, `generic-before?` should use `<`. If the arguments are words that aren't numbers, then `generic-before?` should use `before?` to make the comparison.

What if the arguments are lists? For example, suppose you want to sort on the `artist` field in the albums example. The way to compare two lists is element by element, just as in the `sent-before?` procedure in Chapter 14.

```
> (generic-before? '(magical mystery tour) '(yellow submarine))
#T
> (generic-before? '(is that you?) '(before we were born))
#F
> (generic-before? '(bass desires) '(bass desires second sight))
#T
```

But `generic-before?` should also work for structured lists:

```
> (generic-before? '(norwegian wood (this bird has flown))
                    '(norwegian wood (tastes so good)))
#F
```

What if the two arguments are of different types? If you're comparing a number and a non-numeric word, compare them alphabetically. If you're comparing a word to a list, treat the word as a one-word list, like this:

```
> (generic-before? '(in line) 'rambler)
#T

> (generic-before? '(news for lulu) 'cobra)
#F
```

Sort-on

Now write `sort-on`, which takes the name of a field as its argument and sorts the current database on that field, using `generic-before?` as the comparison predicate.

Add-field

Sometimes you discover that you don't have enough fields in your database. Write a procedure `add-field` that takes two arguments: the name of a new field and an initial value for that field. `Add-field` should modify the current database to include the new field. Any existing records in the database should be given the indicated initial value for the field. Here's an example:

```
> (add-field 'category 'rock)
ADDED

> (edit-record 5)
CATEGORY: ROCK
ARTIST: (THE BILL FRISELL BAND)
TITLE: Where in the World?
YEAR: 1991
BRIAN-LIKES?: #F
```

```
Edit which field?  category
New value for CATEGORY--> jazz
CATEGORY: JAZZ
ARTIST: (THE BILL FRISELL BAND)
TITLE: Where in the World?
YEAR: 1991
BRIAN-LIKES?: #F

Edit which field?  #f
EDITED

> (list-db)
RECORD 1
CATEGORY: ROCK
ARTIST: (THE BEATLES)
TITLE: A Hard Day's Night (original soundtrack)
YEAR: 1964
BRIAN-LIKES?: #T

RECORD 2
CATEGORY: ROCK
ARTIST: (THE BEATLES)
TITLE: Rubber Soul
YEAR: 1965
BRIAN-LIKES?: #T

RECORD 3
CATEGORY: ROCK
ARTIST: (THE ZOMBIES)
TITLE: Odessey and Oracle
YEAR: 1967
BRIAN-LIKES?: #T

RECORD 4
CATEGORY: ROCK
ARTIST: (FRANK ZAPPA)
TITLE: Hot Rats
YEAR: 1970
BRIAN-LIKES?: #F
```

```
RECORD 5
CATEGORY: JAZZ
ARTIST: (THE BILL FRISELL BAND)
TITLE: Where in the World?
YEAR: 1991
BRIAN-LIKES?: #F
```

LISTED

If you like, you can write `add-field` so that it will accept either one or two arguments. If given only one argument, it should use `#f` as the default field value.

Note: We said earlier that each record is a vector but the collection of records is a list because we generally want to mutate fields in a record, but not add new ones, whereas we generally want to add new records, but not replace existing ones completely. This problem is an exception; we're asking you to add an element to a vector. To do this, you'll have to create a new, longer vector for each record. Your program will probably run slowly as a result. This is okay because adding fields to an existing database is very unusual. Commercial database programs are also slow at this; now you know why.

You can't solve this problem in a way that respects the current version of the record ADT. Think about trying to turn the record

```
#((THE BEATLES) "Rubber Soul" 1965 #T)
```

into the record

```
#(ROCK (THE BEATLES) "Rubber Soul" 1965 #T)
```

It seems simple enough: Make a new record of the correct size, and fill in all the values of the old fields from the old record. But does this happen before or after you change the list of current fields in the database? If before, you can't call `blank-record` to create a new record of the correct size. If after, you can't call `get` to extract the field values of the old record, because the field names have changed.

There are (at least) three solutions to this dilemma. One is to abandon the record ADT, since it's turning out to be more trouble than it's worth. Using the underlying vector tools, it would be easy to transform old-field records into new-field records.

The second solution is to create another constructor for records, `adjoin-field`. `Adjoin-field` would take a record and a new field value, and would be analogous to `cons`.

The last solution is the most complicated, but perhaps the most elegant. The reason our ADT doesn't work is that `get`, `record-set!`, and `blank-record` don't just get information from their arguments; they also examine the current fields of the database. You could write a new ADT implementation in which each procedure took a list of fields as an extra argument. Then `get`, `record-set!`, and `blank-record` could be implemented in this style:

```
(define (get fieldname record)
  (get-with-these-fields fieldname record (current-fields)))
```

`Add-field` could use the underlying ADT, and the rest of the program could continue to use the existing version.

We've put a lot of effort into figuring out how to design this small part of the overall project. Earlier we showed you examples in which using an ADT made it *easy* to modify a program; those were realistic, but it's also realistic that sometimes making an ADT work can add to the effort.

Select-by

Sometimes you only want to look at certain records in your database. For example, suppose you just want to list the albums that Brian likes, or just the ones from before 1971. Also, you might want to save a portion of the database to a file, so that you could have, for example, a database of nothing but Beatles albums. In general, you need a way to *select* certain records of the database.

To do this, change the `current-state` vector to have another element: a selection predicate. This predicate takes a record as its argument and returns whether or not to include this record in the restricted database. Also write `count-selected` and `list-selected`, which are just like `count-db` and `list-db` but include only those records that satisfy the predicate. The initial predicate should include all records.

The procedure `select-by` should take a predicate and put it into the right place. Here's an example:

```
> (select-by (lambda (record) (get 'brian-likes? record)))
SELECTED

> (count-db)
5
```

```
> (count-selected)
3

> (select-by (lambda (record) (equal? (get 'category record) 'jazz)))
SELECTED

> (list-selected)
RECORD 5
CATEGORY: JAZZ
ARTIST: (THE BILL FRISELL BAND)
TITLE: Where in the World?
YEAR: 1991
BRIAN-LIKES?: #F

LISTED

> (select-by (lambda (record) #t))
SELECTED

> (count-selected)
5
```

You can't just throw away the records that aren't selected. You have to keep them in memory somehow, but make them invisible to count-selected and list-selected. The way to do that is to create another selector, current-selected-records, that returns a list of the selected records of the current database.

The selection predicate isn't part of a database; it's just a piece of state that's part of the user interface. So you don't have to save the predicate when you save the database to a file.* Save-db should save the entire database.

Save-selection

Write a save-selection procedure that's similar to save-db but saves only the currently selected records. It should take a file name as its argument.

---

* Even if you wanted to save the predicate, there's no way to write a procedure into a file.

Merge-db

One of the most powerful operations on a database is to merge it with another database. Write a procedure `merge-db` that takes two arguments: the file name of another database and the name of a field that the given database has in common with the current database. Both databases (the current one and the one specified) must already be sorted by the given field.

The effect of the `merge-db` command is to add fields from the specified database to the records of the current database. For example, suppose you had a database called `"bands"` with the following information:

```
Artist:                     Members:
(rush)                      (geddy alex neil)
(the beatles)               (john paul george ringo)
(the bill frisell band)     (bill hank kermit joey)
(the zombies)               (rod chris colin hugh paul)
```

You should be able to do the following (assuming `"albums"` is the current database):

```
> (sort-on 'artist)
ARTIST

> (merge-db "bands" 'artist)
MERGED

> (list-db)
RECORD 1
CATEGORY: ROCK
ARTIST: (FRANK ZAPPA)
TITLE: Hot Rats
YEAR: 1970
BRIAN-LIKES?: #F
MEMBERS: #F

RECORD 2
CATEGORY: ROCK
ARTIST: (THE BEATLES)
TITLE: A Hard Day's Night (original soundtrack)
YEAR: 1964
BRIAN-LIKES?: #T
MEMBERS: (JOHN PAUL GEORGE RINGO)
```

```
RECORD 3
CATEGORY: ROCK
ARTIST: (THE BEATLES)
TITLE: Rubber Soul
YEAR: 1965
BRIAN-LIKES?: #T
MEMBERS: (JOHN PAUL GEORGE RINGO)

RECORD 4
CATEGORY: JAZZ
ARTIST: (THE BILL FRISELL BAND)
TITLE: Where in the World?
YEAR: 1991
BRIAN-LIKES?: #F
MEMBERS: (BILL HANK KERMIT JOEY)

RECORD 5
CATEGORY: ROCK
ARTIST: (THE ZOMBIES)
TITLE: Odessey and Oracle
YEAR: 1967
BRIAN-LIKES?: #T
MEMBERS: (ROD CHRIS COLIN HUGH PAUL)

LISTED
```

Since there was no entry for Frank Zappa in the `"bands"` database, the `members` field was given the default value `#f`. If there are two or more records in the specified database with the same value for the given field, just take the information from the first one.

(By the way, this problem has a lot in common with the `join` procedure from Exercise 22.8.)

This is a complicated problem, so we're giving a hint:

```
(define (merge-db other-name common-field)
  (let ((other-db (read-db-from-disk other-name))
        (original-fields (current-fields)))
    (set-current-fields! (merge-fields original-fields
                                       (db-fields other-db)))
    (set-current-records! (merge-db-helper original-fields
                                           (current-records)
                                           (db-fields other-db)
                                           (db-records other-db)
                                           common-field))))
```

This procedure shows one possible overall structure for the program. You can fill in the structure by writing the necessary subprocedures. (If you prefer to start with a different overall design, that's fine too.) Our earlier suggestion about writing a `get-with-these-fields` procedure is relevant here also.

Extra Work for Hotshots

Compare your program to a real database program and see if you can add some of its features. For example, many database programs have primitive facilities for averaging the value of a field over certain records. Another feature you might want to try to implement is two-dimensional printing, in which each column is a field and each row is a record.

Part VII
Conclusion: Computer Science

This is the end of the technical material in this book. We've explored the big ideas of composition of functions, functions as data, recursion, abstraction, and sequential programming. As a review, you might enjoy rereading Chapter 1 to see how the formerly mysterious examples now make sense.

This book is intended both as a standalone programming course for people whose main interest is in something else and as preparation for those who intend to continue studying computer science. The final chapter is directed mainly at the latter group, to tell them what to expect. We confess, though, to the hope that some of the former may have enjoyed this experience enough to be lured into further study. If you're in that category, you'll be particularly interested in a preview of coming attractions.

Structure and Interpretation of Computer Programs

Second Edition

Harold Abelson and
Gerald Jay Sussman
with Julie Sussman

26   What's Next?

We've concluded this introduction to computer science with two examples of "real world" programming—spreadsheets and databases. What may have seemed like a pointless game near the beginning of the book allowed us to write these serious programs.

But we've only begun to explore the ideas that make up computer science. If you're interested in learning more, where do you go from here?

The Best Computer Science Book

The next step is to read *Structure and Interpretation of Computer Programs* by Harold Abelson and Gerald Jay Sussman with Julie Sussman (MIT Press/McGraw-Hill, Second Edition, 1996). Our book was inspired by theirs, and our main goal in writing this book has been to prepare you for that one. If you're a student and your school offers a course based on *SICP*, take it! If not, read the book on your own.

The big organizing idea of *SICP* is abstraction. We've used this idea in several ways. We've talked about *data abstraction* such as inventing the sentence and tree data types. We've also invented more specialized data types, such as positions in the tic-tac-toe program and cells in the spreadsheet program. We've discussed how higher-order procedures abstract a pattern of computation by using an extra argument to represent the function that's abstracted out.

What we've done in this book covers most of the main ideas in about the first hundred pages of *SICP*. But don't skip over those pages. In the footnotes alone you'll find ideas about numerical analysis, cryptography, epistemology (the study of what it means to know something), number theory, programming language design, and the analysis of algorithms.

Because there *is* some overlap between what we teach and what they teach, you may think at first that you can breeze through a course based on *SICP*. Don't fall into that trap; even from the beginning there will be some ideas that are new to you, and after about four weeks it will *all* be new to you.

The core ideas of this book are in the first chapter of *SICP*: functions, recursion, the substitution model, and higher-order functions. The second chapter is about lists and data abstraction, extending the ladder of data abstractions in both directions. (That is, in our book, lists are the fundamental data type used to construct the *sentence* and *tree* abstract data types. In *SICP* you first learn that lists themselves are built of an even more fundamental type, the *pairs* that we mentioned in a pitfall in Chapter 17. Then you learn about several more abstract data types that can be built out of lists.) The idea of data abstraction extends beyond inventing new types. For example, *SICP* uses data structures not only to contain passive information but also to control the algorithms used in a computation. You got a taste of this in the a-list of functions in the `functions` program.

The third chapter of *SICP* is largely about non-functional programming, a topic we only begin in this book. Specifically, *SICP* introduces object-oriented programming, a very popular technique in which the dichotomy between "smart" procedures and passive data is broken down. Instead of a single program controlling the computation, there are many *objects* that contain both algorithms and data; each object acts independently of the others. (This is a metaphor; there is still one computer implementing all this activity. The point is that the programmer is able to think in terms of the metaphor, and the mechanism that simulates the independent objects is hidden behind the object abstraction.)

You may have forgotten by now that *SICP* stands for *Structure and Interpretation of Computer Programs*. We've been talking about the "structure" part: how a program is organized to reflect the algorithm it implements. The "interpretation" half of the book explains how a programming language like Scheme really works—how a computer understands the program and carries out the activities that the program requests. The centerpiece of the interpretation part of the book is the Scheme interpreter in the fourth chapter, a program that takes any other Scheme program as its data and does what that program specifies. (The `compute` procedure that evaluates arithmetic expression trees in Chapter 18 and the `ss-eval` procedure in our spreadsheet program give a hint of what the *SICP* Scheme evaluator is like.) The book goes on to implement different programming languages and illustrate a variety of implementation techniques. Finally, the fifth chapter introduces the study of machine organization: how computer hardware carries out a program.

Beyond *SICP*

Computer science can be broadly divided into three areas: software, hardware, and theory. (Of course not everyone will agree with our division in detail.) This book is about software. *SICP* is also mostly about software, although it introduces some ideas from the other two areas. More advanced computer science courses will concentrate on one particular area.

Software includes programming languages, operating systems, and application programs. You know what a programming language is; there are courses on language design questions (why one language is different from another) and implementation (for example, how to write a Scheme interpreter).* An operating system is a program that maintains disk file structures and allows different programs to run on a computer without interfering with each other. Application programming techniques studied in computer science courses include database management, graphics programming, user interfaces, and artificial intelligence.

The study of computer hardware ranges from physical principles, through the workings of electronic components such as transistors, to large-scale circuits such as memories and adders, to the design of actual computers. This is a range of levels of abstraction, just as there are levels of abstraction in programming. At the higher levels of abstraction, you can think of an electronic circuit as a perfect representation of some function that it implements; that is, the signals coming out the output wires are functions of the signals coming in at the input wires. At a lower level of abstraction, you have to think about the limitations of physical devices. (For example, a device may fail if its output is attached to the inputs of too many other devices. It's as if you could use the return value from a function only a certain number of times.)

Theoretical computer science is a kind of applied mathematics. It includes analysis of algorithms, which is the study of how fast one program runs compared to another. (We touched on this topic when we mentioned that the simple selection sort is slower than the more complicated mergesort. Analysis of algorithms provides the tools to show exactly how much slower.) Theoreticians also study problems that can't be solved by any computer program at all; the most famous example is the *halting problem* of determining

---

* Many beginners think that studying computer science means learning a lot of different programming languages. Perhaps you start with BASIC, then you learn Pascal, then C, and so on. That's not true. The crucial ideas in computer science can be expressed in any modern language; it's unusual for a computer science student to be taught more than two languages throughout college.

in finite time whether some other program would run forever. *Automata theory* is the study of simplified pseudo-computers to prove theorems about the capabilities of computers in general.

A few topics don't fit readily into one of our three groups, such as *numerical analysis*, the study of how computers do arithmetic to ensure that the algorithms used really give correct results. This field involves aspects of programming, hardware design, and mathematics. *Robotics* involves artificial intelligence programming techniques along with electrical and mechanical engineering.

Standard Scheme

As we've mentioned, this book uses a lot of "primitive" procedures that aren't part of standard Scheme. These are procedures we wrote in Scheme and included in the file `simply.scm`, which is listed in Appendix C.

When you use Scheme in some other context, it probably won't come with these procedures included. There are three things you can do about this:

- Learn to love standard Scheme. That means not using the word and sentence functions, not using our implementation of trees, not using our higher-order procedures (`map` and `for-each` are the only standard ones), and not using `read-line`, `read-string`, `show`, `show-line`, `align`, or `close-all-ports`. Also, you may find it necessary to use data types we haven't fully explained: characters, strings, and pairs.

- Load our `simply.scm` and continue to work in the style we've used in this book. The advantage is that (in our humble opinion) we've provided some very convenient facilities. The disadvantage is that other Scheme programmers won't understand your programs unless they've read our book.

- Develop your own collection of tools to match the kind of programming you're doing in the new situations that come up. You can start with some of ours and add new procedures that you invent.

Actually, all three of these are good ideas. If you are going to continue working with Scheme, you'll certainly need to know what's in the standard and what's an extension to the language. After a while you're bound to develop a collection of tools that fit with your own preferred programming style. And sometimes `butfirst` will be just what you need for some project.

You may be curious about the *implementation* of our tool procedures. You've already seen some of them, such as the higher-order procedures whose implementation is described in Chapter 19. The input/output procedures (`show` and its friends) are straightforward once you've learned about the character data type. But you'll find that the implementation of words is quite complicated. Not only did we have to write the obvious `word`, `first`, and so on, but we also had to rewrite all of the arithmetic procedures so they work on words like `"007"` as well as ordinary numbers.

There are two documents that specify exactly what makes up standard Scheme. The first is updated fairly frequently to reflect ongoing experimentation in the language design. As we go to press, the most recent edition is called the *Revised*[5] *Report on the Algorithmic Language Scheme.* The second document is meant to provide a more stable basis for people who depend on a language that's guaranteed not to become obsolete; it's IEEE Standard 1178-1990, *IEEE Standard for the Scheme Programming Language,* published by the Institute of Electrical and Electronic Engineers in 1991. Appendix A tells you how to find both documents.

Last Words

It's hard to wrap up something like this without sounding preachy. Perhaps you'll forgive us this one section since we've been so cool all through the rest of the book.

We thought of two general points that we want to leave you with. First, in our teaching experience at Berkeley we've seen many students learn the ideas of functional programming in Scheme, then seem to forget all the ideas when they use another programming language, such as C. Part of the skill of a computer scientist is to see past surface differences in notation and understand, for example, that if the best way to solve some problem in Scheme is with a recursive procedure, then it's probably the best way in C, too.

The second point is that it's very easy to get a narrow technical education, learn lots of great ideas about computer science, and still have a hard time dealing with the rest of reality. The utilitarian way to put it is that when you work as a computer programmer it's rare that you can just sit in your corner and write programs. Instead, you have to cooperate with other people on a team project; you have to write documentation both for other programmers and for the people who will eventually use your program; you have to talk with customers and find out what they really want the program to do, before you write it. For all these reasons you have to work at developing communication skills just as much as you work at your programming skills. But the utilitarian argument is just our sneaky way of convincing you; the truth is that we want you to know about things that have nothing to do with your technical work. Matt majored in music along with computer science; Brian has a degree in clinical psychology. After you read Abelson and Sussman, go on to read Freud and Marx.

Appendices

A   Running Scheme

The precise incantations needed to start Scheme depend on the particular version you're using and the model of computer and operating system you have. It's beyond the scope of this book to teach you the first steps in using a computer; we assume you've already used other programs, if not Scheme. But in this appendix we suggest a few general ideas and point out some knotty details.

One thing that beginners often forget is that a computer generally has many different programs available, and each one has its own capabilities and its own method of operation. If you think of yourself as interacting with "the computer," you're likely to try to use a command suitable for one program when you're actually using a different program. In learning to program in Scheme, you'll probably use at least three programs: Scheme itself, the operating system's *shell* (which is callled *finder* on the Macintosh and *explorer* on Windows), and a text editor. (The text editor may be part of the Scheme package or it may be an entirely separate program.) The shell allows you to run other programs, such as a printing utility or an electronic mail reader.

If you say (+ 2 3) to your text editor, it won't respond by printing 5. Instead, it will insert the seven characters that you typed into the file that you're editing. If you type the same thing to Scheme, it will evaluate the expression.

The Program Development Cycle

Scheme is an interactive language: You can write a program by typing its definition directly into the Scheme interpreter. This ability to interact with Scheme is a great advantage for one-time calculations and for exploratory work, but it's not the best approach for the systematic development of a large program.

There are two issues to consider. First, when writing a large program, you generally don't get it perfect the first time. You make both typing errors and program logic errors, and so you must be able to revise a definition. Typing directly to Scheme, the only way to make such a revision is to retype the entire definition. Second, Scheme does not provide a mechanism to save your work in a permanent file.

For these reasons, programs are generally typed into another program, a text editor, rather than directly at the Scheme prompt. As we'll explain in the next section, there are several ways in which an editing program can be *integrated* with Scheme, so that the work you do in the editor can be communicated easily to Scheme. But the distinction between Scheme and the editor is easiest to understand if we start by considering the worst possible situation, in which the two are not integrated.

Imagine, therefore, that you have two separate programs available on your computer. One program is a Scheme interpreter. When you start Scheme, you may see some initial message, and then you see a prompt, which is a signal from Scheme that it's ready for you to type something. In this book we've used the character ">" as the prompt. Then, as we explain in the text, you can type an expression, and Scheme will compute and print the value:

```
> (+ 2 3)
5
```

Your other program is a text editor. This might be a general-purpose word processing program, with facilities for fancy text formatting, or it might be an editor intended specifically for computer programs. Many editors "know" about Lisp programs and have helpful features, such as automatic indentation, selection of complete expressions, and showing you the matching open parenthesis when you type a close parenthesis.

To write a program, you use the editor. Although you are typing Scheme expressions, you're not talking to Scheme itself, and so the expressions are not evaluated as you type them. Instead, they just appear on the screen like any other text. When you're ready to try out your program, you tell the editor to save the text in a file. (The command to save the program text is the same as it would be for any other text; we assume that you already know how to use the editor on your computer.) You can give the file any name you want, although many people like to use names like *something*.scm to make it easy to recognize files that contain Scheme programs.

Now you switch from the editor to Scheme. To read your program file into Scheme, you enter the expression

```
(load "something.scm")
```

This tells Scheme to read expressions from the specified file.*

Once Scheme has read the program definitions from your file, you can continue typing expressions to Scheme in order to test your program. If this testing uncovers an error, you will want to change some definition. Instead of typing the changed definition directly into Scheme, which would only make a temporary change in your program, you switch back to the editor and make the change in your program file. Then switch back to Scheme, and `load` the corrected file.

This sequence of steps—edit a file, make changes, save the file, switch to Scheme, load the file, test the program, find an error—is called a "development cycle" because what comes after "find an error" is editing the file, beginning another round of the same steps.

Integrated Editing

The development process can become much more convenient if Scheme and the editor "know about" each other. For example, instead of having to reload an entire file when you change one procedure definition, it's faster if your editor can tell Scheme just the one new definition. There are three general approaches to this integration: First, the editor can be in overall charge, with the Scheme interpreter running under control of the editor. Second, Scheme can be in charge, with the editor running under Scheme's supervision. Third, Scheme and the editor can be separate programs, both running under control of a third program, such as a window system, that allows information to be transferred between them.

If you're using a Unix system, you will be able to take a separate editor program and run Scheme from within that editor. The editor can copy any part of your program into the running Scheme, as if you had typed it to Scheme yourself. We use Jove, a free, small, fast version of EMACS. Most people use the more featureful GNU version of EMACS, which is installed on most Unix systems and available at `ftp://prep.ai.mit.edu/pub/gnu/` and many mirror sites for download.

If you're using a Macintosh or Windows version of Scheme, it will probably come with its own text editor and instructions on how to use it. These editors typically provide standard word-processing features such as cut and paste, search and replace, and saving

---

* If you see an error message about "end of file" or "EOF," it probably means that the file you are trying to load contains unbalanced parentheses; you have started an expression with a left parenthesis, and the file ended before Scheme saw a matching right parenthesis.

files. Also, they typically have a way to ask Scheme to evaluate an expression directly from the editor.

If you're using SCM under DOS, you should read the section "Editing Scheme Code" in the README file that comes with the SCM distribution. It will explain that editing can be done in different ways depending on the precise software available to you. You can buy a DOS editor that works like the Unix editors, or you can ask SCM to start a separate editor program while SCM remains active.

Finally, if you're running Scheme under Windows or another windowing operating system (like X or the Macintosh Finder), you can run any editor in another window and use the cut and paste facility to transfer information between the editor and Scheme.

Getting Our Programs

This book uses some programs that we wrote in Scheme. You'll want these files available to you while reading the book:

simply.scm	extended Scheme primitives
functions.scm	the functions program of Chapters 2 and 21
ttt.scm	the tic-tac-toe example from Chapter 10
match.scm	the pattern matcher example from Chapter 16
spread.scm	the spreadsheet program example from Chapter 24
database.scm	the beginning of the database project
copyleft	the GNU General Public License (see Appendix D)

In particular, the file simply.scm must be loaded into Scheme to allow anything in the book to work. Some Scheme systems allow you to load such a "startup" file permanently, so that it'll be there automatically from then on. In other versions of Scheme, you must say

```
(load "simply.scm")
```

at the beginning of every Scheme session.

There are three ways to get these program files:

- If you have access to the Internet, the most recent versions of all these files can be found at ftp://anarres.cs.berkeley.edu/pub/scheme/

- If you know someone who already has these files, you may copy them and distribute them freely. (The programs are copyrighted but are provided under a license that allows unlimited redistribution on a nonprofit basis; see Appendix D.)

- If you're stranded on a desert island with nothing but a computer and a copy of this book, you can type them in yourself; complete listings for all six programs, plus the GNU Public License, appear in the text of the book.

Tuning Our Programs for Your System

Almost all of the programs we distribute with this book will work without modification in the popular versions of Scheme. We've included "defensive" procedures that allow our programs to work even in versions that don't conform to current Scheme standards in various ways. However, there are a few details that we couldn't make uniform in all versions.

1. Many versions of Scheme include a `random` procedure to generate random numbers, but the standard does not require it, and so we've provided one just in case. If your Scheme includes a primitive `random`, it's probably better than the one we provide, because we have no way to choose a different starting value in each Scheme session.

Before loading `simply.scm` into Scheme, do the following experiment:

```
> (random 5)
```

If you get an error message, do nothing. If you get a random number as the result, edit `simply.scm` and remove the definition of `random`.

2. Do the following experiment:

```
> (error "Your error is" "string")
```

If the message you get doesn't include quotation marks around the word `string`, then do nothing. But if you do see `"string"` with quotation marks, edit `simply.scm` and change the definition of `error-printform` to

```
(define (error-printform x) x)
```

3. Although the Scheme standard says that the `read` procedure should not read the newline character following an expression that it reads, some old versions of Scheme get this wrong.

After loading `simply.scm`, do the following experiment:

```
> (read-line)
```

End the line with the **return** or **enter** key (whichever is appropriate in your version of Scheme) as usual, but don't type a second **return** or **enter** yet. If Scheme prints `( )` right away, skip this paragraph; your version of Scheme behaves correctly. If, on the other hand, nothing happens, type another **return** or **enter**. In this case you must edit `functions.scm` and remove the invocation of `read-line` on the first line of the body of the `functions` procedure.

4. There is a substantial loss of efficiency in treating strings of digits as numbers in some contexts and as text in other contexts. When we're treating 1024 as text, we want to be able to take its `butfirst`, which should be 024. But in Scheme, `024` is the same as `24`, so instead `butfirst` returns a string:

```
> (butfirst 1024)
"024"
```

Yet we want to be able to do arithmetic on this value:

```
> (+ 3 (butfirst 1024))
27
```

To accomplish this, we redefine all of Scheme's arithmetic procedures to accept strings of digits and convert them to numbers. This redefinition slows down all arithmetic, not just arithmetic on strange numbers, and it's only rarely important to the programs we write. Therefore, we've provided a way to turn this part of the package off and on again. If your programs run too slowly, try saying

```
> (strings-are-numbers #f)
```

If you find that some program doesn't work because it tries to do arithmetic on a digit string and gets an error message, you can say

```
> (strings-are-numbers #t)
```

to restore the original behavior of our programs. We recommend that you leave `strings-are-numbers` true while exploring the first few chapters, so that the behavior of the word data type will be consistent. When you get to the large example programs, you may want to change to false.

Loading Our Programs

Scheme's `load` procedure doesn't scan your entire disk looking for the file you want to load. Instead, it only looks in one particular directory (DOS/Unix) or folder (Macintosh/Windows). If you want to load our programs, you have to make sure that Scheme can find them.

The first way to accomplish this is to give the full "path" as part of the argument to `load`. Here are some examples:*

```
UNIX-SCHEME> (load "/usr/people/matt/scheme-stuff/simply.scm")

WINDOWS-SCHEME> (load "c:\\scheme\\simply.scm")

MAC-SCHEME> (load "Hard Disk:Scheme Folder:simply.scm")
```

Under Unix, directories in a path are separated by forward slash characters. Under Windows and DOS, directories are separated by backward slash characters, which have a special meaning to Scheme. So you must use double backslashes as in our example above. On a Macintosh, you separate the parts of a path with colons. (However, most versions of Scheme for the Macintosh or Windows have a load command in one of the menus that opens a standard file selection dialog box, so you can use that instead.)

The other possibility is to put the files in the place where your version of Scheme looks for them. In many versions of Scheme, `load` looks for files in the folder that contains the Scheme program itself. Put our files in that folder.

On Unix, the default loading directory is whatever directory you're in at the moment. If you want to work on different projects in different directories, there's no way to make it so that `load` will always find our files. (But see our suggestion about writing `book-load`.)

---

* Suggestion for instructors: when we teach this class, we define a procedure like

```
(define (book-load filename)
  (load (string-append "/usr/cs3/progs-from-book/" filename)))
```

so that students can just say

```
(book-load "functions.scm")
```

Versions of Scheme

There are lots of them, both free and commercial. Three places to look for pointers are

```
http://swissnet.ai.mit.edu/scheme-home.html
http://www.schemers.org
http://www.cs.indiana.edu/scheme-repository
```

In general, there are four things you should be sure to learn about whatever version of Scheme you choose:

- Most versions of Scheme include a *debugger* to help you find program errors. If you call a primitive with an argument not in its domain, for example, Scheme will start the debugger, which will have features to let you find out where in your program the error occurred. These debuggers vary greatly among versions of Scheme. The first thing you should learn is how to *leave* the debugger, so you can get back to a Scheme prompt!

- Many versions of Scheme will read an *initialization file* if you create one. That is, when you start Scheme, it will look for a file of a particular name (something like `init.scm`, but not usually exactly that), and if there is such a file, Scheme will `load` it automatically. You can copy our `simply.scm` file to the proper filename for your version, and you'll have our added primitives available every time you start Scheme.

- Most versions of Scheme provide a `trace` capability, but the format of the trace results are quite different from one version to another.

- If you are using a Macintosh, one thing to watch out for is that some versions of Scheme expect you to use the ENTER key at the end of an expression, while others expect you to use the RETURN key.

Scheme Standards

The Web sites listed above will provide the latest version of the *Revisedⁿ Report on the Algorithmic Language Scheme.* You can get the document in either Postscript or HTML format.

IEEE Standard 1178-1990, *IEEE Standard for the Scheme Programming Language,* may be ordered from IEEE by calling 1-800-678-IEEE or 908-981-1393 or writing IEEE Service Center, 445 Hoes Lane, P.O. Box 1331, Piscataway, NJ 08855-1331, and using order number SH14209 ($28 for IEEE members, $40 for others). ISBN 1-55937-125-0.

B   Common Lisp

The two most popular dialects of Lisp are Scheme and Common Lisp. This appendix, which assumes that you have finished the rest of this book, describes the most important differences between Scheme and Common Lisp so that you will be able to use Common Lisp if you need to. Common Lisp is the most popular language among Artificial Intelligence researchers, so AI courses often use Common Lisp.

Why Common Lisp Exists

Since the beginning of Lisp, many versions of the language were developed. Each dialect reflected different ideas about the most important capabilities to include in the language. This diversity made Lisp an exciting arena for research, but it also meant that a Lisp program written for one dialect couldn't be used elsewhere.

In 1984, a group of Lisp developers decided to define a version of Lisp that would combine the capabilities of all their favorite dialects, so that in the future they would all use the same language; thus the name "Common" Lisp. Common Lisp was not the first attempt at a universal Lisp dialect, but it was more successful than earlier efforts. In 1985 a revision of the language was begun under the aegis of ANSI, the American National Standards Institute. This ANSI sponsorship gave Common Lisp an official status that has contributed to its growing acceptance.

Since Common Lisp was designed by combining the capabilities of many earlier dialects, it's an enormous language with nearly 1000 primitives, including versions of several programs in this book. There is a primitive `sort` procedure, a procedure like `number-name` that spells numbers in English, and a `substitute` procedure identical to the one you wrote in an exercise, to name a few.

If you're writing your own programs in Common Lisp, you can ignore all the extra features and just use the capabilities you already know from Scheme. If you're trying to read someone else's Common Lisp program, we expect that you will have to look up many primitive procedures in a reference manual.

Defining Procedures and Variables

One minor difference between Scheme and Common Lisp is in the way procedures are defined. In Common Lisp,

```
(defun square (x)
  (* x x))
```

means the same as Scheme's

```
(define (square x)
  (* x x))
```

In Scheme, `define` is used both for procedures and for variables whose values aren't procedures. In Common Lisp, procedures are given names by a mechanism separate from the general variable mechanism; `defun` is only for procedures. To define a variable, use `defvar`:

```
common-lisp> (defvar x 6)
6

common-lisp> x
6
```

In Common Lisp, `defvar` returns the name of the variable you define. If a variable has already been defined, `defvar` will not change its value; for that you must use `setq`.

The Naming Convention for Predicates

In Common Lisp, names of predicate procedures end in a "p" (for "predicate") instead of a question mark. Unfortunately, this convention isn't followed strictly. For example, Common Lisp's version of the `null?` predicate is just "null," not "nullp."

No Words or Sentences

We've mentioned that Scheme doesn't really have words and sentences built in; neither does Common Lisp. So none of the following procedures have Common Lisp equivalents: `accumulate`, `appearances`, `before?`, `bf`, `bl`, `butfirst`, `butlast`, `count`, `empty?`, `every`, `first`, `item`, `keep`, `last`, `member?`, `se`, `sentence`, `word`, and `word?`. (Common Lisp does have lists, though, and list-related procedures such as `map`, `reduce`, `append`, and so on *do* have equivalents.)

True and False

Common Lisp doesn't have the Boolean values `#t` and `#f`. Instead, it has a single false value, `nil`, which is also the empty list.

```
common-lisp> (= 2 3)
NIL

common-lisp> (cdr '(one-word-list))
NIL

common-lisp> '()
NIL
```

Nil is a strange beast in Common Lisp. It isn't a variable with the empty list as its value; it's a special self-evaluating symbol. There is also `t`, a self-evaluating symbol with a true value.

```
common-lisp> 'nil
NIL

common-lisp> nil
NIL

common-lisp> t
T
```

Like Scheme, Common Lisp treats every non-false (i.e., non-`nil`) value as true. But be careful; in Common Lisp

```
common-lisp> (if (cdr '(one-word-list)) 'yes 'no)
```

has the value NO, because the empty list is `nil`.

In Common Lisp's `cond`, there is no equivalent to `else`; Common Lisp programmers instead use `t` as the condition for their last clause, like this:

```
(defun sign (n)
  (cond ((> n 0) 'positive)
        ((= n 0) 'zero)
        (t 'negative)))
```

Files

Common Lisp's mechanism for dealing with files is trivially different from Scheme's. What Scheme calls "ports," Common Lisp calls "streams." Also, there is only one procedure for opening streams; the direction is specified this way:

```
common-lisp> (defvar out-stream (open "outfile" :direction :output))
#<OUTPUT STREAM "outfile">

common-lisp> (close out-stream)
T

common-lisp> (defvar in-stream (open "infile" :direction :input))
#<INPUT STREAM "infile">

common-lisp> (close in-stream)
T
```

Note that the `close` procedure closes both input streams and output streams.

To `read` from an input stream, you must invoke `read` with three arguments:

```
common-lisp> (read stream nil anything)
```

The `nil` indicates that reaching the end of the file should not be an error. If `read` does reach the end of the file, instead of returning a special end-of-file object it returns its third argument. It's possible to choose any value as the indicator for reaching the end of the file:

```
(let ((next (read stream nil 'xyzzy)))
  (if (equalp next 'xyzzy)
      'done
      (do-something next)))
```

It's important to choose an end-of-file indicator that couldn't otherwise appear as a value in the file.

Arrays

In Common Lisp, vectors are just a special case of the multidimensional *array* data type that you invented in Exercise 23.15. There are quite a few differences between Common Lisp arrays and Scheme vectors, none very difficult, but too numerous to describe here. If you need to use arrays, read about them in a Common Lisp book.

Equivalents to Scheme Primitives

Other than the word and sentence procedures, here is a table of the Scheme primitives from the table on page 553 that have different names, slightly different behavior, or do not exist at all in Common Lisp. Scheme procedures not in this list (other than the word and sentence ones) can be used identically in Common Lisp.

Scheme	Common Lisp
align	Common Lisp's `format` primitive has a similar purpose.
begin	`progn`
boolean?	Doesn't exist; see the section in this appendix about true and false values.
c...r	The same, but (`c...r nil`) is `nil` instead of an error.
children	You can use our version from Chapter 18.
close-...-port	`close`
close-all-ports	Doesn't exist.
cond	The same, except for `else`; use t instead.
datum	You can use our version from Chapter 18.
define	Either `defun`, for procedures, or `defvar`, otherwise.
display	`princ`
eof-object?	See the section on files.
equal?	`equalp`
even?	`evenp`
filter	`remove-if-not`
for-each	`mapc`
integer?	`integerp`
lambda	Discussed later in this appendix.
list?	`listp`, except that `listp` also returns true for improper lists.
list-ref	`nth`, except that the arguments come in reverse order.
list->vector	See the section about arrays.
make-node	You can use our version from Chapter 18.
make-vector	See the section about arrays.

map	mapcar
newline	terpri
null?	null
number?	numberp
odd?	oddp
open-...-file	See the section on files.
procedure?	functionp
quotient	truncate
read	Identical except for end of file. See the section on files.
read-line	Doesn't exist. (Common Lisp's read-line is like our read-string.)
read-string	read-line
reduce	The same, but computes (f (f a b) c) instead of (f a (f b c)).
remainder	rem
repeated	Doesn't exist.
show	Doesn't exist but easy to write.
show-line	Doesn't exist.
vector-*anything*	See the section about arrays.
write	prin1

A Separate Name Space for Procedures

All of the differences noted in this table are fairly minor ones, in the sense that the translation needed to account for these differences requires little more than renaming. There is one major conceptual difference between the two languages, however, in the way they treat names of procedures. Common Lisp allows a procedure and a variable to have the same name. For example, the program

```
(defun three-copies (list)
  (list list list list))
```

is perfectly legal.

```
common-lisp> (three-copies '(drive my car))
((DRIVE MY CAR) (DRIVE MY CAR) (DRIVE MY CAR))
```

How can Common Lisp tell that one of the lists means the primitive procedure, but the other ones mean the formal parameter? Symbols in the first position in a list (right after an open parenthesis) are taken to be names of globally defined procedures.

In Chapter 7 we introduced the image of a blackboard with all the global variables written on it, which all the Scheme little people can see. In Common Lisp, there are *two* blackboards: one for global variables, just as in Scheme, and another one for procedures.

The procedure blackboard contains the primitive procedures and the procedures you define with `defun`. Names in the first position of an expression are looked up on the procedure blackboard.

Therefore, the names of procedures are not variables and cannot be used as actual argument expressions:

```
common-lisp> (sqrt 144)
12

common-lisp> (mapcar sqrt '(9 16 25 36))
ERROR: The variable SQRT is unbound.
```

(Common Lisp's equivalent of `map` is named `mapcar`.)

How, then, do you tell Common Lisp that you want to use the procedure named `sqrt` as data? You must use the `function` special form.*

```
common-lisp> (function sqrt)
#<PROCEDURE>

common-lisp> (mapcar (function sqrt) '(9 16 25 36))
(3 4 5 6)
```

`Function`'s job is to look up names on the procedure blackboard. (`Function` actually has a more general definition, as you'll see in a few paragraphs.)

Lambda

In Common Lisp, as in Scheme, procedures can be named or unnamed. Just as procedure names in Common Lisp are meaningful only in certain contexts, so are `lambda` expressions. They make sense at the beginning of an expression:

```
common-lisp> ((lambda (x) (* x x)) 4)
16
```

---

* Common Lisp uses the word "function" to mean "procedure," whether or not the procedure implements a function.

or as the argument to `function`:

```
common-lisp> (function (lambda (x) (* x x)))
#<PROCEDURE>

common-lisp> (mapcar (function (lambda (x) (* x x))) '(3 4 5 6))
(9 16 25 36)
```

but they're meaningless on their own:

```
common-lisp> (lambda (x) (* x x))
ERROR: LAMBDA is not a function

common-lisp> (mapcar (lambda (x) (* x x)) '(3 4 5 6))
ERROR: LAMBDA is not a function
```

More about `Function`

The official rule is that `function` returns the "functional interpretation" of its argument. If the argument is a symbol, that means looking up the procedure associated with that name. If the argument is a `lambda` expression, it means creating a new procedure. `Function` uses the same rule that's used to interpret the first element of a procedure invocation.

Since `function` is a very commonly used special form, it has an abbreviation:

```
common-lisp> (mapcar #'(lambda (x) (* x x)) '(3 4 5 6))
(9 16 25 36)

common-lisp> (mapcar #'cdr '((hey jude) (eleanor rigby) (yes it is)))
((JUDE) (RIGBY) (IT IS))
```

Don't confuse

```
#'(lambda (x) (* x x))
```

with

```
'#(lambda (x) (* x x))
```

The first of these is a function that squares its argument; the second is an array containing three elements.

It's unfortunate that the abbreviation for function contains a single quote mark, because the job of function is nothing like the job of quote. You'll just have to get used to the "hashquote" notation.

Writing Higher-Order Procedures

Think about this attempted translation of the map procedure:

```
(defun map (fn lst)                              ;; wrong!
  (if (null lst)
      '()
      (cons (fn (car lst))
            (map fn (cdr lst)))))
```

(In Common Lisp, null is one of the predicates whose names don't end in "p." Otherwise, this is the same program we showed you in Chapter 19, except for the defun, of course.)

According to our rule about names in the front of a list, this procedure doesn't work. Think about what happens when we say

```
(map #'square '(1 2 3 4 5))
```

According to the substitution model, the parameters fn and lst are replaced in the body with #'square and '(1 2 3 4 5). But Common Lisp makes an exception for the first element of a compound expression. It uses the procedure blackboard instead of substitution:

```
(if (null '(1 2 3 4 5))
    '()
    (cons (fn (car '(1 2 3 4 5))
          (map #'square (cdr '(1 2 3 4 5)))))))
```

Note that one of the appearances of fn was left unchanged. Since there is no global procedure named fn, this program will produce an error:

```
common-lisp> (map #'square '(1 2 3 4 5))
ERROR: FN is not a procedure.
```

How, then, do you write higher-order procedures in Common Lisp? The answer is that you must use funcall:

```
(defun map (fn lst)
  (if (null lst)
      '()
      (cons (funcall fn (car lst))
            (map fn (cdr lst)))))
```

Funcall takes one or more arguments. The first is a procedure and the rest are arguments for that procedure. It applies that procedure to the given arguments.* Since fn is no longer at the beginning of a compound expression, the corresponding argument, #'square, is substituted for it.

---

* This is a lot like apply, you may have noticed. Look at the difference:

```
common-lisp> (funcall #'+ 1 2 3)
6

common-lisp> (apply #'+ '(1 2 3))
6
```

In the first case, each argument to + is a separate argument to funcall. In the second case, a list of the arguments to + is a single argument to apply. Apply always takes exactly two arguments, the procedure and the argument list.

C   Scheme Initialization File

Many of the procedures we talk about in this book aren't part of standard Scheme; we wrote them ourselves. Here is a listing of the definitions of those procedures.

```
;;; simply.scm version 3.13 (8/11/98)

;;; This file uses Scheme features we don't talk about in _Simply_Scheme_.
;;; Read at your own risk.

(if (equal? 'foo (symbol->string 'foo))
    (error "Simply.scm already loaded!!")
    #f)

;; Make number->string remove leading "+" if necessary

(if (char=? #\+ (string-ref (number->string 1.0) 0))
    (let ((old-ns number->string) (char=? char=?) (string-ref string-ref)
          (substring substring) (string-length string-length))
      (set! number->string
            (lambda args
              (let ((result (apply old-ns args)))
                (if (char=? #\+ (string-ref result 0))
                    (substring result 1 (string-length result))
                    result)))))
    'no-problem)

(define number->string
  (let ((old-ns number->string) (string? string?))
    (lambda args
      (if (string? (car args))
          (car args)
          (apply old-ns args)))))
```

```scheme
;; Get strings in error messages to print nicely (especially "")

(define whoops
  (let ((string? string?) (string-append string-append)       (error error)
        (cons cons) (map map) (apply apply))
    (define (error-printform x)
      (if (string? x)
          (string-append "\"" x "\"")
          x))
    (lambda (string . args)
      (apply error (cons string (map error-printform args))))))


;; ROUND returns an inexact integer if its argument is inexact,
;; but we think it should always return an exact integer.
;; (It matters because some Schemes print inexact integers as "+1.0".)
;; The (exact 1) test is for PC Scheme, in which nothing is exact.
(if (and (inexact? (round (sqrt 2))) (exact? 1))
    (let ((old-round round) (inexact->exact inexact->exact))
      (set! round
            (lambda (number)
              (inexact->exact (old-round number)))))
    'no-problem)

;; Remainder and quotient blow up if their argument isn't an integer.
;; Unfortunately, in SCM, (* 365.25 24 60 60) *isn't* an integer.

(if (inexact? (* .25 4))
    (let ((rem remainder) (quo quotient) (inexact->exact inexact->exact)
          (integer? integer?))
      (set! remainder
            (lambda (x y)
              (rem (if (integer? x) (inexact->exact x) x)
                   (if (integer? y) (inexact->exact y) y))))
      (set! quotient
            (lambda (x y)
              (quo (if (integer? x) (inexact->exact x) x)
                   (if (integer? y) (inexact->exact y) y)))))
    'done)
```

```
;; Random
;; If your version of Scheme has RANDOM, you should take this out.
;; (It gives the same sequence of random numbers every time.)

(define random
  (let ((*seed* 1) (quotient quotient) (modulo modulo) (+ +) (- -) (* *) (> >))
    (lambda (x)
      (let* ((hi (quotient *seed* 127773))
             (low (modulo *seed* 127773))
             (test (- (* 16807 low) (* 2836 hi))))
        (if (> test 0)
            (set! *seed* test)
            (set! *seed* (+ test 2147483647))))
      (modulo *seed* x))))


;;; Logo-style word/sentence implementation

(define word?
  (let ((number? number?) (symbol? symbol?) (string? string?))
    (lambda (x)
      (or (symbol? x) (number? x) (string? x)))))

(define sentence?
  (let ((null? null?) (pair? pair?) (word? word?) (car car) (cdr cdr))
    (define (list-of-words? l)
      (cond ((null? l) #t)
            ((pair? l)
             (and (word? (car l)) (list-of-words? (cdr l))))
            (else #f)))
    list-of-words?))

(define empty?
  (let ((null? null?) (string? string?) (string=? string=?))
    (lambda (x)
      (or (null? x)
          (and (string? x) (string=? x ""))))))
```

```scheme
(define char-rank
  ;; 0 Letter in good case or special initial
  ;; 1 ., + or -
  ;; 2 Digit
  ;; 3 Letter in bad case or weird character
  (let ((*the-char-ranks* (make-vector 256 3))
        (= =) (+ +) (string-ref string-ref) (string-length string-length)
        (vector-set! vector-set!) (char->integer char->integer)
        (symbol->string symbol->string) (vector-ref vector-ref))
    (define (rank-string str rank)
      (define (helper i len)
        (if (= i len)
            'done
            (begin (vector-set! *the-char-ranks*
                                (char->integer (string-ref str i))
                                rank)
                   (helper (+ i 1) len))))
      (helper 0 (string-length str)))
    (rank-string (symbol->string 'abcdefghijklmnopqrstuvwxyz) 0)
    (rank-string "!$%&*/:<=>?~_^" 0)
    (rank-string "+-." 1)
    (rank-string "0123456789" 2)
    (lambda (char)                        ;; value of char-rank
      (vector-ref *the-char-ranks* (char->integer char)))))

(define string->word
  (let ((= =) (<= <=) (+ +) (- -) (char-rank char-rank) (string-ref string-ref)
        (string-length string-length) (string=? string=?) (not not)
        (char=? char=?) (string->number string->number)
        (string->symbol string->symbol))
    (lambda (string)
      (define (subsequents? string i length)
        (cond ((= i length) #t)
              ((<= (char-rank (string-ref string i)) 2)
               (subsequents? string (+ i 1) length))
              (else #f)))
      (define (special-id? string)
        (or (string=? string "+")
            (string=? string "-")
            (string=? string "...")))
      (define (ok-symbol? string)
        (if (string=? string "")
            #f
            (let ((rank1 (char-rank (string-ref string 0))))
              (cond ((= rank1 0) (subsequents? string 1 (string-length string)))
                    ((= rank1 1) (special-id? string))
                    (else #f)))))
```

```scheme
        (define (nn-helper string i len seen-point?)
          (cond ((= i len)
                  (if seen-point?
                      (not (char=? (string-ref string (- len 1)) #\0))
                      #t))
                ((char=? #\. (string-ref string i))
                 (cond (seen-point? #f)
                       ((= (+ i 2) len) #t)   ; Accepts "23.0"
                       (else (nn-helper string (+ i 1) len #t))))
                ((= 2 (char-rank (string-ref string i)))
                 (nn-helper string (+ i 1) len seen-point?))
                (else #f)))
        (define (narrow-number? string)
          (if (string=? string "")
              #f
              (let* ((c0 (string-ref string 0))
                     (start 0)
                     (len (string-length string))
                     (cn (string-ref string (- len 1))))
                (if (and (char=? c0 #\-) (not (= len 1)))
                    (begin
                      (set! start 1)
                      (set! c0 (string-ref string 1)))
                    #f)
                (cond ((not (= (char-rank cn) 2)) #f)   ; Rejects "-" among others
                      ((char=? c0 #\.) #f)
                      ((char=? c0 #\0)
                       (cond ((= len 1) #t)   ; Accepts "0" but not "-0"
                             ((= len 2) #f)   ; Rejects "-0" and "03"
                             ((char=? (string-ref string (+ start 1)) #\.)
                              (nn-helper string (+ start 2) len #t))
                             (else #f)))
                      (else (nn-helper string start len #f))))))

        ;; The body of string->word:
        (cond ((narrow-number? string) (string->number string))
              ((ok-symbol? string) (string->symbol string))
              (else string)))))

(define char->word
  (let ((= =) (char-rank char-rank) (make-string make-string) (char=? char=?)
        (string->symbol string->symbol) (string->number string->number))
    (lambda (char)
      (let ((rank (char-rank char))
            (string (make-string 1 char)))
        (cond ((= rank 0) (string->symbol string))
              ((= rank 2) (string->number string))
              ((char=? char #\+) '+)
              ((char=? char #\-) '-)
              (else string))))))
```

```
(define word->string
  (let ((number? number?) (string? string?) (number->string number->string)
        (symbol->string symbol->string))
    (lambda (wd)
      (cond ((string? wd) wd)
            ((number? wd) (number->string wd))
            (else (symbol->string wd))))))

(define count
  (let ((word? word?) (string-length string-length)
        (word->string word->string) (length length))
    (lambda (stuff)
      (if (word? stuff)
          (string-length (word->string stuff))
          (length stuff)))))

(define word
  (let ((string->word string->word) (apply apply) (string-append string-append)
        (map map) (word? word?) (word->string word->string) (whoops whoops))
    (lambda x
      (string->word
       (apply string-append
              (map (lambda (arg)
                     (if (word? arg)
                         (word->string arg)
                         (whoops "Invalid argument to WORD: " arg)))
                   x))))))

(define se
  (let ((pair? pair?) (null? null?) (word? word?) (car car) (cons cons)
        (cdr cdr) (whoops whoops))
    (define (paranoid-append a original-a b)
      (cond ((null? a) b)
            ((word? (car a))
             (cons (car a) (paranoid-append (cdr a) original-a b)))
            (else (whoops "Argument to SENTENCE not a word or sentence"
                          original-a ))))
    (define (combine-two a b)                    ;; Note: b is always a list
      (cond ((pair? a) (paranoid-append a a b))
            ((null? a) b)
            ((word? a) (cons a b))
            (else (whoops "Argument to SENTENCE not a word or sentence:" a))))
    ;; Helper function so recursive calls don't show up in TRACE
    (define (real-se args)
      (if (null? args)
          '()
          (combine-two (car args) (real-se (cdr args)))))
    (lambda args
      (real-se args))))
```

```
(define sentence se)

(define first
  (let ((pair? pair?) (char->word char->word) (string-ref string-ref)
        (word->string word->string) (car car) (empty? empty?)
        (whoops whoops) (word? word?))
    (define (word-first wd)
      (char->word (string-ref (word->string wd) 0)))
    (lambda (x)
      (cond ((pair? x) (car x))
            ((empty? x) (whoops "Invalid argument to FIRST: " x))
            ((word? x) (word-first x))
            (else (whoops "Invalid argument to FIRST: " x))))))

(define last
  (let ((pair? pair?) (- -) (word->string word->string) (char->word char->word)
        (string-ref string-ref) (string-length string-length) (empty? empty?)
        (cdr cdr) (car car) (whoops whoops) (word? word?))
    (define (word-last wd)
      (let ((s (word->string wd)))
        (char->word (string-ref s (- (string-length s) 1)))))
    (define (list-last lst)
      (if (empty? (cdr lst))
          (car lst)
          (list-last (cdr lst))))
    (lambda (x)
      (cond ((pair? x) (list-last x))
            ((empty? x) (whoops "Invalid argument to LAST: " x))
            ((word? x) (word-last x))
            (else (whoops "Invalid argument to LAST: " x))))))

(define bf
  (let ((pair? pair?) (substring substring) (string-length string-length)
        (string->word string->word) (word->string word->string) (cdr cdr)
        (empty? empty?) (whoops whoops) (word? word?))
    (define string-bf
      (lambda (s)
        (substring s 1 (string-length s))))
    (define (word-bf wd)
      (string->word (string-bf (word->string wd))))
    (lambda (x)
      (cond ((pair? x) (cdr x))
            ((empty? x) (whoops "Invalid argument to BUTFIRST: " x))
            ((word? x) (word-bf x))
            (else (whoops "Invalid argument to BUTFIRST: " x))))))

(define butfirst bf)
```

```scheme
(define bl
  (let ((pair? pair?) (- -) (cdr cdr) (cons cons) (car car) (substring substring)
        (string-length string-length) (string->word string->word)
        (word->string word->string) (empty? empty?) (whoops whoops) (word? word?))
    (define (list-bl list)
      (if (null? (cdr list))
          '()
          (cons (car list) (list-bl (cdr list)))))
    (define (string-bl s)
      (substring s 0 (- (string-length s) 1)))
    (define (word-bl wd)
      (string->word (string-bl (word->string wd))))
    (lambda (x)
      (cond ((pair? x) (list-bl x))
            ((empty? x) (whoops "Invalid argument to BUTLAST: " x))
            ((word? x) (word-bl x))
            (else (whoops "Invalid argument to BUTLAST: " x))))))

(define butlast bl)

(define item
  (let ((> >) (- -) (< <) (integer? integer?) (list-ref list-ref)
        (char->word char->word) (string-ref string-ref)
        (word->string word->string) (not not) (whoops whoops)
        (count count) (word? word?) (list? list?))
    (define (word-item n wd)
      (char->word (string-ref (word->string wd) (- n 1))))
    (lambda (n stuff)
      (cond ((not (integer? n))
             (whoops "Invalid first argument to ITEM (must be an integer): "
                     n))
            ((< n 1)
             (whoops "Invalid first argument to ITEM (must be positive): "
                     n))
            ((> n (count stuff))
             (whoops "No such item: " n stuff))
            ((word? stuff) (word-item n stuff))
            ((list? stuff) (list-ref stuff (- n 1)))
            (else (whoops "Invalid second argument to ITEM: " stuff))))))
```

```scheme
(define equal?
  ;; Note that EQUAL? assumes strings are numbers.
  ;; (strings-are-numbers #f) doesn't change this behavior.
  (let ((vector-length vector-length) (= =) (vector-ref vector-ref)
        (+ +) (string? string?) (symbol? symbol?) (null? null?) (pair? pair?)
        (car car) (cdr cdr) (eq? eq?) (string=? string=?)
        (symbol->string symbol->string) (number? number?)
        (string->word string->word) (vector? vector?) (eqv? eqv?))
    (define (vector-equal? v1 v2)
      (let ((len1 (vector-length v1))
            (len2 (vector-length v2)))
        (define (helper i)
          (if (= i len1)
              #t
              (and (equal? (vector-ref v1 i) (vector-ref v2 i))
                   (helper (+ i 1)))))
        (if (= len1 len2)
            (helper 0)
            #f)))
    (lambda (x y)
      (cond ((null? x) (null? y))
            ((null? y) #f)
            ((pair? x)
             (and (pair? y)
                  (equal? (car x) (car y))
                  (equal? (cdr x) (cdr y))))
            ((pair? y) #f)
            ((symbol? x)
             (or (and (symbol? y) (eq? x y))
                 (and (string? y) (string=? (symbol->string x) y))))
            ((symbol? y)
             (and (string? x) (string=? x (symbol->string y))))
            ((number? x)
             (or (and (number? y) (= x y))
                 (and (string? y)
                      (let ((possible-num (string->word y)))
                        (and (number? possible-num)
                             (= x possible-num))))))
            ((number? y)
             (and (string? x)
                  (let ((possible-num (string->word x)))
                    (and (number? possible-num)
                         (= possible-num y)))))
            ((string? x) (and (string? y) (string=? x y)))
            ((string? y) #f)
            ((vector? x) (and (vector? y) (vector-equal? x y)))
            ((vector? y) #f)
            (else (eqv? x y))))))
```

```scheme
(define member?
  (let ((> >) (- -) (< <) (null? null?) (symbol? symbol?) (eq? eq?) (car car)
        (not not) (symbol->string symbol->string) (string=? string=?)
        (cdr cdr) (equal? equal?) (word->string word->string)
        (string-length string-length) (whoops whoops) (string-ref string-ref)
        (char=? char=?) (list? list?) (number? number?) (empty? empty?)
        (word? word?) (string? string?))
    (define (symbol-in-list? symbol string lst)
      (cond ((null? lst) #f)
            ((and (symbol? (car lst))
                  (eq? symbol (car lst))))
            ((string? (car lst))
             (cond ((not string)
                    (symbol-in-list? symbol (symbol->string symbol) lst))
                   ((string=? string (car lst)) #t)
                   (else (symbol-in-list? symbol string (cdr lst)))))
            (else (symbol-in-list? symbol string (cdr lst)))))
    (define (word-in-list? wd lst)
      (cond ((null? lst) #f)
            ((equal? wd (car lst)) #t)
            (else (word-in-list? wd (cdr lst)))))
    (define (word-in-word? small big)
      (let ((one-letter-str (word->string small)))
        (if (> (string-length one-letter-str) 1)
            (whoops "Invalid arguments to MEMBER?: " small big)
            (let ((big-str (word->string big)))
              (char-in-string? (string-ref one-letter-str 0)
                               big-str
                               (- (string-length big-str) 1))))))
    (define (char-in-string? char string i)
      (cond ((< i 0) #f)
            ((char=? char (string-ref string i)) #t)
            (else (char-in-string? char string (- i 1)))))
    (lambda (x stuff)
      (cond ((empty? stuff) #f)
            ((word? stuff) (word-in-word? x stuff))
            ((not (list? stuff))
             (whoops "Invalid second argument to MEMBER?: " stuff))
            ((symbol? x) (symbol-in-list? x #f stuff))
            ((or (number? x) (string? x))
             (word-in-list? x stuff))
            (else (whoops "Invalid first argument to MEMBER?: " x))))))
```

```scheme
(define before?
  (let ((not not) (word? word?) (whoops whoops) (string<? string<?)
        (word->string word->string))
    (lambda (wd1 wd2)
      (cond ((not (word? wd1))
             (whoops "Invalid first argument to BEFORE? (not a word): " wd1))
            ((not (word? wd2))
             (whoops "Invalid second argument to BEFORE? (not a word): " wd2))
            (else (string<? (word->string wd1) (word->string wd2)))))))


;;; Higher Order Functions

(define filter
  (let ((null? null?) (car car) (cons cons) (cdr cdr) (not not)
        (procedure? procedure?) (whoops whoops) (list? list?))
    (lambda (pred l)
      ;; Helper function so recursive calls don't show up in TRACE
      (define (real-filter l)
        (cond ((null? l) '())
              ((pred (car l))
               (cons (car l) (real-filter (cdr l))))
              (else (real-filter (cdr l)))))
      (cond ((not (procedure? pred))
             (whoops "Invalid first argument to FILTER (not a procedure): "
                     pred))
            ((not (list? l))
             (whoops "Invalid second argument to FILTER (not a list): " l))
            (else (real-filter l))))))
```

```
(define keep
  (let ((+ +) (= =) (pair? pair?) (substring substring)
        (char->word char->word) (string-ref string-ref)
        (string-set! string-set!) (word->string word->string)
        (string-length string-length) (string->word string->word)
        (make-string make-string) (procedure? procedure?)
        (whoops whoops) (word? word?) (null? null?))
    (lambda (pred w-or-s)
      (define (keep-string in i out out-len len)
        (cond ((= i len) (substring out 0 out-len))
              ((pred (char->word (string-ref in i)))
               (string-set! out out-len (string-ref in i))
               (keep-string in (+ i 1) out (+ out-len 1) len))
              (else (keep-string in (+ i 1) out out-len len))))
      (define (keep-word wd)
        (let* ((string (word->string wd))
               (len (string-length string)))
          (string->word
           (keep-string string 0 (make-string len) 0 len))))
      (cond ((not (procedure? pred))
             (whoops "Invalid first argument to KEEP (not a procedure): "
                     pred))
            ((pair? w-or-s) (filter pred w-or-s))
            ((word? w-or-s) (keep-word w-or-s))
            ((null? w-or-s) '())
            (else
             (whoops "Bad second argument to KEEP (not a word or sentence): "
                     w-or-s))))))

(define appearances
  (let ((count count) (keep keep) (equal? equal?))
    (lambda (item aggregate)
      (count (keep (lambda (element) (equal? item element)) aggregate)))))
```

```
(define every
  (let ((= =) (+ +) (se se) (char->word char->word) (string-ref string-ref)
        (empty? empty?) (first first) (bf bf) (not not) (procedure? procedure?)
        (whoops whoops) (word? word?) (word->string word->string)
        (string-length string-length))
    (lambda (fn stuff)
      (define (string-every string i length)
        (if (= i length)
            '()
            (se (fn (char->word (string-ref string i)))
                (string-every string (+ i 1) length))))
      (define (sent-every sent)
        ;; This proc. can't be optimized or else it will break the
        ;; exercise where we ask them to reimplement sentences as
        ;; vectors and then see if every still works.
        (if (empty? sent)
            sent                   ; Can't be '() or exercise breaks.
            (se (fn (first sent))
                (sent-every (bf sent)))))
      (cond ((not (procedure? fn))
             (whoops "Invalid first argument to EVERY (not a procedure):"
                     fn))
            ((word? stuff)
             (let ((string (word->string stuff)))
               (string-every string 0 (string-length string))))
            (else (sent-every stuff))))))


(define accumulate
  (let ((not not) (empty? empty?) (bf bf) (first first) (procedure? procedure?)
        (whoops whoops) (member member) (list list))
    (lambda (combiner stuff)
      (define (real-accumulate stuff)
        (if (empty? (bf stuff))
            (first stuff)
            (combiner (first stuff) (real-accumulate (bf stuff)))))
      (cond ((not (procedure? combiner))
             (whoops "Invalid first argument to ACCUMULATE (not a procedure):"
                     combiner))
            ((not (empty? stuff)) (real-accumulate stuff))
            ((member combiner (list + * word se)) (combiner))
            (else
             (whoops "Can't accumulate empty input with that combiner"))))))
```

```
(define reduce
  (let ((null? null?) (cdr cdr) (car car) (not not) (procedure? procedure?)
        (whoops whoops) (member member) (list list))
    (lambda (combiner stuff)
      (define (real-reduce stuff)
        (if (null? (cdr stuff))
            (car stuff)
            (combiner (car stuff) (real-reduce (cdr stuff)))))
      (cond ((not (procedure? combiner))
             (whoops "Invalid first argument to REDUCE (not a procedure):"
                     combiner))
            ((not (null? stuff)) (real-reduce stuff))
            ((member combiner (list + * word se append)) (combiner))
            (else (whoops "Can't reduce empty input with that combiner"))))))

(define repeated
  (let ((= =) (- -))
    (lambda (fn number)
      (if (= number 0)
          (lambda (x) x)
          (lambda (x)
            ((repeated fn (- number 1)) (fn x)))))))


;; Tree stuff
(define make-node cons)
(define datum car)
(define children cdr)


;; I/O

(define show
  (let ((= =) (length length) (display display) (car car) (newline newline)
        (not not) (output-port? output-port?) (apply apply) (whoops whoops))
    (lambda args
      (cond
       ((= (length args) 1)
        (display (car args))
        (newline))
       ((= (length args) 2)
        (if (not (output-port? (car (cdr args))))
            (whoops "Invalid second argument to SHOW (not an output port): "
                    (car (cdr args))))
        (apply display args)
        (newline (car (cdr args))))
       (else (whoops "Incorrect number of arguments to procedure SHOW"))))))
```

```
(define show-line
  (let (( >= >=) (length length) (whoops whoops) (null? null?)
        (current-output-port current-output-port) (car car) (not not)
        (list? list?) (display display) (for-each for-each) (cdr cdr)
        (newline newline))
    (lambda (line . args)
      (if (>= (length args) 2)
          (whoops "Too many arguments to show-line")
          (let ((port (if (null? args) (current-output-port) (car args))))
            (cond ((not (list? line))
                   (whoops "Invalid argument to SHOW-LINE (not a list):" line))
                  ((null? line) #f)
                  (else
                   (display (car line) port)
                   (for-each (lambda (wd) (display " " port) (display wd port))
                             (cdr line))))
            (newline port))))))
```

```
(define read-string
  (let ((read-char read-char) (eqv? eqv?) (apply apply)
        (string-append string-append) (substring substring) (reverse reverse)
        (cons cons) (>= >=) (+ +) (string-set! string-set!) (length length)
        (whoops whoops) (null? null?) (current-input-port current-input-port)
        (car car) (cdr cdr) (eof-object? eof-object?) (list list)
        (make-string make-string) (peek-char peek-char))
    (define (read-string-helper chars all-length chunk-length port)
      (let ((char (read-char port))
            (string (car chars)))
        (cond ((or (eof-object? char) (eqv? char #\newline))
               (apply string-append
                      (reverse
                       (cons
                        (substring (car chars) 0 chunk-length)
                        (cdr chars)))))
              ((>= chunk-length 80)
               (let ((newstring (make-string 80)))
                 (string-set! newstring 0 char)
                 (read-string-helper (cons newstring chars)
                                     (+ all-length 1)
                                     1
                                     port)))
              (else
               (string-set! string chunk-length char)
               (read-string-helper chars
                                   (+ all-length 1)
                                   (+ chunk-length 1)
                                   port)))))
    (lambda args
      (if (>= (length args) 2)
          (whoops "Too many arguments to read-string")
          (let ((port (if (null? args) (current-input-port) (car args))))
            (if (eof-object? (peek-char port))
                (read-char port)
                (read-string-helper (list (make-string 80)) 0 0 port)))))))
```

```
(define read-line
  (let ((= =) (list list) (string->word string->word) (substring substring)
        (char-whitespace? char-whitespace?) (string-ref string-ref)
        (+ +) (string-length string-length) (apply apply)
        (read-string read-string))
    (lambda args
      (define (tokenize string)
        (define (helper i start len)
          (cond ((= i len)
                 (if (= i start)
                     '()
                     (list (string->word (substring string start i)))))
                ((char-whitespace? (string-ref string i))
                 (if (= i start)
                     (helper (+ i 1) (+ i 1) len)
                     (cons (string->word (substring string start i))
                           (helper (+ i 1) (+ i 1) len))))
                (else (helper (+ i 1) start len))))
        (if (eof-object? string)
            string
            (helper 0 0 (string-length string))))
      (tokenize (apply read-string args)))))

(define *the-open-inports* '())
(define *the-open-outports* '())
```

```scheme
(define align
  (let ((< <) (abs abs) (* *) (expt expt) (>= >=) (- -) (+ +) (= =)
        (null? null?) (car car) (round round) (number->string number->string)
        (string-length string-length) (string-append string-append)
        (make-string make-string) (substring substring)
        (string-set! string-set!) (number? number?)
        (word->string word->string))
    (lambda (obj width . rest)
      (define (align-number obj width rest)
        (let* ((sign (< obj 0))
               (num (abs obj))
               (prec (if (null? rest) 0 (car rest)))
               (big (round (* num (expt 10 prec))))
               (cvt0 (number->string big))
               (cvt (if (< num 1) (string-append "0" cvt0) cvt0))
               (pos-str (if (>= (string-length cvt0) prec)
                            cvt
                            (string-append
                             (make-string (- prec (string-length cvt0)) #\0)
                             cvt)))
               (string (if sign (string-append "-" pos-str) pos-str))
               (length (+ (string-length string)
                          (if (= prec 0) 0 1)))
               (left (- length (+ 1 prec)))
               (result (if (= prec 0)
                           string
                           (string-append
                            (substring string 0 left)
                            "."
                            (substring string left (- length 1))))))
          (cond ((= length width) result)
                ((< length width)
                 (string-append (make-string (- width length) #\space) result))
                (else (let ((new (substring result 0 width)))
                        (string-set! new (- width 1) #\+)
                        new)))))
      (define (align-word string)
        (let ((length (string-length string)))
          (cond ((= length width) string)
                ((< length width)
                 (string-append string (make-string (- width length) #\space)))
                (else (let ((new (substring string 0 width)))
                        (string-set! new (- width 1) #\+)
                        new)))))
      (if (number? obj)
          (align-number obj width rest)
          (align-word (word->string obj))))))
```

```scheme
(define open-output-file
  (let ((oof open-output-file) (cons cons))
    (lambda (filename)
      (let ((port (oof filename)))
        (set! *the-open-outports* (cons port *the-open-outports*))
        port))))

(define open-input-file
  (let ((oif open-input-file) (cons cons))
    (lambda (filename)
      (let ((port (oif filename)))
        (set! *the-open-inports* (cons port *the-open-inports*))
        port))))

(define remove!
  (let ((null? null?) (cdr cdr) (eq? eq?) (set-cdr! set-cdr!) (car car))
    (lambda (thing lst)
      (define (r! prev)
        (cond ((null? (cdr prev)) lst)
              ((eq? thing (car (cdr prev)))
               (set-cdr! prev (cdr (cdr prev)))
               lst)
              (else (r! (cdr prev)))))
      (cond ((null? lst) lst)
            ((eq? thing (car lst)) (cdr lst))
            (else (r! lst))))))

(define close-input-port
  (let ((cip close-input-port) (remove! remove!))
    (lambda (port)
      (set! *the-open-inports* (remove! port *the-open-inports*))
      (cip port))))

(define close-output-port
  (let ((cop close-output-port) (remove! remove!))
    (lambda (port)
      (set! *the-open-outports* (remove! port *the-open-outports*))
      (cop port))))

(define close-all-ports
  (let ((for-each for-each)
        (close-input-port close-input-port)
        (close-output-port close-output-port))
    (lambda ()
      (for-each close-input-port *the-open-inports*)
      (for-each close-output-port *the-open-outports*)
      'closed)))
```

```
;; Make arithmetic work on numbers in string form:
(define maybe-num
  (let ((string? string?) (string->number string->number))
    (lambda (arg)
      (if (string? arg)
          (let ((num (string->number arg)))
            (if num num arg))
          arg))))

(define logoize
  (let ((apply apply) (map map) (maybe-num maybe-num))
    (lambda (fn)
      (lambda args
        (apply fn (map maybe-num args))))))

;; special case versions of logoize, since (lambda args ...) is expensive
(define logoize-1
  (let ((maybe-num maybe-num))
    (lambda (fn)
      (lambda (x) (fn (maybe-num x))))))

(define logoize-2
  (let ((maybe-num maybe-num))
    (lambda (fn)
      (lambda (x y) (fn (maybe-num x) (maybe-num y))))))

(define strings-are-numbers
  (let ((are-they? #f)
        (real-* *) (real-+ +) (real-- -) (real-/ /) (real-< <)
        (real-<= <=) (real-= =) (real-> >) (real->= >=) (real-abs abs)
        (real-acos acos) (real-asin asin) (real-atan atan)
        (real-ceiling ceiling) (real-cos cos) (real-even? even?)
        (real-exp exp) (real-expt expt) (real-floor floor) (real-align align)
        (real-gcd gcd) (real-integer? integer?) (real-item item)
        (real-lcm lcm) (real-list-ref list-ref) (real-log log)
        (real-make-vector make-vector) (real-max max) (real-min min)
        (real-modulo modulo) (real-negative? negative?)
        (real-number? number?) (real-odd? odd?) (real-positive? positive?)
        (real-quotient quotient) (real-random random) (real-remainder remainder)
        (real-repeated repeated) (real-round round) (real-sin sin)
        (real-sqrt sqrt) (real-tan tan) (real-truncate truncate)
        (real-vector-ref vector-ref) (real-vector-set! vector-set!)
        (real-zero? zero?) (maybe-num maybe-num) (number->string number->string)
        (cons cons) (car car) (cdr cdr) (eq? eq?) (show show) (logoize logoize)
        (logoize-1 logoize-1) (logoize-2 logoize-2) (not not) (whoops whoops))
```

```
(lambda (yesno)
  (cond ((and are-they? (eq? yesno #t))
         (show "Strings are already numbers"))
        ((eq? yesno #t)
         (set! are-they? #t)
         (set! * (logoize real-*))
         (set! + (logoize real-+))
         (set! - (logoize real--))
         (set! / (logoize real-/))
         (set! < (logoize real-<))
         (set! <= (logoize real-<=))
         (set! = (logoize real-=))
         (set! > (logoize real->))
         (set! >= (logoize real->=))
         (set! abs (logoize-1 real-abs))
         (set! acos (logoize-1 real-acos))
         (set! asin (logoize-1 real-asin))
         (set! atan (logoize real-atan))
         (set! ceiling (logoize-1 real-ceiling))
         (set! cos (logoize-1 real-cos))
         (set! even? (logoize-1 real-even?))
         (set! exp (logoize-1 real-exp))
         (set! expt (logoize-2 real-expt))
         (set! floor (logoize-1 real-floor))
         (set! align (logoize align))
         (set! gcd (logoize real-gcd))
         (set! integer? (logoize-1 real-integer?))
         (set! item (lambda (n stuff)
                      (real-item (maybe-num n) stuff)))
         (set! lcm (logoize real-lcm))
         (set! list-ref (lambda (lst k)
                          (real-list-ref lst (maybe-num k))))
         (set! log (logoize-1 real-log))
         (set! max (logoize real-max))
         (set! min (logoize real-min))
         (set! modulo (logoize-2 real-modulo))
         (set! negative? (logoize-1 real-negative?))
         (set! number? (logoize-1 real-number?))
         (set! odd? (logoize-1 real-odd?))
         (set! positive? (logoize-1 real-positive?))
         (set! quotient (logoize-2 real-quotient))
         (set! random (logoize real-random))
         (set! remainder (logoize-2 real-remainder))
         (set! round (logoize-1 real-round))
         (set! sin (logoize-1 real-sin))
         (set! sqrt (logoize-1 real-sqrt))
```

```
              (set! tan (logoize-1 real-tan))
              (set! truncate (logoize-1 real-truncate))
              (set! zero? (logoize-1 real-zero?))
              (set! vector-ref
                    (lambda (vec i) (real-vector-ref vec (maybe-num i))))
              (set! vector-set!
                    (lambda (vec i val)
                       (real-vector-set! vec (maybe-num i) val)))
              (set! make-vector
                    (lambda (num . args)
                       (apply real-make-vector (cons (maybe-num num)
                                                      args))))
              (set! list-ref
                    (lambda (lst i) (real-list-ref lst (maybe-num i))))
              (set! repeated
                    (lambda (fn n) (real-repeated fn (maybe-num n)))))
       ((and (not are-they?) (not yesno))
        (show "Strings are already not numbers"))
       ((not yesno)
        (set! are-they? #f) (set! * real-*) (set! + real-+)
        (set! - real--) (set! / real-/) (set! < real-<)
        (set! <= real-<=) (set! = real-=) (set! > real->)
        (set! >= real->=) (set! abs real-abs) (set! acos real-acos)
        (set! asin real-asin) (set! atan real-atan)
        (set! ceiling real-ceiling) (set! cos real-cos)
        (set! even? real-even?)
        (set! exp real-exp) (set! expt real-expt)
        (set! floor real-floor) (set! align real-align)
        (set! gcd real-gcd) (set! integer? real-integer?)
        (set! item real-item)
        (set! lcm real-lcm) (set! list-ref real-list-ref)
        (set! log real-log) (set! max real-max) (set! min real-min)
        (set! modulo real-modulo) (set! odd? real-odd?)
        (set! quotient real-quotient) (set! random real-random)
        (set! remainder real-remainder) (set! round real-round)
        (set! sin real-sin) (set! sqrt real-sqrt) (set! tan real-tan)
        (set! truncate real-truncate) (set! zero? real-zero?)
        (set! positive? real-positive?) (set! negative? real-negative?)
        (set! number? real-number?) (set! vector-ref real-vector-ref)
        (set! vector-set! real-vector-set!)
        (set! make-vector real-make-vector)
        (set! list-ref real-list-ref) (set! item real-item)
        (set! repeated real-repeated))
       (else (whoops "Strings-are-numbers: give a #t or a #f")))
     are-they?)))


;; By default, strings are numbers:
(strings-are-numbers #t)
```

D GNU General Public License

The following software license, written by the Free Software Foundation, applies to the Scheme programs in this book. We chose to use this license in order to encourage the free sharing of software—our own and, we hope, yours.

Preamble

The licenses for most software are designed to take away your freedom to share and change it. By contrast, the GNU General Public License is intended to guarantee your freedom to share and change free software—to make sure the software is free for all its users. This General Public License applies to most of the Free Software Foundation's software and to any other program whose authors commit to using it. (Some other Free Software Foundation software is covered by the GNU Library General Public License instead.) You can apply it to your programs, too.

When we speak of free software, we are referring to freedom, not price. Our General Public Licenses are designed to make sure that you have the freedom to distribute copies of free software (and charge for this service if you wish), that you receive source code or can get it if you want it, that you can change the software or use pieces of it in new free programs; and that you know you can do these things.

To protect your rights, we need to make restrictions that forbid anyone to deny you these rights or to ask you to surrender the rights. These restrictions translate to certain responsibilities for you if you distribute copies of the software, or if you modify it.

For example, if you distribute copies of such a program, whether gratis or for a fee, you must give the recipients all the rights that you have. You must make sure that they, too, receive or can get the source code. And you must show them these terms so they know their rights.

We protect your rights with two steps: (1) copyright the software, and (2) offer you this license which gives you legal permission to copy, distribute and/or modify the software.

Also, for each author's protection and ours, we want to make certain that everyone understands that there is no warranty for this free software. If the software is modified by someone else and passed on, we want its recipients to know that what they have is not the original, so that any problems introduced by others will not reflect on the original authors' reputations.

Finally, any free program is threatened constantly by software patents. We wish to avoid the danger that redistributors of a free program will individually obtain patent licenses, in effect making the program proprietary. To prevent this, we have made it clear that any patent must be licensed for everyone's free use or not licensed at all.

The precise terms and conditions for copying, distribution and modification follow.

GNU GENERAL PUBLIC LICENSE

TERMS AND CONDITIONS FOR COPYING, DISTRIBUTION AND MODIFICATION

0. This License applies to any program or other work which contains a notice placed by the copyright holder saying it may be distributed under the terms of this General Public License. The "Program", below, refers to any such program or work, and a "work based on the Program" means either the Program or any derivative work under copyright law: that is to say, a work containing the Program or a portion of it, either verbatim or with modifications and/or translated into another language. (Hereinafter, translation is included without limitation in the term "modification".) Each licensee is addressed as "you".

Activities other than copying, distribution and modification are not covered by this License; they are outside its scope. The act of running the Program is not restricted, and the output from the Program is covered only if its contents constitute a work based on the Program (independent of having been made by running the Program). Whether that is true depends on what the Program does.

1. You may copy and distribute verbatim copies of the Program's source code as you receive it, in any medium, provided that you conspicuously and appropriately publish on each copy an appropriate copyright notice and disclaimer of warranty; keep intact all the notices that refer to this License and to the absence of any warranty; and give any other recipients of the Program a copy of this License along with the Program.

You may charge a fee for the physical act of transferring a copy, and you may at your option offer warranty protection in exchange for a fee.

2. You may modify your copy or copies of the Program or any portion of it, thus forming a work based on the Program, and copy and distribute such modifications or work under the terms of Section 1 above, provided that you also meet all of these conditions:

a) You must cause the modified files to carry prominent notices stating that you changed the files and the date of any change.

b) You must cause any work that you distribute or publish, that in whole or in part contains or is derived from the Program or any part thereof, to be licensed as a whole at no charge to all third parties under the terms of this License.

c) If the modified program normally reads commands interactively when run, you must cause it, when started running for such interactive use in the most ordinary way, to print or display an announcement including an appropriate copyright notice and a notice that there is no warranty (or else, saying that you provide a warranty) and that users may redistribute the program under these conditions, and telling the user how to view a copy of this License. (Exception: if the Program itself is interactive but does not normally print such an announcement, your work based on the Program is not required to print an announcement.)

These requirements apply to the modified work as a whole. If identifiable sections of that work are not derived from the Program, and can be reasonably considered independent and separate works in themselves, then this License, and its terms, do not apply to those sections when you distribute them as separate works. But when you distribute the same sections as part of a whole which is a work based on the Program, the distribution of the whole must be on the terms of this License, whose permissions for other licensees extend to the entire whole, and thus to each and every part regardless of who wrote it.

Thus, it is not the intent of this section to claim rights or contest your rights to work written entirely by you; rather, the intent is to exercise the right to control the distribution of derivative or collective works based on the Program.

In addition, mere aggregation of another work not based on the Program with the Program (or with a work based on the Program) on a volume of a storage or distribution medium does not bring the other work under the scope of this License.

3. You may copy and distribute the Program (or a work based on it, under Section 2) in object code or executable form under the terms of Sections 1 and 2 above provided that you also do one of the following:

a) Accompany it with the complete corresponding machine-readable source code, which must be distributed under the terms of Sections 1 and 2 above on a medium customarily used for software interchange; or,

b) Accompany it with a written offer, valid for at least three years, to give any third party, for a charge no more than your cost of physically performing source distribution, a complete machine-readable copy of the corresponding source code, to be distributed under the terms of Sections 1 and 2 above on a medium customarily used for software interchange; or,

c) Accompany it with the information you received as to the offer to distribute corresponding source code. (This alternative is allowed only for noncommercial distribution and only if you received the program in object code or executable form with such an offer, in accord with Subsection b above.)

The source code for a work means the preferred form of the work for making modifications to it. For an executable work, complete source code means all the source code for all modules it contains, plus any associated interface definition files, plus the scripts used to control compilation and installation of the executable. However, as a special exception, the source code distributed need not include anything that is normally distributed (in either source or binary form) with the major components (compiler, kernel, and so on) of the operating system on which the executable runs, unless that component itself accompanies the executable.

If distribution of executable or object code is made by offering access to copy from a designated place, then offering equivalent access to copy the source code from the same place counts as distribution of the source code, even though third parties are not compelled to copy the source along with the object code.

4. You may not copy, modify, sublicense, or distribute the Program except as expressly provided under this License. Any attempt otherwise to copy, modify, sublicense or distribute the Program is void, and will automatically terminate your rights under this License. However, parties who have received copies, or rights, from you under this License will not have their licenses terminated so long as such parties remain in full compliance.

5. You are not required to accept this License, since you have not signed it. However, nothing else grants you permission to modify or distribute the Program or its derivative works. These actions are prohibited by law if you do not accept this License. Therefore, by modifying or distributing the Program (or any work based on the Program), you indicate your acceptance of this License to do so, and all its terms and conditions for copying, distributing or modifying the Program or works based on it.

6. Each time you redistribute the Program (or any work based on the Program), the recipient automatically receives a license from the original licensor to copy, distribute or modify the Program subject to these terms and conditions. You may not impose any further restrictions on the recipients' exercise of the rights granted herein. You are not responsible for enforcing compliance by third parties to this License.

7. If, as a consequence of a court judgment or allegation of patent infringement or for any other reason (not limited to patent issues), conditions are imposed on you (whether by court order, agreement or otherwise) that contradict the conditions of this License, they do not excuse you from the conditions of this License. If you cannot distribute so as to satisfy simultaneously your obligations under this License and any other pertinent obligations, then as a consequence you may not distribute the Program at all. For example, if a patent license would not permit royalty-free redistribution of the Program by all those who receive copies directly or indirectly through you, then the only way you could satisfy both it and this License would be to refrain entirely from distribution of the Program.

If any portion of this section is held invalid or unenforceable under any particular circumstance, the balance of the section is intended to apply and the section as a whole is intended to apply in other circumstances.

It is not the purpose of this section to induce you to infringe any patents or other property right claims or to contest validity of any such claims; this section has the sole purpose of protecting the integrity of the free software distribution system, which is implemented by public license practices. Many people have made generous contributions to the wide range of software distributed through that system in reliance on consistent application of that system; it is up to the author/donor to decide if he or she is willing to distribute software through any other system and a licensee cannot impose that choice.

This section is intended to make thoroughly clear what is believed to be a consequence of the rest of this License.

8. If the distribution and/or use of the Program is restricted in certain countries either by patents or by copyrighted interfaces, the original copyright holder who places the Program under this License may add an explicit geographical distribution limitation excluding those countries, so that distribution is permitted only in or among countries not thus excluded. In such case, this License incorporates the limitation as if written in the body of this License.

9. The Free Software Foundation may publish revised and/or new versions of the General Public License from time to time. Such new versions will be similar in spirit to the present version, but may differ in detail to address new problems or concerns.

Each version is given a distinguishing version number. If the Program specifies a version number of this License which applies to it and "any later version", you have the option of following the terms and conditions either of that version or of any later version published by the Free Software Foundation. If the Program does not specify a version number of this License, you may choose any version ever published by the Free Software Foundation.

10. If you wish to incorporate parts of the Program into other free programs whose distribution conditions are different, write to the author to ask for permission. For software which is copyrighted

by the Free Software Foundation, write to the Free Software Foundation; we sometimes make exceptions for this. Our decision will be guided by the two goals of preserving the free status of all derivatives of our free software and of promoting the sharing and reuse of software generally.

NO WARRANTY

11. BECAUSE THE PROGRAM IS LICENSED FREE OF CHARGE, THERE IS NO WARRANTY FOR THE PROGRAM, TO THE EXTENT PERMITTED BY APPLICABLE LAW. EXCEPT WHEN OTHERWISE STATED IN WRITING THE COPYRIGHT HOLDERS AND/OR OTHER PARTIES PROVIDE THE PROGRAM "AS IS" WITHOUT WARRANTY OF ANY KIND, EITHER EXPRESSED OR IMPLIED, INCLUDING, BUT NOT LIMITED TO, THE IMPLIED WARRANTIES OF MERCHANTABILITY AND FITNESS FOR A PARTICULAR PURPOSE. THE ENTIRE RISK AS TO THE QUALITY AND PERFORMANCE OF THE PROGRAM IS WITH YOU. SHOULD THE PROGRAM PROVE DEFECTIVE, YOU ASSUME THE COST OF ALL NECESSARY SERVICING, REPAIR OR CORRECTION.

12. IN NO EVENT UNLESS REQUIRED BY APPLICABLE LAW OR AGREED TO IN WRITING WILL ANY COPYRIGHT HOLDER, OR ANY OTHER PARTY WHO MAY MODIFY AND/OR REDISTRIBUTE THE PROGRAM AS PERMITTED ABOVE, BE LIABLE TO YOU FOR DAMAGES, INCLUDING ANY GENERAL, SPECIAL, INCIDENTAL OR CONSEQUENTIAL DAMAGES ARISING OUT OF THE USE OR INABILITY TO USE THE PROGRAM (INCLUDING BUT NOT LIMITED TO LOSS OF DATA OR DATA BEING RENDERED INACCURATE OR LOSSES SUSTAINED BY YOU OR THIRD PARTIES OR A FAILURE OF THE PROGRAM TO OPERATE WITH ANY OTHER PROGRAMS), EVEN IF SUCH HOLDER OR OTHER PARTY HAS BEEN ADVISED OF THE POSSIBILITY OF SUCH DAMAGES.

END OF TERMS AND CONDITIONS

How to Apply These Terms to Your New Programs

If you develop a new program, and you want it to be of the greatest possible use to the public, the best way to achieve this is to make it free software which everyone can redistribute and change under these terms.

To do so, attach the following notices to the program. It is safest to attach them to the start of each source file to most effectively convey the exclusion of warranty; and each file should have at least the "copyright" line and a pointer to where the full notice is found.

```
<one line to give the program's name
  and a brief idea of what it does.>
Copyright (C) 19yy  <name of author>
```

```
This program is free software; you can
redistribute it and/or modify it under the terms
of the GNU General Public License as published
by the Free Software Foundation; either version
2 of the License, or (at your option) any later
version.
```

```
This program is distributed in the hope that it
will be useful, but WITHOUT ANY WARRANTY;
without even the implied warranty of
MERCHANTABILITY or FITNESS FOR A PARTICULAR
PURPOSE.  See the GNU General Public License for
more details.
```

```
You should have received a copy of the GNU
General Public License along with this program;
if not, write to the Free Software Foundation,
Inc., 675 Mass Ave, Cambridge, MA 02139, USA.
```

Also add information on how to contact you by electronic and paper mail.

If the program is interactive, make it output a short notice like this when it starts in an interactive mode:

```
Gnomovision version 69,
Copyright (C) 19yy name of author
Gnomovision comes with ABSOLUTELY NO WARRANTY; for
details type 'show w'.  This is free software, and
you are welcome to redistribute it under certain
conditions; type 'show c' for details.
```

The hypothetical commands 'show w' and 'show c' should show the appropriate parts of the General Public License. Of course, the commands you use may be called something other than 'show w' and 'show c'; they could even be mouse-clicks or menu items—whatever suits your program.

You should also get your employer (if you work as a programmer) or your school, if any, to sign a "copyright disclaimer" for the program, if necessary. Here is a sample; alter the names:

```
Yoyodyne, Inc., hereby disclaims all copyright
interest in the program 'Gnomovision' (which makes
passes at compilers) written by James Hacker.
```

```
<signature of Ty Coon>, 1 April 1989
Ty Coon, President of Vice
```

This General Public License does not permit incorporating your program into proprietary programs. If your program is a subroutine library, you may consider it more useful to permit linking proprietary applications with the library. If this is what you want to do, use the GNU Library General Public License instead of this License.

Credits

Many of the examples in this book revolve around titles of songs, especially Beatles songs. Since titles aren't covered by copyright, we didn't need official permission for this, but nevertheless we want to acknowledge the debt we owe to the great musicians who've added so much pleasure to our lives. The use of their names here does not mean that they've endorsed our work; rather, we mean to show our respect for them.

The cover and the illustrations on pages 4, 10, 34 (top), 102, 90, 91, 216, and 280 were drawn by Polly Jordan.

The illustration on page 16 was drawn using Mathematica^{TM}.

The illustrations on pages 28, 70, 342, 386, and 438 appear courtesy of the Bettmann Archive.

The illustration on page 40 appears courtesy of the Computer Museum, Boston. Photograph by Ben G.

The quotations on pages 44 and 70 are from *Through the Looking-Glass, and What Alice Found There,* by Lewis Carroll (Macmillan, 1871).

The Far Side cartoons on page 56 are reprinted by permission of Chronicle Features, San Francisco, CA. All rights reserved.

The photograph on page 126 appears courtesy of UCLA, Department of Philosophy.

The photograph on page 146 appears courtesy of the Computer Museum, Boston.

The photograph on page 88 appears courtesy of UPI/Bettmann.

The illustration on page 172 is *Printgallery,* by M. C. Escher. © 1956 M. C. Escher Foundation–Baarn–Holland.

The quotation on page 173 (top) is from "I Know an Old Lady," a traditional song of which a recent version is copyright © 1952, 1954 by Rose Bonne (words) and Alan Mills (music).

The illustration on page 188 is *Drawing Hands,* by M. C. Escher. © 1948 M. C. Escher Foundation–Baarn–Holland.

The illustration on page 234 is reprinted with permission from Michael Barnsley, *Fractals Everywhere,* Academic Press, 1988, page 319.

The illustration on page 248 is reprinted from page 234 of M. Bongard, *Pattern Recognition,* Spartan Books, 1970.

The illustration on page 304 is *Flowering Apple Tree,* by Piet Mondrian, 1912. Courtesy of Collection Haags Gemeentemuseum, The Hague.

The illustration on page 326 is a photograph by Ben G.

The illustration on page 366 is from *The Wizard of Oz,* © 1939. Courtesy of Turner Home Entertainment.

Alphabetical Table of Scheme Primitives

This table does not represent the complete Scheme language. It includes the nonstandard Scheme primitives that we use in this book, and it omits many standard ones that are not needed here.

`'`	Abbreviation for (`quote` ...).
`*`	Multiply numbers.
`+`	Add numbers.
`-`	Subtract numbers.
`/`	Divide numbers.
`<`	Is the first argument less than the second?
`<=`	Is the first argument less than or equal to the second?
`=`	Are two numbers equal? (Like `equal?` but works only for numbers).
`>`	Is the first argument greater than the second?
`>=`	Is the first argument greater than or equal to the second?
`abs`	Return the absolute value of the argument.
`accumulate`	Apply a combining function to all elements (see p. 108).
`align`	Return a string spaced to a given width (see p. 358).
`and`	(Special form) Are all of the arguments true values (i.e., not #f)?
`appearances`	Return the number of times the first argument is in the second.
`append`	Return a list containing the elements of the argument lists.
`apply`	Apply a function to the arguments in a list.
`assoc`	Return association list entry matching key.
`before?`	Does the first argument come alphabetically before the second?
`begin`	(Special form) Carry out a sequence of instructions (see p. 348).
`bf`	Abbreviation for `butfirst`.
`bl`	Abbreviation for `butlast`.
`boolean?`	Return true if the argument is #t or #f.
`butfirst`	Return all but the first letter of a word, or word of a sentence.
`butlast`	Return all but the last letter of a word, or word of a sentence.
`c...r`	Combinations of `car` and `cdr` (see p. 286).
`car`	Return the first element of a list.

`cdr`	Return all but the first element of a list.
`ceiling`	Round a number up to the nearest integer.
`children`	Return a list of the children of a tree node.
`close-all-ports`	Close all open input and output ports.
`close-input-port`	Close an input port.
`close-output-port`	Close an output port.
`cond`	(Special form) Choose among several alternatives (see p. 78).
`cons`	Prepend an element to a list.
`cos`	Return the cosine of a number (from trigonometry).
`count`	Return the number of letters in a word or number of words in a sentence.
`datum`	Return the datum of a tree node.
`define`	(Special form) Create a global name (for a procedure or other value).
`display`	Print the argument without starting a new line.
`empty?`	Is the argument empty, i.e., the empty word `" "` or the empty sentence `( )`?
`eof-object?`	Is the argument an end-of-file object?
`equal?`	Are the two arguments the same thing?
`error`	Print an error message and return to the Scheme prompt.
`even?`	Is the argument an even integer?
`every`	Apply a function to each element of a word or sentence (see p. 104).
`expt`	Raise the first argument to the power of the second.
`filter`	Select a subset of a list (see p. 289).
`first`	Return first letter of a word, or first word of a sentence.
`floor`	Round a number down to the nearest integer.
`for-each`	Perform a computation for each element of a list.
`if`	(Special form) Choose between two alternatives (see p. 71).
`integer?`	Is the argument an integer?
`item`	Return the nth letter of a word, or nth word of a sentence.
`keep`	Select a subset of a word or sentence (see p. 107).
`lambda`	(Special form) Create a new procedure (see Chapter 9).
`last`	Return last letter of a word, or last word of a sentence.
`length`	Return the number of elements in a list.
`let`	(Special form) Give temporary names to values (see p. 95).
`list`	Return a list containing the arguments.
`list->vector`	Return a vector with the same elements as the list.
`list-ref`	Select an element from a list (counting from zero).
`list?`	Is the argument a list?
`load`	Read a program file into Scheme.
`log`	Return the logarithm of a number.
`make-node`	Create a new node of a tree.
`make-vector`	Create a new vector of the given length.
`map`	Apply a function to each element of a list (see p. 289).
`max`	Return the largest of the arguments.
`member`	Return subset of a list starting with selected element, or `#f`.
`member?`	Is the first argument an element of the second? (see p. 73).
`min`	Return the smallest of the arguments.

`newline`	Go to a new line of printing.
`not`	Return `#t` if argument is `#f`; return `#f` otherwise.
`null?`	Is the argument the empty list?
`number?`	Is the argument a number?
`odd?`	Is the argument an odd integer?
`open-input-file`	Open a file for reading, return a port.
`open-output-file`	Open a file for writing, return a port.
`or`	(Special form) Are any of the arguments true values (i.e., not `#f`)?
`procedure?`	Is the argument a procedure?
`quote`	(Special form) Return the argument, unevaluated (see p. 57).
`quotient`	Divide numbers, but round down to integer.
`random`	Return a random number ≥ 0 and smaller than the argument.
`read`	Read an expression from the keyboard (or a file).
`read-line`	Read a line from the keyboard (or a file), returning a sentence.
`read-string`	Read a line from the keyboard (or a file), returning a string.
`reduce`	Apply a combining function to all elements of list (see p. 290).
`remainder`	Return the remainder from dividing the first number by the second.
`repeated`	Return the function described by $f(f(\cdots(f(x))))$ (see p. 113).
`round`	Round a number to the nearest integer.
`se`	Abbreviation for `sentence`.
`sentence`	Join the arguments together into a big sentence.
`sentence?`	Is the argument a sentence?
`show`	Print the argument and start a new line.
`show-line`	Show the argument sentence without surrounding parentheses.
`sin`	Return the sine of a number (from trigonometry).
`sqrt`	Return the square root of a number.
`square`	Not a primitive! `(define (square x) (* x x))`
`trace`	Report on all future invocations of a procedure.
`untrace`	Undo the effect of `trace`.
`vector`	Create a vector with the arguments as elements.
`vector->list`	Return a list with the same elements as the vector.
`vector-length`	Return the number of elements in a vector.
`vector-ref`	Return an element of a vector (counting from zero).
`vector-set!`	Replace an element in a vector.
`vector?`	Is the argument a vector?
`vowel?`	Not a primitive! `(define (vowel? x) (member? x '(a e i o u)))`
`word`	Joins words into one big word.
`word?`	Is the argument a word? (Note: numbers are words.)
`write`	Print the argument in machine-readable form (see p. 400).

Glossary

ADT: See *abstract data type.*

a-list: Synonym for *association list.*

abstract data type: A *type* that isn't provided automatically by Scheme, but that the programmer invents. In order to create an abstract data type, a programmer must define *selectors* and *constructors* for that type, and possibly also *mutators.*

abstraction: An approach to complex problems in which the solution is built in layers. The structures needed to solve the problem (algorithms and data structures) are implemented using lower-level capabilities and given names that can then be used as if they were primitive facilities.

actual argument expression: An expression that produces an actual argument value. In (+ 2 (* 3 5)), the subexpression (* 3 5) is an actual argument expression, since it provides an argument for the invocation of +.

actual argument value: A value used as an argument to a procedure. For example, in the expression (+ 2 (* 3 5)), the number 15 is an actual argument value.

aggregate: An object that consists of a number of other objects. For example, a sentence is an aggregate whose elements are words. Lists and vectors are also aggregates. A word can be thought of, for some purposes, as an aggregate whose elements are one-letter words.

algorithm: A method for solving a problem. A computer program is the expression of an algorithm in a particular programming language; the same algorithm might also be expressed in a different language.

apply: To *invoke* a procedure with arguments. For example, "Apply the procedure + to the arguments 3 and 4."

argument: A datum provided to a procedure. For example, in (`square 13`), 13 is the argument to `square`.

association list: A list in which each element contains a *name* and a corresponding *value*. The list is used to look up a value, given a name.

atomic expression: An expression that isn't composed of smaller pieces.

backtracking: A programming technique in which the program tries one possible solution to a problem, but tries a different solution if the first isn't successful.

base case: In a recursive procedure, the part that solves the smallest possible version of the problem without needing a recursive invocation.

body: An expression, part of the definition of a procedure, that is evaluated when that procedure is invoked. For example, in

```
(define (square x)
  (* x x))
```

the expression (`* x x`) is the body of the `square` procedure.

Boolean: The value #t, meaning "true," or #f, meaning "false."

branch node: A *tree node* with *children*. The opposite of a *leaf node*.

bug: An error in a program. This word did *not* originate with Grace Hopper finding an actual insect inside a malfunctioning computer; she may have done so, but the terminology predates computers by centuries.

call: Synonym for *invoke*.

cell: One location in a *spreadsheet*.

children: The *nodes* directly under this one, in a *tree*. (See also *siblings* and *parent*.)

composition of functions: Using the value returned by a function as an argument to another. In the expression (+ 2 (* 3 5)), the value returned by the * function is used as an argument to the + function.

compound expression: An expression that contains subexpressions. Opposite of *atomic expression*.

compound procedure: A procedure that a programmer defines. This is the opposite of a *primitive* procedure.

constructor: A procedure that returns a new object of a certain type. For example, the word procedure is a constructor that takes words as arguments and returns a new word. See also *selector, mutator,* and *abstract data type*.

data abstraction: The invention of *abstract data types*.

data structure: A mechanism through which several pieces of information are combined into one larger unit. The most appropriate mechanism will depend on the ways in which the small pieces are used in the program, for example, sequentially or in arbitrary order.

database program: A program that maintains an organized collection of data, with facilities to modify or delete old entries, add new entries, and select certain entries for display.

datum: The piece of information stored in each node of a tree.

debugging: The process by which a programmer finds and corrects mistakes in a program. No interesting program works the first time; debugging is a skill to develop, not something to be ashamed of.

destructive: A destructive procedure is one that modifies its arguments. Since the only data type in this book that can be modified is the vector, all destructive procedures call vector-set!.

domain: The set of all legal arguments to a function. For example, the domain of the count function is the set of all sentences and all words.

effect: Something a procedure does other than return a value. For example, a procedure might create a file on disk, or print something to the screen, or change the contents of a vector.

empty sentence: The sentence ( ), which has no words in it.

empty word: The word " ", which has no letters in it.

end-of-file object: What the file-reading procedures return if asked to read a file with no more unread data.

expression: The representation in Scheme notation of a request to perform a computation. An expression is either an *atomic expression,* such as 345 or x, or a *compound expression* consisting of one or more subexpressions enclosed in parentheses, such as (+ 3 4).

field: A single component of a database *record.* For example, "title" is a field in our example database of albums.

first-class data: Data with the following four properties:

- It can be the argument to a procedure.
- It can be the return value from a procedure.
- It can be given a name.
- It can be part of a data aggregate.

In Scheme, words, lists, sentences, trees, vectors, ports, end-of-file objects, Booleans, and procedures are all first-class.

forest: A list of *trees.*

formal parameter: In a procedure definition, the name given to refer to an argument. In

```
(define (square x)
  (* x x))
```

x is the formal parameter. (Note that this is not the same thing as an actual argument! When we invoke square later, the argument will be a number, such as 5. The parameter is the *name* for that number, not the number itself.)

function: A transformation of information that associates a *return value* with some number of *argument values*. There may be many different *algorithms* that compute the same function; the function itself is the relationship between argument values and return value, no matter how it may be implemented.

functional programming: A style of programming in which programs are expressed as compositions of functions, emphasizing their arguments and return values. Compare to *sequential programming*.

global variable: A variable created with `define`, which has meaning everywhere in the program. The opposite of a *local variable*.

helper procedure: A procedure that exists to help another procedure do its work. Normally, a user does not invoke a helper procedure directly. Instead, the user invokes a top-level procedure, which invokes the helper procedure to assist it in coming up with the answer.

higher-order procedure: A procedure whose domain or range includes other procedures.

index: A number used to select one of the elements of a vector.

initialization procedure: A procedure that doesn't do any work except to invoke a *helper procedure* with appropriate argument values.

interactive: An interactive program or programming language does its work in response to messages typed by the user at a keyboard (or perhaps indicated with a pointing device like a mouse). Each message from the user causes the program to respond in some way. By contrast, a non-interactive program works with input data that have been prepared in advance.

invoke: To ask a procedure to do its work and come up with a return value. For example, "Invoke the + procedure," or "Invoke the + procedure with the arguments 3 and 4."

keyword: The name of a *special form*.

kludge: A method that gets the job done but isn't very elegant. Usually the result is a program that can't be extended the next time a new feature is needed.

leaf node: A *tree node* with no *children*. The opposite of a *branch node*.

leap of faith: A method for understanding recursion in which you say to yourself, "I'm going to assume that the recursive call always returns the right answer," and then use the answer from the recursive call to produce the answer to the entire problem.

list: A data aggregate containing elements that may be of any type.

local variable: A variable that associates a formal parameter name with an actual argument value. It's "local" because the variable exists only within one procedure invocation. (This includes variables created by `let`.) This is the opposite of a *global variable*.

mutable: A data structure is mutable if its contents can change.

mutator: A procedure that changes the value of a data object. In this book, the only mutable data objects we use are vectors, so every mutator is implemented using `vector-set!`. See also *selector, constructor,* and *abstract data type*.

mutual recursion: The program structure in which one procedure invokes another, and the second invokes the first.

node: An element of a *tree*. A node has a *datum* and zero or more *children*.

parent: The node above this one, in a *tree*. (See also *children* and *siblings*.)

pattern matcher: A program that takes a pattern and a piece of data as inputs and says whether or not that piece of data is one that the pattern describes. We present a pattern matcher in Chapter 16.

plumbing diagram: A pictorial representation of the composition of functions, with the return value from one procedure connected to an argument intake of another.

port: An object that Scheme uses to keep track of a file that is currently open for reading or writing.

portable: A portable program is one that can be run in more than one version of Scheme or on more than one computer.

potsticker: A Chinese dumpling stuffed with meat and vegetables, first steamed and then pan-fried, or sometimes first pan-fried and then simmered in water added to the pan.

predicate: A procedure that always returns a *Boolean* value. By convention, Scheme predicates have names like "`equal?`" that end in a question mark.

primitive procedure: A procedure that is already defined when a Scheme session begins. By contrast, a *compound* procedure is one that the programmer defines in Scheme.

procedure: The expression of an algorithm in Scheme notation.

prompt: A character or characters that an interactive program prints to tell the user that it's ready for the user to type something. In many versions of Scheme, the prompt is a > character.

random access: A data structure allows random access if the time required to locate an element of the structure is independent of its position within the structure.

range: The set of all possible return values from a function. For example, the range of the `count` function is the set of non-negative integers.

read-eval-print loop: The overall structure of a Scheme interpreter. It *reads* an expression from the keyboard, *evaluates* the expression by invoking procedures, etc., and *prints* the resulting value. The same process repeats forever.

record: One complete entry in a database. For example, one album in our database of albums. A record contains several *fields*.

recursion: Solving a big problem by reducing it to smaller problems of the same kind. If something is defined recursively, then it's defined in terms of itself. See *recursion*.

recursive case: In a recursive procedure, the part that requires a recursive invocation. The opposite of the *base case*.

rest parameter: A parameter that represents a variable number of arguments. In the formal parameter list (`a b . x`), x is a rest parameter.

result replacement: A technique people can use to figure out the value of a complicated Scheme expression by rewriting the expression repeatedly, each time replacing some small subexpression with a simpler expression that has the same value, until all that's left is a single quoted or self-evaluating value.

robust: Able to function despite user errors. Robust programs check for likely errors and recover from them gracefully.

root node: The *node* at the very top of a *tree*.

selector: A procedure that takes an object as its argument and returns some part of that object. For example, the selector `first` takes a word or sentence as argument and returns the first letter of the word or first word of the sentence. See also *constructor, mutator,* and *abstract data type.*

self-evaluating: An expression is self-evaluating if, when evaluated, it has as its value the expression itself. Numbers, Booleans, and strings are the only self-evaluating objects we use in this book.

semipredicate: A procedure that answers a yes-no question by returning `#f` for "no," but instead of returning `#t` for "yes," it returns some additional piece of information. The primitive `member` procedure is a good example of a semipredicate. ("Semipredicate" isn't a common term; we made it up for this book.)

sequencing: Evaluating two or more expressions one after the other, for the sake of their *effects.*

sequential programming: A style of programming in which programs say, "First do this, then do that, then do that other thing." (Compare to *functional programming.*)

siblings: Two *nodes* of a *tree* that are the children of the same node. (See also *children* and *parent.*)

side effect: See *effect.*

special form: A Scheme expression that begins with a *keyword* and is evaluated using a special rule. In particular, some of the subexpressions might not be evaluated. The keywords used in this book are `and`, `begin`, `cond`, `define`, `if`, `lambda`, `let`, `or`, and `quote`. (The keyword itself is also sometimes called a special form.)

spreadsheet program: A program that maintains a two-dimensional display of data can compute some elements automatically, based on the values of other elements.

state: A program's memory of what has happened in the past.

string: A *word* delimited by double-quote marks, such as `"A Hard Day's Night"` or `"000123"`.

structured list: A list with *sublists*.

subexpression: An element of a *compound expression*. For example, the expression `(+ (* 2 3) 4)` has three subexpressions: `+`, `(* 2 3)`, and `4`.

sublist: An element of a list that is itself a smaller list. For example, `(c d)` is a sublist of the list `(a b (c d) e)`.

substitution model: The way we've explained how Scheme evaluates function invocations. According to the substitution model, when a compound procedure is invoked, Scheme goes through the body of that procedure and replaces every copy of a formal parameter with the corresponding actual argument value. Then Scheme evaluates the resulting expression.

subtree: A tree that is part of a larger tree.

symbol: A word that isn't a number or a string.

symbolic computing: Computing that is about words, sentences, and ideas instead of just numbers.

tree: A two-dimensional data structure used to represent hierarchical information.

tree recursion: A form of recursion in which a procedure calls itself recursively more than one time in each level of the recursion.

type: A category of data. For example, words, sentences, Booleans, and procedures are types. Some types overlap: All numbers are also words, for example.

variable: A connection between a name and a value. Variables can be *global* or *local*.

vector: A primitive data structure that is mutable and allows random access.

word: A sequence of characters, including letters, digits, or punctuation. Numbers are a special case of words.

Index of Defined Procedures

This index contains example procedures whose definitions are in the text and procedures that you are asked to write as exercises. (The exercises are marked as such in the index.) Other sources of information are the general index, which contains technical terms and primitive procedures (for which there is no Scheme definition); the glossary, which defines many technical terms; and the Alphabetical Table of Scheme Primitives on page 553.

General Index

This index contains technical terms and primitive procedures. Other sources of information are the index of defined procedures, which contains procedures whose definitions are in the text and procedures that you are asked to write as exercises; the glossary, which defines many technical terms; and the Alphabetical Table of Scheme Primitives on page 553.

`#f` 71
`#t` 71
`'` 58
`*` 553
`+` 553
`-` 74, 553
`/` 553
`<` 73
`<=` 73
`=` 73
`>` 73
`>=` 73

A

Abelson, Harold xxi, xxxi, 209, 501
`abs` 74
abstract data type 270, 287, 315, 441
abstraction 5, 47, 134, 270, 434, 501
`accumulate` 108, 110, 331
actual argument 45
actual argument expression 45
actual argument value 45

ADT 270, 287, 315, 441
algorithm 13, 238
`align` 358
`and` 75, 76
apostrophe 58
`append` 283
`apply` 293
argument 6, 32
argument, actual 45
arguments, variable number of 292
arithmetic function 18
array 406, 421
artificial intelligence xviii
`assoc` 291
association list 291
atomic expression 29

B

backtracking 256, 270
base case 178
base cases, simplifying 197
Baskerville, John iv

Beatles xxxii, 551
before? 73
begin 348
bf 61
binary number 237
bl 61
body 42
Bonne, Rose 552
Boole, George 21
Boolean 21, 71
boolean? 73
boring exercise xxiii
bottom-up 142
branch node 305
bridge points 141
butfirst 60
butlast 60

C

c 347
c...r 286
cadr 287
car 282
Carroll, Lewis 45, 551
case, base 178
case, recursive 178
cdr 282
ceiling 554
cell 425
chalkboard model 93, 94
child (in spreadsheet program) 451
children 306
children 308
Chinese food xxxii
Clancy, Michael xxxi
clause, cond 79
Clinger, William 394
close-all-ports 401
close-input-port 388
close-output-port 388
comments 32
complexity, control of 5
composition of functions 26, 47
compound expression 29

compound procedure 8
computing, symbolic xviii, 14
cond 78, 157
cond clause 79
condition 79
cons 283
consequent 79
constant, named 89
constructor 61, 282, 283, 307
control of complexity 5
conversational program 343
cos 554
count 109

D

data abstraction violation 316
data file 387
data structure 149
data type, abstract 270, 287, 315, 441
database 265, 477
datum 306
datum 308
Dave Dee, Dozy, Beaky, Mick, and Tich
    xxxii
debugger 7
debugging xxiii
Dee, Dave xxxii
define 41, 130
definition, global 131
diagram, plumbing 34
Dijkstra, Edsger xvii
display 350, 387
Dodgson, Charles 551
domain 20
double-quote marks 58, 61
Dubinsky, Ed xxxii, xxxi

E

effect, side 345
Ehling, Terry xxxi
else 80
EMACS 429, 436
empty sentence 61, 72

empty? 73
end-of-file object 390
engineering, software xx
`eof-object?` 391
`equal?` 72
`error` 554
error messages 7
`eval` 456
evaluation, order of 31
`even?` 554
`every` 104, 110
exclusive, mutually 80
exercise, boring xxiii
exercise, real xxiii
`exit` 7
expression 29
expression, actual argument 45
expression, atomic 29
expression, compound 29
expression, self-evaluating 30, 61, 62
`expt` 554
extensibility 435
extensions to Scheme xxiv, 59, 525

F

factorial 14, 192
false 71
Fibonacci numbers 213
field 477
file, data 387
`file-map` 391
`filter` 289, 331
`first` 60
first-class 63, 113
`floor` 554
food, Chinese xxxii
forest 308
fork 159
form, special 42, 58, 76, 78, 95, 128, 348
formal parameter 45
forms, special 214
formula 426, 431
Fortran 335
`for-each` 351

Free Software Foundation 547
Freud, Sigmund 505
Friedman, Daniel P. xxi, xxxi, 406
Frisell, Bill xxxii
function 17
function as argument 104
function as data 21
function as object 23
function as process 23
function composition 26, 47
function machine 33, 106
function vs. procedure 43, 104
function, arithmetic 18
function, higher-order 23, 106, 289, 327
function, unnamed 133
functional programming ·17, 27, 89, 348
`functions` 367

G

generalization 46, 327, 392, 434
global variable 131

H

Harvey, Brian 209
Harvey, Tessa xxxi
helper procedure 224
Hennessy, John L. xxxii
higher-order function 23, 106, 289, 327
Hofstadter, Douglas R. xxxii
Hypercard 435

I

ice cream xxxii
identity element 119, 221, 332
`if` 71, 76
IFSMACSE xxxii
imperative programming 417
indentation 35
indentation in a program 11
Indianapolis 405
infix notation 317
initialization procedure 224

`integer?` 554
intelligence, artificial xviii
interactive programming 343
interface, user 360
`item` 114

J

join 402
justify 394

K

Katz, Yehuda xxxi
`keep` 107, 110
`keep` pattern 220
keyboard 343
keyword 42
kludge 157, 162, 165, 333
Knuth, Donald iv

L

`lambda` 127
lambda calculus 128
`last` 60
Latin, Pig 10, 179
leaf node 305
`length` 291
Leron, Uri xxxii
`let` 95
lines of a program 10
Lisp xix
list 281
`list` 283
list, association 291
list, structured 282, 335
`list?` 290
`list->vector` 411
`list-ref` 291
little people 30, 49, 90, 207
`load` 554
local variable 93
`log` 554
Logo xxxi

M

machine, function 33, 106
`make-node` 307
`make-vector` 406
Manilow, Barry 57
`map` 289
mapping 289
Marx, Karl 505
matcher, pattern 249
matrix 421
`max` 554
McCarthy, John xix
`member` 290
`member?` 73, 82
mergesort 238
metaphor 434
Mills, Alan 552
`min` 554
model, chalkboard 93
moon, phase of the 212
mutator 407
mutual recursion 310
mutually exclusive 80

N

named constant 89
naming a value 89, 130
`newline` 350, 387
node 305
node, branch 305
node, leaf 305
node, root 305
`not` 75
`null?` 283
number, binary 237
`number?` 73
numbers, Fibonacci 213

O

object, end-of-file 390
`odd?` 555
`open-input-file` 388

open-output-file 388
or 76
order of evaluation 31

P

parameter, formal 45
parameter, rest 293
parent 306
parent (in spreadsheet program) 451
parentheses 36
parentheses, for procedure invocation 6,
    32, 119
parentheses, for cond clauses 79
parentheses, for let variables 96
Pascal xxi
pattern matcher 249
pattern, recursive 217
pattern: keep 220
Patterson, David A. xxxii
Payne, Jonathan iv
phase of the moon 212
Pig Latin 10, 179
Pisano, Leonardo 213
pivot 159
placeholder 250
plumbing diagram 34
points, bridge 141
port 387
portable 428
position 148
predicate 72
prefix notation 317
primitive procedure 8
printed twice, return value 211
printing 343, 362
Prior, Robert xxxi
procedure 6
procedure as argument 104
procedure vs. function 43, 104
procedure, compound 8
procedure, helper 224
procedure, higher-order 327
procedure, initialization 224
procedure, primitive 8

procedure? 555
program, conversational 343
programming, functional 17, 27, 89, 348
programming, imperative 417
programming, interactive 343
programming, structured xx
programming, symbolic xviii, 14
prompt 6

Q

quadratic formula 94
quotation marks, double 58
quote 57
quotient 555

R

random 410, 555
range 20
read 354, 387
read-eval-print loop 29, 343, 367
read-string 396
read-line 356, 387
real exercise xxiii
record 477
recursion 174, 577
recursion, mutual 310
recursion, tree 312
recursive case 178
recursive pattern 217
reduce 290, 332
Rees, Jonathan 394
remainder 555
repeated 113
replacement, result 33
representation 150
rest parameter 293
result replacement 33
return 17
robust 334
Rogers, Annika xxxi
root node 305
round 555

word? 74
Wright, Matthew 209
write 400

Z

Zabel, David xxxii